Sweet William

Sport and Society

Series Editors
Benjamin G. Rader · Randy Roberts

A list of books in the series appears at the end of this book.

Sweet William

The Life of Billy Conn

Andrew O'Toole

University of Illinois Press

Urbana and Chicago

Frontispiece: Conn against Melio Bettina.
Courtesy the Conn Family Collection.

First Illinois paperback, 2010

⊗ This book is printed on acid-free paper.

Library of Congress Cataloging-in-Publication Data
O'Toole, Andrew.
Sweet William : the life of Billy Conn / Andrew O'Toole.
p.   cm. — (Sport and society)
Includes bibliographical references and index.
ISBN-13: 978-0-252-03224-0 (cloth : alk. paper)
ISBN-10: 0-252-03224-1 (cloth : alk. paper)
1. Conn, Billy, 1917–
2. Boxers (Sports)–United States–Biography.
I. Title.
GV1132.C66O76   2008
796.83092–dc22 [B]   2007024083

Paperback ISBN 978-0-252-07745-6

For my girl,
Mickie

Contents

Photographs follow page 116.

Acknowledgments

There is an old Irving Berlin song,

"A pretty girl is like a melody,
That haunts you night and day,
Just like a strain of a haunting refrain,
She'll start upon a marathon
And run around your brain."

That was their song, Billy and Mary Louise. They met when he was the champion of the world and she was the prettiest girl in the world, and they would remain together more than half a century. Working on this book and telling their story has been a pleasure. Most gratifying was meeting Mary Louise Conn, who graciously opened her home to me on several occasions. Mrs. Conn patiently answered all questions I asked of her and offered up many stories of Billy and their life together. And she is, by the way, still the prettiest girl in the world.

Indeed, without the support and input of the Conn family, this project would not have been possible.

I appreciated Billy Junior's wry sense of humor and his pointed opinions. Billy never blushed at telling the truth, and presented to me his unblinking impression on his dad's life and career.

Billy Conn has no bigger devotee than his son Tim. I met Tim while I was researching my biography of Art Rooney (Tim's godfather). Sitting on his couch, I looked across the room and saw Billy's championship belt framed and hanging on the wall. The idea for this book was sowed at that moment. I cannot thank Tim enough for all his input.

He was always there when I would call with a question or needed to corroborate a point. Anything I needed for my research was offered to me, including fight films, audio recordings of Billy's matches, photographs, and the family's cherished scrapbooks. I might add that at no time has any member of the Conn family asked for approval of the final manuscript or requested to see the book before it went to print.

I would also like to thank Billy's brother Frank and sister Mary Jane, who each gave me their memories of the Conn family growing up in East Liberty. Billy's brother-in-law, Jimmy Smith, was also very helpful, supplying me with entertaining tales and recounting his story of hitchhiking his way to the Polo Grounds with Buzzy Kane to see the Louis–Conn fight.

It's been a pleasure to get to know Robert and Maria Pitler. Robert was very young when his father, Johnny Ray, passed away, but both he and his wife Maria were extraordinarily helpful to my research.

A number of others considerately gave of their time to this project; I'm grateful to each: Ralph Brown, Steve Compton, Ray Connelly, Luckett Davis, Harold L. Gefski, Bob Jacobs, Roy Lamphram, Jack McGinley, Roy McHugh, Allen Rothstein, and Christopher Stokes.

The archives at a number of libraries were essential to my research, including the Carnegie libraries in East Liberty, Allegheny, and Oakland; the Hillman Library at the University of Pittsburgh; the Ohio County Public Library in Wheeling, West Virginia; the Washington Memorial Library in Macon, Georgia; and the International Boxing Hall of Fame. I would especially like to thank Kristen Wilhelm of the National Archives, and George Rugg, special collections at Hesburgh Library, University of Notre Dame.

There by my side at these libraries was my research partner, Courtney Doan. Thank you, Courtney, for all your hard work and the spirited debates on those long car rides. This book would be much the poorer without your efforts.

I owe a debt of gratitude to Frank Deford for his brilliant piece on Billy and Mary Louise, "The Boxer and the Blonde." In his profile, Deford lovingly captured the essence of Pittsburgh and its people better than any writer ever has. Funny, it took a Baltimorean to capture that unique spirit. "The Boxer and the Blonde" is, in my opinion, the finest writing ever on a sporting subject. I thank Mr. Deford for introducing me to the wonderful characters that live in this book.

And finally, my bride Mickie. Thanks always for your love and encouragement.

You and me . . . it's a beautiful thing, this life we have.

Sweet William

One   This Is Easy

The double-decked steel and concrete stands of the Polo Grounds reverberated in anticipation; 54,487 fans filled the permanent seats in the grandstand and the temporary wooden chairs, which were laid out in an orderly grid on the New York Giants playing field. Nothing in sports quite equals the excitement present at a heavyweight championship fight. And this fight, which matched the great Joe Louis against challenger Billy Conn, generated interest not seen since the champion battled Max Schmeling three years earlier, in 1938.

Those in attendance came from all walks of life and from every corner of the country, but no area was better represented than Billy's hometown of Pittsburgh. They came en masse from the Smoky City in trainloads: the Ham and Cabbage Special and the Shamrock Special; it was from these well-lubricated revelers that Conn's most boisterous cheers originated as he made his way from the distant dressing room located in the depths of center field to the ring.

Clad in a white bathrobe, Billy bounced up the steps leading to the ring, slipped through the ropes, blessed himself, and bowed to the roaring throng. He was the picture of confidence.

Thirty seconds later, Louis, wearing a blue robe with red trim and a customary towel draped over his head, entered the ring opposite Conn. As each fighter's cornermen placed gloves on the combatant's hands, Lou Nova, the man in line to face the night's winner, was introduced and shook hands with both Louis and Conn before retreating from the ring.

So much was on the line.

The championship, for sure, but there was also Maggie.

Back home on Fifth Avenue, Billy's mother, whom he adoringly called Maggie, lay sick, unable to travel to New York for the fight. She had been bedridden for more than a year. Her health was so fragile that doctor's orders prevented her from even listening to the bout on the radio. In the solitude of her bedroom, Maggie's prayers for Billy were interrupted by her sister Rose, who delivered updates on the fight. Conn often said a man's mother should be his best friend, and Maggie was indeed his.

Though Conn's two sisters were also at home, listening intently to the radio broadcast with their Aunt Rose, the male Conns were all in attendance at the Polo Grounds.

Westinghouse, Billy's father, sat ringside, where eyewitnesses saw him praying, prayers interspersed with instructions to his son.

"Keep movin' Billy . . . box, box," and then the verbal commands and pleas to a greater entity fell silent. The elder Conn's lips continued moving, though no sounds came forth.

Billy's brothers, Frank and Jackie, were there with their father. No day in the Conn clan was complete without a skirmish en famille of some sort, and this day, the biggest day the family had ever known, was no different. Billy spent a portion of his afternoon, time he should have spent resting for the bout, harassing Jackie. In short, a seltzer bottle, an open mouth, and a sleeping brother—when he should have been resting for the biggest fight of his life, Billy instead decided to try to suffocate Jackie.

Mary Louise, Billy's girl, was at the Waldorf waiting on pins and needles for word of the bout. She had only been to one of his fights, but Mary Lou had walked out on that. She didn't have the stomach for such a brutal display. The young couple had hoped to be married by now but convincing Mary Louise's father, "Greenfield" Jimmy Smith, to give his blessing had been futile. Smith refused to consent to his daughter marrying a pug; they never amount to anything, of this he was certain. Despite much pleading from the couple, Greenfield Jimmy refused to relent in his opposition to their love.

The passion play was reported in all the papers in the days leading up to the fight. Stories were replete with Smith's numerous threats of physical harm should Billy try to sneak off with Mary Lou. Among other forms of corporal punishment, Greenfield Jimmy threatened to "pin back" Billy's ears. Westinghouse took umbrage at Smith's bullying harangue. He interpreted Smith's words as an affront to the family name, and promptly replied in kind. "He might lick Billy, but I'll be damned if he can lick me," the senior Conn boasted.

Billy tried not to be distracted by the interfamily squabbles, though that proved to be a difficult task. "Now I see I got to lick two guys," he mentioned to a reporter early that afternoon, "Louis and Smitty. I know I can lick Louis, but that Smitty is pretty tough, I think I'll steer clear of him."[1]

He would steer clear of him, but he wasn't going to back down. He was a fighter. Professionally, he guessed he was a boxer. To the more refined, he was a pugilist. But one thing was certain; he sure as hell wasn't no pug.

Maybe he wasn't the smartest guy around. He quit on school early because the nuns had tired of him. His lack of education didn't mean he was dumb, though. No, he wasn't dumb. He knew a thing or two about a thing or two, and one thing he knew, Greenfield Jimmy wasn't going to keep him away from Mary Louise.

First things first, however. There was Joe Louis to contend with before he could spirit his young love away.

Billy came in at 174 pounds, and that was with Mike Jacobs's finger on the scale. Jacobs was the promoter of the show. He controlled the boxing game, and without his blessing, Billy would have never had this shot at the title.

Uncle Mike was boxing. Sure there were bigger names. The past had Dempsey and Tunney, and presently nobody could pack them in like Louis, but no man held sway over the game like Jacobs. The normally staid and crotchety Jacobs showed his soft side in the presence of the affable Conn. Uncle Mike had an unabashed affection for Billy. Though Jacobs's fondness was sincere, surely Billy's magnetism as a gate attraction enhanced the promoter's feelings for the fighter. For Mike Jacobs, nothing was as desirable as the almighty dollar—preferably multiple dollars.

Jacobs beefed up Billy's weight in the hope of maintaining interest in the fight. There was a distinct possibility that the public wouldn't consider Conn a serious threat to Louis's throne. The champion was already criticized for the lengthy list of "no-names" he had defeated over the preceding years: Tony Musto, Abe Simon, Clarence Burman,

Tony Galento. These no-names became known as Louis's "Bum of the Month Club." Despite possessing a championship himself in the light-heavyweight division, Conn looked like a pushover for Joe. The actual disparity in weight of thirty pounds was significant, and certainly enough to scare away potential patrons who had no desire to see the scrawny Pittsburgher sacrificed at the Polo Grounds purely for their entertainment. This was something Uncle Mike couldn't have. Tilting the truth, in the name of commerce, was simply good business.

The prefight buildup to this match was extraordinary. Not since Louis and Schmeling met three years prior was a championship fight surrounded by such hype. And even then, it was the political overtones of a Black man squaring off against a representative of Nazi Germany that drew most of the commentary. This bout, though not occurring on such a broad world stage, had many attractive qualities, which newsmen cheerfully relayed to their eager readers.

There was, of course, the mostly unspoken role Billy played as the Great White Hope. Though most followers of the sport recognized Louis as a gracious and great champion, in many those beliefs were overwhelmed by an underlying, sometimes deeply concealed, bigotry. Louis had held the heavyweight crown for the better part of four years, which in the eyes of some was four years too long. The time for a white heavyweight champion was long overdue.

To others, Billy's ethnic background held as much appeal as his race. Conn was Irish through and through, and he proudly wore his heritage on his sleeve. Earlier in the day, a great number of Billy's followers could be seen roaming the boulevards of New York decked out in green, with emerald bowlers nestled neatly upon their heads. Still, the allure of this particular championship bout went deeper than ethnicity and race.

In the days leading up to the fight, Conn was swimming in a sea of juxtaposed emotions and, thanks to vigilant newsmen, the whole country was allowed to peep in on Billy's turbulent personal life. Maggie's worsening condition was regularly updated in the papers. While this story line tugged at heart and sentiments of the most hardened, it was the forbidden love affair between the challenger and his young fiancée that swayed even the most cynical. The story was irresistible. Photos of the stunning couple accompanied accounts of their tale, most of which were snapped at the shore. They were pictured prancing through the sands of Ocean City, her, the blonde beauty queen, and him, the gorgeous athletic specimen; together they were the All-American couple.

Indeed, this fight had something for everyone, and seemingly everyone who wasn't at the Polo Grounds had an ear pressed to the radio, anxiously waiting to learn how these story lines would play out.

Louis began the fight on the offensive; Billy started on the run, backpedaling his way through the first round. By the end of the second, it looked as though Conn was well on his way to joining the other bums on Joe's lengthy list. Then, in the third and fourth, Billy got off his bicycle and the fight began in earnest.

The crowd's emotional state and attentiveness steadily increased with each succeeding round. "Feigned amusement; then deep interest," reported the *Pittsburgh Press,* which gave way to "profound amazement, and finally sheer delirium."[2]

The eighth started slowly. Billy circled to his left, throwing jabs; Louis came in with a right and left to the head and fired several combinations to Conn's body. Billy was cautious, stepping away as Louis continued to be on the offensive. Then, as quick as that, the fight turned on a dime.

Billy lashed out with a right and a left to Joe's head, and followed that one-two with another. A hard right to the jaw, and then another, brought the crowd to their feet. Conn tied Louis up and, as they broke, caught Joe cleanly with a left hook to the jaw. Another right, and Louis pulled Billy to him in a clinch. Conn fought his way out of Joe's hug and delivered a trio of hard blows as the bell brought the round to a close.

Billy strolled back to his corner. "I got him," he told his seconds.[3]

Dancing through his mind were visions of Mary Louise on his arm, the two of them walking along the Jersey shore. The champ and his girl. Passersby would gaze admiringly at the handsome couple. *There goes the man who knocked out Joe Louis.*

Conn felt so secure in his lead that he began to pop off to Louis, just as he had done during the training period when he kept his mouth running to the press corps. He would take Joe out for sure, Billy claimed, and said so repeatedly in the weeks leading up to the fight: "If that guy thinks I'm going to be his next 'bum of the month,' he either don't know what month it is, or he has been so used to looking at bums that he thinks everybody is one."[4]

By the tenth, Joe knew he was in a fight as the champ began to show the effects of Billy's barrage of hooks and jabs. In the twelfth, Billy showed that his punches packed some wallop despite what some of those critics said. He hurt Louis. Conn landed with everything he threw and at the close of the round, Joe was in trouble. In the champion's corner following the twelfth, Jack Blackburn urged his fighter: "Chappie," Blackburn said, "you're losing. You gotta knock him out."

Across the ring, a beaming Conn told his manager, Johnny Ray, that the fight was in the bag.

"This is easy, Moonie," Billy told Ray. "I can take this sonofabitch out this round."

Ray couldn't believe what he was hearing. Their plan had worked to perfection thus far.

"No, no! Billy stick and run. You got the fight won. Stay away. Just stick and run, stick and run . . ." The bell, Billy's cue, interrupted Johnny's exhortations.

Conn shot up from his stool, ready to lay claim to his glory. Indeed, the only thing between him and the championship was three rounds . . . nine minutes. . . .

There he goes. There goes the man who knocked out Joe Louis.

Two A Kiss from Heaven

She had the voice of an Irish angel.

Margaret McFarland Conn filled her home with the melodies and songs of the Emerald Isle, singing lullabies from the Old Country to her children.

> It's the one place on earth
> That heaven has kissed
> With melody, mirth
> And meadow and mist

She was born to Annie and Peter McFarland in 1900. Both Peter and Annie were native to County Down, and though Margaret's birthplace was the small English seaport town of Milan, Cumberland, she was Irish through and through. She immigrated to America in 1914 with her parents and five siblings via third-class steerage. They settled in the industrial Pittsburgh neighborhood of East Liberty.

William Conn was born a hardscrabble fella in Pittsburgh. Like Margaret, William's people hailed from Ireland; the Conn family came from a small village outside Belfast. A Protestant, Joseph Conn converted to Catholicism when he married Jane McNeely. The Conns came to America and initially resided in Cincinnati before establishing a home in Pittsburgh. A fightin' Mick was Joseph, and he also was known to tip back a pint occasionally, two avocations he passed on to his son. "Did he like to drink?" William liked to say of his daddy, setting himself up for his own well-worn punch line. "Was the Pope Catholic?"

Indeed, the Pope was of the Catholic faith, and it was true—the Conns could drink and fight with the best of them.

Margaret was a handsome lass; tall, blue eyed, raven haired, and buxom. She would carry with her a hint of her native brogue for her whole life. Though barely sixteen years old when she met William Conn, Margaret was smitten by William's understated good looks, and was won over by his sure Irish charm. Atop Conn's head was a neat head of dark hair, a wisp of a mustache lay above his lip, and his eyes, when unprovoked, twinkled with a hint of mischief.

Following a brief courtship, Margaret and William were wed at their parish, Sacred Heart, and their firstborn arrived on October 17, 1917. The child was christened William David Conn. Billy, as he came to be known, was soon followed by two brothers, Frank and Jackie, and two sisters, Mary Jane and Peggy Ann. Though she loved all her children with equal fervor, Margaret felt a special bond with her firstborn, and he with her. When he was old enough to talk, Billy began calling his mother "Maggie," a term of endearment that would continue until Margaret's death.

The young family made their home in a tenement row house on Shakespeare Avenue, which ran directly behind Penn Avenue in East Liberty. The Conn home sat at the end of the row house, a modest two-story dwelling with three bedrooms. Though theirs was a household of limited means, Margaret wanted her children to always be dressed nicely, and made certain they were well scrubbed. No one would ever say the Conn kids looked like ragamuffins. She was a devout Catholic and tried, with modest success, to impress her faith upon her boys. While Margaret was trying to instill in her children the importance of studying hard, maintaining a neat appearance, and, above all, abiding by the Holy Spirit, William set a different agenda for his sons. Nothing was more vital to a growing boy than learning the art of self-defense and understanding how to implement such teaching on the street. From the moment a boy is first cut loose from his mother's apron strings, he'll find his courage tested. William engendered in his sons the tenet that, should a Conn's toughness be brought into question, then they were to stand and fight. Not only were they to fight, but by God, they better win. No one gets the better of a Conn.

And so it was that Billy, Frank, and Jackie learned the fine art of street fighting from one of the town's premier scrappers. They would say, about the boys anyway, that they had a bit of "Wild Bill" Conn in them. For William, learning the art of self-defense was a rite of passage. If he was to leave his boys with nothing else, William was determined that his sons know how to handle themselves.

For a time, Conn walked the beat as an East Liberty cop, and then he caught on as a steamfitter at Westinghouse in East Pittsburgh. When hours were short at the plant, Conn worked as a bouncer at a local bar. It was William's employment at Westinghouse that inspired Billy to bestow a nickname upon his father. From here on out, he wouldn't be "dad," or "pop," or any such nonsense. Instead, William was simply "Westinghouse."

Conn was a good provider for his family; even in the depths of the Depression, Westinghouse was never out of work. Still, he could be sorely lacking as a father. Far too often, William enjoyed a glass or two. Drink and Conn's temperament were not compatible, though. When filled with a few toots, Westinghouse could become mean spirited and any perceived slight would send him into a fighting rage. "Wild Bill," an apt moniker, would take on anyone if challenged. His uncontrollable disposition landed Conn in trouble on more than one occasion.

After classes one afternoon, Billy was walking home from Sacred Heart when he saw his father, chained to a telephone pole, taking a beating from two of East Liberty's finest. Following another incident, Westinghouse was hauled into the police station. While in custody and being restrained by a few officers, another cop smacked Conn upside the head with a blackjack. A couple of weeks later, Maggie and Westinghouse were out for an evening at a local theater when Conn spied the cop who had given him the cheap shot. Officer of the law or not, fair is fair, so Westinghouse ran the cop down and beat the hell out of him.

His was a peculiar legacy to pass on to his sons. Fighting became second nature to the Conn boys, especially Billy and Jackie. Frank was the more passive of the brothers, but he took no guff from anyone. They fought among each other mostly, but nothing slowed a Conn from defending the family's honor against an outsider.

Years later, after Billy became a national figure, a number of magazine essayists and newspaper columnists liked to pinpoint Billy's leaving organized schooling to the moment when Sacred Heart nuns asked him to please move along. He was simply getting too big to remain in the same grade year after year as he had been doing, the sisters supposedly said. The truth was far simpler, though not as humorous. Billy simply wasn't geared toward schooling.

One school day during Billy's eighth-grade year, his teacher addressed her class. "Why don't some of you big boys get out of this school," the sister pleaded. "You don't learn anything, and all you do is keep the smaller children out. Why don't you go to the trade school?"

While Billy was hardly the model student, he did exhibit a genuine talent as a sketch artist. One particular drawing Billy made of Notre Dame football coach Knute Rockne was an exceptional likeness of the legendary gridiron genius. Conn mailed the portrait to Rockne, which duly impressed the coach, who returned the sketch with his signature attached. Still, despite his demonstrated artistic potential, the nuns at Sacred Heart never encouraged Billy to pursue his gift.

Rather than nurture his artistic skills, Conn took his teacher up on her suggestion, left Sacred Heart, and enrolled in Washington Trade school. He took up the vocation of automobile mechanic in his new school. "They give us a wheel with wooden spokes out and told us to put them back," Billy later explained. "And I says to myself, 'What are we doing this for? They don't have wheels with spokes on automobiles.'

"I stuck around for a couple of days and then went on the hook for nineteen days. I figured I wouldn't get anywhere in that school so [I] went in and asked for a transfer to another trade school."

Unfortunately, Conn's second choice for trade school refused his request of a transfer. "So," Billy said, "I went on the hook for a few days more and then I went to another school and they asked me where I came from and I said, 'I came from Cincinnati and I don't have no transfer.' So they let me in, but I didn't like that school either and I quit."

Billy was just fourteen years old and through with structured education. Westinghouse knew that no good could come from a boy wandering aimlessly on the street. What Billy needed, his father reasoned, was a lesson on life's reality. Conn took his son to the Westinghouse plant in East Pittsburgh.

"Without schooling, this is where you're going to end up," Westinghouse ominously warned Billy.

Years later, Billy could still recall that visit and the feelings that washed over him at that moment. "It scared the hell out of me," Conn admitted. Still without an education, what else would a young man do for a living other than laboriously struggle in some unforgiving industry?

Junior and Moonie

Located above an Irish pub on Penn Avenue sat a ratty one-room hall, which served as the home of Johnny Ray's gym.

It was a dingy room. A room that gave birth to imaginings, improbable dreams of fame and glory, riches that would keep the romantic from toiling in one of the burg's many mills. Reality always set in, though, and boxing became nothing more than a side occupation at best, a pursuit that delayed life's dreary certainty.

A couple of heavy bags, a dusty ring, and a speed bag or two were positioned throughout the gym. The wooden floor was littered with discarded cigarette butts. The air was ripe with the aroma of stale sweat and ever-lingering smoke, a nauseating blend to the uninitiated. To the indigenous, though, the scent wafted about, sweet as the perfume of a gardenia . . . atmospheric to the job at hand.

Into this hazy second-story gymnasium, Westinghouse brought his eldest son. Knowing what the streets will do to an aimless youth, Conn went to Johnny Ray; some time in the gym would keep the kid out of scrapes with the boys in blue, and learning how to fight would always come in handy, Westinghouse reasoned.

"He's having trouble with bigger kids around home, and I want him to have a fair chance to take care of himself," Conn explained to Ray.

Johnny was acquainted with Billy Sr.; the two often conversed over an afternoon drink at a nearby tavern. "Tell you what I'll do," Westinghouse said to Ray. "I'll give you a buck a week—if you let him in the gym and teach him about boxing."[1]

That offer, modest as it was, caught the attention of Ray. A buck to Johnny was "a couple of meals, or four drinks"—certainly nothing to turn up his nose at, not when he was just scratching by. Ray had opened his modest gym after retiring from the ring. His was hardly an extravagant lifestyle. "Sometimes," he remembered, "you had the rent and enough left over for a steak or a hamburger."[2]

In these times, Conn's offer of a buck a week was not something Johnny could dismiss out of hand.

From January 13, 1913, when he entered the ring as a 105-pound flyweight, until January 28, 1924, when he fought as a 133-pound featherweight, Johnny Ray fought in too many professional matches to either count or remember. The official record credits Johnny with 138 fights, though other sources claim he had as many as 300. Thanks to porous recordkeeping, the truth lies somewhere in between. During the breadth of his career, Ray fought for as little as a buck and as much as $3,000; more often than not, however, his payday was much closer to the former than the latter.

He faced fellas like George "Kayo" Chaney, Johnny Kilbane, Rocky Kansas, Johnny Dundee, and Jack Zivic. Despite taking on some of the tougher guys in the business, Ray was never knocked out. In fact, Johnny only hit the canvas once, and that happened when he got tangled up in his feet.

He fought a number of Patsys. Four of them in fact: Scanlon, Gallagher, Brannigan, and Haley . . . Patsys all. There was also Young Lightning, Young Ketchell, Young Henry, Young McGovern, and Young Mendo. The nicknames were neither imaginative nor diverse, but the unoriginal fighters provided Ray with a regular payday, however paltry.

He was born Harry Pitler in Pittsburgh's Hill District on December 14, 1896.

It was while Harry was working as a newsboy at Penn Station that he first met local fight manager James "Red" Mason. "I used to fight with the other kids there and I had 'em all scared of me," he later said. "Red Mason used to buy papers from me—that is, he didn't exactly buy 'em. He'd read them and then hand them back to me."

Mason was well known in Pittsburgh's sporting sect. He worked as a manager of boxers, and often as a promoter, referee, and announcer as well—whatever was required to put on a good show. He was a gambler who loved to place a wager on damn near any event where they kept score. Red never bet against his beloved Fighting Irish of Notre Dame, and even when he knew better, Mason still put his money on the Pirates. He was a frequent visitor to Forbes Field, and his bellicose voice could be heard razzing opposing pitchers throughout the grandstand. Years earlier, when Connie Mack managed the Pirates, Mason served with the club as a trainer. But boxing was his area of expertise, and Mason had built up a fine stable of fighters that was recognized throughout the country. He originated the rather unsanitary act of spraying his fighter in the face with a mouthful of water as the boxer returned to the corner between rounds.

Mason took note of the way young Harry handled himself with the other kids around the railway station and saw potential in the scrawny kid. Always on the lookout for another young man who could potentially make him a few bucks, Mason offered to add Pitler to his stable. First thing, though, he needed a different name. Fistic crowds had a fondness of rooting for fighters who shared their nationalities, and Irish boxers were proven to be a bigger draw than Jewish brawlers. For his new name, one he would retain until his death, Harry "borrowed" from a two-a-day vaudeville team he enjoyed, Johnny and Emma Ray.

Now known as Johnny Ray, Harry joined Al Grayber, Cuddy DeMarco, Bricky Ryan, "Red" Robinson, Buck Crouse, and the great Harry Greb as men governed by Mason. It was Red's philosophy to nurture his young fighters along slowly, carefully choosing their opponents until they were ready, and then placing them in the ring frequently and against all comers.

Life between the ropes sure beat hustling newspapers, but it was far from an alluring existence. In the ring, Johnny was a very clever fighter. Opponents found it difficult to lay a glove on Ray, who put up a formidable defense with his arms and elbows, wrapping them protectively around his head. Johnny was also a genius at timing a last-minute rally to close each round. This technique was effective in not only rattling his opponent, but also impressed scoring officials with his strong close. His style brought both victories and the respect of his foes, but life as a small-time fighter, especially one managed by a skinflint, was hardly a glamorous world.

Mason's tight-fisted nature wasn't limited to his distaste for purchasing newspapers. "He managed me on the same basis," Johnny explained. "The only time I could ever get a dollar out of Red was when he'd get drunk, and then I'd roll him."

To save a few bucks on train fare, Mason took advantage of Johnny's youthful looks and diminutive size. Sometimes Mason would pay half-fare for Ray, the rate the railroads charged for children. On other occasions, Red pocketed the entire amount. "I spent most of my time in the women's toilet. You could travel for nothing there," Ray reasoned. "The conductor wouldn't unlock the door. I went from Pittsburgh to St. Louis and back that way once. Red Mason would throw me in the minute we got on the train, I'd lock the door and I wouldn't come out until he gave the secret knock."

Mason would not be stymied if the ladies restroom weren't available. "If we couldn't get away with that, Red used to hide me under a seat, throw his overcoat over me and pile a couple of bags up against me so nobody could see me. It was pretty confining, but we got there."

Johnny didn't own his first pair of long pants until he was twenty-two. Showing signs of a heart and generosity, Mason broke open his wallet and splurged, spending $12 on Ray's first pair of long pants. This moment of largesse occurred following Johnny's impressive, though too prideful, effort against Johnny Kilbane. Kilbane was fresh off knock-out victories over Willie Jackson, Irish Patsy Kline, and George Kayo Chaney. Johnny, most observers figured, was "to be sucker number four."

"Kilbane was champion of the world then. I was just a punk and I boxed him in Pittsburgh," Ray remembered. Using his effective, offensive-defensive approach, Johnny seemed to have the fight in hand ("he couldn't hit me on the taillight with a buggy whip"). And the manager did his part by placing a sympathetic official in the ring with the boxers. Yet Red didn't take into account his spirited fighter.

"Mason had his own referee in and everything was under control. It was a six-rounder. The ref wanted to give [a] round to me on a foul, but like a sucker, I wouldn't take it. . . . Mason almost killed me when I got back to the dressing room for not taking the round when it was offered. Mason was much tougher than Kilbane in my book."

His new trousers, an unofficial initiation into manhood, still didn't provide Johnny with a seat in the rail cars. Into the women's loo, or under a pile of coats and baggage, Ray went, his traveling station remaining unchanged. After all, Red needed to compensate for the unscheduled outlay of twelve bucks.

Johnny's final fight was held on January 28, 1924, at East Liberty's Motor Square Garden. Leading up to the match, the talk was that Ray was on his way to a date with Benny Leonard for the lightweight championship. Following Johnny's disappointing loss to Jack Zivic that evening, though, any possibility of a title shot was gone. In the opinion of those present, the "blonde from the Hill District" was now in the "has beens class."[3] There was some solace to be found in defeat for Johnny. His 25 percent take of the record-setting $10,000 Motor Square gate sent him into retirement with one of the largest purses of his career.

"So you want to be a fighter, eh? Well, you know how to start on your career don't ya? Ya start by sweeping out this joint, and makin' yourself generally useful around here."[4]

Billy arrived at Johnny's the next afternoon, his unsubstantiated reputation preceding him. "I hear you're a thief," Ray said to Billy.

Without a whisper of denial or a word in self-defense, Billy answered Ray's accusation like a true street punk. "What am I going to steal around here? Sweatsocks?"

With that, Johnny sent Billy up the street to Julie the bootlegger to procure an adult beverage, a pint of moonshine for fifteen cents. When the youngster returned with Johnny's refreshment, he was promptly told to sweep the gym while Ray returned to training his established fighters. This scene played out day after day, a beverage then a broom, as Johnny tested the sincerity and commitment of the wayward four-teen-year-old.

On the fifth day, when he thought no one was paying any attention, Billy set aside his broom and started shadowboxing off in a corner. Ray, however, noticed the solitary teenager fighting an imaginary foe. "So help me," Johnny later recounted, "as soon as he put up those little fists and made his first move, I fell in love with him."[5]

That day, when Ray was through with his fighters and after Billy was finished cleaning the gym, Johnny pulled the boy over and told him he was ready to learn the art of boxing. The old fighter was so impressed with Billy's obvious aptitude for the sport that he decided to accept just one week's "pay" from Westinghouse. "I told him I'd work for nothing providing he would allow the boy to become a professional fighter when the time was right, and that I'd manage him."

From that date forward, Billy and Johnny were practically insepa-rable. In time, the two would be bound by an abiding sense of loyalty. Theirs was a friendship and partnership that would lift each out of the doldrums of life in a mill town. In their familiarity, Ray and Conn became "Moonie" and "Junior."

Billy followed Johnny around like a newborn pup. He stayed in the gym from early morning until late in the evening. He would pull up a chair and sit entranced as Johnny's palookas worked out. Everyone that set foot in the gym was taken by his enthusiasm. Ray gave him pointers, while Johnny's fighters taught him everything they knew. In addition, to gather further experience, Billy served as a sparring partner for visiting fighters.

He immediately took to Ray's tutelage and was diligent in tending to practice. While other neighborhood kids played the sport of the season, be it baseball, football, or just plain fighting in the street, Billy was in the gym at Johnny's side. He listened to Ray's every word of advice: how to block a punch; how to hold his hands properly; the basic philosophy of the left jab; how to attack an opponent; and when to lay off.

Billy listened to Ray and studied the few pros that Johnny managed. The boys in Ray's stable were run-of-the-mill, or just plain run-down, but they helped out the eager Conn. The fight game interested him like nothing at Sacred Heart ever did or could. He was the proverbial sponge, soaking up every ounce of boxing knowledge he could in Johnny's ratty old gym.

On the top of his head Ray had an unruly mop of sandy hair, which usually fell softly over his eyes. His virtues outweighed his imperfections, though his character blemishes were notable and manifest. He smoked entirely too much, drank enough to perpetually stay one step ahead of sobriety, and tended to gamble beyond his means. His cheery face revealed his true nature, though. Beyond his vices, Johnny Ray was a kind and gentle soul. He took to Billy and treated him as a son. Likewise, Johnny became a second father to Billy, nurturing him to the ways of the world while teaching him the intricacies of his chosen vocation.

Time in the ring was imperative to Billy's education. There were other lessons, however, to be garnered beyond the four walls of Johnny's second-story gym. Ray frequently took Conn on walking tours of local saloons and gambling dens. Inside, Ray would inevitably find a familiar face. "Look, see that guy?" he would point out to Billy. "He was once a good fighter. Now he's a bum on account of rum. If I ever catch you takin' a drink, I'll kill you."

From the gin joint they would traverse to another house of iniquity. "Junior, see that guy looking for a handout? He used to get $10,000 a fight. If I ever catch you gambling, I'll break your neck."[6]

When the day was through, Billy would pester Johnny, begging to hear about the old days and the fighters Moonie knew back in his day. Ray would wax nostalgic about a Frank Klaus or Al Grayber, maybe Jack McCarron. Patiently Billy would sit as Johnny reminisced about his old friends and foes. But there was one name that sparked his interest more than any other: no one could touch Harry Greb—not the myth or the man.

Though Billy was too young to have actually witnessed the "Pittsburgh Windmill" in action, Greb had been his idol since he was in short pants. Westinghouse, though, *had* seen the great Greb in the ring and would regale his son with tales of Harry's exploits. Long before Billy had ever dreamed of following a fistic trail, he was enamored with Greb. But Westinghouse only knew of Greb from a distant seat in a local hall and through news gathered from the local papers. Johnny, however, could lay claim to not only being Harry's stablemate, but also his friend, and Billy couldn't get enough of Moonie's memories.

"How did Greb hold his hands?"

"What did Harry usually eat before a match?"

"How did he set his feet?"

The questions were never ending.

More than two years of apprenticeship passed and Ray believed the boy was ready to turn pro. He asked Bill Sr. to the gym for a talk. "Your kid is a hell of a fighter. In my book he's ready to make money. I'm asking for your okay."

The boy was hell-bent on being a fighter, Johnny told the already aware Westinghouse. For that line of employment, a formal education was unnecessary. In fact, Ray said, "The dumber you are the better. So why don't you let me have him from now on? If he ain't gonna make the grade, I'll get him a job in a steel mill, and make him go to work for a living."[7]

It's no coincidence that a slew of memorable and great fighters arose from the Depression era. Hard times limited available employment, and many young men who may have, in normal economic times, taken to a trade instead found deliverance in the boxing ring. This life wouldn't be glamorous, though, that much was certain. But the other option was the mills—or maybe Westinghouse like the old man. In Billy's way of thinking, there was no doubt which way to go. Billy's feelings were cemented when his father took him to Westinghouse and showed him around the plant, showed him what would await him there. That, Billy later said, scared the shit out of him. Yep. He was done with school and he sure as hell didn't want to work for a living. That left hustling on the streets or making his way in the ring, and with the confidence Billy had in his ability, there really wasn't any choice.

Starting off his career as an amateur was not an option for Billy. His two years in the gym had thoroughly grounded him in every fundamental of boxing. Johnny saw no advantage in spending even one round among the echelon of the unpaid. "Why should you fight for tin watches when you can be making good money from the same work?" Ray liked to say. He dismissed the feasibility of amateur boxing. "A kid'll get a beating just the same as the pros, and all he sees at the end, and that's if he's successful, is some dime-store prize."

His was sound reasoning, though it was a belief that went against the grain. Most fighters came up through the amateur ranks. Working their way through the Golden Gloves tournaments where the more talented youthful pugs caught the eye of promoters and newsmen. Ray would have none of that for his Junior.

"You can't learn anything from guys you can lick, but get in there with a guy like Mickey Walker and you'll come out a fighter."

For Ray, the next few years would be reminiscent of his days traversing the country with Red Mason. Johnny and Billy trekked between the small river towns of West Virginia and mill towns of western Pennsylvania. They slept in flea-ridden motels and ate according to their budget—that is to say, very little or very creatively. They ate hero sandwiches, which, Billy explained, "was half a loaf of bread, sliced lengthwise, stuffed with spicy Italian sausages and soaked in hot peppery sauce." These sandwiches were a favorite of Italian laborers as well as Ray and his protégé. Thanks to their prodigious size, it allowed the boys the equivalent of a full meal for a scant dime.

Another expense for Ray was the frequent acquisition of shoes for the still-growing Conn, who, Johnny claimed, went through footwear faster than anyone he'd ever seen. "I used to buy his shoes for seventy-five cents a pair, at stores were they hung out front like a bunch of bananas."

On June 28, 1934, at the age of sixteen years, eight months, and twenty days, William David Conn made his professional boxing debut. This initial foray took place Fairmont, West Virginia, against middling veteran Dick Woodward. A "tin watch" probably would have looked pretty good in the aftermath of his four-round loss. Instead of second-rate jewelry, Billy received four bits, his share of the modest $2.50 purse.

"Why fifty cents?" Billy protested. "Where's the rest of my money?"

"We gotta eat," Johnny answered.

"Yeah, but how's come I'm paying outta my share?" Conn complained.

Simple, Ray answered. "You were the one who lost."[8]

The edification of young Billy hardly ceased once he turned professional. Some lessons, such as the harsh reality of the pittance to be made as a preliminary fighter, were harder to absorb than others. Inside the ring, Johnny looked to match his Junior up against older, more experienced boxers, men who would tutor Billy with their gloved fists.

With his next outing in Charleston, West Virginia, Conn scored his first victory with a knockout over Johnny Lewis. He followed that with another win, this time over Bob Dronan in Parkersburg.

Following a victory over Paddy Gray in his professional debut in Pittsburgh, Billy stepped into the ring to spar against a seemingly superior opponent. Mickey Walker came to Pittsburgh for his fight with Tait Littman, scheduled for November 26. In the days prior to his bout with Littman, the Toy Bulldog worked out at the Pittsburgh Lyceum. The Lyceum was located on Washington Street in the lower Hill, and was run by Father O'Connor, pastor of the Epiphany Church, which sat across the street from the gym. All good fighters visiting Pittsburgh trained at the Lyceum when in the city. That is, all *White* fighters; Black athletes were ardently barred from the establishment. When Billy wasn't at Johnny's, he was at the Lyceum studying the visiting boxers and occasionally sparring with them. Walker gave the gym-fly just such an opportunity. Billy impressed Walker with his speed and courage.

"The lad has what it takes," he declared after three hard-fought rounds with the pugnacious Conn. For his efforts, Walker tipped Billy ten bucks, five of which he promptly handed over to his manager.

A few months later, on January 11, 1935, Billy's tutelage continued, though under more unusual circumstances. On that evening, Conn landed the position of holding the spit bucket in the corner of Detroit native Joe Louis. A top contender for the heavyweight crown, Louis was in town to take on Hans Birkie at Duquesne Garden. For his troubles, Billy was treated to an illuminating display by the masterful Louis, who had his way with Birkie, knocking the German out in the tenth round. Before vacating the ring, Louis nodded to Billy and instructed his manager to "give that kid twenty bucks."

More and more, Billy began spending time at Johnny's home. Ray rented a cottage on Stratford from the father of composer Oscar Levant. For $14 a month, Johnny got what he paid for, a roof over his head with no frills. "We used to tie the beds to the windows so they wouldn't roll around the room, the floors sloped so," explained Ray.

The accommodations were modest, for sure, but Johnny saw brighter days ahead for him and his fighter. This hole was nothing more than a way station. The city was theirs for the taking. With a scrawny arm wrapped around Billy's bony shoulders, Ray promised his adolescent prodigy, "In no time we'll own this place."

Three I Can Lick Anyone Johnny Ray Tells Me I Can Lick

"Keep your eye on this kid . . . his name is Billy Conn."
—Havey Boyle, *Pittsburgh Post-Gazette*

Billy had been boxing professionally for a little more than a year when Havey Boyle formally introduced him to Pittsburgh fight fans. "He's got a great future in the fight game," continued Boyle in his "Sports Stew" column, which appeared in the *Post-Gazette*. "He can punch, is developing into a good boxer, and is cool as a veteran of three or four years' experience. If we were to pick out a fighter in the preliminary ranks today as the youth most likely to become a star, Billy Conn would be that boy."[1]

Conn was doing his best to fulfill Boyle's prophecy. Though his record consisted of just eight victories in his first fourteen fights, Billy ended 1935 with a streak of five consecutive victories, and lengthened that run as the calendar turned to a new year.

The purses were still modest rewards for their efforts, but Ray knew bigger paydays were on the way. Though few people recognized it at this early stage, Johnny already saw the potential for greatness in Junior. Ray was confident in his own ability to train Billy in the ring, and he was also sure he could manage the boxing facet of Conn's career, but Johnny was honest in evaluating his aptitude when it came to the business aspect of the game. Admittedly, Ray was something less than a financial wizard. Money slipped through Johnny's hands quicker than he earned it, and Ray understood the need to bring aboard someone to assist in managing the monetary side of things. He also needed someone to help defray some of the expenses that had begun to swell. Johnny looked around the local boxing scene, and one name stood out over all others, Johnny McGarvey.

The fifty-seven-year-old McGarvey possessed a genial face, which was set off by big, welcoming eyes. What precious little remained of his dark hair was combed neatly to the right side of his head. He was a fight man through and through, and no one was more respected in Pittsburgh fight circles than McGarvey. Known for honesty and square dealing, Johnny built his good reputation by promoting a number of big shows, including several of Harry Greb's hometown bouts. Indeed, McGarvey was credited with doing more than anyone else to elevate the sport to a high standard in the city.

In 1908 he entered the fight game in the role of matchmaker while working out of the old Northern Club. He later moved his efforts to Motor Square Garden, and was able to boast of never putting on a show in East Liberty that showed a financial loss. Motor Square had a varied and storied history. Renowned architects Peabody and Stearns of Boston designed the facility, which could best be described as a combination of Roman and Renaissance styles. Situated on Baum and Centre Streets, Motor Square Garden opened in 1898 as the Liberty Market House where fresh meats and vegetables could be purchased in what was billed as "the most modern food emporium in Pittsburgh."

The building took on a new use in 1915 when it was taken over by the Pittsburgh Automotive Association and was renamed Motor Square Garden. For the next few years, a wide variety of events took place at Motor Square including expositions, auto shows, and circuses. Though the arena had housed some boxing matches in the previous few years, it wasn't until 1925, when matchmaker McGarvey teamed up with promoter John J. Bell and brought some of the games most attractive fighters to East Liberty, that Pittsburgh moved to the forefront of the boxing world.

Johnny left boxing in the mid-twenties for several years before turning up again in 1935 when he helped with the production of the Teddy Yarosz–Vince Dundee championship bout at Forbes Field. With McGarvey back in the game, Ray approached his old friend and proposed sharing the managerial duties of Conn. Though McGarvey had never managed a fighter before, Ray knew he was perfectly suited for the role and there were few men who knew boxing better than the old promoter. McGarvey thought well of Ray; the two had become well acquainted years earlier when Johnny performed on a number of the promoter's cards. McGarvey was also impressed with young Billy, and he too envisioned great things to come for Conn. McGarvey and Ray struck an accord. They would share managerial duties of Billy, each man receiving 25 percent of the take, while McGarvey fronted the cash for expenses.

Though Johnny McGarvey had taken leave of the profession, Pittsburgh still could claim nearly as many fight promoters as fight venues. The men who operated the game in town were as diverse as the settings in which they put on their shows.

The most likable of the local promoters was the energetic and affable Jake Mintz. With his smashed-in nose and a profound knack of mangling the English language, Mintz was a popular figure in Pittsburgh's sporting clique. Jake became well known about town for proficiently peppering his discourse with malaprops. So the story goes, Mintz's all-out assault on the King's English originated when he was handed a speech to deliver on the radio, a discourse he read from the last page forward, ending with the beginning. By all accounts, the address was a huge hit with listeners, a result that only encouraged Mintz the orator.

Jake immigrated to America from Russia as a young child. After taking leave of school at a young age, Mintz tried his hand at a number of vocations. Among other occupations, Mintz at one time was a carnival barker, a police officer, a salesman, and a boxer. In the ring the diminutive Jake fought under the pseudonym of "Fighting Jack O'Boyle," an Irishman who wore the Star of David on his trunks. "I wanted to have the whole house going for me," he explained.[2]

In summer months, Mintz put on his shows in Millvale's Hickey Park Bowl. Since Jake purchased Hickey Park from Bus Vogel in 1935, he had become a prominent player in the local fight game. With five rows located ringside and another eight elevated above the ropes, the small, square-shaped edifice seated 4,200 people. Not all were willing to fork over their cash to Mintz, however. A number of fight fans avoided paying the entry fee by taking in Hickey Park shows from an adjacent hillside. An enterprising woman who owned the parcel of land charged a scant dime to view the fights from her property. Wanting every nickel he could squeeze from each program, Mintz put up a canvas to hinder these spectators. Instead of being thwarted, the frugal enthusiasts simply moved further up the hill to take in the proceedings below.

Later, on October 1 of the same year that Mintz took over Hickey Park, Jake opened the doors of the Northside Grotto to fight fans. Previously, before Mintz brought boxing to the building, the Grotto had been used solely for fraternal ceremonials and dance bands. With its ornate lobby, luxurious balcony, and beautiful lighting, holding a fight in such lush accommodations would have seemed absurd before Mintz gave it a shot.

Jake faced stiff competition on several fronts. Northsider Bill Dumer ran shows at Greenlee Field in the Hill District with tickets priced between sixty cents and two dollars. Jules Beck and Bunny Buntag each offered quality programs also, but theirs were usually modest affairs. Buntag ran shows out of the Moose Hall on Penn Avenue, downtown. The Moose Hall provided an intimate setting from which to watch a fight. The ring was built out from a stage in the ballroom, leaving patrons with a bird's-eye view of the proceedings below. Buntag's ability to draw the bigger cards in town was hampered by the hall's limited seating capacity of just 2,000.

Mintz's number-one rival, however, was Elwood Spitsenberg Rigby, who was known in the boxing community as the "boy promoter." The hefty Rigby enjoyed oversized cigars, good beer, fast cars, and fine brandy. He managed grapplers Strangler Ed Lewis and Ed Don George and was credited with bringing the first successful incursion of professional wrestling to Pittsburgh. Elwood made his mark in the more respectable world of boxing when he put on the Al Gainer–John Henry Lewis fight at Forbes Field in Oakland.

The popularity of boxing in Pittsburgh waned in the years immediately following Harry Greb's heyday. The spate of local fighters, which had seemed endless in the early twenties, dried up as the decade came to a close. As the effects of the Depression deepened, however, young men discovered that the ring offered opportunity—opportunity they couldn't find elsewhere. Suddenly Pittsburgh was awash with quality homegrown pugs. Once again the city blossomed as a fight town. Out-of-town fighters trekked to the Smoky City where they earned themselves a nice payday and, thanks to the renewed interest, the number of fight shows increased exponentially. Competition was fierce and during the summer season, Jake Mintz's Hickey Park played host to the more attractive programs. But as the weather turned and the shows moved out of the elements, the finer cards were put on at Duquesne Garden.

Located in the Oakland district, wedged between Craig and Neville Streets, was Pittsburgh's largest indoor arena, the Duquesne Garden. Forbes Field may have been the home to the city's largest fight cards; however, of the indoor arenas, the Garden was considered far and away the finest venue in Pittsburgh. Though the official name used the singular "Garden," to most townspeople, the building's name was plural. The Gardens had a seating capacity of 7,500 with unobstructed views of the ring, which was placed in the center of the auditorium. It was at the Gardens that local boxing developed a semblance of propriety. Before the first matches were put on in the Oakland arena in 1909, fights were held on river barges or in "sneak" joints in surrounding towns like Carnegie, McKees Rocks, or Millvale.

The Gardens was built in 1890. Constructed of brick with sandstone trim, the facility served as a "car barn" for the street trolleys of the Duquesne Traction Company. Before the turn of the century, the fad of indoor ice-skating gave the building a new purpose. Sessions were held three times daily at a rate of twenty-five cents. Ice-skating led to hockey. In time, the Hornets, Yellow Jackets, and Pirates would all skate at the Gardens while representing the city of Pittsburgh in various hockey associations. Still, it was boxing that breathed life into the Gardens and gave the hall its allure.

When 1936 began, Billy Conn was just another preliminary fighter, albeit one with potential. The ensuing months saw his profile steadily increase as he abandoned the prelim ranks. By the close of the year, Billy had become a top draw in a town replete with quality fighters.

An integral aspect of Johnny's curriculum centered on getting his young fighter plenty of work. Though Ray lined up eighteen bouts for Billy throughout the course of the year, the duo never left the city. The venues varied: Hickey Park, Moose Hall, Islam Grotto, Motor Square, Greenlee Field, Northside Arena, Duquesne Garden, and Forbes Field. The opponents, too, varied, but not much. Multiple dates with Steve Nickleash, Teddy Movan, General Burrows, Kid Cook, and Honey Boy Jones made up the bulk of Conn's work year.

Johnny's repetitious scheduling strategy was being noticed and commented upon by local writers. "One of these nights when they have nothing else to do, Conn and Movan probably will get together and try to figure out somebody they can fight besides each other."[3]

Movan had just arrived in Pittsburgh from an extended stay in New York, where Teddy had won seven of eight matches he had in the city. When he returned home, Movan found that Pittsburgh's pugilistic crowd had taken to the up-and-coming Conn. "Get that guy for me," Movan told his manager. "He hasn't licked me yet."

Having already defeated Billy once, the McKeesport native was certain that he deserved the praise being given Conn. Teddy was still disgruntled that their second meeting, held the previous October, had been declared a draw. Their third encounter was on the undercard of a John Henry Lewis–Al Gainer bout at Greenlee Field. However confident he may have been prior to the fight, Movan learned shortly after entering the ring that he was facing a distinctly different fighter than he did in the fall. Conn easily won an eight-round decision in which he fully reminded Harry Keck of his tutor and manager.

"On the defensive work [he] is becoming more and more a carbon copy of Johnny Ray, who really seemed to have too much defense to please the fans," Keck wrote. "But Conn is a stronger hitter than Ray was and is much more aggressive."[4]

Despite the lopsided margin of victory for Conn, Movan remained certain that he was the better fighter, and Teddy wanted one more shot. The duo's fourth match, their second in eleven days, was the main bout at Hickey Park on August 11. This Jake Mintz production settled the question and quelled any doubt regarding who was the better boxer between the two local products.

In the bout, after taking things easy in the opening round, Billy soundly thrashed Movan for the remaining seven rounds. Teddy was saved from a technical knockout only because of a generous call by referee Red Robinson, who stepped in to stop the fight moments before the final bell. Though Robinson had clearly moved in before the sound of the bell, he did not credit Billy with a TKO. "I'd hardly call that a technical knockout," Robinson said. "The bell beat me to it."[5]

Whether by decision or TKO, Conn clearly won the fight and his development in the ring was obvious. Billy's conspicuous growth in the ring could in some part be credited to Ray's redundant scheduling philosophy. Conn consistently looked better the second or third (or fourth) time he met a man. By the fourth match with Movan, the talent gap between the two was unmistakable.

On May 27, Billy fought Honey Boy Jones for the first time. Jones, whose given name was Richard, fought in Gus Greenlee's stable of fighters. Greenlee, a prominent businessman in the city's Hill District, aspired to have a fighter in each weight class. Along with Jones, there were Jim Thompson, Jackie Wilson, and Red Bruce, among others. Though these men were capable in the ring, none matched the skill of John Henry Lewis. When Lewis defeated Bob Olin on October 31, 1935, he became the sole Black champion in the sport and Greenlee became the first Black man to manage a Black champion.

Although Jones wasn't in the same class as Lewis, he was a gifted boxer, one who consistently gave his opponents trouble with a brutal style of in-fighting. The Conn–Jones bout was a Jules Beck show at Greenlee Field, part of the undercard of John Henry Lewis–Charlie Massera. Conn won the tightly contested battle, which was such a crowd pleaser that Beck brought the two youngsters back seven days later at the same venue.

Few fans ventured out on the unseasonably chilly June night. Those who did were industrious and kept themselves warm by building a bonfire in the grandstand. Though Izzy Singer and Red Bruce later provided a disappointing main bout, in Billy's first ten-round match he and Jones thrilled the sparse crowd with another tremendous fight. Honey Boy began the fight soundly beating Conn about the body. However, the tide turned in the middle rounds when Billy won the fourth, fifth, and sixth. The stage for a fiery close was set when Jones took the subsequent two rounds. With the fight virtually even through eight, the two boys spent the final six minutes whaling away on one another, each desperately gunning for a knockout. Both fighters remained standing at the sound of the final bell, each equally convinced he was deserving of the decision. An exhausted Conn was awarded a close but unanimous decision and in the process evoked memories of his mentor. "Even if you didn't know Johnny Ray was coaching Billy Conn, the city's newest fistic pride, you could guess Johnny had something to do with Bill from the way the latter uses his elbows," Harry Keck observed.[6]

On September 8, Billy met Honey Boy for the third time in three and a half months. Though Jake Mintz had advertised the Jackie Wilson–Tommy Spiegel bout as the main event, an announcement was made from the apron that a coin flip would decide which match would close the show. Such shenanigans drew the wrath of the *Sun-Telegraph*'s Keck, who was growing weary of the lack of professionalism often displayed in the local fight scene. "Maybe next week a four round opener will be put in the top spot unless the silliness season closes before then," Keck wrote, the sarcasm quite apparent.[7]

Despite losing the coin flip, Conn and Jones gave the Hickey Park crowd a match worthy of top billing with one of the finest fights in the city's summer season. By Keck's count, Billy won only two rounds, the third and fifth. At several different points Conn seemed as if he were on the verge of being knocked out by Jones; each time, however, Billy came roaring back, much to the delight of the partial crowd. What Keck saw as a one-sided fight, with Jones the clear victor, was viewed quite differently by the two judges who disagreed with both the writer and the referee. In a split decision Billy was named the winner, though had the judges been color-blind, Billy would have arguably suffered the seventh loss of his young career.

Billy's popularity gradually increased as 1936 wore on, and not just with local fans. The men who covered the fight game for the city's newspapers had begun to recognize that something quite special was blossoming before their all-too-cynical eyes. Proof lay in the prose of these men. In fight accounts drawn from the beginning of the year, Conn was always described as Billy Conn "of the Hill" or "of the East End." Slowly, as his profile increased, Billy became the "baby-faced assassin" and "Sweet William."

Since 1927, when the *Telegraph* merged with the *Sun* and the *Post* merged with the *Gazette Times,* the city was a three-daily town. From Conn's very first days on the scene as a gangling prelim boy, three men were there to chronicle his career. This trio of local writers provided the narrative for Billy's career, detailing the lanky teenager as he developed into a champion and captured the nation's imagination as Conn made a stab at the most prized crown in sports.

Harry Keck, the sports editor of the *Sun-Telegraph,* was obsessed with boxing, writing about the sport almost to the exclusion of everything else. He gained a national reputation when he was one of a handful of writers to pick Gene Tunney over Jack Dempsey in their fabled match. Keck received some inside dope from Harry Greb, who believed Tunney had the edge over the seemingly indestructible Dempsey. Unlike his friend and colleague at the *Post-Gazette,* Havey Boyle, boxing was Keck's sole sporting passion. He rarely attended baseball or football contests, but Keck could always be counted on to be seated ringside at any local match.

Regis Welsh covered boxing for the *Press* and was perhaps the most popular writer in town reporting on the sport. He was well respected and carried with him deep knowledge of the local scene. Like Keck, Welsh too went back to the days of Greb, and also Johnny Ray. Both reporters took a keen interest in Conn's development thanks to his association with Johnny, whom they each recalled fondly from his days in the ring. Often, these writers who remembered Ray's style made comparisons between teacher and pupil. The examples were numerous and appeared after many of Billy's fights. Certainly, Conn was bigger in size than Ray, but the pupil carried the unmistakable style of fighting embedded into him by Johnny.

The dean of the town's sportswriters, Havey Boyle was both beloved and respected throughout town. He knew Pittsburgh and Pittsburghers as well as anyone. From the Mellons to the workingman in the mill, from the Fifth Avenue mansions to the tenements on the Hill, Boyle had the pulse of the town. With prose that was rich in humor, witty, and refined, Boyle captured the character of the city in his column "Sidewalks of Pittsburgh," which ran for several years in the *Sun-Telegraph.* Havey later left that newspaper to join the *Post-Gazette,* where he began his tenure as that daily's sports editor in November 1929.

Boyle became Pennsylvania's boxing commissioner when Governor Gifford Pinchot appointed him to the post in 1923, the same year boxing took on legal status within the state. A number of people in the know credited Boyle with not only popularizing the sport in the state, but also making certain that the sometimes disreputable exercise was aboveboard. Havey's tenure continued uninterrupted until 1931, when he was replaced by Dr. William D. McClelland. Due to political machinations, McClelland and Boyle spent the next four years swapping the position back and forth. The dizzying carousal stopped for a period in 1935 with McClelland holding the post.

Before relinquishing the position, however, Boyle met the precocious Conn for the first time. Havey thought well of Johnny and had great respect for Ray as a "ring warrior and as a student of boxing form and relative values."[8] However, when John brought Junior by the commission office one day, Boyle believed Ray had lost his mind. Thinking that Johnny was helping a wayward youth blow off school, Boyle chastised Ray. "You ought to be ashamed of yourself, and if you don't take that child home right now I'll have your butt arrested."

But Johnny would hear none of it. "This kid," Ray insisted, "was a future champion, just wait and see," he told Havey. Boyle may have thought Johnny was off his rocker, but he took note of Ray's young fighter, and before long Havey was closely following the burgeoning career of the prodigy.

On December 2, Conn scored an impressive victory over Jimmy Brown at Motor Square Garden. The groundwork for Billy's technical knockout was laid in the fifth round when he gave the Canton, Ohio, native a terrible body beating against the ropes, the effects of which were evident in the following round when Brown went down three times, first for a count of nine, again for nine, and a third time for a count of one . . . without even being struck by Billy.

"Everyday, in every way, the fact is dawning upon fight fans that Pittsburgh once more is on the verge of fistic fame," Regis Welsh wrote in his fight account the following morning. "But this time, instead of one fighter to bring national prominence, like a Greb, a Moran, a Klaus, or a Chip—it's twins."[9] In addition to Conn, Welsh was referring to Fritzie Zivic, who fought Harry Dublinsky on the same Motor Square card. "It was a great night for the two kids, each envious of the other's reputation, and each more eager to fight one another than the promoters seem willing to match them."

A proposed fight between Zivic and Conn began when Fritzie's loquacious manager, Luke Carney, issued a direct challenge to Billy. Carney's provocation angered Ray and McGarvey. Their fighter was young and inexperienced in contrast to Zivic. Putting Billy in a position where he would be forced to turn down the chance to fight Zivic was nothing more than a dirty trick, they believed. McGarvey confronted Carney on the issue and angry words were exchanged between the two men, as Johnny accused Luke of poor sportsmanship, among other things. Carney replied that he was only looking out for the interests of his fighter; Conn was getting all the publicity around town and it was time for Zivic to get his fair share.

What may have begun as a publicity grab by Carney quickly took on a life of its own. Fight fans around town started taking sides and columnists began examining the merits of such a bout. At the same time, Ray was weighing his options and examining the risk of pitting his Junior against the older and more practiced Zivic. After much contemplation, Johnny decided to accept the challenge, a decision Carney had not anticipated. The tables had been turned. Now Carney was reluctant to agree to a fight with Conn. There wasn't much to be gained by his fighter, and much to lose, Carney thought. Why should Zivic risk a loss against the relatively unknown and untried Conn? That he had initiated the whole controversy was now lost on Carney. Painted into a corner by Ray, Carney became bitter.

"Fritzie is after the welterweight title and he will never get it fighting Conn," Carney penned in a letter to Jules Beck, one of the local promoters bidding on the fight. The manager was writing without the consent or knowledge of his fighter. Carney and Zivic, like Conn and Ray, worked without a contract. Unlike Billy, however, Fritzie occasionally made deals on his own without the approval or endorsement of his manager. For his part, Zivic had no qualms about facing Conn. In response to local writers who asked if he would like to square off against Billy, Fritzie didn't hesitate or stutter before answering. "Sure," he said with a confident ease.

Not surprisingly, Conn too was willing to take on anyone. "I'll fight Joe Louis if I get paid for it," he said, referring to the current heavyweight champ. "Get me Zivic. I think it will be a great fight."

The pressure was building on many fronts for Carney to come to the bargaining table and negotiate. Even with both combatants willing, several factors came into play that slowed down the prospects for a fight. Foremost was the percentage of the gate being awarded to the participants. The Pennsylvania Boxing Commission would not sanction any bout in which the boxers were guaranteed more than 55 percent of the receipts. Elwood Rigby, on more than one occasion, had tested this regulation only to have the commission order him to restructure the contracts. Both Zivic and Conn had turned down an initial offer of either $2,000 apiece or 30 percent of the gate each.

Another point of contention was the disparity of weight between the fighters. Zivic's backers believed that Billy at 159 pounds and Fritzie at 147 pounds was too large a gap. If there was going to be a fight, Carney argued, there was to be no more than ten pounds difference in weight.

Ray and McGarvey were both incensed by Carney's oblique handling of the whole proposition. The rival manager had initiated the prospect of a bout and then immediately backpedaled, insisting that his fighter deserved a larger share of the purse. Such a stipulation was reasonable enough to Conn's team. After all, Zivic had more prestige than Conn, having established a reputation in Pittsburgh and beyond. What the two Johnnys took umbrage with was their perception that Carney wasn't negotiating in terms of what he believed Zivic was worth, but rather on what Conn was going to receive.

"We were offered 30 percent by both Rigby and Jules Beck," McGarvey said, referring to the competing promoters. "And as to the disparity in weights, we had nothing to say about that. It was Luke Carney who came out with the declaration that Zivic wanted to get into the middleweight competition."[10]

Finally, after weeks of negotiation in the newspapers, the two sides came together on December 17 at the Pittsburgher Hotel. With Johnny McGarvey by his side, Billy signed to fight Zivic on December 28 at the Duquesne Garden. Each contestant posted $1,000 forfeiture. Zivic agreed to weigh no less than 150 pounds; Conn, no more than 160.

The newspapers were awash with commentary on the impending fight. Foremost in the mind of most columnists was whether Conn was ready to face an opponent with the skill and experience of Zivic. For the first but certainly not the last time, local critics called Johnny Ray's managerial judgment into question. He was rushing Billy, they believed. Zivic was far too learned a fighter for Conn at this point in his career. But Billy had already run through the local preliminary boys, and all that was left were some washed-up middleweights. In addition, Ray was having a hard time getting promoters to agree to matches that were clearly designed to solely gain Billy experience. Besides, Johnny had studied Fritzie on numerous occasions and was completely confident Junior could take the tough welterweight.

As could be expected, Billy had unshakable faith in his manager's decisions. "I think I can lick anyone Johnny Ray tells me I can lick," said Conn. "I know if I do what Ray tells me that I will be all right against anyone he picks."[11]

Ray had picked up a habit carried by his old manager Red Mason, who wouldn't speak to his counterpart during negotiations or in the days prior to the match. Johnny and Luke Carney were well past the cold-shoulder treatment, though. Following the December 2 show at Motor Square, the two men came to blows before being separated. The acrimony between the managers continued even after the rival sides reached their agreement to meet on the 28th.

The lithe but eager Ray didn't shy away from the full-bellied Carney, and Johnny freely admitted to being more "worked up" about the upcoming bout than any match he fought in his heyday. Intentional or not, Carney's machinations were certainly grating on Johnny. In an open letter printed in Havey Boyle's *Post-Gazette* column, Elwood Rigby noted than in all his experience, he had never seen more animosity between opposing camps. At a meeting in the commission's office, it took both Jake Mintz and Rigby to keep the raucous managers apart. The promoter feared all who were present, Billy and Fritzie included, would break into a free-for-all at any moment.

The gathering broke up with no blows exchanged; Zivic, however, called Rigby over for a word. "There is only one way for me to get even with that gang over there," Fritzie said from the hallway, nodding inside to Johnny, Billy, and McGarvey, "and that is for me to knock that pink-cheeked kid right into the laps of Mr. Ray and Mr. McGarvey."[12]

Moments later McGarvey passed Zivic and Carney in the hallway and called them "everything from Pittsburgh to Los Angeles and back."[13]

Fritzie Zivic was the pride of Lawrenceville. Fritzie, along with brothers Eddie, Jack, and Pete, comprised the "Fighting Zivics." Arguably, the quartet was the greatest collection of siblings in boxing history. Their father, Joseph, immigrated to America from his native Croatia in 1890. He found work in Pittsburgh's Black Diamond Steel Works, scrupulously saved his money, and sent for his love, Mary Kepele of Slovenia. The couple married, and soon the new Mrs. Zivic was bearing Joseph bouncing boxing babies.

To say Fritzie was a handsome soul would be generous. He did, however, present an engaging appearance despite all his God-given restrictions. Led by his eyes, he continually gave the impression that he got the punch line moments before the rest of the room. He wore a perpetual smile, an expression that seemed to be permanently attached to his mug, and proudly sported a pug's well-worn nose. Zivic's warm and welcoming face turned cold upon entering the ring, however. With Fritzie, the gentlemanly aspect of the sport went by the wayside. At the sound of the bell, sparks flew, heads butted, "misdirected" blows landed down below, and epithets hung heavy in the air.

In retirement, Fritzie commented on his resourceful fighting style. "I'd give 'em the head, choke 'em, hit 'em in the balls, but never in my life used my thumb because I wanted no one to use it on me. But they accused me of that." Indeed, Zivic's reputation, though seemingly something of legend, was not embellished, but rather founded in reality and well earned.

"I used to bang 'em pretty good," he said. "You're fighting, you're not playing the piano, you know."[14]

With all the buildup, the fight seemed destined to be anticlimatic. To the delight of the more than 5,100 who jammed into Duquesne Garden, the bout was an instant classic . . . an all-out brawl that left the crowd roaring its approval, and many howling at the close.

The lead of the *Post-Gazette's* account of the match set the scene.

"The fight last night in Duquesne Garden between Billy Conn and Fritzie Zivic, as a wild-eyed crowd looked on, was to be a pleasing boxing bout between pals, but as it worked out, the boys used everything but knives, with the result that the town was treated to as swell a boxing feud as you would gaze at."[15]

Zivic got off to a fast start, easily taking the first two rounds. In the third Billy continued to struggle, appearing tired and leg weary. Sixty seconds into the period, Fritzie was warned for an attempted head butt by the referee, Al Grayber. No sooner had Zivic received the reprimand than Billy woke from his malaise and joined the fight with a solid right hand delivered under Fritzie's heart. Conn had absorbed Zivic's best and he was still standing.

Regis Welsh recognized the exchange as a pivotal moment in the bout. "Zivic, a rip-tearing, slam bang artist, stalking what looked like a well-beaten foe, lusting for the expected kayo, winced," Welsh wrote in the *Press*. "And with that wince, with that one punch, Conn came through."[16]

From that instant on, each fighter was charged. Conn and Zivic stood toe to toe, inflicting maximum punishment on one another. In the seventh and eighth, Billy put on an exhibition, as he transformed from puncher to boxer. "He danced and feinted," Welsh wrote, "pranced and punched, his left hand working like a piston, with Zivic's corrugated nose on the end of every thrust."[17]

On two occasions, Grayber had to step between Fritzie and Billy, as the two continued to throw punches after the bell had sounded. Conn was getting a taste of Zivic's freewheeling style of fighting. He wasn't to be bullied about by his more experienced opponent, however. Billy gave as good as he got, but the lessons he learned that December evening at the Duquesne Garden stayed with him long after his days in the ring were over.

"He was a great teacher," Conn said of Zivic in retirement. "That was like going to college for five years, just boxing him ten rounds. He'd do everything in the world to you. The minute you did something to him, he would holler and scream, you'd have to have the police to keep him quiet. He put an awful face on me, busted me all up with everything. He did everything but kick you."[18]

As they touched gloves at the start of the tenth, each man knew the fight was too close to call at that moment. The winner of the final round would in all likelihood take the fight. Both Zivic and Conn fought the final three minutes as if a world championship was at stake, each slugging from the heels in a frightening demonstration of close-in boxing.

"The fight wound up in the bloody tenth," Havey Boyle reported, "with each swinging from downtown, as Zivic, with Conn backed against the ropes, whipped in lefts and rights to the body and head, and with Conn, coming out for momentary cover, would slash out with a head-rocking hook and whipping right to the body."[19]

With the judge's decision in his right hand, ring announcer Ray Eberle proceeded to the microphone. Grayber scored the fight in favor of Zivic. Judges Jap Williams and George McBeth each viewed Conn as the winner, however. The announcement set off an array of reaction throughout the hall. Standing ringside, anxiously awaiting Eberle's declaration, was eleven-year-old Jackie Conn. Upon hearing his brother's name, young Jackie fainted dead away. The crowd at large was split in their reaction to the decision, though no one in the Gardens matched young Jackie's emotive response. Loud cheers and roars of approval filled the room, as a good portion of the crowd had taken to Billy and viewed the nineteen-year-old as the underdog despite his weight advantage. But Fritzie had his fair share of loyal backers, also. Their howls of protest fused with the boisterous approval of Conn supporters, creating a combustible din that shook the walls of the old car barn.

Between the ropes, Zivic and Conn had put on an exhilarating exhibition, tearing into one another with a fury that bordered on the sadistic. Afterward, onlookers were amazed to see the two young men carrying on like school chums. As Billy emerged from the shower in the dreary dressing room, Fritzie was there to offer a towel and a congratulatory hand.

Billy then sat back and relished a victory few thought would be his. Conn had great respect for his rival, but he wasn't taking a backseat to any fighting soul. "I learned a lot in that fight with Fritzie," he said, holding a glass of milk in his right hand. "He's a tough guy, but I believe I'm just as tough."[20]

Boxing tradition almost always called for a rematch, especially in the wake of a controversial decision. Not surprisingly, the demand was high to see a repeat of Conn and Zivic. Regis Welsh recognized the controversy over the verdict. He also understood the impulse for fans and promoters alike to call for a rematch. "But," Welsh penned, "let's not have it. There was glory enough for both last night."[21]

Four Like a Thief
He Kept Running

Immediately following the vicious match at the Gardens, Luke Carney began negotiations with Rigby and Ray for a proposed January 13, 1937, rematch at the same venue. Carney, though, wanted the same terms as the first time around, both financially and the weight restrictions. Johnny would not hear of it. His boy won and deserved, at the minimum, an equal percentage, if not more than Zivic.

In search of new worlds to conquer, shortly after the start of the new year, Billy traveled west with Johnny along with Harry Krause and another member of Ray's stable whose name is lost to history. The quartet set out from Pittsburgh by automobile for the coast with no matches in hand, hoping to entice a promoter to line up a payday or two. Though his fighting companions secured a couple of modest paying bouts, there were no offers for Billy, much to his consternation. It was a slight that Billy vowed not to forget. Still, he managed to make the venture memorable thanks to his phenomenal appetite and sublime performance against a formidable opponent.

On a dreary northern California morn, the two roustabouts were sitting in an Oakland diner. "Billy was always hungry, but when we unexpectedly found ourselves with money, he was always hungrier than usual," Johnny recounted. "This time he was real puckish. Almost in less time than it takes to tell it, he ate thirteen fried eggs, a pound of bacon, a plateful of flapjacks, figs and cream and coffee. An hour later he went into a gym and boxed three rounds with Max Baer—and the big guy hasn't hit him yet. When he came out, Billy tugged at his belt and asked me, 'Hey Johnny, how about a nice thick steak and some French fries, huh?'"

Johnny, long since finished with his meal, left Billy to his stack of hotcakes and went to Duffy's gym to rustle up some work for his boy. Conn, surrounded by a group of gaping waitresses, had just lifted a fork to his mouth when Johnny came rushing into the eatery.

"Billy, don't eat anymore. Baer is down at the gym and he promised to go three rounds with you."

Baer? Who wanted to fight? Billy was still hungry.

Ray was incredulous. How could the kid brush off this opportunity? "Max Baer! One-time heavyweight champion!" Johnny hollered, hoping to snap some sense into Conn. "This is not only an honor, but it'll get in all the papers and it'll save a year on the road. Come on, we box in two hours."

At 6 feet ½ inch Billy was four inches shorter, seventy-five pounds lighter, and eight years younger, yet for three rounds he not only survived, but also shook Baer with his speed and deceptive power. At the close of the session, Johnny was practically shedding tears of joy when he embraced his Junior. The champ walked across the ring, shook Billy's hand, and with a broad grin told him, "My only advice to you son, is don't grow up . . . at least not until I retire."

"Conn whipped a left hook to Baer's body," Eddie Muller wrote in the *San Francisco Examiner.* "He crossed with a whistling right to Baer's whiskers and the ex–heavyweight champion's knees buckled."

Muller and the others in Duffy's gasped at what was taking place in front of them. "Who was this kid that took such liberties and banged Mr. Baer around like that?"[1] The next morning, another West Coast sportswriter who was present in the gym told his readers that "this young Conn is a little boy who throws snowballs at silk hats of the fistic world."[2]

An ecstatic Ray took his "baby" back home to Pittsburgh. They went back to East Liberty and couldn't wait to tell everyone about their memorable travels. "That big bum couldn't lay a glove on my Junior," Johnny told anyone that would listen.

Though suffering ill health, Ray always brightened when the subject of his protégé was brought up. On the eve of Billy's much-ballyhooed follow-up to Zivic, Johnny Ray was feeling especially ebullient. "We're going to have another champion in Pittsburgh," Ray declared. "My

Billy Conn!"[3] The March 11 fight wasn't a title bout; he would be facing Babe Risko, the former middleweight champion. Once again local writers feared that Johnny was pushing his fighter along too quickly. Risko was no over-the-hill ex-champ; he had just lost the title to Freddie Steele the previous July. The Polish sailor was too strong for Billy; he had too much experience. Most experts agreed that, by any measure, Risko simply overmatched Conn.

Johnny heard and read all the critical analysis prior to the fight. The second-guessing and backbiting bothered him not one bit. His skin was thick, but his nerves, always frayed as a fight closed in, were in tatters the afternoon before Billy was to meet Risko. Just prior to the start of the preliminary bouts, Johnny's frail condition gave way and he collapsed in the lobby of the Gardens. He was immediately transported to nearby Mercy Hospital and examined. Though the *Post-Gazette* reported that Ray had suffered a heart attack, the diagnosis was doubtful. More likely, his poor health coupled with the added nervous tension was too much for the little man to bear. Against the orders of his doctor, Harold Kuehner, Johnny left the hospital and returned to the arena. Ray did, however, listen to the good doctor's plea not sit in the corner and direct his fighter. Ashen-faced and gaunt, Johnny delivered final instructions to Billy before leaving the dressing room and taking a seat not too far removed from his customary position. In his stead, Ray reluctantly left Johnny McGarvey, former fighter Val Gruenewald, and Bill Heckman to run things in Billy's corner.

Though the consensus deemed that Risko's brute strength would sway the fight in Babe's favor, the former champion's corner tried to gain an edge with some gamesmanship. Before the first bell rang, Risko's seconds complained to officials about the type of gloves Billy was using. Nothing came of the feeble protest; the gloves were regulation, and Conn was not shaken in the least by the remonstration. Then, at the sound of the bell, Babe stormed across the ring, virtually in a sprint. The frenzied attack was intended to confuse Billy and distract him from Ray's final directives. Though Risko won some early points with the furious onslaught, the strategy didn't have the intended effect of confusing Billy. Conn simply stood his ground before taking the offensive himself. What followed amazed the skeptics sitting on press row. The fight turned in the fourth round when Billy delivered a devastating right to Risko's stomach. Babe slumped forward into a clinch and let out a guttural grunt. From that point forward, Conn knew the fight was his. Risko's punches no longer had any potency and his legs had obviously weakened from Billy's punishing body attack.

By the eighth, Risko was weary and bleeding from both eyes and clearly was a defeated man. An unblemished Billy begged his cornermen to let him abandon the fight plan and finish the ex-champ off.

"No," McGarvey sternly told him; a decision was all they needed.

Conn did as instructed. Even in the tenth, with the outcome a foregone conclusion, Risko made no attempt to try for a knockout, his only hope for victory. Billy breezed to the upset, taking apart his opponent and leaving Babe bitter in defeat.

Following the fight, Billy strode across the ring to shake hands with Risko, but Risko had already left in a spate of temper. A bemused Conn shrugged his shoulders as he watched his foe storm off. From ringside someone shouted, "What's the matter, Billy, is he sore?"

With a smile Conn answered, "I guess so."

The Zivic bout had impressed them, but Risko wowed 'em.

"Conn fought a smart fight. He fought a game fight. He fought a thrilling fight," enthused Harry Keck.

"What a youngster!" continued the *Sun-Telegraph's* sports editor. "A youngster who has the earmarks of becoming not only a good but a great ringman, still has a boyish smile and hasn't forgotten to address his elders as 'Mr.' and 'Sir' and on the whole is one of the most polite 19–year-olds you'll run across in a month of Sundays in these rather flippant times."[4]

Conn stepped from down from the ring apron and was greeted by a fatigued but joyful Johnny Ray. Though he fought a near-perfect fight, Johnny's well-being weighed heavy on Billy throughout the match. The sight of Ray elated Billy. He grabbed his manager by the arms and unashamedly placed a kiss on Johnny's lips.

Sitting near ringside during the fight and watching Conn with great interest was Ray Foutts, manager for Teddy Yarosz. One row behind Foutts was his fighter, equally attentive. A victory by Billy and now surely the locals would be clamoring for a match between Yarosz and Conn—which is precisely what happened. For the immediate future, however, it looked as if Teddy would be traveling to Seattle for a shot at Freddie Steele, an opportunity to reclaim the middleweight title he held briefly.

The weeks subsequent to Billy's brilliant performance against Risko were filled with speculation. Who would be the next opponent for Conn? Yarosz? That was certainly the favorite matchup among the hometown fans. Fred Apostoli? Or maybe Solly Krieger; all were top challengers for Freddie Steele's middleweight title. One name not mentioned was former champion Vince Dundee, who was in the midst of a modest comeback. Just shy of his thirtieth birthday, Vince had returned to the ring in March after spending nearly two years recuperating from a severe beating administered at the hands of Steele. In just three rounds of their July 30, 1935, bout, Steele knocked Dundee down to the canvas *eleven* times before the referee put a merciful stop to the carnage. The Dundee that Johnny signed on for Billy to face was a bit long in the tooth, but coming off of four straight victories.

Local scribes watching Dundee work out at the Lyceum came away impressed. Physically the ex-champ looked as good as he did when he held the title, and mentally Dundee seemed sharper and more confident than at any time since Steele administered such a brutal beating on him.

"I never felt better in my life," Dundee admitted. "I've never seen Conn fight, but from what I've heard and read I'm pretty sure that I can knock him out; that is if he stands up and fights and doesn't use a cycle. I understand he's pretty good in a defensive way but all I want him to do is to fight and keep his elbows to himself."[5]

The two, the cherub-faced boy from East Liberty and the grizzled Baltimore veteran, thrilled the Duquesne Garden crowd with an action-packed match. Throughout the fight, Dundee kept a running discourse going with Billy. Unlike most of his brethren, however, Vince wasn't venting profanity-laced diatribes; he was simply offering an ongoing dialogue, practically a blow-by-blow analysis. With every punch and jab, Dundee surrendered his critique. *Nice going kid, keep it up.*

Johnny's instructions, hollered above the din inside the Gardens, were met with Dundee's approval. *Listen to him kid; he knows what he's talking about.*

The civility continued even as Billy accidentally landed a blow below the belt. *I'm sorry, Mr. Dundee.*[6] The apology was accepted without retaliation.

Billy won eight of the ten rounds; his youth, speed, and stamina were clearly evident. Throughout the May 3 fight, however, Dundee displayed great courage, never wilting or bending under Conn's persistent attack. The decision was unanimous for Conn. He was the aggressor and sharper puncher, but the Gardens crowd was equally boisterous in their praise of Dundee. In defeat, the ex-champ had won over the paying customers with his valor and grit.

After the decision was announced over the PA system, Billy graciously addressed his opponent. "Mr. Dundee," he said as the two foes shook hands. "I learned more tonight than all my other fights. I want to thank you for the lesson."

Together they left the ring to great cheers from an appreciative house. Sitting on a rubbing table in his dressing room afterward, Dundee shook his head in wonder. "Imagine that—calling me Mr. Dundee, I must be somebody," he laughed. "I've never seen a boy like him. All through the bout he was calling me 'Mr. Dundee' and I couldn't figure it out at first. He is a polite, clean-cut kid, and I don't mind losing to him."[7]

The former champion sang the praises of more than just Billy's good manners; Dundee saw a great future for Conn. "I hope he goes a long way. He's a little bit green right now, but he's all right. He keeps popping you with a left hand. His right hand is not as dangerous as it looks. He throws it too far. But he'll shorten it up. Yes, sir, he's a great prospect."

Over in the winner's room, Billy made no attempt to contain his enthusiasm. He was as excited by the experience as he was with his well-earned victory. "Look at my mouth," Conn told the small crowd of newsmen gathered around him. "Cut and split by his left hands. He hits you with a lot of them. And he's hard to hit back. He's moving and weaving and bobbing all the time. I guess I missed more punches tonight than I ever did. . . . It certainly was a great experience. He's the best I ever fought. It was my toughest fight."[8]

The clamor continued for a date between Yarosz and Conn. Three former middleweight champs in a row! It was a natural for promoters and newsmen alike. The sought-after bout would have to be put on hold for a little while longer, however.

Shortly after the Dundee match, Johnny Ray signed to fight Oscar Rankins, the "Red Terror" from Chicago. One week subsequent to the Conn–Dundee clash, Rankins met Solly Krieger at the Gardens. Though Rankins won the match, he came away from the battle with two "bad" eyes. When Ray contractually agreed to meet Rankins, he was of the belief that his fighter could dispatch the partially disabled Chicagoan with ease. Before the show could be put on, however, Billy developed ear trouble and the match had to be postponed. By the time Conn was healthy, Rankins was also—and a healthy Rankins was dangerous.

In the nearly three years that Johnny had been directing Billy's career, he had made no major mistakes managing his young fighter. With Rankins, Ray had painted himself into a corner. He had no intention of taking on an able-bodied Rankins. Such a prospect was too big a threat to Billy's meteoric climb. Yet he was bound by the contract. Pressured by Commissioner W. D. McClelland, Ray cleverly tried to sidestep the issue. He would let Conn fight Rankins, Johnny said, next Christmas. The humor in such a proposal was missed by Dr. McClelland, who dismissed any such proposition. Conn's next fight would be Rankins, or he would face a suspension, the commissioner ordained.

Acquiescing, Ray met with Rankins's representative, George Traftin, and set a date for May 27 at the Gardens. Though he had struggled in his recent bouts, Rankins possessed a fine résumé. He "ruined" Al Quaill, kept Red Bruce in the prelim ranks, and took Krieger out of contention for the middleweight crowd. Win or lose, Rankins always gave the paying customer his money's worth, fighting with flair, determination, and guts. The Conn camp feared Oscar's powerful body deliveries and sneaky left hook.

The night of the fight, Johnny's apprehensions were realized. Rankins proved to be every bit the fighter Ray anticipated and more. Leading up to the match, pundits and fight fans had one remaining question concerning Conn's makeup: whether he was made of championship timbre. "Can he take it?" Against Oscar, Billy answered all skeptics.

In the second round, for just a moment, Conn let his guard down, the defense that had served him so well in recent matches. All Rankins needed was a slight opening; from a crouch, he threw a short right hand, catching Billy high on the jaw.

Conn went down. He went down seemingly in slow motion, paralyzed by the devastating blow. Collapsing on his nose, to all present Billy looked out for the count. At two he slowly rolled over. At four he was prostrate. At seven he was on one knee. Red Robinson continued his deliberate count. At nine he was up—woozy, but up. He survived the remaining moments of the round by retreating and holding onto Rankins for dear life. Try as he might with a number of numbing body blows, Oscar could not put Billy away before the bell.

Newsmen who normally expressed no emotion in their prose couldn't help themselves when detailing Billy's gutsy stand. "Well," a usually crusty Regis Welsh gushed, "if you had seen that kid, dropped with one of Oscar Rankins' best short-chop rights to the chin, get off the floor and go on to a slugging victory you would be the last to question his gameness."[9] Ray and McGarvey revived their fighter, dousing his groggy head with cold water. By the time the chime of the bell called him back, Billy had shaken the cobwebs from his head and he was dancing about the ring, ready to take the fight back.

According to Welsh's scorecard (though admittedly, the writer seemed to be in the bag for Billy this time around), Conn won all the remaining rounds with the exception of the third and eighth. In particularly the fifth and sixth stanzas, Billy set a heart-racing pace that had the crowd atop their seats, roaring.

In the *Sun-Telegraph,* Harry Keck was reporting on a seemingly different fight than his *Press* counterpart. "If ever a fighter won a bout here Rankins won last night," Keck wrote.[10] By his estimation, Keck had Rankins winning six rounds, which, taken with the second round knockdown, should have easily tilted the match toward the Chicagoan. Luckily for Billy, and perhaps more so for manager Ray, Keck wasn't among the judges who decided the fight. At the close of ten hard-fought rounds, one judge, George McBeth, voted Rankins as the winner. The other judge, George Kutzbauer, and referee Red Robinson selected Conn, however. The split decision was greeted with cheers by the Gardens crowd, though a great many of them walked away thinking that Billy had gotten away with one.

Whether Conn deserved the ten-round decision was certainly debatable; nonetheless, officially the victory was his. Billy's winning streak continued and so too did the call for Teddy Yarosz. With each fighter's schedule finally cleared, the Conn and Yarosz camps agreed to meet June 30, 1937, at Forbes Field. Sporting Pittsburgh braced itself for the biggest fight the town had seen in many a year.

Though drumming up hype for the long-anticipated match was probably unnecessary, Chester Smith did his part in the prefight buildup. "There isn't room for both Yarosz and Conn in Pittsburgh," the *Press* editor declared in his column, "especially when both are anxious to sit on the top shelf."[11]

When he was coming up through the ranks, Teddy dispatched the locals standing in his way: Young Rudy, Buck McTiernan, and Tiger Joe Randall. So, too, did Conn need to push aside the "Pugnacious Pole."

Born in the North Side in 1910, Yarosz moved to Monaca when he was ten years old. His father, a Polish immigrant and sandblaster by trade, regularly rebuked his boys, Thaddeus and Ed, for beating the tar out of each other. When his father died, Teddy quit high school and went to work at the Jones and Laughlin mill in Aliquippa. In the evenings, he and his brother Ed hitchhiked their way to boxing tournaments. As an amateur, Teddy dominated his competition: Yarosz won thirty-seven fights and was a finalist in the national AAU welterweight championships.

Yarosz was obviously ready to make the jump to the pros, and he began begging Ray Foutts, a promoter who staged fights in East Liverpool, Ohio, for a chance to prove his wares. Thinking that Yarosz would leave him alone after receiving a good beating, Foutts eventually relented and put Teddy on one of his cards.

Like Conn, Yarosz wasn't known for his powerful punch. What he lacked in power, though, he more than made up for with quantity. Yarosz inundated his opponents with a seemingly endless parade of punches. Such tactics required that Teddy be in excellent condition. A six-mile run every morning was followed by sparring sessions and skipping-rope exercises in the afternoon. Twice a month, Teddy would walk the thirty miles between Monaca and Pittsburgh.

Yarosz had won the middleweight title on September 11, 1934, when he defeated Vince Dundee at Duquesne Garden. A little more than a year later, Teddy relinquished the title at Forbes Field to Babe Risko. His continuing pursuit to regain the crown was Yarosz's motivation as he headed into the match with Conn. A decisive victory over Billy would place Teddy in contention for a date with Freddie Steele and the middleweight title.

On June 29, Yarosz's final day at Madame Bey's training camp in Summit, New Jersey, Teddy worked out fifteen rounds, boxing for twelve. He sparred with Walter Woods, who would be facing Lindsay Rossi on the same Forbes Field bill, and Ben Joby. At Eagle's Rest in Millvale, nearly a thousand fans watched Billy box twelve rounds in preparation for the following day's match. He sparred with Barney Ruffner, John Henry Thomas, and Al Quaill.

The next morning, both fighters appeared at McClelland's office in the Law and Finance Building for the prefight weigh-in and compulsory physical. Accompanied by trainer Ray Arcel and manager Ray Foutts, Yarosz was the picture of athletic beauty. His body was well toned from his monthlong preparation for the fight, his skin bronzed by the sweltering Jersey sun.

Following the official weigh-in (in which both men came in at 161), McClelland asked Yarosz, Conn, and their representatives into his private office for a chat. "You two boys have been a credit to the fight game, not only in Pittsburgh but in a national sense," the commissioner said. "Tonight's fight is the culmination of a great ambition for both of you." Then, after instructing each fighter that any fouls would not be tolerated, McClelland addressed the controversy surrounding the selection of a referee. The debate originated following Yarosz's fight with Krieger in New York. Foutts had heard rumors in the aftermath that the referee was "in the bag" for Solly. To protect his fighter's interest, Foutts went to the Boxing Commission and submitted a list of referees that were suitable to him. Publicly, McClelland had remained silent on the issue. Offering a comment would only lend credence to such suspicions. Privately, in his office, the commissioner chose to address the matter directly with the fighter.

"Since this match has been made, various rumors have been afloat concerning the attitude of the Commission," McClelland said. "I have no interest in either of you, except that this fight be fought cleanly and to the best of your ability. I will pick the referee I think stands the least chance of being unconsciously swayed by crowd psychology. That is important in any bout involving two local boxers, where the sentiment is bound to be keener than at any other time. It is vital that all officials close their ears to the crowd, and the men we choose will be those who are best at that."[12] And with that explanation, McClelland shook hands with each fighter and wished them both well.

Billy seemed oblivious to the excitement he and Teddy had stirred up in the city. Throughout the examination, Conn maintained an air of confidence that belied his age. Or perhaps it was a confidence born in youthful ignorance. As the hour of ten o'clock approached, and the town's collective heart rate quickened, Billy remained blissfully calm.

Following a morning shower, the skies above Oakland remained threatening throughout the afternoon. Elwood Rigby's crossed fingers seemingly did the trick, though, as the rain held off. The promoter forgot one minor detail, however. Ring announcer Ray Eberle was left without a PA system to introduce the fighters to the Forbes Field crowd. Eberle made do with his natural timbre, but still struggled to be heard above the din of the anxious crowd.

"In the far corner, wearing black trunks with red trimming, the Pride of Monaca, Teddy Yarosz. In this corner, wearing purple trunks, from East Liberty, Billy Conn."

The judges were split in their decision of the match. The crowd, boisterous and near riotous, struggled to agree on what they had just witnessed. The critics, however, were unanimous in their appraisal of the much-ballyhooed fight—exhilarating.

Chester Smith wrote approvingly of the match, "One of the most vicious middleweight hooligan brawls this town has ever seen. . . . The marbles are down for keeps and they are at each other from the first clang of the bell to the last."[13]

"No matter how you took the decision it was a rootin' good battle," Jesse Carver gushed in the *Sun-Telegraph*. "It had the customers wild-eyed and hoarse-throated in one of the grandest cheering duels we've heard at a fight here since beer was a nickel."[14]

The fight began in a whirlwind of punches as Yarosz landed time and again with both hands. His blows were effectively mixed, right crosses interspersed with left hooks, an attack that kept Conn on the defensive for much of the first three rounds. When Billy did attempt to go on the attack, he usually found that Teddy had beaten him to the punch.

Despite dominating the initial rounds, Yarosz could not take Billy out. Following the third, after enduring a big round by Teddy, Conn strolled to his corner and exhorted, "Am I in condition!" to Johnny Ray. His confidence was obvious to all within earshot.

By the fourth, Teddy began to tire while Conn seemed energized. The sudden turnaround began with a hard hook to Teddy's head, which set Yarosz to holding and grabbing and, quite out of character for him, backpedaling. The blow not only stunned Yarosz, but also, more important, bolstered Billy. He learned that he could hurt Yarosz. At the close of six rounds, most observers had the fight scored even at three rounds apiece.

"Under the terrific pace which Conn had unleashed, Yarosz became visibly leg weary and arm tired," Regis Welsh reported. "A right-handed smash to the head in the middle of the fifth skidded Teddy across the ring and, as the thing wore on it seemed that Yarosz could not shake off the effects of this tide-turning wallop."[15]

The most vicious exchange yet occurred in the seventh when Yarosz was knocked back on his heels by a jolting left to the jaw. Stunned, but standing, Teddy retaliated with a punishing combination, including a couple of devastating right hands under Conn's heart. Once again Billy displayed courage beyond his years. A less audacious fighter would have withered under the Yarosz assault, but Billy gathered himself quickly and again went on the offensive.

Between the eighth and ninth, Billy sat in his corner and called to a reporter sitting nearby, "How'm I doing?" he asked.

The reporter advised Conn that he was behind and to "jam his foot down on the throttle."[16] Billy winked at his unpaid consultant and went back into battle with those words of instruction, along with Johnny's between-round schoolings.

Yarosz was effectively tying Billy up by clutching and holding. Conn's only recourse was an occasional slap to the back of Teddy's head, which brought the consternation of the referee. At one point, Grayber warned Conn against using the rabbit punch; "I can't hit him any other place when he keeps holding," Billy protested.[17]

Tempers flared following Grayber's verbal reprimand in the tenth. As a token of sportsmanship, Conn offered his glove to Yarosz. Rather than acknowledging this understood act of contrition, Teddy threw a punch to Billy's head. Infuriated by the cheap shot, Conn continued fighting well after the bell sounded, ending the chaotic round.

Order was restored for the final two stanzas, though the action continued unabated. As the match neared its end, Conn proved too strong for Yarosz. Teddy, however, refused to give in, and continued slugging away at Billy. Nevertheless, Conn forced the fight in the closing minutes, and these efforts were certainly fresh in the minds of the judges as they made their decision.

Judge Jap Williams had Conn winning on his card. Judge George McBeth selected Yarosz. Al Grayber, the referee, cast his deciding vote for Conn. When the decision was announced by Ray Eberle, Conn backers let out a tremendous roar of approval, a clamor that was quickly drowned out in a chorus of boos and catcalls by Yarosz supporters. "They threw everything loose in the general direction of the ring," Carver reported. "But they played hell with Gus Miller's nice red and blue cushions. In practically no time at all, they had the floor of the ring waist deep in same."[18]

Before the fighters could vacate the ring, numerous seat cushions, courtesy of a local entrepreneur, came raining down from the stands. Irate Yarosz boosters coupled their vocal displeasure with a more unbecoming behavior. Some chairs were heaved, but mostly the angry horde used the leather seat pillows as their missile of choice. Though not as damaging as a thrown chair, the seat cushions, waterlogged from an earlier downpour, packed a smart wallop. One such cushion plunked Chester Smith behind his right ear. Though momentarily stunned, the writer soon began plucking away at his typewriter as anarchy reigned all around him.

Bottles came crashing down from the bleachers. Punches were thrown just as freely as bottles and seat pillows. Some were delivered to knowing targets, others thrown for the sheer sport of it. Amazingly, through all the bedlam, no one was injured.

Following the main bout, the scheduled fight between Johnny Duca and Al Quaill was delayed due to the small-scale riot. The crowd remained sour tempered throughout the closing match, as debris continued to fill the Oakland air and effectively subdued a victorious night for Quaill.

Such chaos and controversy, however, fueled the immediate talk of a rematch.

In the dressing quarters, Ray Foutts damned the judges' verdict. "That decision stinks," the manager flatly declared. Sitting silently on a rubbing table, his back resting against the wall, Yarosz nodded in agreement. Teddy's disappointment at the outcome, though, did not spill over into his views on Conn. "Billy is a good boy, but I was certain I beat him," said Yarosz. "He's a good fighter. He's game and he's strong. He didn't hurt me at all. If we meet again, and I would be glad to do so, I am sure I would be able to make it so decisive the officials wouldn't rule against me."[19]

"Billy surprised me," he continued. "I didn't think he'd keep coming after I nailed him with those rights under the heart and on the jaw. But he did. . . ."

What was next for him? "I don't know," Teddy said with a shrug. "It was to be a title bout with Freddie Steele next, but this sort of spoils it. I guess I'll have to fight Billy again."[20]

Across the way, the first words out of Billy's mouth when he reached the Pirates' dressing room at Forbes Field were, "Gee, I wish that the fight were just starting." Yarosz's desire to meet again was passed on to Conn, who readily agreed to a rematch. "Sure," he said. "I'll fight him again."[21]

Before reporters had their chance at him, family, friends, Ray, and McGarvey all had an opportunity to congratulate Billy and give him a pat on the back.

"Were you hurt, Billy?" a writer finally asked.

"No, he didn't hurt me at all, but he was a hard man to fight. He does more infighting than I do, and that is where he got in the hardest blows, but they still did not hurt me."

Conn continued, "He is the third former champion I have fought and he did not give me as much trouble as Dundee and Risko. Both of them hit harder than Teddy, but Teddy is a better boxer than either."

"Did that blow in the first round hurt you?" Billy was asked.

"No, after the third round I knew Teddy could not hurt me."[22]

He then noticed Harry Keck standing in the crowd. "Well, I did what you told me to do at the weigh-in," he said.

"What was that?" Keck asked.

"You told me my chance to win lay in doing my fighting during the time I was in the ring and not in figuring out the next day what I should have done. You told me to keep punching, and that's what I did."[23]

Few fights had ever been interpreted so differently. McBeth gave Conn three rounds, Williams gave him six, and Grayber five.

McBeth scored Yarosz the winner in eight of the twelve rounds; Williams gave Teddy four, as did Grayber. McBeth scored one round a draw, Williams two, and Grayber four.

No two people agreed completely on what they had witnessed. Sure, there were some aspects of the fight beyond dispute. Yarosz took the first three rounds without a doubt. After that, however, every patron (or newsman) told a different tale of what had taken place. No amount of arguing could sway the Yarosz fans present at Forbes Field, which made up a predominance of the crowd. Equally fervent in their opinion were the legions of Conn boosters. The outcome of the fight, as well as the unseemly demonstrations afterward, ensured a rematch and fueled what was sure to become an unequaled rivalry.

A footnote to Billy's defeat of Yarosz was Teddy's capturing of the state middleweight championship. Though in retrospect the title was a relatively modest accomplishment, it was a matter of great pride to Teddy. Yarosz had held the belt as Pennsylvania's best middleweight since August of 1933.

There were no imminent plans to place Conn back in the ring. Ideally, Johnny wanted to take a few weeks off and then get Billy a tune-up fight before setting up a date with Fred Apostoli. For the time being, Ray did not have his sights on Freddie Steele. Since the beginning, Ray had been studious and deliberate while planning his fighter's future. To the public, the next move for Conn seemed natural: either an immediate rematch with Yarosz or a shot at Freddie Steele and the championship.

Two days after the fight, Ray and Foutts agreed in principle for a return engagement; this time, the bout was for a proposed fifteen-round match. Each side, however, tried to hold up local promoters for prohibitive terms. The wrangling continued for several weeks, until it was too late to stage a rematch for the outdoor season. Still, at this juncture, Billy had little to gain from meeting Yarosz so soon after their first match. A loss to Teddy in the shadow of his stirring victory would only damage Conn's mystique. Oh, they would face Yarosz again, and in the not-too-distant future, but before that meeting, Johnny had other plans for Junior. As for Steele and the title, Johnny wanted to give his fighter more time to mature, perhaps a year.

In the previous eight months, Billy had proven that he could fight and win in front of a friendly audience. Even against Zivic and Yarosz, when a substantial portion of the crowd was pulling for his opponent, Conn had his fair share of fans rooting for him. The next step in his learning experience would be for the boys to take their act on the road. Just six months earlier, Ray had taken Billy and Harry Krause to northern California only to be shunned by West Coast promoters. Before leaving California in February, Johnny told local promoter Tony Palazola, "The next time we come out here you will send for us."[24]

Indeed, Johnny's prognosis proved correct. Following Conn's impressive string of victories, San Francisco promoter Palazola sent Ray a letter. "You were right," Palazola wrote. "I am now sending for Conn and am also sending three round-trip tickets for him and his handlers."[25] In addition to expenses, the contract called for Billy to receive a guarantee of $3,500 or 30 percent of the gate, whichever was higher. Conn's first appearance in front of a hostile crowd was set for August 13 at Dreamland Auditorium; his opponent, Young Corbett III.

Though born Raffaele Capabianca Giordano in Campania, Italy, Corbett was a favorite son of San Francisco locals. As a child, he immigrated with his family to Fresno, California. In 1919, Raffaele began boxing under the name of Young Corbett III while still a newsboy of just fourteen. Along his long journey up the ranks, Corbett became a headliner in the clubs along the coast. Finally, on February 22, 1933, Corbett defeated Jackie Fields for the welterweight title. His reign as champion was brief, as Corbett lost to Jimmy McLarnin just three months later. The veteran Young had since abandoned the welterweight division, and had recently defeated Johnny Diaz, Mike Bazzone, and Gus Lesnevich. With his experience and hometown advantage, Young was installed as a 10 to 8 favorite.

The fact that Corbett was a southpaw also added to his favor. Billy had never faced a lefty before. In fact, Conn had never even sparred with a southpaw previously. He had, however, worked out with right-handers who assumed the lefty stance. Learning to fight a "backward" boxer was essential to Billy's growth in the ring, but Ray made it clear they weren't traveling all that way just to procure Junior a lesson. "We would never have taken this match if we didn't think Conn could take Corbett to the cleaners, despite the fact that he's a portsider," Johnny asserted.[26]

Before they hit the coast, however, Johnny set up a tune-up for Conn in Youngstown. On Wednesday, August 2, Ray, McGarvey, and Billy boarded a train bound for Youngstown, their first stop on the way to California. Fight fans in the Ohio mill town had heard about the young up-and-coming Pittsburgh pugilist, but only a scant number had ventured to Billy's hometown to see him in person. Johnny agreed to the August 4 date at Idora Park to appease Youngstown fight fans, but Ray also saw a way to gather a middling payday with very little danger. Conn's opponent was a familiar one. Ten months earlier, Billy met Ralph Chong at Duquesne Garden. Still, the Billy Conn that Ralph Chong fought the previous October was an entirely different fighter than the young man he encountered in Youngstown. Unlike their first meeting, which went the distance, the second time around Billy easily dispatched Chong in five rounds with a TKO. The outcome was never in doubt.

The following morning, Conn boarded a train with his managers and the trio continued their voyage westward. They arrived in San Francisco to find themselves in the midst of a controversy. Word had reached the coast of a Les Biederman piece published in the *Pittsburgh Press,* which alleged Conn had been "propositioned to take a dive." Supposedly, according to Biederman's account, Ray and Conn were approached on their previous trip to California. Johnny and Billy's refusal to throw a fight, Biederman wrote, was the reason they couldn't scrounge up a match earlier in the year. By Biederman's telling, there was something suspect in West Coast boxing circles. Was it a coincidence that Conn, with his fine record, couldn't find work in California, while a number of lesser Eastern fighters had no trouble getting dates (and losing)? Donn Shields of the California State Athletic Commission investigated the matter before issuing Conn a license. Following his query, Shields exonerated both Ray and Conn of any wrongdoing and okayed Billy to fight in the state.

West Coast fans and writers were wondering the same thing; why was this up-and-coming kid venturing across the country to face such a tough opponent? As usual, Ray had a plan mapped out. An East Coast fighter who traveled to the left coast and defeated a formidable boxer in his own backyard would then be given proper respect. "In the East, promoters and fans alike regard Corbett as a great fighter," Ray told Eddie Muller of the *San Francisco Examiner.* "They think if an eastern fighter can whip him in San Francisco he deserves to get first crack at the middleweight championship. We're taking a short cut trying to get at Freddie Steele."[27]

The match had barely begun when Conn suffered a debilitating injury. Midway through the second round, the two fighters lunged toward one another. When they separated, Billy's face was awash in crimson. The result of the collision was a three-inch gash above Conn's left eye, which immediately began oozing blood. From Billy's corner came the cry of foul. Corbett had obviously butted their fighter, Ray and McGarvey proclaimed. They were not alone in their interpretation of the exchange. The consensus ringside was that Corbett's action was not accidental.

Intentional or not, there was no debate that Conn fought at a definite disadvantage following the head butt. Shortly after the injury was incurred, Corbett knocked Billy down for a count of two. Young caught Conn with a left cross to the jaw, which sent Billy tumbling to the mat. Thankfully, for Billy's sake, the round was near its end, and Corbett was unable to finish his woozy opponent off.

The remaining eight rounds were filled with furious exchanges. As the blood continued to flow down Billy's face, he fought with a grit and determination that stirred the northern California sportswriters. "Conn made a decided impression with skill, courage and aggressiveness," wrote Jack Rosenbaum of the *San Francisco News.*[28]

Despite his tenacity, the injury and the home crowd was too much for Billy to overcome. The split decision, announced by referee Jack Downey, rankled good boxing men in the crowd who believed Conn had been robbed. Writing under the headline, "Corbett Butts His Way to Win over Conn," Dick Frienlich of the *Chronicle* believed the second-round foul was the difference in the fight.

"Certainly Conn would have emerged the victor if he hadn't run afoul of the butting match because from the fourth round to the ninth rounds he gave Corbett a fine body punching." Frienlich continued, "In spite of the handicap, Conn fought back so viciously that many ringsiders went away convinced he should have won the nod or received no worse than a draw."[29]

The normally loquacious Conn had little to say afterward. He did, however, indicate that he believed the decision was a "hometown" verdict, and Billy wanted another shot at Corbett. Such a close and controversial outcome set the stage for a rematch. In the disappointing aftermath of the fight, Johnny met with Palazola and discussed the possibility of arranging another meeting. Before any dates could be set, the wound over Billy's eye needed time to heal. The party set off for Pittsburgh without an agreement with Palazola, though Ray left open the possibility that they might return to the coast. One thing all parties agreed to; a rematch would draw considerably better than the $4,500 the first bout grossed, a losing proposition for Palazola.

During the Oscar Rankins fight in late May, Johnny McGarvey had suddenly taken ill. His doctor diagnosed McGarvey's malady as a liver ailment, and following a brief hospitalization, Johnny was permitted to recuperate at his East Liberty home. Several weeks of bed rest and Johnny was seemingly back in good health. Indeed, McGarvey's vigor had returned, and his physician had okayed the long cross-country trip to San Francisco for the Young Corbett fight. On the way home from the West Coast, however, Johnny was suddenly stricken again. When they arrived at Penn Station, Conn and Ray stood by as their friend was taken from the train in a wheelchair. For the next three weeks, McGarvey's condition remained dire. Finally, on September 17, Johnny succumbed and passed away at his home on West Penn Place.

The Pittsburgh sporting world went into mourning for the late boxing promoter. For more than three decades, McGarvey earned the reputation as a "square shooter"; it was a standing he lived up to 'til his dying day.

Johnny Ray was taken aback by the loss of his partner and friend. Their relationship went back nearly twenty years. McGarvey helped nurture him as a young boxer, and on more than one occasion he was there to offer Ray a helping hand. He was also there to provide Ray with much-appreciated insight into the finer points of the business side of the game. A good portion of Johnny Ray's nearly flawless managing of Conn's career could be attributed to McGarvey's guidance, a fact that Ray would readily admit.

For Billy, the loss was also profound. Like Ray, who had essentially become a second father figure to Conn, McGarvey had also served as a mentor to Billy. As he had with Ray, McGarvey passed along his vast knowledge to the young boxer. Though Conn was too young to fully appreciate the deep reservoir of wisdom he was receiving, Billy welcomed and was grateful for the paternal interest McGarvey exhibited in him.

On September 20, Johnny was buried at Calvary Cemetery following mass of requiem at St. Lawrence Catholic Church. Immediately after the rite, Billy resumed training for his much-anticipated rematch with Teddy Yarosz. Just days before McGarvey passed away, on September 14, Ray Foutts and Johnny Ray met at the office of boxing commissioner W. D. McClelland. The two managers agreed to have their fighters meet at the newly refurbished Duquesne Garden on the 30th of that same month. McClelland released a statement declaring that the second Conn–Yarosz bout would be an elimination match. The winner would be recognized as the middleweight title challenger and eligible to face Freddie Steele, either in Pittsburgh or elsewhere in the state.

In August, Ray had returned to Pittsburgh to learn that he was the subject of criticism in the local press. Why travel across the country for a relatively paltry sum of money, to a town where Corbett invariably came out on top? Not to mention the fact that his fighter came back home with a nasty cut above his eye. Now Ray had signed on to face Yarosz again, for what was sure to be even more ballyhooed than the first meeting. The second fight, though, would be held at the Gardens rather than Forbes Field. Instead of a possible $30,000 gate, the show would draw roughly half that amount. Not all the blame for the delay in signing for a rematch could be laid at Ray's feet. Foutts also held out for a better deal for his fighter. Still, it was Johnny who drew the brunt of the criticism from local pundits.

McGarvey's death left a marked impression on Conn. His performance in the days following Johnny's passing was, to be kind, lackluster. During one sparring session, Harry Krause stopped in mid-round and asked Billy what was bothering him. Wearing headgear to protect his cut eye, Conn paused for a moment but didn't offer a reply, only a wave of his gloved hand signaling Krause to continue. Harry's inquiry alone didn't snap Conn from his doldrums. With each succeeding day, though, Billy looked sharper and more focused in the ring.

A handful of reporters came to Eagle's Rest where Conn began preparing for the fight. Following his workout, writers began peppering Billy with questions. "What did you learn from your last fight with Yarosz?" he was asked.

"I learned this," Conn replied, "that he cannot hurt me. I learned also that I can avoid a lot of those harmless punches that he throws. I also discovered that I have a punch—and I am willing to bet right now that if I don't knock him out he will be so badly beaten there will be no question about it."

Billy then went on to tell reporters that he wanted his fans in town to know that Yarosz would most likely be his last fight as a middleweight. "It takes quite an effort for me to get down to 162 pounds," explained Billy. "The next fight that I engage in will be among the light heavyweights. I would like to postpone taking on the heavier fellows, but I cannot do it. . . . I think it will be better for me if I let nature take its course and from now on I believe I will have to fight those so-called champions like Gainer, Fox, and John Henry Lewis."[30]

Not surprisingly, Yarosz was equally sure of victory. "I have too much on the ball for the kid," Teddy told newsman. "I will not outpoint him and I will out punch him in such a way that there will be no question about it. I have a pride in my work in front of Pittsburgh audiences and I am not going to let down fans who thought I won the last time. I also think, and I know, that I won the last fight and I will be out here tonight to keep that confidence that my friends have in me."[31]

Originally Teddy planned on training for the fight at home in Monaca. He quickly changed his mind, and on the 16th, Yarosz boarded a train for New Jersey where, under the tutelage of Ray Arcel, Teddy prepared for Conn at Madame Bey's. Unlike the first meeting, when Teddy returned to Pittsburgh the evening before the fight and was able to sleep just an hour the night before, Yarosz came home several days early from New Jersey. On Sunday the 26th, Teddy stepped off his train at Penn Station looking robust and fresh. The following afternoon, Yarosz and Arcel were scheduled to pick up where they left off in New Jersey at the Lyceum downtown. By chance, Billy had also relocated his training regiment to the same facility, and he too was slated to work out Monday, though the gym was reserved for Conn two hours prior to Teddy's two o'clock date.

In an act of gamesmanship, Billy began his session late, entering the ring just minutes before Teddy was scheduled to start his drilling. Arcel and Yarosz arrived at the gym only to find a large crowd watching Conn spar with Harry Krause. Red-faced, Arcel tried in vain to have Billy expelled from the ring before the duo grabbed their equipment and headed to the Centre Avenue YMCA for Teddy's workout.

At the close of his session, Billy noticed that his opponent had taken leave of the gym. Knowing he had just won a psychological battle, Conn believed the physical fight, three days hence, would be his to take also. "He can't hurt me, no matter what the distance," Billy told the handful of newsman who stayed through the workout. "And if he can't hurt me, he's not going to stop me. I'm going to punch it out with him this time, as he won't be able to stand up under it for fifteen rounds."

The boastful nature of Conn's comments took the local writers aback. They hadn't yet seen this side of the fighter. Though Billy exuded confidence, he had rarely, if ever, spoken so frankly before a match. "Don't be surprised if I knock him out. I'm going to try to put an end to all the argument the other one caused."[32]

Already having had his fun, Conn did not try to tweak Yarosz any further in the subsequent days leading up to the fight. Though both worked out at the Lyceum, schedules were adhered to and no further controversy ensued. Indeed, each camp conspicuously avoided the other altogether, opting instead to save all stored up animosity for Thursday evening.

The grand buildup was nearly all for naught. The boxers and their agents met at McClelland's office at two o'clock for the official weigh-in. First on the scale was Yarosz. The contract set the limit at 161, give or take a pound, and Teddy came in exactly the prescribed weight of 161. Next up, deputy boxing commissioner Stanley Waechter put Billy on the scale. "162¾." Waechter said.

Impossible, Ray blurted out, the scale must be off.

Again, Waechter had Billy step up, and again the weight read the same.

Still certain his fighter had reached weight, Johnny again dissented.

Giving in to Ray's protest, Waechter repeated the act a third time only to read off the same disputed figure. Convinced now that he and his fighter had failed to fulfill the contractual agreement, Ray fretted that McClelland would call off the match.

Instead, the commissioner pulled both fighters and their managers aside for a private talk away from the media present. Some time passed before McClelland resurfaced and told the waiting scribes that Conn would be required to shed the extra weight before the fight could be sanctioned. Johnny and Billy briefly exited the office only to return fifteen minutes later. Whatever Ray prescribed did the trick. At long last, after four tries at the scale, the fight was finally on.

"They don't carry winners out of the ring in a state of sheer exhaustion," penned Regis Welsh in beginning his fight summary. But, Welsh acknowledged, "Neither do they award decisions to the fighter who has only won five out of fifteen rounds and gained an even break in two others."[33]

Through twelve rounds, Teddy held the edge by outthinking and outpointing Billy. He was able to deftly avoid Conn's punches while scoring with his own. For eleven rounds, Yarosz looked like the champion he once was. Billy seemed perplexed by Teddy's method. He forgot all about his potent left, and when he used his right, Conn most often missed. At one point, Billy stood, both feet even, seemingly ready to fight as a southpaw, such was the extent that Yarosz had him confused.

By the middle of the twelfth, however, Teddy began to noticeably tire. Most on hand thought Billy's only chance for victory as the fight entered the thirteenth was to knock out his adversary. And the potential for *that* to happen, many believed, was minimal given Conn's lack of a knockout punch.

Despite his poor showing through much of the fight, Conn never lacked in spirit. Even as Yarosz danced around him, snapping off left and straight rights, Billy looked lively. It seemed to observers that Conn was simply biding his time, but the hour was growing late.

Early in the thirteenth, Billy noticed a slight buckle in Yarosz's knees. He quickly leapt to take advantage of the opening. Visibly exhausted,

Teddy began to clutch and hold onto Conn, who shrugged off his weakened opponent and wildly hurled untold rights and lefts at a diminished target.

Surviving the Conn onslaught, in the following round Yarosz threw a right that missed its intended objective. Teddy crumpled to the canvas from the exertion of the fruitless attempt. Swiftly Yarosz righted himself, but he had barely returned to his feet when Conn was upon him, unleashing a relentless rain of punches. To the surprise of many, Teddy somehow managed to remain upright under the punishing torrent.

Though he had already fought for forty-two minutes, Billy entered the ring for the final round looking as fresh as he did in the first. Regis Welsh took note of Conn's condition and what he believed were the first signs of life shown by the fighter in the whole match. "Riding the crest with youthful stamina undiminished by the boxing lesson he had absorbed, unbounded courage and a will to win for the first time, tore in like a wild man," wrote Welsh.[34]

For three full minutes, Billy cuffed Yarosz about, from one end of the ring to another. When it seemed as if Teddy couldn't take one more blow, the bell sounded, saving Yarosz from what seemed to be an inevitable knockout. The frenzied finish had worked the crowd up into a state of delirium. Surprisingly, given their condition just a few moments earlier, the crowd of 6,843 reacted with a curious calmness when Ray Eberle announced the split decision. By every manner of scoring—greater aggressiveness, more punches thrown—Yarosz easily won the fight. Still, judges Karl Koehn and George Kutzbauer gave the verdict to Conn, while referee Freddie Mastrean voted for Yarosz.

As Eberle raised Billy's hand in triumph, Teddy went to his corner and collapsed onto his stool. A doctor looked over Yarosz while a group of friends hovered nearby. A full fifteen minutes passed before Teddy was able to leave the ring. Once the Yarosz party reached his dressing room, Ray Arcel and Dr. Fleming laid Teddy out onto a training table and applied restorations to the beaten fighter.

Despondent and in tears, Teddy had nothing to offer reporters. "I don't want to talk about it," was all Yarosz said in response to the handful of questions posed. Respectfully, the local media left the fighter alone and moved on to his trainer, Arcel, who theorized that the smoke in the Gardens may have been responsible for Teddy's drastic falloff in the last three rounds. Arcel did not elaborate or explain why the smoke didn't equally afflict Conn.

Ray Foutts was nearly apoplectic. He wasn't as diplomatic as Arcel; the smoke in the hall wasn't the cause of Teddy's defeat. No, Foutts intimated that something more nefarious was afoot. He was "convinced that it is impossible to beat Conn in Pittsburgh unless he is knocked out." The implication in Foutts's assertion was clear to reporters, who asked the manager if he wanted to modify his comments for attribution.

"You can't make it too strong," Foutts sputtered. "I have seen Conn lose several fights here in which he received the decision, but this is the worst. Yarosz tonight gave a masterful exhibition of boxing to completely befuddle Billy and win by a mile, only to be the victim of such an absurd ruling."[35]

In the opposite dressing room, a beaming Conn was more than happy to oblige a needy press corps with his comments. "Yes, I'm happy to win," Billy said, "but I had to come back strong. Ted had me worried. That right of his hurt me more than once, but if he would have fought me the same way as he did the first time, I would have won hands down. . . . I realized that I was behind when the late rounds arrived, but I wasn't beaten. I was encouraged by the thought that Ted couldn't hurt me, but I'll admit that he made things pretty miserable. . . . Sure," Conn declared, "I'll meet him again, and I'm pretty sure I'll beat him."[36]

Though the official decision was split in favor of Conn, the town's boxing writers were unanimous in their belief that Yarosz was the rightful winner. In the *Post-Gazette,* Havey Boyle credited Teddy with the victory, but he believed Yarosz had only himself to blame for the controversial decision. His poor showing in the final two rounds did Teddy in, Boyle asserted. "It is entirely possible Teddy collapsed from his own exertions and not any thing produced by Conn, but the testimony against him, whether his condition was self-imposed or induced by Conn was weighty."[37]

In two meetings, Yarosz and Conn had produced two entertaining fights with two controversial outcomes. Hopefully, Regis Welsh wrote, a third meeting wouldn't be in the offing. The young fighters more than proved their courage and worth in their two bouts, and neither had anything left to prove.

"Decisions in record books will show that Conn beat Yarosz twice, regardless of what you think," Welsh opined. "But only memory will recall the vivid circumstances of those wins, and losses by two kids with the hearts of lions, the will to win, and the ability to drive usually sane-minded persons on the verge of delirium. . . . Let them both go their way, they have given all of us enough to remember them by."[38]

The evening after the fight, Ray Foutts filed a formal complaint with the state boxing commission. In a letter to Dr. McClelland, Foutts asked the commission chairman to reverse the decision. The argument for reversal was laid out in reasoned prose for McClelland to contemplate.

1. Pittsburgh newspaper stories were unanimous in declaring Yarosz the winner on the basis of the majority of rounds won. One paper stated that Yarosz won thirteen out of fifteen rounds.
2. It is my understanding that the number of rounds won determines the winner of a fight in Pennsylvania.
3. The referee, the man who was in the best position to judge the fight, gave nine rounds to Yarosz, four to Conn, and two even.
4. The general opinion of the public supports my request in asking for a reversal of the verdict.
5. My request seems to be in order, in keeping with the previous policy of the state athletic commission in reversing uniform verdicts.[39]

One week later, McClelland responded. The commissioner did not address Foutts's grievance, but rather the side agreement negotiated by Yarosz's manager and Elwood Rigby. The undisclosed deal prompted the indefinite suspension of both men by McClelland and a severe verbal reprimand. "The existence of any side agreement other than the contract filed and approved by the commission cannot be tolerated," McClelland wrote in a public statement.

"In his last promotion, in spite of the largest gate in the history of indoor boxing, promoter Rigby demonstrated a lack of financial responsibility. Billy Conn has not yet been paid in full. This matter will be brought to the attention of the bonding company, and immediate steps [will be] taken to recover the balance of the $1,815.55 due Conn."[40]

Feelings for Billy throughout Pittsburgh were anything but apathetic. He certainly had a strong base of supporters, but there was also a growing contingent of boxing fans that had no use for him. Members of this group found any number of reasons not to like Conn. Reason one, he was vastly overrated as a boxer, they believed. Another, Billy received far too much attention, especially when taking into account his accomplishments to date. Not coincidentally, a substantial number of Conn's detractors counted themselves among Yarosz's followers.

And they wholeheartedly believed their hero had been robbed twice of victories at the hands of Billy.

Gone were the days when Billy was playing with house money. Two very questionable victories over Yarosz sandwiched a loss to Corbett. It was in this setting that Johnny signed on to face Corbett again. This time, though, the fight would take place on Billy's home turf. A victory over the Californian in their rematch was vital if Conn was to continue his rise up the ranks and develop a national standing in the sport.

The reputation of Pittsburgh as a respectable boxing town was also on the line. Nationally, boxing critics were beginning to question the ethics of local officials. Conn's victories over Zivic, Rankins, and Yarosz were viewed as suspicious wins in some circles.

To the great relief of all the local parties, Conn at long last won a match in which no controversy followed. The lead in the *Press* fight account recognized the significance of Billy's unblemished victory, as well as the lack of controversy in the postfight fallout.

"For the first time since the East Liberty flash has become a big shot attraction hereabouts, there has been no argument, no cushion throwing, no derisive howling, no heated post mortems to take credit from the kid who, despite his brilliant record, has been a dubious winner to more than a few fans who know fight game angles."[41]

Though he had carried it to a ridiculous extreme the last time out against Yarosz, Billy had fallen into the habit of starting off his fights slowly. To combat this irritating and potentially fatal flaw in Billy's game, Ray had his fighter "box" for three rounds prior to entering the ring against Young. Johnny's plan worked to perfection as Conn came out and quickly took control of the fight. Holding the edge over his opponent with height and weight, Billy forced the fight all night long. Not until the fourth was Young able to mount an effective offensive, and that round proved to be his finest of the evening. Billy's only real mistake in the match came in that same round when he moved about high on his toes with his guard down. Corbett saw an opening for an overhand hook. He delivered four in a row, but the punches seemed to have no effect on Billy. Realizing that he had taken the best Young had to offer and yet was not fazed one iota, Conn took the fight inside without any fear of reprisal from Corbett.

Later, in the ninth, Young hit Conn with a left uppercut that violently snapped Billy's head back. The blow had no discernable effect on Conn, however, as he came back from the blow and delivered two swift rights to Young's head. Following the fight, Conn admitted that Corbett's ninth-round left was the only punch he felt all night, and that one didn't even hurt him.

The fourteen-year veteran was no pushover. Despite Billy's more aggressive style, Young bravely fought on. Overpowered and over-matched, Corbett's only recourse was his savvy. Experience wasn't enough for Young, however. The final bell rang with Billy well ahead on points, leaving no doubt about the decision of the judges. Young accepted the defeat graciously, and had nothing but praise for his adversary following the fight.

"Billy's a great boy," Corbett said. "I thought he was a better fighter today than he was when I met him out on the coast. . . . He is learning real fast and will keep on learning. He is young and strong and has all the requirements of a great fighter."

Surrounded by a number of well-wishers, Billy was pleased with his performance and particularly with settling the score with Young. "I felt pretty good all the way, and was confident of winning," a jovial Conn said from his Duquesne Garden dressing room. Billy then described the strategy he employed, an approach he determined would be effective following their first meeting. "I tried to center most of my punches at his stomach because I learned in our first fight that he didn't care much for blows there. Every time I hit him there, he would say, 'Break,' and I figured I would weaken him with those blows."[42]

Earlier that afternoon Westinghouse had fallen ill and was forced to take to bed. The news of his father's condition was kept from Billy until he began getting dressed following the fight. It was the first time the elder Conn missed his son perform locally. His absence, though, was duly noted because Westinghouse always made his presence at Billy's fights known. The elder Conn was often a distraction to his son as Billy battled in the ring. While Billy battled for pay between the ropes, Westinghouse scuffled in the stands, often with very little provocation. Early in his career, Billy asked his father to stop coming to his bouts; his behavior was embarrassing.

"I have enough problems with the fight," he told Westinghouse. "I can't be worried about you." But Billy's pleads were shrugged off. Only illness could keep Westinghouse away from one of his boy's bouts. Strangely, when his father was finally absent, Billy found he missed the ruckus Westinghouse brought to the show.

A lack of proper police presence outside the Gardens before the most recent Conn–Yarosz fight led to an unruly scene in which ticket holders were roughly manhandled and were forced to fight their way into the arena. Criticism of Elwood Rigby was rampant as he once again was guilty of shoddy crowd control.

"The handling of the crowd was the usual disgrace," Havey Boyle wrote. "It keeps on getting worse. There will be the usual statements, excuses and apologies, with a promise that the next time everything will be hunky-dory."

One thing was certain to Boyle; Pittsburgh was not ready for a big-time event. "New York, Chicago and other spots handle World Series crowds and heavyweight title fights with not one moment's confusion—In Pittsburgh, it is the rule to buy a ticket, for which there is no seat, to fight your way into the hall, after an hour's milling, and then find your seat occupied—and the show about half over."[43]

Boyle's contemporary, Harry Keck of the *Sun-Telegraph,* also saw the need to clean up the local scene. "A wholesale cleanup of the boxing situation here, including closer supervision of all of the promoters, is in order at once. . . . The sport cannot endure if the paying customers are herded and pushed about like so much cattle."[44]

The Conn–Corbett fight epitomized the efforts of local promoters. Corbett's $4,000 guarantee, plus his expenses, which came to $700, equaled nearly 47 percent of the $9,926 gate; 30 percent went to Conn, and 15 percent for the rental of the Garden. More than 90 percent of the revenue generated had been spent before officials, security, preliminary fighters, and ushers had been paid. A relatively successful card such as Conn–Corbett still turned out to be a losing proposition for Jake Mintz.

The crash was bound to come. The three most prominent promoters in the city, Mintz, Jules Beck, and Elwood Rigby, had been recklessly conducting business while trying to outdo one another. Unreasonable guarantees were handed out indiscriminately. This practice did much to lure the top names in the industry to Pittsburgh, but also made turning a profit a distant memory. In their competition with one another, the three promoters cared less about a show's profitability than swiping matches from one another. Unwittingly, Barney McGinley, a saloon owner from Braddock, enabled this careless practice by backing all three of the aforementioned promoters on different occasions in 1937. With McGinley's money behind them, Rigby, Beck, and Mintz had no need to concern themselves with any losses incurred.

Into this chaotic scene entered a new promotional team that promised to stabilize the fight scene in Pittsburgh. Art Rooney, the owner of the Pittsburgh Pirates football club, and McGinley combined their friendship and passion for the sport to form the Rooney-McGinley Boxing Club. The stout Rooney once acquitted himself well in the ring. Though he fought only twice professionally, Art built quite an impressive résumé as an amateur. Smartly, Rooney opted to hang up the gloves undefeated in his two pro bouts, and instead ventured into a wide array of business interests. Some, like backing semipro sports clubs, were aboveboard. Others, however, crossed the sometimes-blurred line of legality. Art and his partner, Milt Jaffe, capitalized on the Volstead Act by plying parched customers with the banned libation of their choice. Jaffe and Rooney also operated a gambling hall on the North Side called the Showboat. In addition, Art was also a great handicapper of horses. On one day in 1936, Rooney took the pumps for 250 grand at Saratoga. The boxing club would be a strictly legitimate endeavor for Barney and Art, though the connections the duo had made through their wide variety of interests would assist them in making the club a success.

There was an air of casualness to the business in Pittsburgh. The Rooney-McGinley team, while making a noble attempt at stepping into the big time, still operated much like a mom-and-pop store. Though they were the only outfit in town operating out of an office, the promoters ran their business out of the same Fort Pitt Hotel office that served as the home of the Pirates. Ducats for the gridiron game in one drawer, boxing tickets in another. There was something charming and quaint about the enterprise.

For these promoters, the biggest expense was the boxers. The rent, printing tickets, paying officials, the main event (who received a percentage), the undercard (who received a flat fee that varied depending on whether they were four-, six-, or ten-round bouts), plus transportation for out-of-town fighters—everywhere you turned, there was another cost. The most important part of promoting is knowing what a fight will draw. There was an art to the whole process, but unforeseen circumstances could throw even the best-laid plans to the wind. Poor weather could wreak havoc with an outdoor show, making a sure winner a losing card.

Nobody, not Mintz, Eberle, Rigby, or Rooney and McGinley, was going to get rich promoting fights in Pittsburgh. Certainly, when everything came together, there was money to be made by all. But there were also many bouts for which the gate was miniscule, and with the fighters to be paid and the house to be paid for, it took some money to put the whole place together; sometimes when everyone got their cut, there was nothing left for the promoter but unpaid bills.

Word of the twenty-year-old kid from Pittsburgh was beginning to spread beyond the parochial boroughs of western Pennsylvania. New York City, the place where stars were made, was now open to Billy. In the aftermath of Conn's impressive performance against Young Corbett, Johnny received several offers to bring his Junior to New York. Harry Keck, for one, believed Ray would be a fool not to jump at the chance to leave the soot and grime of the Smoky City for an opportunity to perform under the bright lights of Gotham.

"[Conn] has fought four former world champions," Keck stated. "He might as well meet opposition of this caliber in New York's Madison Square Garden as here, and reap the benefit of national, if not worldwide, ballyhoo."[45]

Inexplicably, Ray politely turned down the New York overtures and instead signed on with Jake Mintz for a December 16 bout at Duquesne Garden. Billy's opponent was a twenty-eight-year-old Jewish middleweight from Brooklyn, New York. On the surface, Solly Krieger did not match up against the high-quality foes Conn had faced in the preceding months. Krieger was a well-experienced club fighter who turned professional after winning the Golden Gloves championship in 1928.

Krieger's "iron chin" held out against the relentless pounding of Oscar Rankins on October 22, 1936, awing all in Duquesne Garden that evening. If Rankins's powerful blows couldn't persuade Krieger to the canvas, what chance did Billy have? Similar questions had been raised in each of Conn's matches throughout the year. Time and again, Billy rose up to meet the challenge, and those in his corner believed that the "East Liberty flash" would once again find the resolve to counteract his opponent's strength. They hadn't taken into consideration, however, a secret weapon secured by Solly's people.

In Krieger's corner was Ben Finkle, of the Ninth Street Finkles in Washington, D.C. Professionally known as "Evil Eye" Finkle, this hired gun was brought aboard by Solly's manager, Hymie Caplin, to work his distinctive magic on Conn. Born with a "bum glimmer,"[46] Finkle was an eye for hire, who used his bad left eye to place a hex on the opponent of whomever bought his employ. With a penetrating glare, the thirty-nine-year-old Evil Eye stared his subject into submission.

Mr. Finkle took his work seriously. His unusual gift of nature did not leave him lacking in confidence. "Once I give 'em the evil eye, they might just as well fold," he explained. "They know they are licked. You know how that is—like Germany knew it was licked in the World War and threw in the towel."[47]

Having developed an outstanding reputation in boxing circles, the freelance hex-maker found himself in great demand. Satisfied customers such as Vince Dundee, Walter Woods, Lou Ambers, and Joey Archibald sang Finkle's praises. In accepting Caplin's offer to work for Krieger in Pittsburgh, Finkle balked out of a deal with Chino Alvarez, who was fighting Norment Quarles in Tampa. (Without the help of Evil Eye, Alvarez fell to Quarles.)

"I can't help it," Finkle blushed. "The eye is now in a position to turn down all minor league jobs. From now on, we are taking only the best offers."[48]

Shortly before the headliners were to enter the ring, Finkle strolled into Conn's dressing room, ready to earn his pay. Lifting his green-rimmed sunglasses, Evil Eye gave Billy the once-over with his good right eye before applying the whammy with his supernaturally powerful left eye. Full of himself and the unyielding powers he possessed, Finkle smugly told reporters later, "I could see Conn wilting as I looked at him."[49]

Finkle would attribute Billy's sluggish performance later that evening to his malevolent stare; however, Havey Boyle questioned whether Conn had overtrained for Krieger. Both Johnny Ray and Billy knew going into the fight that Solly Krieger would test Conn's endurance, and the duo prepared accordingly.

Though Solly lacked the polished boxing skill possessed by Conn, he made up for his deficiencies with raw power. Krieger's mauling style, with punches thrown haphazardly from every conceivable angle, made for an interesting contrast to Billy's more refined ring manner.

As the bout began, Evil Eye sat in the Krieger corner gazing intently at his prey. Solly took the offensive at the sound of the first bell. Using a wild windmilling attack, Krieger had Conn backpedaling early in the match. Billy spent the first three-quarters of the fight on his bicycle, to counteract Solly's aggressive tactics. When he was able to successfully land a punch, Krieger's jaw of concrete harmlessly absorbed the blow.

Twice, early in the fight, Billy slipped to the canvas because of a wet ring surface. In the eighth, however, Conn went down for a count of eight, the result of a Krieger left hook to the body. Unhurt, Billy sardonically smiled as he watched the timekeeper. Rising at the count of eight, Conn was none the worse for wear after the knockdown, though his ego was bruised. Krieger set forth with his most damaging attack of the night in the ninth: a barrage of blows, including the coup de grâce, a left uppercut placed squarely on Conn's chin. Though his head snapped back in a frightening manner, Billy's legs remained upright.

At the start of the tenth, Conn began a modest rally out of which a left hook came and connected flush with Krieger's jaw. The best punch thrown all night by Billy didn't faze Solly whatsoever. He took the best Conn had to offer, kept moving swiftly about the ring, and at the close of the round looked as fresh as he did at the start of the fight. Again in the eleventh, Conn took the fight to Krieger, scoring with his deft punching, but the best he could manage for the round was a draw. Entering the twelfth and final round, Billy was so far behind in points that it was beyond question that he needed a knockout to win the match. In both the tenth and eleventh, Conn threw everything he had left into knocking Krieger out for the count. Game to the end, Billy was nonetheless spent by the beginning of the twelfth. Krieger finished strongly. With numbing body blows and stinging uppercuts, Solly battered a tired but unrepentant Conn. Blood streamed down Billy's face, oozing from a gash above his right eye, at the sound of the final bell.

Two fights in a row ended with no dispute or controversy. The victory was awarded unanimously to Krieger, and rightfully so.

"He's a good, strong kid," Krieger said afterward from his dressing room. "Knows a lot about the fight game and should be a good fighter some day." Though Solly was normally reluctant to discuss the specifics of his fights, he answered the inquiries of the local press. "He started to bother me late in the fight, that's why I made that fast finish. I wanted to win this one and when the twelfth round came up I didn't want to let anything stand in the way. But Billy is a good fighter. He should go somewhere."[50]

Where Conn was going next certainly wasn't New York. The loss wasn't devastating to Billy, but it was a setback. He was, after all, only twenty years old, and though the momentum had been momentarily stifled, his potential remained vast.

In the midst of the Krieger fight, Jake Mintz visited his friends on press row and informed them that he had signed Billy as the headliner for a card to be held at Motor Square Garden. According to Jake, Conn was the star attraction in what was set to be an all-star show consisting of local talent. The card would be held the next month, on January 14, 1938, according to the promoter.

Who was slated to face Conn, Mintz was asked?

Before answering, Jake took a step back and threw his arms up in a defensive mode. He was certain the writers wouldn't like his reply. "Honey Boy Jones," Mintz said, and prepared for the hue and cry.

On the surface the match held no intrigue. Conn had already defeated Jones three times, and he had seemingly moved beyond the club fighters, of which Honey Boy could be cast. In the shadow of Billy's decisive loss to Krieger, however, the Mintz card looked a bit more interesting. After all, it wasn't as if Billy had soundly beaten Honey Boy in their previous meeting. Jones himself was certain that he was the rightful victor in at least one of those bouts, if not two. In each of the fights, Honey Boy jumped off to a lead before tiring later in the bout, allowing Billy to close strongly for the decision. Another hindrance to Billy was reaching the middleweight limit of 165. Against Krieger, two factors undoubtedly hurt Billy. The first was overtraining for the bout. The other was reaching the prescribed weight. It was getting more and more difficult for Conn to make weight, and the ordeal certainly sapped his strength.

Billy was growing at a pace that was making Ray uneasy. Making the limit of 165 was getting more difficult with each succeeding fight. For Jones he came in at 165 exactly when weighing in at Commissioner McClelland's office, though instead of appearing tired and spent as he had at recent weigh-ins, Billy looked vigorous and fresh. An edge of seven pounds over Jones would be of great advantage if the fight were to reach later rounds.

As the fight began, Conn was already in a foul mood. Whether his disposition could be attributed to his poor showing against Krieger or a personal resentment of Jones born from their three previous meetings was unclear, but Billy began with a fury, both physically and verbally. Conn's punches were mixed with an "inarticulate epithet" that Billy directed at Jones.[51]

For ten rounds Conn unloaded on Jones with everything in his arsenal. A sturdy, stubborn foe, Honey Boy stood fast as Billy delivered his shellacking, refusing to give an inch. As the fight wore on, however, Conn began to tire—seemingly from the sheer number of punches he had thrown. In the eleventh, Honey Boy turned aggressor, chasing Billy from rope to rope. A left hook caught Conn flush and sent Billy to the floor (though he later claimed to have slipped on the canvas). He rose quickly and the two rivals rejoined their brutal display.

For a bout that was met with yawns when initially announced, the nearly three thousand in attendance walked away believing they had witnessed the most exciting match in the sixteen-year history of Motor Square Garden. The twelfth and final round capped the memorable bout, as both Jones and Conn stood toe to toe, inflicting unrestrained punishment on one another. Only the final bell offered a respite from the deluge of violence. "Each boy scorned any defense whatsoever in the closing stanza," reported Havey Boyle, "and as they backed and milled around the ring each cut loose with rapid-fire hooks to the body, jabs and uppercuts to the jaw, right crosses and in fact everything but a solid kick."[52]

Without question the victory was Billy's, but in defeat Jones won the admiration of most, if not all, in attendance. Fight coverage extolled the courage of the Hill District native who refused to wilt under Conn's relentless attack. It was only after the fight was over and Jones was safely out of sight of the audience that he showed the effects of the terrible body beating inflicted upon him. In his dressing room, Honey Boy doubled over in pain and exhaustion, and suffered several spells of vomiting.

In his jubilant quarters, Billy was overheard paraphrasing radio comedian Milton Berle, and his famed phrase, "For today I am a man."

"For today I'm a light-heavyweight," Conn said for all to hear.

He was going to take some time off and, ideally, work toward a summer date at Forbes Field against light-heavyweight champion John Henry Lewis.

True to his word, Billy took more than two months off before again entering the ring. Following a tour of several southern states and a brief stay in Miami, Conn returned home tan and fit; however, three square meals a day did little to add heft to his frame. Remarkably, after months of griping about the continual struggle he faced trying to reach the limit as a middleweight, Billy tipped the scales at only 167½ for his April 4 debut as a light-heavy.

Though his opponent, Italian "importation" Domenic Cercerelli, wasn't the most formidable, Billy looked impressive as he entered the new class. Only the bell saved Cercerelli from a first-round knockout, as the referee's count reached five at the close of the stanza. The bald-headed Italian stayed in the fight, though at times the match seemed to be little more than a sparring session for Conn. In the ninth, Billy once again knocked Cercerelli down, this time for a count of nine when the bell once again saved Domenic. These were Billy's first knockdowns since Conn sent Jimmy Brown to the canvas in December 1936. Though not facing top-flight competition, Billy showed that he was ready for the heavier weight class. Indeed, he needed some more work before confronting John Henry Lewis, and most experts believed Conn's next opponent was an obvious choice. In fact, Ray all but promised Al Quaill of nearby Brookline the slot. However, following Quaill's loss to Erich Seelig on Valentine's Day, Johnny reneged on the handshake agreement. Instead, Ray replaced Quaill with Seelig for a May 9 date at Hickey Park.

A feud between Johnny and Quaill's management figured largely in the alteration. Simply, Ray didn't like Quaill's handlers, Dan Ryan and Philip Goldstein. Both men frequently went about town and talked up their fighter, often to the detriment of Ray's. Quaill would not only beat Conn, they bragged, he would knock Billy out. Johnny had had it up to here with such braggadocio, and Quaill's loss to Seelig allowed him an out.

Though the Conn–Seelig match was scheduled to be the opening of the town's outdoor season, it was instead delayed a day due to inclement weather. Rather than risk another postponement, Jake Mintz moved the fight indoors to Motor Square Garden. Another delay and Mintz ran the risk of competing head to head with Teddy Yarosz and Al Quaill, who were to fight on the 12th at Duquesne Garden.

The changed date and venue made little difference to Billy. Another mostly innocuous foe, Seelig did nothing to hinder Conn's progression toward a possible championship date later in the summer. Seelig, a German native, used some of the same tactics that worked so well for Solly Krieger the previous December. Early in the bout, Seelig tied Billy up on the ropes in an attempt to wear Conn down with a steady rain of punches to the body. At 169½, Conn was at his heaviest yet, and outweighed his opponent by four pounds. This added weight, however slight, helped Billy withstand Seelig's attack. Once Erich's onslaught had fizzled of its own volition, Conn began his own assault. As he had with Honey Boy Jones, Billy unfurled an unremitting number of blows on his German counterpart. Frustratingly, despite being thoroughly ahead through five rounds, Conn was unable to send his opponent to the canvas. A burly and durable adversary, Seelig recognized that his only hope of a victory was to put Billy down for the count. Through the middle rounds Erich rallied, flailing at Conn with unyielding fervor. Billy, though, revealed his growing maturity. Though obviously shaken by a couple of Seelig's deliveries, Conn successfully distanced himself from a continued attack long enough to regain his composure. A strong finish by the hometown boy eased any pressure that may have been on the judges. Billy was awarded a unanimous ten-round decision, but again he was unable to dispel the growing notion that he "lacked a punch." Few critics questioned Conn's skill as a boxer, but as his opponents grew in stature and girth, these commentators wondered if "skill" alone would be enough to take care of business.

On April 22, 1938, while attending the Pirates home opener at Forbes Field, Johnny Ray suddenly took ill and was forced to leave the game during the third inning. Ray left the Oakland ball yard and admitted himself into Mercy Hospital, complaining of terrible pain in his chest. Doctors examined Ray, and determined that, in addition to being a chronic alcoholic, Johnny was suffering from pleurisy and influenza. To his doctor, Ray admitted to drinking too much, about a quart a day, he estimated. Johnny's dependency played no small part in his condition, but physicians struggled to cure Ray. Numerous tests were conducted, and still doctors couldn't pinpoint the exact cause of Johnny's distress.

His condition remained poor as the Seelig fight approached in early May, and it soon became apparent that Johnny would be unable to take his usual place in Billy's corner. For forty-nine bouts, Conn knew Ray was there for him. Billy not only had Johnny in his corner, but Ray's was the only voice he'd ever heard giving instructions between rounds. Nobody spoke except Johnny. The change would be drastic, but against Seelig, Billy had two friendly faces working as his seconds,

Bill Heckman and Harry Krause. Though he was served well by Heckman and Krause, Billy sorely missed Ray.

As June came and summer fast approached, Johnny's condition showed slight improvement. He was discharged from Mercy Hospital during the first week of June, and left for a week of relaxation on the shore at Atlantic City. Upon returning to his home on South Dallas Avenue, though, Ray suffered a relapse. The chest-rattling cough returned, even worse than before. Again, on June 17, Johnny admitted himself into Mercy Hospital. He complained of the incessant cough, "night sweats," and an overwhelming feeling of weakness. Doctors were puzzled; they had ruled cancer out, but could not isolate the source of Johnny's infirmity. Once again, Ray underwent a battery of tests.

The hospital bills mounted, and not having great resources at his disposal to begin with, Ray found himself in dire financial condition. Money never had stayed in Johnny's keep for long, but with Billy's steadily increasing earning power, Ray had been able to sock away a few bucks. The swelling hospital bills quickly ate up his modest savings, however. Pittsburgh's sporting society was a close-knit, if not a sometimes fractious, world, and word of Johnny's growing monetary problems were well known throughout the clique of local sportsmen.

Milt Jaffe paid a visit to Johnny and offered to relieve Ray's financial burden. Jaffe, a native of the Hill, was a professional gambler. He possessed innate knowledge about all games of chance, be they roulette, craps, poker, whatever; Jaffe made the odds work for him. To Johnny, Milt proposed that he step into the shoes left vacant since the passing of Johnny McGarvey. He would help Ray with the escalating hospital bills, Jaffe continued, and also cover Johnny and Billy's training expenses. In return, Ray would give Milt half his interest in Conn. Reluctantly, Johnny agreed to Jaffe's proposal, under the agreed-upon condition that he continue to have complete say over Junior's career.

No sooner had Milt agreed to be nothing more than a silent partner than he stepped out of that role and attempted subvert Ray's authority. Jaffe and Art Rooney tried to convince Conn to work with Bill Duffy in New York for training and experience. Conn rejected the idea out of hand. "Where were you when we were busted?"[53] Billy angrily asked. They were on the eve of some big paydays, and he wasn't turning his back on Moonie now. Indeed, Conn was sticking with Johnny, and he was sure Ray would be out of the hospital before long; until then, Billy would just bide his time.

Any chance of a meeting between John Henry Lewis and Billy for the light-heavyweight championship in the coming summer months was put to bed when Gus Greenlee accepted a $25,000 guarantee for his fighter to face Adolph Heuser in Berlin that August. All hands agreed that Greenlee would not permit Lewis to risk his title prior to the lucrative date in Germany.

With Johnny offering advice from his hospital bed, Jaffe negotiated his first deal for Conn. Though the hoped-for meeting between Lewis and Conn was off the table indefinitely, the next most sought after fight locally was yet another meeting of Billy and Teddy Yarosz. Short of a championship bout, there was certainly no other pairing that could generate the fan interest of Conn–Yarosz. In early June, contracts were signed and a date of July 25 at Forbes Field was set. Complications soon set in, however. Yarosz was unhappy with the terms negotiated by his manager, Ray Foutts. Surprisingly, after a nine-year relationship that saw Teddy reach the pinnacle of his profession, Yarosz suddenly terminated his relationship with his manager. Foutts offered a different explanation for the separation, though. He wasn't fired; rather, it was he who stepped aside when he learned that Yarosz was displeased with his work.

"I always received the best purses possible for Teddy in all of his bouts, and when he felt I wasn't getting a just amount for the Conn bout, I decided to chuck it all," Foutts told Jimmy Miller of the *Sun-Telegraph*. "I wish him all the luck in the world and sincerely hope he ties up with a pilot who will be as good to him as I have been."[54]

With his brother Eddie, Teddy went to Commissioner McClelland and asked if the contract could be reopened. After inspecting the agreement, McClelland voided the deal. The commissioner, upon learning that Foutts had signed Yarosz's name to the document, had declared the agreement invalid. Foutts was still under suspension, an edict that the commissioner had passed down the previous October. Until reinstated, Foutts was not permitted to act in a managerial capacity.

A new contract was worked up. Monetarily, Teddy was satisfied with the new deal. He was to receive 20 percent of the gate, while Billy agreed to a $3,000 guarantee. The fight was changed from a twelve-round bout to fifteen in the new contract, a concession to the Conn party. A longer fight was also a dig by Yarosz at his old manager, who insisted on twelve rounds in the initial contract. Teddy wanted to prove Foutts wrong—twelve or fifteen rounds, it made no difference; he was going to win the fight. Ray and Jaffe were equally confident that a longer fight benefited Conn.

Billy's path to a championship may have been diverted by meeting Yarosz a third time, but among local fans, the fight held great import. The local press was building up the bout as a "grudge" match between two young men who were developing a distaste for one another. Conn was a fan favorite when he performed in his hometown, but only when he wasn't paired against another local fighter. In both his earlier matches with Yarosz, the majority of the crowd was in Teddy's corner. The Monaca Mauler, despite his defensive mode of fighting, always held sway with Pittsburgh crowds, and there was no reason to believe the same wouldn't be true at Forbes Field on July 25.

Conn trained at Nathan Liff's Eagle's Rest in Millvale, while Teddy remained isolated at his camp in Monaca until the official weigh-in. Yarosz did break from training long enough to issue a statement saying, in effect, he had beaten Conn twice and would do it again. However, there was reason to doubt Teddy's ability to back up his brash talk. The last time out, on June 6, Teddy had lost a decision to Georgie Abrams in Washington D.C. In fact, since he last faced Billy, Yarosz had won only three of his six outings. Yet another loss to Conn, some in the local press believed, might convince Teddy to hang up his gloves and instead take to his pipe and slippers. Still, in Conn's camp there was no disputing that Teddy was a formidable opponent.

In the days leading up to the show, Jake Mintz was busily hyping the gate as a possible $25,000 draw. The resourceful promoter was doing all he could to make the card an enticing program for local fans. In addition to placing area fighters on each of the four bouts, Mintz hoped pitting boys of different nationalities against one another would heighten the animosity between combatants in the ring and the rooting interest in the crowd. Besides Conn–Yarosz, Mintz set Billy Soose of Farrel, Pennsylvania, against Al Quaill; Washington, Pennsylvania's, Sammy Angott against Leo Radak; and Emil Josephs, the "Pride of Millvale" against Carmen Notch of Lawrenceville. While much of the world was on the brink of war, Jake thought the added flavor of Hungarians, Poles, Italians, and Irish fighting one another, a virtual "all-nations" show, would entice a few more paying customers out to Oakland for the festivities.

As he had every day since Johnny entered the hospital, the evening before the fight Billy stopped by to visit with Moonie. This day, however, Conn was not allowed admittance to Ray's room. Johnny's doctors informed Billy that his manager's condition had worsened. Moonie's life was hanging in the balance, they told Conn, and Johnny would be lucky to make it through the night. Distraught, Billy left Mercy Hospital and aimlessly wandered the streets of Oakland. That night, Billy surrendered to his emotions. He cried until the tears would no longer come. None of what he had achieved thus far in his career would have been possible without Johnny's guiding hand. And nothing that might come in the future, including a championship belt, would matter without Moonie there in his corner. The fight later that evening was an afterthought. Johnny was all that was on Billy's mind as he walked and prayed all night long.

Shortly after sunrise, friends who had been searching for Conn all night discovered him curled in the backseat of his car, which was parked on an East Liberty backstreet. They found Billy sobbing and in no condition to face Yarosz later that night. They delivered the news that Ray had survived the night and his doctors believed his chances of recovery were greatly improved. The information brightened Billy's spirits greatly, but did little to relieve him of his sleepless night. He was due at McClelland's office in several hours. A short nap before weigh-in and another following the ritual were all Conn could rustle before the match.

The undercard was interesting and the matches certainly had merit, but it was the blood feud of the headliners that Mintz was banking on and had the town's fight fans talking. Those anticipating a brutal scrum were treated to an affair that had to make the most hardened avert their glances.

The nattily dressed Ray Eberle proffered an air of dignity as he introduced the headliners. The participants, in their prefight state, resembled two observant altar boys. Before the fight was a minute old, though, each had dropped the guise and stepped into the more fitting character of bona fide street ruffians. Who threw the first questionable blow was not a matter of contention. In the first stanza, Conn hit Yarosz with several rabbit punches and a number of blows to Teddy's kidneys (thirty-eight by Regis Welsh's exaggerated count). The veteran Yarosz did not stand idly by and turn the other cheek, however. Billy was attempting to play outside the rules with a fighter who knew all the tricks and wasn't bashful about using that knowledge. In fact, Teddy most assuredly preferred a fight of this nature. Though he wouldn't admit it to anyone, Billy was his superior as a boxer, and Yarosz's best chance at winning was to disrupt Conn from his training; to get inside his head and stir that Irish blood to a slow boil. Whether Teddy went into the bout with these nefarious intentions or if the thought occurred to him after Billy instigated the foul play is uncertain. But it is beyond question that Yarosz worked his opponent perfectly.

At the close of the second and fifth, the fighters continued their hostilities long after the bell had brought the round to a close. In both instances the instigator was Yarosz, as he was in the ninth when, after committing a foul of some sort, Teddy extended his left glove as a gesture of apology. While Billy reached out to accept Yarosz's offering, he was sideswiped by a left hook to the jaw.

Referee Fred Mastrean made only a couple of feeble attempts to maintain order. He failed to assert his authority and offered only a few empty warnings to each fighter. Had Mastrean threatened to expel both fighters from the ring and hold their purses, quite possibly the hooliganism would have stopped. By failing to convincingly put a halt to the nonsense, the boys took Mastrean's indifference as an endorsement of their tactics. Conn continued with the rabbit punches occasionally interspersed with a blow to the kidneys. Yarosz ably used his thumbs in an effort to pop Billy's eyeballs from their sockets.

Though each fighter was equally guilty of bringing their sport down to the level of an alley fight, reporters placed the onus on Conn's shoulders. In their fight reports and commentary, these sportswriters rued Billy's lost composure. "[He] has too much Irish in him to control his fighting ability once he gets 'burned up,'" wrote Regis Welsh. Conn completely abandoned whatever fight plan he entered the ring with and instead fought in a blind rage. "The East Liberty youngster lost his head completely as Yarosz repeatedly tied him up—and in the last few rounds Conn's glare was about his best fighting asset," continued Welsh.[55]

Chester Smith offered similar observations. "[Conn] worked up a hate which ruins his boxing and all that goes with it. He has no timing, he forgets to punch, all he wants to do is bare his teeth and glare at the Monaca Pole," Smith wrote.[56]

In Conn's corner were Val Gruenewald, Bill Heckman, and Harry Krause. None held sway with Billy like Ray. Their pleas to "fight clean" fell on deaf ears. With each sound of the bell, Conn's rage was stoked.

Though Billy threw the first dirty blow, Yarosz effectively egged on such actions in a well-devised strategy to divert Conn from his teachings. After the fight, Billy admitted as much in his dressing room. Teddy had outsmarted him and riled him, Billy told reporters. He then showed the writers surrounding him the swelling under both of his eyes, the result of Yarosz's gouging. His own fouls, the low blows and rabbit punches, were justifiable; after all, how else could he fight a man who remained in a perpetual crouch? And yes, Johnny's absence hurt, Conn said. Perhaps Ray would have been able to soothe Billy's anger and help him maintain focus to the task at hand.

"I don't mind losing to a fellow who will stand up and fight me, but that guy won't," Conn groused. "He stabs and chops and then goes for cover, and you can't hit him anywhere else. I still think I can out fight him, although I fought a bad fight tonight and lost."[57]

Revenge was sweet for Yarosz, and Teddy was making no apologies for the methods he used to win the match—a decision that he believed was rightfully his the previous June. An added pleasure for Yarosz was having his arm raised in victory in front of his old manager Ray Foutts, who was present at the match after paying his way into the ballpark.

Prior to Yarosz, Conn seemed poised to be in line for a chance at the middleweight crown. His previous defeats had been brushed aside as learning experiences for the still-evolving young boxer. However, the tone of the prose penned by Pittsburgh's sports columnists changed drastically following the brutal display at Forbes Field. Chester Smith believed Yarosz had capped a fine career; Billy, his potential derailed before he hit the big time.

"A good many of us go away with the idea that Yarosz can't go much further," wrote Smith, "[and] Conn isn't going anywhere. . . ." The *Press*'s sports editor opined that Conn lacked the mental makeup needed to become a champion, and Billy's performance against Yarosz went a long way to establishing such a belief. Even Harry Keck, long a booster of Billy, had written in his column that he believed Conn had been surpassed by Charley Burley as the local fighter with the most potential.

In the wake of the defeat, Billy was despondent. He had lost before, but never had he been so roundly criticized. Each and every barb stung, and the cutting remarks were many. Johnny's dubious health also played heavily on Conn's mind and added to his depression. A couple of days passed before Ray was completely out of danger and able to receive visitors. One of the first through his hospital-room door was Junior. Gone was the buoyant and confident young man who just days before was considered a top contender for the middleweight championship. Looking as if he hadn't slept since the fight, a disheveled Billy shuffled his way into Ray's room, sorely in need of a pat on the back. Instead, he received a kick in the rear.

"Get out of here, and don't come back 'til you get a grip on yourself," Johnny bellowed. "I know how you feel. Your pride is hurt. You don't want to face your friends and have to explain to them why you look so bad. So you're moping around and looking for a place to curl up and die."

Ray wasn't yet finished with his dressing down of Billy. "Scram. Get yourself a shave and a new suit and dress up and walk down Fifth Avenue like you own it. Don't run away from people and hide. Go on out and face them. You fought a bad fight—so what? So go out and fight a good one and make them forget that one. And don't come back here 'til you can look me in the face and smile."[58]

The transformation didn't happen overnight. The lashing he took in the press hurt Billy, but seeing Johnny vibrant made all the difference. He did as Ray directed. A haircut and new suit, as they usually did, gave Conn a sense of assurance. Slowly the bounce returned to his step, the smile reappeared on his face, and his appetite to fight once again returned.

Billy was a daily visitor to Mercy Hospital. Of course, the conversation was often dominated with talk of boxing, Conn's career in particular. Though Johnny kept himself up to date through the newspapers and Rosey Rowswell's radio broadcasts, Billy also delivered daily briefings on the Pirates and their run for the National League pennant.

One summer afternoon, Ray told Billy of a number he had dreamed. Johnny was so certain the number would hit, he gave Conn two dollars and told him to go play it for him. In dreams, Johnny was no luckier than in his wakening moments, and suffice to say, his number did not come in. Billy was deeply concerned that, in his frail state, Ray couldn't withstand the disappointing news. He was certain that Johnny would suffer a relapse if he learned the truth. Conn's solution was as generous as it was impulsive. Only a close friend of both men was able to convince Billy not to withdraw $1,400 from the bank to pay off a number that did not hit.

More than three months had passed since Johnny first suffered from severe chest pain, but his doctor, G. C. Weil, finally pinpointed the source of Ray's illness. Weil determined that Johnny had acute and chronic bronchitis abscess of the left lung. An operation was necessary to clean the lung of excessive sputum. The operation took place on August 3, but after a few days it became obvious that Weil failed to completely remove all expectorate from Ray's chest. Another operation was conducted on the 11th. Following the second operation, Johnny was seemingly out of the woods.

When Ray was ready to receive visitors, one of the first men through the door was Harry Keck. "What's the matter with you sportswriters?" Ray bellowed at Keck from his hospital bed. On the day Keck stopped by room 332 at Mercy Hospital, Johnny was feeling particularly vigorous and the two had a long talk about the Pittsburgh boxing scene. The conversation became volatile when Johnny addressed the poor press his Junior received in the aftermath of the Yarosz match.

> You all took Billy for a ride on that Yarosz fight. It wasn't his fault. Some of it, yes, but not all of it. Say the kid's only 21 years old, and he's fought four world champions and he's lost only three fights since he's been in the windups. . . . What do you fellas want him to do? He's going to become a great fighter. He needs a lot of work and that's why I'm going to take him away for a while to places where he won't have to fight champions every time out."[59]

Billy's next opponent was never mistaken as a champion, or even a champion in waiting, and once again he would be traveling far from home to fight. Still, Ray Actis was considered a tough customer in the ring. "Who's the bastard who matched you with this guy?" Billy was asked. "He's a light-heavyweight and you're a middleweight. You're only going to get three hundred bucks and knocked out."[60] Knocked out? Conn didn't even consider the prospect, but he did get more than he bargained for.

On September 14, Conn met Actis in San Francisco for Ray's first appearance in his hometown in more than a year. At the San Francisco Exposition Auditorium, the two men put on a "vicious, bloody duel." In the third, Actis put Billy on his behind with a terrific hook to the chin, but was unable to finish Conn off. Billy rose from the canvas and surprised his foe with a gripping flurry.

For the remainder of the evening, Conn and Actis entertained and enthralled the partisan crowd with what Eddie Muller of the *Examiner* called "a blistering swatfest."[61] Referee Joe Gorman finally called a halt to the fight at two minutes thirty-one seconds of the eighth, when a wobbly Actis could no longer defend himself from Conn's unmerciful attack. Billy was thankful to get out of the Auditorium with a win. He was ready to pack his bags and head back home.

Billy remained absent from the local scene for three months. With Johnny still recuperating from his lengthy illness, Conn was reluctant to square off against an unknown entity or, for that matter, a boxer of great proficiency. The only appealing offer Ray and Jaffe received was yet another bout against Honey Boy Jones. Sure there were other proposals, more alluring names, but everyone in Billy's camp agreed to wait until Johnny was back in the corner before taking on another challenging foe.

Conn–Jones V was a coheadliner in a Jake Mintz production at Duquesne Garden. Sharing top billing with Conn was Fritzie Zivic, who was returning home after a successful eastern tour. Zivic's opponent was a highly regarded welterweight, Baby Sal Saban. Opening the show, in a scheduled four-round match, was Billy's little brother Jackie, who was making his professional debut against Philadelphian Mickey Whelan.

As they had in the two previous fights that Ray was unable to attend due to his infirmity, Harry Krause, Bill Heckman, and Hal Gruenewald were once again in Billy's corner. Following Zivic's impressive win over Saban, Billy gave Honey Boy the most decisive beating yet in their five meetings. Though he had proved in their previous bouts to be a superior boxer to Jones, the fifth encounter left no doubt that Billy and Honey Boy were no longer in the same class. Over the course of ten rounds, Conn had his way with Jones, easily connecting with his right and his left. Jones's only course of defense all evening was to clutch and grab Billy, which proved effective enough to withstand a knockout.

After losing only once in his amateur career, in his pro debut Jackie entertained the Gardens crowd, who "liked his effort and acted as though they wanted to see more of him."[62] Two Conn victories in one night, and to top it off, Johnny's release from the hospital was imminent.

The day after Billy defeated Jones, Jaffe released the news that Conn had received two offers, one on each coast. He was wanted in New York to face Lloyd Marshall on a November 18 card featuring Fred Apostoli and Young Corbett. Promoters in San Francisco also wanted to have Billy again, this time for a Christmas Day fund-raising show. Johnny was left to determine when he should unveil Billy at Madison Square Garden. San Francisco was easier to turn down; Billy had already been out there several times, but New York offered new possibilities. He was certain Billy was ready for the grand stage, not to mention Marshall, an up-and-coming light-heavy. The Apostoli–Corbett card was attractive, but still Johnny was going to turn it down. Ray wanted Junior to go to New York, and soon. But when Billy went to New York, he was going as a headliner or not at all.

On November 1, Solly Krieger defeated Al Hostak in Seattle and in the process captured the world middleweight title. In the vicious championship fight, Hostak broke both his hands early in the fight and was knocked down for the first time in his career. Krieger's impressive victory nearly coincided with Johnny's release from Mercy Hospital. Ray's first order of business was meeting with Jake Mintz and Krieger's manager, Hymie Caplin.

All three parties were eager to reach an accord when they convened during the second week of November. The promoter, of course, wanted a top draw and matching a world champion against a local product certainly should entice boxing fans. Johnny was eager to get back into the game himself, the sooner the better. More important, though, after Actis and Jones, Junior badly needed to face a high-quality opponent. For nearly a year and a half following the Zivic fight, Billy had been the darling of the Pittsburgh boxing press. The local fight commentators fell over one another singing Billy's praises; however, they also tried to outdo one another following the third Yarosz fight in condemning his poor showing. Four months later, despite two victories in the in-terim, Billy's career was stagnant and sorely in need of a jump start, and a win over Krieger would rightfully bring Conn's name back into the discussion of top contenders for the light-heavy crown.

Caplin and Krieger loved performing in Pittsburgh, having appeared there seven times previously. When Mintz tendered a guarantee of $3,000, the duo had all the more reason to hail the hospitality of the town. The generous guarantee was easily the largest post of Solly's career, far outstripping the $1,670 he received for the title bout against Hostak. Caplin quickly agreed to face Conn in a twelve-round nontitle fight November 25 at Duquesne Garden. "We don't care if we ever fight in New York," Caplin gushed. "Pittsburgh is our second home. We like it here and we like to fight here."[63]

The day of the bout, an unexpected snowstorm crippled Pittsburgh and the surrounding area. Public transportation continued to service commuters, but schedules were sporadic at best. In addition, most local roads were impassable for vehicles. By early afternoon, it seemed obvious that Conn and Krieger would be fighting before a hall full of empty seats. Caplin suggested delaying the fight several days, a gracious offer in light of the fact that neither he nor Krieger would suffer financially from a poor turnout. Mintz and Ray readily agreed and the fight was rescheduled for Monday, November 28.

"There comes a time in the life of every great fighter on the way up when he suddenly finds himself," Harry Keck penned in the *Sun-Telegraph*. "This appeared to be Billy's night."[64]

In his rematch with Krieger, Conn fought a near perfect fight. He won nine of twelve rounds, with two, the third and tenth, deemed even, and only the eleventh round scored in favor of Krieger. Having Ray back in his corner made a marked difference. Any semblance of the angry, unhinged boxer who squared off against Teddy Yarosz was gone. Conn looked and fought as if he were reborn. For twelve rounds Billy stayed poised as he meticulously went about his business of slashing and cutting up Krieger. He deftly kept his distance, dancing to all corners of the ring, all the while effectively avoiding Solly's powerful right hand. He lost the first bout with Krieger trying to go toe to toe with Solly, and Billy remembered all too well how that turned out.

As Caplin cut the gloves from his hands, Krieger seemed a bit shellshocked. He entered the ring a 10 to 8 favorite and fully cognizant of the fight a year earlier when he handled Conn with relative ease. "I don't know what was the matter," he said. "I couldn't get going. Didn't have any zing. Felt slow. And he kept running and throwing lefts."[65]

Even in his stunned state, Krieger handled defeat as a sportsman and gentleman. He patiently waited for Billy to emerge from the shower. Quietly, the two exchanged words and a handshake before Solly returned to his dressing room. There, Hymie Caplin was courting the local press. Sure, Billy was a great kid and he fought a beautiful fight, Caplin told the gathered scribes, still, "You gotta give Solly credit for chasin' him. All through the fight he chased him and made it a good fight, takin' those stabs in the mush and keepin' going. . . . Say, the way that guy kept givin' that left in the mush and kept running like a thief. Yeah, like a thief he kept runnin'. And you can put that in the paper. Like a thief he kept runnin' with my Solly chasin' him."[66]

It was a near perfect night for Conn. The only sour note came when he received his share of the purse, a payday that came to slightly more than $600. Delaying the fight three days did nothing to bolster the gate, which was only $5,393.

The paltry remittance was easy to look past. New York promoter Mike Jacobs was keeping a close eye on the happenings in Pittsburgh. Before the night was out, Johnny Ray received an invitation to come to New York and meet with Jacobs concerning a proposed date with Fred Apostoli.

Five A Fistic Star Is Born

Immediately following the lopsided victory over Solly Krieger, Johnny Ray boarded a train for New York where he met with fight promoter Mike Jacobs and Larry White, the manager of Fred Apostoli. Negotiations were swift and straightforward, as Ray was anxious to bring his boy to the glitter and limelight of Broadway. Earlier in the fall, Johnny rejected the offer for Billy to fight on the undercard of the November 18 Apostoli and Young Corbett match. Billy wasn't coming to New York as a prelim boy. No, when he went to New York, he was arriving as a headliner, just as his record merited. The agreement Ray reached with Jacobs and White on December 1 did just that. Billy would make his debut in Gotham on January 6, against the New York state recognized middleweight champion, Fred Apostoli. For the fight, Billy was not to weigh more than 168, for Krieger came in at 165½.

The twenty-five-year-old Apostoli had made his professional debut in 1933. At that time, Fred was also employed as a concierge at a hotel in his hometown of San Francisco. Aptly, the nickname of the "'Frisco Bellhop" was strung upon the darkly handsome Apostoli. A year previously, Fred made his debut on the East Coast when he defeated Solly Krieger with a TKO. His style in the ring was quite similar to Billy's. Apostoli was "one who rips, rather than hurts, and who renders an opponent helpless rather than paralyzing him," according to Regis Welsh.[1]

Apostoli, with his impressive résumé, didn't intimidate Billy. Nor did the vast stage of Madison Square Garden offer the young man a moment's pause. "It ought to be just like any other," he told Welsh, "and Apostoli is just another fighter. If he is as good as they say he is, maybe it will mean something beating him. I fought guys just as tough as he is, and I'm still here. And he'll know I'm there too, once the bell rings."[2]

Sportswriters commonly referred to the Garden as the mecca of boxing, and rightly so. Reaching Madison Square Garden had been the goal of every fighter since the building's doors were first opened. Havey Boyle likened a boxer's first appearance at the Garden to that of an opera singer's debut at the Metropolitan Opera or an old vaudevillian playing at the Palace. As Billy well knew, Pittsburgh fighters had a dubious history at Madison Square. It was at the Garden that Harry Greb lost his title to Tiger Flowers. Where a young local hopeful, Buck McTiernan, lost to Ignacio Ara. And Jack Zivic defeated Tommy Milligan (twice). No other Steel City fighter had performed on boxing's center stage.

There was no doubt in Billy's mind that he would succeed where his hero Greb had failed. "This is the chance I've wanted since I first started boxing," he said. "You don't think I'm going to blow it without trying, do you? I'll box Apostoli's ears off—and he's not going to hit me like he did Solly Krieger, Glenn Lee or Young Corbett. Even if he does manage to clip me, I'm sure he can't hit any harder than Krieger, Ray Actis, or Oscar Rankins. And I beat the three of them."[3]

Though his title was not at stake, Apostoli still had much riding on the fight. The state of New York went out on a limb when it declared him to be champion in the aftermath of his victory over Corbett. On the calendar for February was a championship bout with Krieger. A loss to Billy wouldn't affect Fred's claim on the title, but would, at the very least, prove embarrassing.

Billy arrived in New York two and a half weeks prior to the fight, and, as he was leaving Pittsburgh, someone remarked that it would be the first Christmas he'd ever spent away from home. "I'm not worried about that," Conn replied with complete earnestness. "The fight is all that matters. I *have* to win this one."[4]

The New York fight crowd was taken with him immediately. His ebullient personality, his charming disposition, and his matinee idol good looks won over Broadway practically upon arrival. The normally cynical New York press wore out their typewriters singing the praises of the kid from the Smoky City. The big question was, could this kid fight?

For the first time since the heyday of Harry Greb, Pittsburgh fans were traveling en masse to see a hometown fighter perform in New York. In addition to the four hundred who ventured to New York via automobiles, another four hundred Pittsburghers boarded the Ham and Cabbage Special, a train chartered by local tavern owner Owney McManus. Periodically, over the previous few years, McManus contracted similar trips, which followed the Pirates football team around the East Coast. The charter's unusual name came simply from the cuisine served aboard the train, though the Irish grub was cheerfully supplemented with a plethora of intoxicating beverages.

The rollicking rail trip was filled with Pittsburghers donning green bowlers and puffing corncob pipes. Steel City natives weren't the only people aboard the Conn bandwagon, though. Billy's most recent opponent, Solly Krieger, jumped on with both feet. "Apostoli won't hurt him," he said. "As a matter of fact, outside of Joe Louis, I don't know anyone who might hurt him now. . . . I tackled Billy Conn in the same ring a year ago, won 12 of 12, had him on the deck and everything. But what went on last December didn't go this last trip, which should give you a rough idea of how far and rapidly Conn has come on."

Krieger then offered a bold prediction, a forecast that would have seemed absurd just a few months earlier, when some in Pittsburgh believed Billy had already seen his better days. "I wouldn't be surprised if he lifted Joe Louis's heavyweight crown before another three summers roll by," Solly stated with a straight face.[5]

Upon arriving in New York, one of the boys' first stops was Pioneer Gym in midtown Manhattan. Johnny knew, with the move to the big time, he needed to find Billy a trainer. The best available was Freddie Fierro, who worked out of the Pioneer.

Fierro had been following Conn's career through the newspapers ever since Fritzie Zivic, whom Freddie had worked with for a period of time, told him of a kid back in Pittsburgh. "A young punk who moves like a greyhound and jabs better than Barney Ross," Zivic told Fierro. "His name is Conn, an Irish kid."[6]

Zivic's commendation may have brought Conn to Fierro's attention, but the trainer was understandably impressed by the list of champions Billy had fought through with relative ease. Still, Freddie had no inkling that he would be working with the up-and-coming boxer, and was surprised when the opportunity to work with a fighter possessing immense potential came through the doors of his New York City gym.

The two came to Gotham dressed for the big time. Johnny looked dashing sporting a light-brown suit over his slight frame, and Billy wore an exquisite camel hair overcoat, chewing on a toothpick, when the duo entered Pioneer Gym in search of Fierro.

"You Freddie Fierro?" Ray asked of the man working with a prelim fighter. Setting down the water bottle, Freddie walked over toward the visitors.

"That's me."

"I'm Johnny Ray. This here is Billy Conn." Billy removed the toothpick from his mouth, nodded and greeted Fierro.

"Hi there, Fat," he said, in an unusually informal greeting.

Obviously put off by Conn's wiseacre style, Fierro fired a fierce look toward the young punk. "Don't mind him," Ray offered apologetically. "He's always sounding off. Don't mean no harm, though."

Hoping he successfully soothed the ruffled Fierro, Johnny explained why he and Billy were there. "We heard a lot about you from Fritzie Zivic. Says you're the best trainer in the business. I'd like you to take care of Billy."

Though the fight was just over two weeks away, Fierro readily accepted Ray's proposal with the stipulation that he receive the usual trainer's fee. With a chance to make amends for his impolite salutation, Billy, leaning in the doorway throughout the meeting, opted instead to depart with an equally rude adieu: "I'll be seeing you, Fat."

Understandably, Fierro was put off by Conn's brash attitude. He walked over to Billy and without a stitch of humor in his voice asked, "Where do you get this 'Fat' routine?"

"I dunno," Conn answered with a wry smile, "you look 'Fat' to me."

Training began immediately. Fierro readied Billy for Apostoli by working him out the equivalent of fifteen rounds everyday. During one of these preparatory sessions, a visitor entered Pioneer Gym. With the exception of Conn, all present in the hall were familiar with the shadowy figure, and with their recognition came the cessation of all movement.

Frankie Carbo had an illustriously dark and menacing résumé. Born on the East Side of Manhattan in 1904, Frankie copped to his first manslaughter shortly after his twentieth birthday. In time, there would be more killings; homicides generally committed in the line of business.

Having already penetrated many walks of American life, members of organized crime were always on the make for a new opportunity to hustle a buck. The fight game was relatively open to infiltration by the underworld, and no one recognized the possibilities more than Frankie Carbo. In the mid-thirties, Carbo wrested his way into the sport as the manager of Babe Risko in partnership with Gabe Genovese, a cousin of future mob boss Vito Genovese. With time he gained control of several other fighters, and in so doing, acquired power and prominence in the business by fulfilling favors asked of him by numerous fighters, promoters, and managers. Once in his debt, these men were under his control.

By the late thirties, Carbo was no longer known as a "manager" of fighters, but had graduated to a "promoter" of fights. In this role, his hold on the game only strengthened.

He would move in by asking for a piece of a fighter. It's what he did. He muscled in on the backs of fighters and managers trying to make an honest go of things. If the manager of the boxer in question refused to comply, Frankie the "promoter" made it difficult for the fighter to find action, let alone have a chance at the title. As evidenced by his résumé, Carbo was not above resorting to violence, and the threat thereof swayed those who resisted his proposition.

With his gray fedora, ominous demeanor, and piercingly fierce dark eyes, Carbo looked the part he played. With businesslike precision, Frankie made the purpose of his visit to Pioneer Gym known immediately. Pulling Ray aside, Carbo informed Johnny that he wanted a piece of Billy. Ten percent would do.

From across the room, Billy overheard Johnny arguing with Carbo and headed toward the dispute.

"What's the matter, Moonie?" Conn asked.

Ray snapped at his fighter, "You mind your own business. Don't get mixed up with this."

Billy sized up the situation quickly and a flash of anger overwhelmed him. "Look, Johnny's my manager. I don't need nobody else."[7]

With a glint of appreciation for the young fighter's chutzpah, Carbo simply nodded and left the room, his message delivered.

Unlike most fighting teams, Johnny and Billy had some recourse in the face of Carbo's implied threat. For some time, Billy had been exposed to fellas of this ilk; it was impossible to exist in professional boxing and not be. Two men, Art Rooney and Milt Jaffe, had a hand in it to some extent. Rooney the gentlemanly sportsman had not made his living from his moribund, deficit-wielding football outfit. Rather,

Rooney provided for his family (and kept his Pirates afloat) through his cunning knowledge of thoroughbreds and other, more nefarious means. It was said that he "ran" the North Side of Pittsburgh. Along with Jaffe, he operated the Showboat Casino, which was located at the foot of the Sixth Street Bridge on the Allegheny. Rooney was well versed in the intricacies of Carbo's world; however, neither he nor Jaffe possessed the cold-blooded streak in 'em that Carbo possessed. Nonetheless, Rooney was acquainted with someone who certainly did.

Some twenty years later, Jimmy Cannon credited Johnny Ray with saving Billy from the clutches of Frankie Carbo. Such a story made for good copy; however, as the newsman well understood, Johnny's scrawny fists were no match for the brutality of Carbo's gun. What *did* make Carbo think twice about his demand was the polite, but firm, request that he back off of Conn by a man more murderous than he.

If sized up by an unknowing soul, Owney Madden did not physically intimidate. This mattered little, as nearly all of Owney's disagreements were not settled with fists. Rather than testing his mettle in a corporeal manner, Madden preferred any number of armaments to settle disagreements, including brass knuckles or a lead pipe swathed in newspaper. More often than not, though, Madden chose a pistol as an arbiter in most disputes. For pure viciousness, Owney, known as the "English Killer," made Frankie Carbo look like a dilettante.

He made his dough in all the usual places, including bootlegging and bookmaking. Madden also wet his beak in the fight game. The most notable fighter in his stable was Primo Carnera, whom Owney helped guide to the heavyweight championship in 1933.[8]

At the request of Art Rooney, whom Madden knew to be a man of principle, Owney stepped in and told Carbo in no uncertain terms to leave Conn alone; this new fighter was off-limits to Frankie's mercenary ways. Wisely, with due consideration to his personal well-being, Carbo heeded Madden's directive.

Johnny and Billy went back to business.

All eyes in the great hall were focused upon Billy as he walked down the aisle toward the ring. The "oohs" and "ahhs" from the female members of the crowd were audible; boxers weren't *this* pretty. With bouncy dark curly hair, gleaming white teeth, a handsome face with nary a mark upon it; this Billy Conn looked like a matinee idol, not a boxer. Draped in a green silk robe that had his name emblazoned on its back, Billy slipped through the ropes and waved to the (mostly) adoring crowd. Before he had thrown his first punch in New York City, the crowd was taken by Conn. If he could fight, they would *love* him. An Irishman who could box—New York had been pining for one since the heyday of Jimmy Slattery.

Smitten though fans may have been, the smart money was on Apostoli. Having easily dispatched Krieger, Young Corbett, and Freddie Steele by way of knockout, Apostoli seemed to most handicappers to be invincible. Still, with the arrival of the Ham and Cabbage contingent, Pittsburghers backed their hometown boy with their wallets, putting much money on the 2½-to-1 underdog. And no one was going to clean up more from a Conn victory than Milt Jaffe, who was taking bets left and right from Apostoli boosters.

The ceremonial prefight introductions of boxing notables included heavyweight champion Joe Louis. Like most of those present in the hall, Louis had heard much about this kid from Pittsburgh and he was curious to learn if Conn could live up to the newspaper hype. The champ walked from center ring to Billy's corner and offered an outstretched hand to Conn.

"How are you feeling?" he asked Billy.

With other, more pressing matters at hand, the normally loquacious Conn kept the patter short. "All right," he answered. Billy then looked past Louis, to Apostoli, and patiently waited for the bell.

Going against personal precedent, Billy started the fight quickly and effectively rather than in his usual slumber. Using his left almost entirely to the exclusion of his right, Conn "stabbed," "hooked," and "crossed"[9] repeatedly to Apostoli's jaw, sweeping the first three rounds. In the fourth, Freddie found an opening when, in a show of overconfidence, Billy was caught with a hook to the chin. Staggered by the blow, Conn stumbled backward toward the ropes. Sensing his opportunity, Apostoli moved in for the kill. Swinging wildly with both hands, Freddie landed a left to the chops and followed that with a right. Visibly dazed, Billy took two more lefts to the head and a solid blow to the body. The Pittsburgh delegation collectively held their breath, when, miraculously, Billy snapped to. With a left, Conn knocked the mouthpiece from Apostoli's mouth. Two more stinging blows caught Freddie flush in the face—then, the bell.

The crowd was taken by Billy's resurgence and roared its approval as Johnny enlivened his fighter by stuffing Conn's head in a bucket of water. The fight was his. Apostoli had his chance and couldn't take him down. From the fifth on, with a brief flurry by Freddie in the sixth, Conn owned the bout while putting on as fine a boxing exhibition as the old town had seen in some time.

One spectator marveled at Billy's adroit footwork, which he found akin to "a mixture of adagio and sentry duty." Conn's dexterous dance baffled Apostoli, making him at times resemble "a suburbanite chasing yesterday's train."[10]

Billy kept Apostoli off balance and thereby neutralized the Fightin' Bellhop. In the ninth, frustration settled over Apostoli when he realized the fight was all but lost to him. Two blows below the belt elicited boos from the crowd but had little effect on Conn. His dancing continued around the mystified Apostoli; with more jabs to Fred's head, Billy unleashed his whole repertoire.

The tenth and final round began with the combatants grudgingly touching gloves before each man wildly tore into one another. Needing a knockout for victory, Apostoli let loose a last-gasp flurry. With a minute and a half to go in the fight, Freddie had Billy on the run. Following several blows to the body and head, Conn showed no sign of reciprocating Apostoli's punches, and offered little defense. Then, as he had done in the fourth, Conn, as if snapped backed to life, straightened up and delivered a numbing hook to Apostoli's head followed by a right to the chin. This stifled Freddie's assault. Though the round was lost, Billy finished the tenth and the fight with a mad whirlwind of punches, including a definitive right to Apostoli's head as the bell brought the electrifying fight to a close.

There wasn't a dissenting voice among the crowd of 10,918 when referee Billy Cavanaugh announced the unanimous decision.

Billy celebrated his triumph at Leon and Eddies, a Gotham nightclub, where he held court into the wee hours of the morning as a steady procession of celebrities, old friends, and new admirers stopped by and congratulated him on the great victory. He awoke the next afternoon to find that he was the darling of the New York sporting press.

"It was a story of Conn-fidence and Conn-quest," Bill Corum wrote in the New York *Journal American*. "The lad is a upstanding, handsome, cool and sharp punching fellow—a bit of a throwback to the stand up fighters of old English print days. He has a left hand that would warm the hearts of old-timers."[11]

"A new fistic star is born," the New York dailies declared the following morn.

Hype Igoe was already looking ahead to the day when Billy would be aiming for Joe Louis's crown. "It's silly to look too far into the future, but the Conn of two years from now, filled out to maturity and with added ring knowledge by keeping in action and condition, may be the answer to future heavyweight problems."[12]

In the exhilaration following the surprising upset, everyone wanted a piece of Billy. Larry White wanted a rematch for his boxer. Mike Jacobs wanted to put on another show with his newfound attraction. Hymie Caplin cornered Ray in the dressing room, pleading with Johnny to match Conn with his fighter, Solly Krieger, before committing to another match. Jake Mintz beseeched Ray for the opportunity to promote Billy's next fight in Pittsburgh. And Johnny—he was ready to capitalize on Junior's unanticipated fame with a quick, substantial payday.

White, Ray, and Jacobs came to a rapid and straightforward agreement. The day after Billy's victory over Apostoli, it was decided the fighters would meet again February 8, 1939, at the Garden. Pointedly, the rematch was a scheduled fifteen-round fight. This stipulation was of great significance to those who observed the January 6 bout. Many in attendance at the first fight were of the belief that, had it been scheduled fifteen rounds rather than ten, Billy would have come out on the losing end. Seemingly, in the tenth, Conn began to tire. Despite such conjecture, Ray had faith that his fighter would have continued his dominance against Apostoli.

"He did appear tired in the tenth round," Johnny agreed, "and maybe he was, but I have seen him tired after a round in other fights, and got worried about him, and then he would go out and put on one of his best punching and speed displays."[13]

In the locker room following the fight, Ray questioned Billy, who erased any notion that he was tiring. "No," Conn assured his manager. "I wasn't bothered one bit, in fact, just about a half minute before the bell that ended the round, I found myself hitting harder than I had hit all night. I would not have minded it a bit if the fight kept going. I sorta had my second wind."[14]

Like many times before, the Pittsburgh media questioned whether Johnny Ray was biting off more than Billy could chew. Time and again, however, Ray's instinct had been proven correct. Fighting Apostoli once more, with so little time elapsed, again elicited criticism from some quarters. Ray's decision was a calculated move. A loss would be a slight setback to Billy, though a knockout would unquestionably be a blow to his ego. In defeat or victory, 25 percent of an anticipated $50,000 gate was worth the risk, however minimal a risk it was. Such an opportunity was made possible by the largesse of Mike Jacobs.

The normally staid promoter was taken immediately with Billy. Conn altered Uncle Mike's stone-faced ambivalence toward the action in the ring. Jacob's main priority—in fact, his only interest—lay in the receipts tucked away in the box office. The exuberance and personable zeal on display when Conn performed in the ring, however, rubbed off on the dour Jacobs. Mike took to Billy, and something of a father-son dynamic was born between the two. Their collaboration would take Billy to the heights of the sporting world (and, along the way, earn Uncle Mike a hefty sum).

A genius of business is blessed with foresight, daring, compunction, and resolve; resolve to try again should one brainchild fail, or expand should one flourish. Mike Jacobs was born with the innate ability to visualize profits where others saw nothing. "I saw there was money to be made," Jacobs said after he had found his fortune, "but not the way some of the boys were getting it.[15]

"I also saw that the slow plodding way was both too tough and too long. I decided that early. To be a promoter of one sort or another."

Born on March 17, 1880, at 17 Washington Street in New York City, Michael Strauss Jacobs was still a young man when he began working the ferryboats at the Battery. While still in his early twenties, Mike implemented his first cunning business idea. The opportunity sprung from the chaos that persistently surrounded the ticket window at Battery Park. The confusion often resulted in the boat setting sail before all patrons would be waited on. With great acumen, Jacobs decided to begin buying ferry tickets early and scalping them to customers arriving at the docks late. This ingenious venture provided Mike with a nice profit as commuters and tourists readily anted up a premium to avoid the disorder found at ticket counters. Almost simultaneously, Jacobs acquired the rights to all concessions on all boats departing the Battery. These successes led to Mike chartering his own boats. Jacobs's ambition far outreached the tidy proceeds he procured from these enterprises. The next step was ticket brokering. Sporting events, the theater, and opera—anything that required a ducat for entry, Mike made available to the public.

Finding success with simple scalping, Jacobs then began to buy out the house for opening nights. The 1911 World Series, however, made Mike. Demand for tickets was high as New York's Giants faced off against Connie Mack's Philadelphia Athletics. It was said that Jacobs cleared more than $100,000 over the course of the six-game series. How did Mike come into so many premium tickets? Such queries drew an indignant response from Jacobs. "I take big chances, I should make some profit," he said. "How I get first-class tickets is nobody's business."[16]

Some years earlier, on September 3, 1906, Mike Jacobs met Tex Rickard at the Joe Gans–Battling Nelson fight. The match was the first promoted by Rickard, who would go on to become the preeminent force in the fight game. The two men became friendly; Jacobs helped Rickard get acquainted with and involved in the New York set, and Mike profited from brokering tickets to Tex-promoted matches and occasionally investing in some of the same.

Rickard established his hold on the sport when he promoted boxing's first $1 million gate, which pitted Jack Dempsey against French challenger Georges Carpentier. In 1925, Tex established the Madison Square Garden Corporation, an entity devoted distinctly to the promotion of sporting events. That same year, Rickard built a new Madison Square Garden at Forty-ninth Street and Eighth Avenue.

Tex died on January 6, 1929, leaving behind a burgeoning and dominant sporting enterprise. Rickard left this world with barely a penny to his name. Such a fate, Jacobs swore, would not befall him. His fortune, however, would have to wait. Some nine months after Rickard's death, on October 19, the Great Crash came. Professional sports were not immune from the repercussions of the Crash, and in the wake of the financial calamity came a downward turn for the business of boxing. Replacing Rickard as the head of the Garden Corporation was Bill Carey, a solid and successful businessman. But Carey was no Rickard, nor was he Mike Jacobs. Following several nondescript years, during which Jacobs proved his mettle by successfully promoting a series of benefits for the Milk Fund, a charity pushed by Mrs. William Randolph Hearst, fortuitously, Joe Louis happened upon the scene; Uncle Mike had found his meal ticket.

After viewing several of Louis's bouts in late '34 and early '35—fights that saw the Detroit heavyweight obliterate the likes of Natie Brown, Willie Davis, Stanley Pordea, and Hans Birkie, Jacobs became a believer. "Rickard had his Dempsey, I am going to have my Joe Louis," Mike declared.[17] Since 1933, when he formed the Twentieth Century Sporting Club with three New York reporters, Jacobs had been promoting fights at the Hippodrome and other small venues. Mike instantly recognized that Louis was his ticket to the big time.

Following the Brown fight in Detroit, Jacobs met with Louis and his representatives, Julian Black and John Roxborough. Though there hadn't been a Negro champion since Jack Johnson, Mike convinced the group that he could get Joe a shot at the title. Skeptical at first, Black, Roxborough, and Louis soon began to buy into Mike's fervor. The two sides came to an agreement in the Motor City "colored" night spot, the Frog Club. A boisterous party in honor of Joe's victory forced them to retreat to the men's room to sign their accord. Jacobs was to be Louis's sole promoter for three years, with an option for renewal. The benefits of the arrangement were mutual. Louis and his handlers were pleased because they finally would be able to break into the Eastern markets while Jacobs rode the Detroit fighter to the top of the fight game. Their first venture together was September 24, 1935, when Joe defeated Max Baer in front of 88,000 at Yankee Stadium.

The house built by the exploits of Babe Ruth was nice enough, but the venue that Mike most coveted was Tex Rickard's Garden. With the Henry Armstrong–Petey Sarron featherweight championship fight of October 27, 1937, Mike's Twentieth Century Sporting Club promoted its first fight at Madison Square Garden. From that day, until he eased himself out of the business in 1949, Jacobs had a hand in every fight of significance in New York City, the undisputed capital of the boxing world. Under Jacobs's guidance, the Garden had become a pugilistic mecca.

A chain smoker and coffee drinker by the gallon, Jacobs was a tightly wound bundle of nervous energy. Often Mike would put in an eighteen-hour workday, and no day was more hectic than the day of a scheduled fight. On those occasions, he would arrive at the venue early in the morning, overseeing each and every aspect of the show. His hands-on approach, while efficient and resourceful, also had its drawbacks. For all his kindness and geniality, Jacobs had another side to his persona, an aspect not an all endearing or pleasant.

Nat Fleischer profiled Jacobs in *The Ring,* offering a less than glowing glimpse at Uncle Mike. "In many respects Mike has a Jekyll and Hyde personality," Fleischer wrote. "He was cruel, at times, to his help particularly when things didn't go as he planned."[18]

No detail was too minor for Jacobs, who wanted shows bearing the Twentieth Century name to be first class through and through. At times his perfectionism caused him to become crabby, and he would snap, bellowing to underlings, barking in his responses to friends. Following these outbursts, Mike was always apologetic and regretful. Shortcomings and all, Jacobs was, by 1939, the undisputed emperor of his chosen domain; the man who bestowed crowns on make-believe kings.

Jacobs couldn't believe his good fortune. In Conn he had everything a promoter could ask for in a fighter: looks, style, personality, and, above all else, ability.

"My two fists are my referee," a jovial Conn said from his training "headquarters," once again Pioneer Gym. "Apostoli is a cinch. Only this time I'll do a better job. I was too nervous and tense in my last start. I can fight better than that."

Among the writers watching Billy's workouts was Regis Welsh, who reported back to his readers that Pittsburgh's pride was sparing no sweat in preparing for his rematch with Apostoli. "Conn," Welsh wrote, "has been training as never before" and "looked to be in great shape."[19] Two weeks before the fight, Freddie was a 2 to 1 favorite, but thanks to Billy's impressive workouts in the days leading up to the match, prices dropped. By the time the bell rang, Apostoli was an 11 to 10 favorite.

Both men had a track record of improving when facing an opponent for the second time. Apostoli first beat Krieger in a ten-round decision before knocking him out in five. He lost to Young Corbett in ten, then kayoed him in eight. Freddie Steele knocked out Apostoli in ten before the Bellhop returned the favor. Billy, of course, rebounded from defeats to Yarosz, Corbett, and Krieger with victories. What this would mean on February 10, no one could decide.

The prefight build up was relatively blasé. The interest was certainly present, as Conn had captured the imagination of New Yorkers. And, once again, hundreds of Pittsburghers were riding the Ham and Cabbage to take in the event. Indeed, there most certainly was no indication in the weeks prior to the fight of the acrimonious affair to come.

Following their meeting on January 6, neither fighter expressed any unusual disdain for his opponent. Prefight talk was nothing out of the ordinary. Each boxer offered generically confident quotes for the press to disseminate. "I know what he does now, and I'll tag him early," Apostoli said. "I won't waste six or seven rounds looking foolish [this time]."

"I whipped him once, I can whip him again," Billy told gathered newsmen. "I won't try to act cute like I did before. I'll tend to business and box him off his feet."[20]

Shortly after the bell rang to begin round two of the rematch, however, Conn and Apostoli partook in a riotous display, an exhibition that cast aside the sissy rules of decorum dispatched by the Marquis of Queensbury.

In a career chalk full of slow starts, the second Apostoli fight marked one of the worst yet for Billy. A head butt in the second, initiated by Fred, set off what Havey Boyle described as "a slashing, bitter battle with no quarter asked and none given."[21] Conn backed away from the collision, his right eye cut, his face smeared with blood, and looked to referee Frank Fullam for justice. Fullam ignored Conn's pleads, and the fighter waved his gloves in angry protest.

Stepping back into the fight, Billy was greeted with a thumb in the eye. Stunned, bloodied, angry, and hurt, Billy put up little fight for the remainder of the round as Freddie handily thrashed him about the body and head. Finding no solace from the official's judgment, Billy let loose a torrent of unprintable (for the next day's papers at least) invective at his opponent.

"Listen, you dago bastard, keep your thumb out of my eye," Conn spewed.

"Listen, you Irish sonofabitch, quit beefin' and c'mon and fight," Apostoli retorted.

"We were hot at one another," Billy recalled years later. "I had two paisans in my corner and a drunken Jew. So Apostoli hit me a left hook in the stomach just before the bell, so I go back to the corner. They started hollering at me for calling Apostoli names."[22]

Billy paid the reprimand from his cornermen no mind, though he would later be embarrassed to learn that, thanks to a microphone placed under the ring, members of the Garden crowd up to a dozen rows out were able to hear the colorful exchanges between the fighters.

Despite having his dander raised to an irreversible pitch, Billy was soundly whipped in the third and fourth before taking charge of the match. Conn retaliated, not just with vivid verbiage, but also with a couple of well-placed blows that landed below Apostoli's belt. In fact,

Billy lost two rounds, the eleventh and thirteenth, due to such fouls. In addition, he was warned by Fullam to curb the blue language (which went unheeded).

Writing in the *New York Post,* Jack Miley had some fun with the dirty tactics that took place during the bout, suggesting that perhaps the fighters should be wired in order to notify officials of foul blows.

> I wonder if the protective cups those pugilists wear couldn't be wired for sound, the way they do when one fencer nudges another with a swift thrust of his épée, this contact against a vital organ causes a bell to ring. . . . If Fred Apostoli, for instance, should hit Conn anywhere south of the equator it would be nice to hear a bell clang, so we'd all know what had happened. If it were just a light blow, there could be a soft, silvery tinkle. And if it were a good, substantial smash the gong would be made to resound like the engines clattering off to a four-alarm conflagration on the water front.
>
> The boys could park batteries and buzzers in their britches and they'd sound like a troupe of Swiss bell ringers.[23]

Between head butts, prodding thumbs, and punches thrown below the equator, a mighty fine fight took place. Both men swung freely and from the heels at their opposite's inviting chin. Body punches were so vicious members of the crowd winced in pain and cheered in admiration for the pugnaciousness of the combatants.

Bill Corum reported simply, "It was a honey of a fight."[24]

The highlight for Billy came in the tenth when he electrified the Garden with a steady salvo to Freddie's belly and jaw. Despite the pummeling, Apostoli endured to win four of the final five rounds, though two of the rounds were due to Conn's revenge-induced fouls.

The fifteenth found both fighters all but spent after a high-spirited initial fourteen rounds. Seemingly, Apostoli sensed that he was behind on the judge's scorecards. The final three minutes were spent trying to find the one good punch that would send Billy to the canvas. Conn, however, seemed imperturbable to Freddie's blows, which lost much of their luster en route to delivery.

In front of the largest crowd he had every played to, nearly 19,000, Billy had survived. The decision was unanimous. Fullam's scorecard read 8–7 in favor of Conn, and both judges ruled it 9–6 in Billy's favor. He set aside an injured right eye (the result of an Italian thumb), a strained leg (sustained when he slipped on the wet canvas in the sixth), and a damaged left eye (also incurred during the sixth when Fred landed a violent hook). He overcame a furious foe that threw everything, legal and illegal, at him.

Billy was cut so badly that someone suggested that photographs be taken at an angle so as not to show the damage inflicted by Apostoli. Milt Jaffe wouldn't hear of it: "What's the difference?" he said. "He won. Let the people see what he looks like."[25]

The next morning, a photo appeared in the *Pittsburgh Press* along with the caption, "If this is the winner, what does the loser look like?" Pictured was Billy, his face swathed in cloth, only his bruised eyes and puffy lips not covered by the bandages. The photograph would become a favorite of Conn's, though his counterpart believed the snapshot to be evidentiary of his victory.

"Look at me. Not a mark on me," Apostoli protested in the locker room afterward. "And then look at the other fellow. That's the answer as to who won the fight. He was hitting low all night, and those were the only punches that hurt me. . . . He's a good boy and I guess it's no disgrace to lose to him, but you may say for me that I didn't think I lost."[26]

Larry White also thought the decision was a farce. "I admit Conn had an edge last time," said the manager. "But Fred won easily tonight. Talk about burglary!"[27]

With a grin, Billy waved away all such talk. He won, and he knew it. "If I hadn't yelled at him when he started thumbing in the second round he would have gouged out my eyes."[28]

Covering the fight for the *New York Post,* Jack Miley saw no dispute with the decision. "Willy was a frightful nuisance. The belting bellhop from San Francisco hit him with everything he had, which wasn't nearly enough. For Silly Willy just kept laughing at him and jabbing his kisser out of shape with that timeless left. If there was ever a bout there was no doubt about before the official numbers went up, this was the one."[29]

Again the experts were enamored by what they witnessed from Conn in the ring. Billy was the embodiment of a captivating and successful boxer. "He has superb boxing ability, the courage that is characteristic of his ancestry, a physique that a sculptor couldn't improve on, and the innate intelligence that is rarely encountered in the ring, but," Dan Parker wrote, "Billy couldn't punch a dent in a firkin of [beer] on the Fourth of July."[30]

This criticism, in the shadow of all his attributes, had followed Conn around for several years and would continue to plague him for some time. "If he were a puncher," Joe Dawson wrote in the *New York Times,* "Conn surely would have knocked out [Apostoli]. He might conceivably beat a Joe Louis if he had a paralyzing blow. He might never have such a weapon; he is not the type."[31]

Billy's share of the gate was $10,467.01, an amount that stupefied but also tickled him. "I had heard there was that much money in the world, but I was always puzzled just how to get it. Now, I know."[32]

With a portion of his take, Conn would once again do his part for the development of the automotive industry. "I'm going out and buy myself a new car," Billy called out to Johnny through the din of the postfight chaos.

Ray had heard this postvictory declaration before. "Okay kid," he said, before addressing reporters gathered near. "Every time Billy won a fight in the past, he would trade in his old car for a new one. . . . He's not working for me and him, but for General Motors."[33]

Sparkling new vehicle or not, Billy wasn't going big time. He was offered the use of the penthouse at Park Avenue's Hotel 70 that night and any time he was in the city. This kid knew where he came from. "The West Side YMCA has always been good enough for me," he said. "And if they ain't got room there, I can hit the kip at Mills Hotel No. 8."[34]

Prior to the fight, Johnny was asked what they would do following a second victory. Traveling was on Ray's mind then, perhaps Ireland, and maybe they would make it a working vacation by booking a couple of fights for Billy in his ancestral homeland. In the immediate moments subsequent to the vicious brawl, however, the manager had altered his plans.

A happy though nerve-wracked Johnny told gathered boxing scribes that he needed a respite from the ring. "Maybe Billy can stand the strain of so many tough fights in quick succession, but I can't," Ray sputtered between drags on his cigarette. "I want a rest, and Billy needs one, and I think it will do him some good. He will put on some weight and be a full-fledged light-heavyweight."[35]

With Apostoli, Johnny declared, Billy was through with the middle-weights.

There was talk of facing Conn off against John Henry Lewis. Just a couple of weeks earlier, Lewis was soundly beaten by Joe Louis in the first heavyweight championship to pit two Black men against one another. Other rumors surfaced also. Reportedly, Mike Jacobs offered to give Billy a shot at Melio Bettina and the light-heavy title sometime in March. A Bettina match would certainly be held in Madison Square Garden, while the proposed Lewis fight was to take place in Chicago on St. Patrick's Day. There were also proposals to bring Billy to both Detroit and Philadelphia to face as-yet unnamed opponents.

No one was more cognizant than Johnny Ray of the uncertainty facing Conn and how unsettled his future was just six months earlier. And now that they had finally made it in New York, and made it big, they were going to take it slow. Though Johnny had announced that Billy was no longer fighting middleweights, he also acknowledged that his fighter needed to beef up from the 167 pounds he weighed for Apostoli. In addition to adding some bulk to his frame, Billy needed to mend from the beating endured at the hands of the San Franciscan fighter.

"They're not as bad as they look," Ray said of the cuts blemishing Conn's face. "One of them, under the right eye, that one he got in the second round, is more a rip than a cut. Apostoli did that early, after he got away with the old trick of biting the thumb of his left glove until he wore it down to a razor edge."[36]

Billy's skin, Ray explained, was as tender as a baby's, and needed to be toughened up. "The head-butt cut rather deeply, but Billy's young and it shouldn't do him any harm if he takes proper care of himself."

This, Johnny was sure Junior would do. Ray was also quite certain that his fighter would not get a big head now that he was in great demand. "Even though he is pretty much new to all this hurrah stuff that comes when you reach the top or near it, he has a pretty good head and doesn't figure to go haywire."[37]

Once again Ray was making the proper decision for his fighter. The lure of big money was there for the taking, and it was certainly tempting to make a grab for it, but Johnny was seeing beyond the day. There was no denying Billy's future; he was going places and there was no reason to rush the trip, especially for a quick buck. There would be bigger paydays to come.

The morning after Apostoli, Billy flew home to Pittsburgh and was immediately admitted to Mercy Hospital. There he received treatment for the cuts under his eyes (which were not considered serious) and got some much-needed rest. A handful of local writers were allowed in Billy's room and granted brief access to boxing's newest idol.

"How does it feel to be a hero, a fellow who whipped the great Fred

Apostoli twice within five weeks, and now has the boxing world bubbling of his exploits?"

Ever self-effacing, Billy responded, "Shucks, I'm still the same fellow who was booed here last summer."

Conn was a newsman's delight. His answers weren't cluttered with diplomatically empty sound bites. Though he was deferential and courteous to his opponents, he answered questions honestly with any thought that came to mind. Billy simply held court while the enchanted reporters scribbled his brash and honest thoughts into their notebooks.

"Apostoli is the best fighter I've ever met. But he's one of the dirtiest. He hit me a pretty good smack under the left eye and that's how I got that cut. But he would sit in his corner at the end of each round biting the thumbs of his gloves to stretch them. Then he'd come out and poke that thumb in my eye. . . . I must have had a lot of friends in the Garden. Gosh, how they cheered for me, why, there must have been 3,000 persons jamming the aisles and crowding around my dressing room when I tried to get through after the fight.

"And I did get telephone calls, telegrams and letters. Ha, here's a funny one. Some girl in Orange, N.J, sent me a letter with her picture and a crushed flower. She said she wanted me to say hello to her on the radio. Imagine that!"[38]

Six Gone to the Fight

He wasn't through with the middleweights just yet.

Conn's immediate future following the second Apostoli match was a couple of days in Mercy Hospital before an auto trip to Hot Springs with Johnny and Milt Jaffe. From there, the three headed to Hollywood; the highlight of the trip was a meeting with Zeppo Marx. The much-needed three-month vacation came to a close on May 12 when Billy once again met Solly Krieger; this time the venue was Madison Square Garden.

Yet another Krieger–Conn fight was met by apathy. Pittsburghers had long been hearing of Billy's run toward a championship belt; still here was another detour. This was not only a deviation away from a title; this was another middleweight, another repeat opponent. The bout failed to capture the imagination of Pittsburgh fight fans or the city's sports editors. Neither the *Press* nor the *Sun-Telegraph* sent a correspondent to cover the fight. Instead, these newspapers depended on wire service reports for their coverage of the match. Only Havey Boyle of the *Post-Gazette* made the trip.

Even the Ham and Cabbage Special wasn't leaving Penn Station for this one. Owney McManus offered a simple explanation for the cancellation of the charter train. "I just don't give a damn who wins, and neither does anyone else," he said.

This matchup was the handiwork of Mike Jacobs, a further irritant to local fans. The recent marriage of Johnny Ray and Jacobs made the natives uneasy. It was becoming exceedingly obvious that Billy was no longer the sole property of Pittsburgh. Mike Jacobs and New York was now laying their own claims to the attractive fighter.

"The impression grows that Master Conn and his superintendent of actions, Johnny Ray, have turned their future over to Mike Jacobs and his Manhattan mélange," lamented Chet Smith. "This is something of a disappointment to us yokels in this end of the province, who had hoped that Billy would consent to come home to open the outdoor boxing season next month. Instead, Mr. Ray starts talking in terms of telephone numbers and war debts whenever the matter is mentioned. If he feels that way, we think the best way is to let him go. He will be back someday looking for his old friends."[1]

Smith's criticism of Ray was off the mark and unfair. Johnny would have been lax in his duties as Billy's manager if he didn't take the best offer available for his fighter; New York was where the big money lay. Regardless of Smith's condemnation, Conn was one of the few fighters who fought for Jacobs, yet remained free of obligation for any future fights. For this, Ray deserved praise. Sure, he had entered a relationship with Jacobs but, as Havey Boyle noted, "Usually when you sign for a match with Jacobs in New York you sign away both the oil rights and the privilege of flying over your own premises."[2] Still, provincial concern took priority over Conn's career interests.

Traipsing along with Billy and Johnny was Jackie, who was going to make his New York debut on the undercard of his big brother's bout. In his role as the brothers Conn chaperone, Ray spent several days in a nervous titter as he tried to keep them from killing one another.

Following the duo during their stay in New York was Jack Miley of the *New York Post,* who kept his readers posted on their unruly antics.

"Yesterday Billy hit Jackie a punch on his little pug nose that set him back on his heels and had the gore spurting down his chest," Miley reported. With blood streaming from his nose onto a recently laundered shirt, Jackie blubbered. "That dirty bum," he cried, "two years from now he won't do that."[3]

Hours later, in the lobby of the Edison Hotel, the boys had to be separated by Ray. What spurred this disagreement? "Aw, Billy told me to stop looking at tall buildings," Jackie complained to a sympathetic Miley. "He said everybody'd know I was a hick from Pittsburgh. Just because he's been to New York before he's a wise guy."

On their first full day in the city Jackie loaded himself up with pop, candy, and cakes, much to the disgust of Billy. "I'll knock you around until that stuff comes out of your ears," Billy threatened. That afternoon, following their session at Pioneer gym, Jackie was standing tall and running his mouth. "Well, I don't see that pie coming out of my ears."

Before leaving their hotel for the fight Billy offered some brotherly advice to his slightly cowed sibling who was intimidated by the grand stage of Madison Square Garden. "Aw, this place is just like Duquesne Gardens, only there's more of it," said Billy reassuringly. "Forget those people and keep your eye on the guy's right hand. Hit him first and the show's over. It's a breeze."

Besides, he added, "They're not coming to see you, they're coming to see me."[4]

Pittsburghers may not have been intrigued by the Conn–Krieger matchup, but New Yorkers certainly were. Only Joe Louis was a bigger attraction than Billy, and 11,000 paid more than $25,000 to see him take on Krieger. The bout itself did nothing to quell the public's thirst for Conn. Joseph Nichols, in his *New York Times* fight account, likening Krieger to an animated punching bag. "Using a left hand to the face that rarely missed its mark, the Pittsburgh athlete dominated the proceedings almost completely from long range," Nichols reported while also calling Billy's performance a "masterpiece of boxing."[5]

Though he wasn't at his best, Billy far outclassed Krieger. He was never in any danger, and finished the fight unblemished except for a slight cut above his right eye. Only Solly's jaw of granite kept him upright, however, as Billy's new "secrete weapon" proved most effective. He had added a new punch to his repertoire, a spanking inside right uppercut. The punch, Billy explained, was devised by Ray to stifle Krieger's desire to in-fight.

"Johnny told me to keep moving with my hands up and to jab and hook short and fast and occasionally shoot a right when I had an opening and to work the uppercut inside," Conn said. "That's all there was to it. I felt great and didn't tire. I could have kept going indefinitely."[6]

What about Jackie, Billy was asked? The newsmen were impressed by Jackie's TKO over Harlem product Freddie Lewis, but Conn appraised his younger brother's fighting prospects with a shrug. He was an all right boxer, Billy said of Jackie, but he could be much better if he'd lay off eating nickel pies and drinking soda pop.

"How'd I do Billy? How'd I do?" Jackie asked when he returned from the ring.

Victory or not, Billy was unimpressed. His appraisal of his brother's performance was succinct and completely void of sentiment. "Get a job," Billy told Jackie. "You're going to get killed."

Billy returned to the Edison Hotel and got a sound night's sleep before he was up and on an airplane heading back home. He arrived in Pittsburgh less than twelve hours after he'd left Madison Square Garden the evening before. Though he had scarcely showed the effects the night before, Billy had been troubled for days by infected tonsils and was rushing home to have them removed.

His recovery from the minor surgery was rapid. On Monday, May 15, Johnny and Billy sat ringside at Duquesne Garden closely watching the match between Melio Bettina and Italo Colonello. Junior and Moonie studied Bettina intently, knowing that Billy's route to a championship now led through the Italian from Beacon, New York. Melio exhibited impressive punching power, taking just two rounds to knock out the huge, if unskilled, Colonello. Though he plainly took note of Bettina's brawn and skill, Conn wasn't intimidated by the prospect of facing him. "He won't hit me with those punches," Billy stated, as a matter of fact.

Clearly, the next fight for Billy would be against Bettina. Immediately following the Krieger match, Ray Foutts, who was working for Rooney-McGinley as a matchmaker, approached Johnny. Foutts tried to entice Ray into a summer match at Forbes Field against Bettina. Unfortunately for Foutts and Pittsburgh fight fans, Bettina was tied to Mike Jacobs. No fight would be put together without Uncle Mike's okay, and Jacobs wasn't about to cede the rights to such a lucrative match. Ray was near a deal that would finally put Billy in the ring, fighting for a championship, against Bettina. The terms of the contract, however, would be dictated to Ray and not by him; such is the life of the challenger.

Ever the entrepreneur, Jacobs began looking ahead before Billy exited the Garden ring on May 12. Conn–Bettina was definitely his first choice. That match, he figured, would take place sometime in mid-July. Another possibility was a third Apostoli–Conn fight. However, even Uncle Mike would have to admit that would be a tough sell. The promoter preferred to pit Apostoli against Krieger for the middleweight crown. For public consumption, Johnny Ray let his preference be known. He didn't care who they fought as long as they were paid well. Privately, though, Ray wanted the title for Billy. He wanted the title more for Junior than he ever wanted it for himself.

The day after the Krieger match, Johnny met with Mike Jacobs and agreed to a deal that would have Billy fight in New York sometime in July. His opponent wasn't immediately announced, however. It wasn't until late June that it was confirmed; Conn would meet Melio Bettina on July 13, 1939, at Madison Square Garden. The fight was to be the first time Melio risked his belt, which he gained when he defeated Tiger Jack Fox in an elimination tournament the previous February. Though Melio was recognized by most states as the champion following his victory over Fox, the New York Boxing Commission arbitrarily vacated the title when it ruled John Henry Lewis ineligible to defend his crown due to health considerations. The winner of Conn–Bettina would be recognized by the state of New York as the titleholder.

The matchup against Bettina was a favorable one for Conn, who had several natural advantages over his opponent, including height and reach. "This is just one of the steps Billy will be taking toward that shot at Louis," Ray said. "I talked with Mike Jacobs and he has his mind set on the idea that next year he will meet Joe Louis for the heavyweight crown."[7]

Louis . . . boxing experts couldn't resist projecting a Conn–Louis bout. The possibility was first uttered by Solly Krieger months before—the thought that, given time to fill out, Billy was the best bet to take away Joe Louis's title. Now most everyone was looking forward to the time when Conn would be facing the heavyweight champion. Many were even looking past the imminent match against Bettina toward that far-off day. That kinda stuff was for writers and fans, however. Billy was steadfast. His mind was firmly fixed on a squat Italian from Beacon and capturing *his* crown.

The New York press was intoxicated with Billy's charm and wit. Reporters simply opened their notebooks, asked a question, and let the garrulous kid ramble. The subject of conversation ran the gamut. Human-interest notes took precedence over the normal staid boxing fare, as the fairer sex was eager to learn more about this handsome young fighter.

> Who was his favorite singer?
> *Bing Crosby*
> Favorite actor?
> *Groucho Marx*

Favorite dish?
Corned beef and cabbage
Baseball player?
Jim Tobin
Song?
"Ireland Must Be Heaven"

More than any other topic, the contingent of New York sportswriters was taken with the "Fightin' Conns." "My brothers love to fight," Billy admitted. "My old man loves to fight. And my grampappy loves to fight. My grampappy is the only one of them who can fight a lick."

Aw, the old man is a fighting man, he's a fighting Mick himself. He's the best fighter in the family. Up till a year ago I used to fight with him out in the backyard.

I'm getting too good for him now. After all, he's 41 years old. There are plenty of guys he can still fight—for fun that is. He knows where to find his fights around Pittsburgh. I don't know about here. Give him a day or two, I guess, and he'll get guys to slug it out with.

My old man once battled it out with my manager, Johnny Ray. They were taking a bunch of fighters, including me, from Pittsburgh to Erie, Pa. On the way back Johnny said something the old man didn't like. He swung, Johnny swung. When it was finished Pop had a broken nose and Johnny had lost a tooth. That made them pals.

There was another time when an Irish club was having a big party in Pittsburgh. A fellow was playing the piano and singing a song that finished like this, "There never was a coward in the land where shamrocks grow." As soon as he finished my old man jumped up and shouted, "You're damn right, brother. Play that tune again. The Conns will fight anybody."

That old man of mine goes around Pittsburgh telling everybody I'm a cinch to beat Joe Louis right now. I figure I can beat Louis, but it ain't nice to go talking about it. My old man don't stop at just saying that. He steps right out on the floor and shows them how I'll do it—a hook, a jab, a feint, you know.

Some day I have to go over to Ireland and find out what made my old man's family like this. My old man says he comes from a family of fighting kings and that they chased all over the country winning battles, then fighting among themselves when there wasn't anything else to do. He says he does his best to live up to the old custom. I do, too, so why must Johnny Ray hold me back when I want to swing at those guys who bump into you on the street?"[8]

Harry Keck, who had much personal experience with the Conn brothers, allowed his readers a taste of the unique experience of being in the company of Billy and Jackie. Keck gained exclusive access to the troublesome duo as they rode to the official weigh-in. Freddie Fierro manned the wheel as Jackie rode shotgun. Billy comfortably sat in the backseat with Keck, as a moment of calm receded into familiar turbulence. No sooner had Keck begun the interview than Billy told his brother, "Why don't you get a haircut?"

Jackie, used to such harassment, didn't bother turning around before replying, "Why don't you mind your own business?"

Keck tried to get the boys on track. The newsman asked Jackie if he would have become a fighter if Billy hadn't. "Sure," he responded, "we started out together."

The reply was Billy's cue to jump in, "What was that, punk?" he prodded. "We started out *together?* Why I'm almost twenty-two, and you were a baby when I started. Where do you get that 'started out together' stuff?"

Jackie shrugged off Billy's harangue, and continued his conversation with Keck. "Well, almost together. And everybody says I'm a better fighter now than you were when you were my age."

As expected, Billy took Jackie's boast as a challenge. "Is that so? Well, you'll have to grow fast to join my league. You'll never see the day you'll be able to lick me."

"All right Chump—I mean Champ. Give me a few more years and you won't be saying that. I'll take you, all right."

Later that afternoon Keck met with Maggie, who had arrived in New York following a visit to Baltimore, though she had no intention of attending the show. Were her boys this playful at home, Keck asked?

"Not only them, but their father as well," Mrs. Conn said. "You know, he's only 41 and he still thinks he's as young as they are. Every morning, when they have fights on, Billy and Jackie get up early and go out on the road to do their running together. Almost invariably they are arguing and they're into it, punching and wrestling. It may be in the living room or the dining room or kitchen. They're not a bit fussy about picking a spot. Along about that time their dad comes home from his night trick at Westinghouse, and the first thing I know he's into it too, and the three of them are tosseling about. Only he finds out after a few minutes that he's not as young as he used to be and has to give up when his wind deserts him."

Is all this fighting a strain on her, Keck asked? "You can't get along with them and you wouldn't know what to do without them. Many a time I've taken a broom to the whole lot of them. But I'd miss them and their fussing if they ever decided to settle down and behave themselves."[9]

With Conn's growing popularity came more demands on his time. To help with these newfound hassles, Billy's sister Mary Jane served as his Girl Friday. She took phone messages, answered fan mail, packed Billy's bags, and ran errands for her brother. Unfettered by menial tasks, Conn was free to pursue the laurels that came from his newly found fame. He would go out on the town, but Billy didn't fall for the playboy aspect of celebrity. He didn't drink or smoke and Conn's moves in the ring didn't translate well to the dance floor. Billy had an eye for the girls, all right, but he couldn't overindulge. They weakened the legs, you know.

Billy also now had an open-ended invitation to visit Mike Jacobs's estate in Rumson, New Jersey. Uncle Mike bent over backward to make Conn comfortable. Billy had the use of Jacobs's duplex at Central Park West and vacationed at the promoter's Miami hideaway. He even was allowed to borrow Mike's sporty, cream-colored convertible. Yes sir, this fame stuff was all right.

"Bettina will win," Melio's manager, Jimmy Grippo, stated. "He must win. I've told him so." Grippo was a self-styled magician who, when necessary, would cast a "spell" on adversaries.

What if Melio should fail? Grippo was asked. "Then," he said, "I will do my last trick, the Indian rope trick. I'll toss one end of a rope up in the air. It will hang there. I'll climb up the rope, and disappear."[10]

Though some found Grippo's act amusing, John Phelan of the New York Boxing Commission did not. Phelan warned Grippo that his antics would not be accepted during the bout. There was to be no hypnotic spells cast in the midst of the fight. A couple of days prior to the fight, Grippo attempted to work his magic on Conn in the Boxing Commission office where the parties central to the fight had gathered for instructions.

"Now, none of that monkey business around here, young man," Phelan said, admonishing Grippo. "We're not running a medicine show here." The chairman had made his point; Grippo's carnival act would not be tolerated, either in the ring or in his office.

The day of the fight, the town of Beacon, New York, was practically shut down. Signs filled the windows of Beacon establishments: "Gone to the fight," they read; no other notice was needed. Several days earlier, the townspeople got their bloodthirst up when they burned Conn in effigy at a large civic gathering. They carried this passion downstate for the big bout. More than 1,500 Beaconites traveled to New York to root on their native son. They brought along with them a couple of brass bands, which sat opposite one another in Madison Square Garden; the resulting cacophony of sound filled the hall with festive spirit.

Jolly Pittsburghers refused to have their exuberance drowned out in a brass dissonance. "You'll have to have more than a band to lick an Irishman," a Conn backer shouted as one of the bands bellowed out a raucously disjointed tune.[11] Several hundred fans arrived in New York from Pittsburgh. They came by auto and airplane, but the majority came via the two special trains chartered by Owney McManus, who decidedly *did* care who won this bout. Billy sent a message to his hometown fans who made the eastward pilgrimage to support him. "I won't let anybody down," he promised. "He'll have to knock me out to win."[12]

The atmosphere inside the Garden took on the celebratory aura of a collegiate football contest. Not even the nauseating heat inside the hall, caused by a malfunctioning air-cooling system, quelled the enthusiasm of the boisterous fight patrons. Bettina's rooters marched around the ring bearing a variety of signs, all praising their Melio—"Beacon, New York's World Champion, Melio Bettina"; "Our Man Is Melio." The animated Bettina boosters had a practice run when Jackie was introduced to the crowd before his match with Lou Vallente. Their hoots, howls, and catcalls filled the room as the name *Conn,* however briefly, reverberated through the hall.

They were ready, then, for the headliners. "The Garden was an amplified boiler factory when the main bout contestants were introduced," Dan Parker wrote in the *New York Daily Mirror.*[13] The roustabouts from Dutchess County practically tore the roof off the Garden when their Melio was announced. They then equaled that delight with a venomous displeasure directed at the Pittsburgh Pretty Boy. Billy certainly had his supporters, but they unfortunately lacked the spirited backing of a band.

Sporting his lucky purple trunks, Conn sat calmly in his corner taking in the festivities. He turned to Fierro and with an assured grin promised Fat, "I hate to ruin the night for these people, but Beacon ain't gonna have a champion an hour from now."

The fight had barely begun when Ray and Conn both realized that they had underestimated Bettina. Through the first four rounds, Billy tried to fight Melio rather than outbox him. This made him wide open for the bone-jarring hooks the left-handed Bettina tirelessly threw. His timing was off, and he missed with more than he landed. Billy answered the bell in the fifth with a complete change in style; up on his toes, moving, stabbing with his left, and delivering short jolting blows with his right. As the round neared its end, referee Frankie Fullam stepped in to separate the fighters, who had become tied up in a clinch. After the break, Billy nailed Bettina with a hard right, nullifying all his hard work in the round when Fullam told officials that he was awarding the stanza to Melio because of the Conn foul. On most every score sheet, official and unofficial, Bettina started the fight with a nearly insurmountable lead.

Ironically, neither Ray nor Conn viewed the fight that way. Unbelievably, both men believed they were ahead. "I held Billy back in the early rounds, and I told him to play it safe in the last round," Ray told Harry Keck following the match. "I thought he was miles ahead. Bettina never hurt him at any time, and he blocked most of those early rushes. I guess it was because he let Bettina crowd him into the ropes and swing in close that the spectators thought Billy was being punished."[14] Apt perception or not, Billy *was* behind on all the scorecards that mattered, five rounds to none.

Built close to the ground, Bettina was described by one writer as a "swarthy squat-sized southpaw." Handsome he was not. But champion he was, and Billy desperately wanted the crown Bettina wore. It took some time, and Billy had dug himself a cavernous hole, but he finally solved Melio's unorthodox style. He took the sixth, seventh, eighth, and ninth easily. With a confident air, Billy danced and jabbed while slowly cutting into Bettina's large lead.

The first of three excellent knockout chances came for Billy in the eleventh. The action turned in during this round was the most harried of the evening. Reborn, Bettina began rushing Billy and scored with a number of solid blows to the body. This onslaught was ended when Conn caught Melio with a hard right. All life immediately slipped out of the stunned Bettina. Though standing, he dropped both hands and ceased putting up a fight. Rather than move in and administer the pièce de résistance, Conn stayed back, moving around the perimeter of the ring, allowing Melio to recover from his momentary paralysis.

Another great opening came for Billy two rounds later when, after a hard hook to the body followed by a right cross to the jaw, Bettina's legs turned to rubber. This time Conn didn't let the moment slip away without trying to finish off his opponent. Billy tore into Bettina, igniting the crowd into a frenzy. In an act of self-preservation, Melio buried his head in his arms hoping Billy would punch himself out. The stifling heat in the Garden did more to slow Conn than any defensive tactic Bettina put forth; this much was confirmed by Billy following the fight. His strength somewhat sapped by the humidity in the arena, Conn had missed his best chance of the night to knock out Bettina.

The fourteenth was more of the same. Billy was taking the fight to Melio, who was doing all he could to hold on. Grabbing and clutching at Conn was Bettina's only defense. Somehow, as the final round began, Bettina summoned the strength for one last gasping offensive. A few of his punches found their mark; one hook caught Billy flush and sent him reeling to the ropes. Still, Conn continued to return fire, though at long range. Bettina's offensive was enough for him to take the round.

The decision was unanimous.

"The winner, and new light-heavyweight champion of the world, Billy Conn."

Though Johnny was just a few feet from Billy, Westinghouse, who leapt up from his seat in press row, slipped through the ropes and was the first to shake his son's hand in congratulations.

Moments later, inside the jubilant winner's dressing room, friends and family surrounded Billy. Westinghouse, drenched in sweat and smiling profusely, sat next to his eldest son with Jackie and Frank nearby. Milt Jaffe, of course, was there, as were Art Rooney and the brothers Wolk, Charley and Curley.

"It was hot, and I didn't have my old zip," Billy explained. "I really thought I could go in and finish him anytime I pleased, but Johnny wouldn't let me."[15]

Ray acknowledged as much. "If he would have lost it would have been my fault," he said.[16] Holding Billy back, in the early rounds in particular, Johnny said, could have been very costly. In defeat, one could have second-guessed Ray's strategy. In the aftermath of victory, however, Johnny came out smelling like a rose.

"The only thing he complained about was the heat," Ray told reporters, "but so did Bettina. The Garden was like an oven. But he stood the heat better than Bettina, although he didn't have his old zip. He'll knock Melio out when they meet again," Johnny promised.[17]

Dan Parker believed the fight was won and lost by the cornermen and not by the boxers themselves. "Billy had the benefit of excellent advice from one who had been through the mill and knows what it's all about," Parker told his readers. "Johnny Ray helped him solve the awkward southpaw's style which had him so baffled for the first four rounds. On the other hand, Bettina had a hypnotist in his corner who succeeded only in hypnotizing himself. Jimmy Grippo is a pleasant, entertaining fellow, but a correspondence school Svengali is a poor substitute for a good handler like Ray Arcel or Whitey Bimstein who not only knows when a fighter is following the wrong course but also has the remedy for it."[18]

Bettina had no answer for Billy's new tactics when the direction of the match changed in the fifth and Grippo offered no solutions. Repeatedly Melio looked to his corner for guidance, but received nothing in return except a feeble gaze of helplessness from Grippo. Foolishly, the hypnotist cum manager spent much of the early rounds casting imbecilic spells on Conn rather than tending to his fighter.

In the loser's dressing room, Bettina wept bitter tears. He had won. He was sure of it. Grippo was equally sure. Since when, Jimmy asked, did the judges begin awarding fights to challengers who "did all the running?"[19]

The dethroned champion reiterated his manager's protest. "I don't think I lost," Melio complained. "They took my title away and gave it to a fellow who ran. I did all the forcing."[20] The fight was certainly close, and Bettina's complaint in the shadow of a hard-fought contest was understandable. Still, when Frankie Fullam raised Billy's right arm in triumph, nary a sound of protest was heard from the large Beacon contingent present. Indeed, the fight was Billy's fair and square, and Melio would get his chance in the inevitable rematch sure to come later in the summer.

Also unavoidable was the question of Joe Louis and when would Billy face the heavyweight champ. "I'll fight him," Conn said, "but Johnny says I'm a year away from Louis. I'll always do as he says. Why shouldn't I? Here I am, a champion of the world. Johnny's advice has been better than my father's could have been up to now."[21]

In fact, Johnny was every bit the father figure to Billy that Westinghouse had been. Ray was determined not to allow Junior's career to fall short of his great expectations and wither on the vine, as he had done with his own. Johnny had the talent to be a champion, but he was not faithful to his craft. He trained sporadically, never hard enough to reach the top level of his sport. Johnny also had far too many late nights, his potential undermined by the lure of the bottle. When his days in the ring had come to a close, all Ray had to his name were a few bad habits. This would not happen to Junior, Johnny determined. He saw much of himself in Billy, the salvageable element at least, and Ray vowed to keep Conn on the straight and narrow. Luckily for the two men, Billy bought into everything Johnny sold, and now the long hours in two-bit gyms had paid off with a championship—a championship earned through diligence and hard work; one shared with mutual love and admiration.

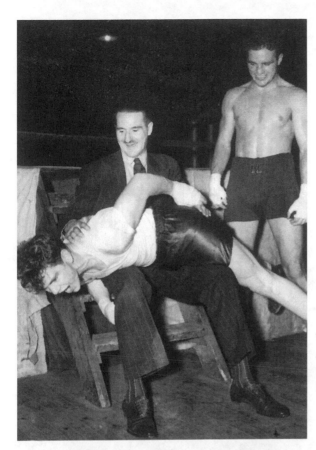

Westinghouse spanks
Jackie as Billy looks
on approvingly (Conn
Family Collection)

Maggie and Billy (Conn Family Collection)

Fritzie Zivic enjoys Billy's damaged nose (Conn Family Collection)

Greenfield Jimmy Smith
with the 1919 Cincinnati
Reds (Conn Family
Collection)

Conn (*left*) against Melio Bettina (*right*), at their rematch on September 25, 1939, at Forbes Field (Conn Family Collection)

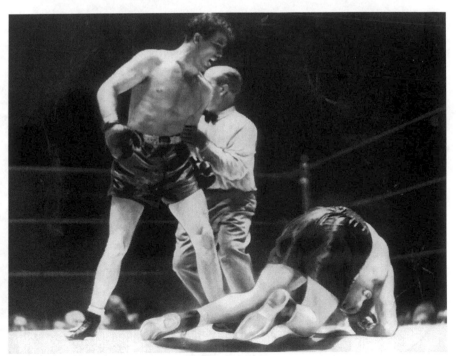

Conn standing over Bob Pastor, September 6, 1940 (Conn Family Collection)

Junior and Moonie (Conn Family Collection)

Mary Louise Smith (Conn
Family Collection)

Billy and Mary Louise, running along the Jersey Shore (Conn Family Collection)

Louis and Conn, June 18, 1941, at the Polo Grounds (Conn Family
Collection)

LOUIS K.O.'S CONN IN THE 13

(*Above*) Billy goes down in
the thirteenth, June 18, 1941
(Conn Family Collection)

Burying the hatchet with
Greenfield Jimmy (Conn
Family Collection)

Harry Pitler, aka "Johnny Ray," circa 1921 (courtesy of Robert and Maria Pitler)

Mary Louise and Billy (Conn Family Collection)

Seven Fighting Is My Business

"Billy Conn, a cinema god by birth and a Celtic blooded prizefighter through choice, today holds the light heavyweight championship of the world in the palm of his hand and isn't quite sure what he can do about it."
—Hype Igoe, *New York Journal American*

Jubilation, rightly earned, filled Billy's dressing room. He basked in the deeply satisfying emotion only a champion could appreciate. Surrounding him, filling the room, were well-wishers. The usual lot was present: Conn's brothers, Frank and Jackie, were there, as was Westinghouse. A great photograph was snapped for the papers; it showed Westinghouse kissing the right cheek of a grinning Billy, while Johnny planted one on Junior's left cheek.

Jaffe was also there, as was Milt's business partner, Art Rooney. Rooney and Jaffe were just two of Pittsburgh's sportsmen who'd been following Billy's career since his prelim days. This championship was a shared realization for these men. Billy was one of their own, and they embraced him fully. Among these longtime hometown admirers of Conn's pugilistic pursuits was the well-known and respected businessman "Greenfield" Jimmy Smith.

Smith was born in the Greenfield section of Pittsburgh on May 5, 1895. The eldest of five children, Jimmy's mother came to America from Wales, while his father had emigrated from Ireland. Most everyone in the predominantly Irish area of Greenfield worked the steel mills. Jimmy's father was no exception, nor were his uncles Thomas and Johnny. James L. Smith was a blacksmith at the Jones & Laughlin mill, while his brothers were both puddlers. Of all the backbreaking labor found inside a mill, the puddler had it the worst. The puddlers were a special breed of men; they did the physically unforgiving work of raking the impurities out of the molten steel.

James provided well for his family, which allowed young Jimmy an opportunity to envision life beyond the mills. Even as a young man, Jimmy displayed great ambition and his chosen path to escape a life of deadening labor was baseball. Such a dream was a long shot to be sure, but Smith possessed talent. He began his foray into professional baseball in St. Mary's, Pennsylvania, with a local semipro team. Smith was easily the finest player on his club, and while playing on the sand-lots of eastern Pennsylvania, Jimmy caught the eye of a major league scout.

Smith played his first major league game on September 26, 1914, with the Chicago Whales of the Federal League. He returned to the "outlaw" league the next year, splitting the season between the Whales and Baltimore's Terrapins. What followed for Smith was five different teams in six seasons. A stint with his hometown Pirates in 1916 saw Greenfield Jimmy spell the legendary Honus Wagner at shortstop for twenty-six games. Though Smith's teams reached the World Series twice (New York Giants in 1917 and Cincinnati Reds in 1919), his career was rather unspectacular.

He was the prototypical "no hit, good field" player. What he may have lacked in aptitude, Smith more than made up for in spirit. Jimmy's finest attribute, however, was something not found in a box score. Smith's snappy wit, bellicose voice, and complete lack of fear propelled him to great heights as a bench jockey.

While with the Giants, manager John McGraw asked his utility in-fielder to use his unusual gift on Eddie Collins of the Chicago White Sox during the '17 Series. Though Smith had rightfully earned the nickname "Serpent Tongue Jimmy Smith," he was off his game during the Series. Throughout the six-game set, Jimmy heckled the college-educated Collins unmercifully. Nothing was sacred, not even the woman Eddie was then seeing socially.

"How's Frances, Ed?" Jimmy repeatedly inquired, loud enough for patrons in the first few rows behind the Giant dugout to hear. Such a breach of decorum rankled Collins. Certainly, Smith was getting under the skin of Chicago's second baseman, but the incessant chatter didn't affect Collins's play on the field. The future Hall of Famer starred in the Series, batting .409 and scoring the decisive run in the deciding game six.

As a Giant, Smith became one of McGraw's favorite ballplayers. Sure, he wasn't a star, but Jimmy possessed the mettle that McGraw loved to see in his men. The Giants manager used his utility infielder as a buffer with Jim Thorpe, an incorrigible outfielder. And Thorpe didn't question Smith, not after he witnessed Jimmy challenge the entire Brooklyn Dodgers team, "individually, or all at once." There were no takers stepping forward from the Brooklyn dugout.

His final major league game came with the Philadelphia Phillies in 1922, but Smith continued to pursue professional baseball for several years with the Toronto Maple Leafs of the International League. The career prospects for a poor-hitting, tough-talking bench jockey were unstable at best. This reality was not lost on Smith. With Prohibition in full effect, Smith discovered he had other talents: a great business acumen that overshadowed his abilities on the playing field.

The law of supply and demand was simple to decipher. More than a few speakeasies in the states were in need of booze, and in Canada liquor was legal and plentiful. A thinking man, Smith understood that a sizeable, if not honest, buck could be had if one could deliver the goods to stateside gin joints. Using the Maple Leafs team train as his mode of transportation, Jimmy purchased countless cases of Canadian liquor and stored the contraband in lockers aboard the train. Before long, Greenfield's income from bootlegging dwarfed his meager minor league salary.

Smith discovered something else while in Canada; Jimmy found that he had fallen in love with a beautiful, self-determined brunette named Nora Bailey. The ambitious, rum-running ballplayer disarmed the well-read Miss Bailey, who was swept away by Smith's charm. Unfortunately, Nora's parents weren't as enamored with her beau as was their daughter. When Jimmy blasted a line drive off a sign in Maple Leaf Park that read, "Hit me and win a diamond ring," he took his prize and asked for Nora's hand in marriage. The Baileys were English Episcopalian by faith, and Nora was raised to look down upon Irish Catholics. She was warned repeatedly by her parents, "You'll regret the day you ever married that Catholic," but love prevailed. Without her parents' blessing, Nora and Jimmy eloped to Detroit.

The newlyweds were enjoying the fruits of Smith's labors. His income from bootlegging had swelled to nearly $50,000 a year. When comparing it to his $5,000 baseball salary, Smith realized it was time to hang up his spikes. The couple returned to Pittsburgh and settled into a home on Bigelow Street in Squirrel Hill. Just a short drive from his home, Jimmy opened a "private club" on the corner of Shady and Penn in East Liberty. He named it the Bachelor's Club.

Already well known and respected in his role as a major league baseball player, the popularity of Jimmy's new establishment helped expand his sphere of influence. Greenfield was a connected man, a man about town who made friends in the right places. Local politicians were among those who Smith counted as his friends. Smartly, he used the influence garnered from these relationships to pay off elected officials and law enforcement.

Following the repeal of the Volstead Act, the Bachelor's Club was transformed from a speakeasy into a classy show club. A restaurant was added and patrons were treated to floor shows from some of the country's finest musical and comedy acts. "It was a good clean place," one member said, "where you could take your wife and know she would be safe."[1]

The Bachelor's Club was strictly a members-only establishment. To join, one needed a member to vouch for him. Upon their first visit, newcomers were asked their birthday; the information was kept in a card system. The next time the new member visited, doorman Al Turner would ask their birthday before allowing admittance. Turner only asked the information once, though, for he had an amazing memory and a knack for recalling faces.

Once okayed by Turner, patrons passed through the first of several steel doors and into a vestibule. Through another steel door and there lay a splendidly appointed lobby, paneled with wood salvaged from the demolished mansion of R. B. Mellon. Then, patrons went up a red-carpeted stairway lined with mirrors to another steel door. Inside there was a large room where top-of-the-line entertainers performed and club members danced, ate, and drank. The room was decorated in the latest art deco fashion. The tables were red and gray and set off with red leather chairs with gray leatherback inserts. Placed on the wall behind a red leather and chrome bar was the only picture in the room, a portrait of Harry Greb.

Through the last of the steel doors was the gaming room. Red carpeting covered the floor and exquisite chandeliers lit the space. A beautifully hand-carved fireplace, which Jimmy also bought from the Mellon manse, was the centerpiece in the venerably decorated room. Smith offered a wide array of games of chance for his clientele to partake of in the exquisite surroundings. A roulette wheel, several craps and poker tables, and numerous slot machines filled the room.

His unrelenting ambition and lucrative business enterprises didn't prevent Smith from becoming a successful family man. Nora gave Jimmy four children—Nora, Jimmy, Tommy, and, the apple of her father's eye, Mary Louise. Each summer the Smith family would vacation on the shore of Atlantic City. As his children grew, so did Greenfield's financial circumstances. In 1934, while much of the country was still mired in the hardships brought on by the Great Depression, Jimmy built a three-story, red-brick home in Ocean City, New Jersey. This would be the family home from June until September every summer.

And this is where Greenfield Jimmy Smith invited Billy Conn to visit. Smith had learned that the newly crowned champion had never been to the shore, and when the moment presented itself, Jimmy asked Billy if he would like to come to Ocean City for a few days. Greenfield had been a fan of Conn for some time. The two men, though, had become acquainted years earlier when Billy was still running the streets of East Liberty.

Neighborhood kids, Conn included, enjoyed letting the air from the tires of Smith's Bachelor Club patrons on a daily basis. Greenfield struck a deal with the ringleader of the group, Billy. If they stopped with the petty vandalism, Jimmy would give them a buck a day. This hazy memory wasn't rehashed in the Madison Square Garden dressing room. There would be time to reminisce later. . . . Billy eagerly accepted the offer to visit the shore.

The ocean was nice, and so was the beach, but nothing could match the splendor Billy found in Jimmy Smith's youngest daughter. Just sixteen years old, Mary Louise was a beauty queen–in-waiting. Despite her age, the attractive young blonde was not without a bevy of suitors. Fraternity boys from Villanova and prep school boys from Philly, all from money, had showered Mary Louise with attention. Despite his good looks and charm, Billy barely made an impression on Miss Smith. She didn't know who Conn was when she met him; sports figures were a dime a dozen around the Smith household, they were all the same to her. Had he not declared his intention to one day marry her, Mary Louise may have forgotten him completely after he left Ocean City.

What do you do when you're the champ? You remember where you came from. You remember who ridiculed you. Right after winning the belt, Billy ventured into an East Liberty tavern, Nick the Greek's. Inside were a number of fellas who had razzed Conn over the years about hanging around "that drunken Jew." Billy laid his cash on the bar. "Hey all you Dago bastards and Irish sons of bitches," Conn called out. "Have a drink on me. This is the last time you'll see me."[2] Billy turned and left, never to look back.

You also remember who was right there with you all the way. For Maggie, the sky was the limit. Anything she wanted was hers for the asking. And though she didn't ask for it, Billy bought her a new home, a home that befitted the queen of his life. From the overcrowded, worn-down tenement on Shakespeare Avenue, the Conn family, all seven of them, relocated to the ritzy address of Fifth Avenue in Shadyside.

The great boulevard was the well-known home to many of Pittsburgh's wealthiest citizens. Now another family could be added to the upper echelon of Pittsburgh society, the Conns. Maggie, though, wasn't sure if the new neighborhood was for her. "I don't know anyone on Fifth Avenue," she told Billy. That trifling fact didn't deter him. His mother was going to live on the Boulevard of Millionaires.

"You know the Conns were always poor," Billy told a newsman. "There wasn't much money for so many of us. When I started to make money with my fists it seemed like a dream. It's wonderful to have money and some of the comforts and pleasures it brings."

His success was hard earned, but Billy took nothing for granted. He was thankful for his good fortune and the niceties that resulted. Providing a better life for Maggie was the most gratifying thing to come from this boxing business, but Billy enjoyed some of the amenities of prosperity himself.

"We moved out of the old house we were raised in not long ago," Conn told famed boxing writer Hype Igoe. "Moved into a new house. I fitted it with wonderful new furniture. I have a beautiful room all for myself. You should see my bed. Fit for a king, I tell you. I have an extension phone right at my elbow. The Conns never had that kind of luxury before."

An extension phone—now that was practically an obscene opulence.

"When it was installed I used to call up all my friends. I'd get them up out of bed first thing in the morning, just to get a kick out of the extension. A lot of them thought I was daffy, but Santa Claus had come and I was playing with the new toys."

Billy even played his boyish pranks on Maggie, sometimes calling downstairs to his unsuspecting mother.

"Good morning Missus William Margaret Conn of East Liberty, State of Pennsylvania, USA. The top of the morning to you, gracious madam."

Taken aback by the strange greeting, Maggie stammered, "Wh-wh-who is this, please?"

"You are speaking to the light-heavyweight champion of all this wide, wide world, your son, William David Conn, of the East Liberty Conns, who will be downstairs in ten minutes for his creamed quail and toast."

One person could still put William David Conn, the light-heavyweight champion of all the wide, wide world in his proper place, and that was Maggie. "Look here, Willie Conn. You stop putting on such airs. We're the casual Conns around here, still. You'll come down and get ham and eggs like the rest of them."[3]

Maggie wasn't the only one who thought Billy might be putting on airs. Some Pittsburgh fans thought Conn had gotten too big for his britches (and they hadn't even been on the receiving end of one of Billy's extension phone pranks). He hadn't fought in Pittsburgh since defeating Krieger the previous November, and the locals' discontent was felt and heard when Billy was introduced at a Forbes Field all-star show several days after claiming the light-heavy crown from Bettina. On July 17, 1939, Conn sat ringside for a card that presented Al Gainer–Teddy Yarosz, Charley Burley–Fritzie Zivic, and Sammy Angott–Petey Sarron. When Billy's name was announced to the hometown crowd, boos filtered through the stands and into the champion's ears. Outwardly Billy didn't let on that the surly reception bothered him. He rose from his seat, beamed that smile that weakened many a female knee, waved to the crowd, and sat back down.

But he heard, and he would remember.

Though Johnny insisted that Billy's first defense of the title take place in their hometown, Mike Jacobs once again delayed Conn's return to Pittsburgh. The day after Billy's victory over Bettina, Jacobs announced that Art Rooney and Barney McGinley would promote a

Conn–Gus Lesnevich bout at Forbes Field in early September or late August. In the subsequent days, Jimmy Grippo objected to the proposed match. His boxer was promised the first chance at Billy, he protested. "Conn and his manager, Johnny Ray, can't hold a championship fight without my consent," he stated.[4] Grippo's complaint fell on deaf ears. Lesnevich as an opponent would fall by the wayside, but Bettina stayed on the back burner. Offers came in from a number of cities: Philadelphia wanted Billy; so did Cleveland and St. Louis. The City of Brotherly Love, however, won out. Conn's first fight as the light-heavyweight champion was a nontitle bout against heavyweight Gus Dorazio on August 14 at Philadelphia's Shibe Park.

"After Dorazio and Bettina, I won't pass up any bouts," Billy told the *Philadelphia Evening Public Ledger.* "Johnny Ray plans to take me out to the coast next winter. No one will want for a fight. I'll be a fighting champ."[5]

He spoke with local writers upon his arrival in Philadelphia on August 7. Conn was feted with an official welcome at City Hall. Later that same afternoon, Billy left for nearby Leiperville where he and Johnny set up training camp for Dorazio.

"Yes, you can say I'll be ready in the summer of '41. I'll be twenty-three, and at least fifteen pounds heavier. Louis will be twenty-seven and on the downside . . . maybe." No sir, there was no doubt where he was heading. Dorazio was simply a stepping-stone toward his ultimate goal. "There's no 'ifs' or 'buts' about it," Billy stated as a matter of fact. "I'll be the heavyweight champion of the world."[6]

Dorazio, a twenty-two-year-old slugger from South Philly, had been fighting professionally since 1935. His defeat of Bob Pastor the previous December had put Gus on the map. Since that victory, though, the two-fisted bruiser had struggled, losing three of his six fights in 1939 (a bout against Tommy Tucker was called a draw). Regardless of his recent run, Dorazio took Conn's confident ramblings as a personal affront, and an entertaining war of words filled the sports pages in the days leading up to the fight. "This guy ain't nothing," Dorazio said. "What's he gonna beat me with? He can't punch a lick. I'll rip him to pieces."[7]

Billy returned the barb in kind. "I see this Dorazio says he'll win, because he feels he can beat me," a laughing Conn said. "He doesn't always feel that way, it seems. Well he must be a swell Kiyoodle. I think I can win any fight. Sure, I'm ready for Dorazio. Or Joe Louis for that matter. Fighting is my business."[8]

More than 12,000 came to Shibe Park on the evening of August 14 and watched Billy back up every word of his braggadocio. Sitting empty, though, were twenty ringside seats Conn had set aside for Mary Louise Smith and her schoolmates.

At her father's decree, Miss Smith had gone across the state to attend school. Greenfield Jimmy sent his daughter to Rosemont College and directed the university's mother superior to keep Billy Conn away from Mary Lou. Smith had seen Billy's reaction upon meeting his little girl, and he wasn't taking any chances. No prizefighter was going to corrupt his daughter, champion or not. Out of the ring, they're all the same; they're bums who add up to nothing, Smith believed.

Mary was bemused by her daddy's caution. She didn't mind going to school in Philadelphia; she had wanted to get out of Squirrel Hill anyway. As for Billy, Mary Lou thought little of his infatuation. Conn sent cards and presents. She was flattered and enjoyed the attention, but nothing would ever come from Billy's adoration, of this Mary Louise was sure. When she learned that he had sent enough tickets for her and all her friends, Mary thought it might be fun to go. Unfortunately, Rosemont's mother superior put the kibosh on any such plans, and Mary Louise was exiled to her dorm for the evening.

Billy entered the Shibe Park ring and loosely danced about the canvas. His broad grin diminished when Conn looked down ringside and saw a large section of empty seats. For a moment Billy's buoyant confidence was dashed. Dorazio and the task before him had vacated his mind momentarily, but the first solid blow snapped Billy back to the job at hand.

Following his slow start, Conn completely outboxed his opponent. Through the first seven rounds, Billy had lost one and another was called a draw. At the close of the seventh, Dorazio's face resembled a crimson mask, as blood streamed down his brow from a badly cut left eye. Referee Leo Houck went to Dorazio's corner, studied the damaged eye, and called for a halt of the proceedings.

From Dorazio and handlers came a pleading cry, "No!" "No!"

The physician on hand for the match, W. P. G. Terry of the Pennsylvania Boxing Board, came up the stairs to Dorazio's corner, examined the eye, and overrode Houck's opinion. "Okay, let it go on," Terry said. Still, the doctor warned that he would order the bout stopped if the bleeding began anew.[9]

In a show of sheer desperation, Dorazio unleashed everything he had, but only met vicious opposition. Showing no mercy, Billy attacked Dorazio's injury with two quick lefts, reopening the wound. The flow of blood began anew, spilling down his left cheek. With a portion of the crowd shouting, "Stop it," at one minute, fifty two seconds into the eighth, referee Leo Houck stepped between the two fighters and ended the fight. The decision was not endorsed by all as jeers filled the sultry summer air, and Dorazio's cornermen protested to Hauck to no avail. "One Good Punch Gus," his face cut to ribbons by Conn's slicing blows, refused to concede anything in defeat. "He didn't hurt me," Dorazio insisted. "Give me a return match and I'll beat him. I can whip him anywhere, anytime. Even after I was butted, I'd had done it if that referee hadn't stopped the fight. What's the matter with that guy? I don't think Conn's a great champion."[10]

A little sour grapes from a sore loser wasn't going to dampen Johnny's enthusiasm. "The first time Junior fought a light heavyweight he licked him for the title," Ray said. "The first time he fights a heavy, he knocks him out. What more can you ask?"[11]

Hype Igoe was completely taken by Billy: "He's one of the pleasures of writing about boxing," Igoe wrote. "His kind doesn't bob up so often. What an expert job he did on Dorazio."[12]

Murray Lewin of the *New York Mirror* thought Billy should forsake the light-heavies and concentrate on the heavyweight division. "I'd like to see Johnny Ray take the boy and put him in the woods for about six to eight months to make his shoulders bulge a little more and thicken his neck, say, with 10 more pounds, I think he would give that Nova a very nice punching around right now."[13]

Early the next morn, Billy hopped in a car and drove home for a brief stay. Just one day in Pittsburgh gave Billy time to fill up on Maggie's home cooking before he was off again. On the 16th, Conn was on his way to New York where he was honored at the Court of Peace at the World's Fair. More than 8,000 people attended the August 17 "Irish Day" program where a number of great boxing champions were introduced. Jack Dempsey, then Benny Leonard, Gene Tunney, Jim Braddock, Barney Ross, and Henry Armstrong. The crowd roared its approval with each succeeding name; then came the guest of honor. The president of the Fair Corporation, Grover Whalen, spoke in tribute of Conn's "character and those qualities which make a champion."[14] Whalen then presented to Billy an oversized white boxing glove that was inscribed

with the names of numerous boxing champions. He could now rightfully place his name alongside all the greats that came before.

When the proposed Lesnevich bout was scrapped in early August,
Johnny Ray and Mike Jacobs opted to fulfill their contractual obligation with Jimmy Grippo and Melio Bettina. Quite possibly, Lesnevich
was just a ploy all along, concocted by Jacobs and Ray to get Grippo's
goat. If so, the ruse worked to perfection. On August 4, they let him off
the hook when the Twentieth Century Sporting Club issued a press
release announcing Billy's first title defense. Jacobs, with the assistance
of Jake Mintz, would promote a Conn–Bettina rematch September 23
at Forbes Field. The agreement quieted Grippo's newsprint politicking
for the time being. The egocentric Grippo couldn't stay silent long,
however. Shortly after Billy's victory in Philly over Dorazio, Grippo
again began manipulating the media to get his message out in a public
forum. Sports editors didn't mind the exploitation as long it made for
entertaining reading. Three weeks before the combatants entered the
ring, Grippo fired his first salvo. In an "open letter" published by the
Sun-Telegraph, Grippo sent his message to Pittsburghers that he was
pleased that Bettina was getting a chance to regain the title—the title,
Jimmy made clear, that was wrongly taken from him.

"I want to let you and the people of Pittsburgh know how happy
Melio Bettina and I are that Melio is getting an opportunity to fight Billy
Conn again when for a time it appeared that we would be deprived of
the opportunity," he began.

"Bettina has been in fine spirits since learning that he is to fight
Conn again and under fairer circumstances than before." Grippo then
launched into a plaint: Billy's victory in July, perhaps all victories prior
also, was tainted because of Conn's exploitation of the rules. "I believe
the referee will see to it that Conn does not hit on the breaks or his low
and will make him use his left hand as it is intended to be used. The
so-called beautiful left jab of Conn's is in reality a flick with the open
glove. It looks good from a distance, but it is a flagrant violation of the
rule which states that all hitting should be done with a closed fist."

Grippo also wished to set the record straight; he was a hypnotist,
not a spell caster in the mold of Ben Finkle. Using the July 13 fight as
evidence, Grippo explained how his hypnotic powers strengthened his
fighter. "Post hypnotic suggestions are made to the subject," Grippo

wrote, "who must cooperate as Bettina does. Although Bettina was handicapped in the Madison Square Garden fight by the warm, smoke-filled air, he responded well and made a strong finish in the fifteenth and final round."

Grippo had seemingly forgotten that the New York State Boxing Commission reprimanded him in July for unsporting behavior. The admonishment stemmed from Grippo's actions at the weigh-in when he waved his hands and wiggled his fingers in the direction of Conn, putting the "whammy" on Billy.

"I do not use the 'evil eye' on an opponent but I do maintain that the post hypnotic suggestions were responsible for improvement of Bettina's physical strength and mental alertness during the Garden fight, the suggestions working through his subconscious, faster in his movements, and generally accelerating his mind and body."[15]

Harry Keck, hoping to secure a newsworthy comment, let Johnny Ray read Grippo's piece prior to publication. Ray wasn't going to add fuel to an already combustible rivalry, at least not yet. After looking over Grippo's handiwork, Johnny paused and simply said, "That Grippo writes a pretty good letter, doesn't he."[16]

The deluge of propaganda continued to flow from Bettina headquarters. After conducting his preliminary training at Greenwood Lake, New York, Melio arrived in Pittsburgh on August 7 with his manager. They set up camp locally at Eagle's Rest in Millvale. From there, Grippo issued his daily musings, which rarely varied. His main talking points were "we wuz robbed," concerning the first match, and "we're going to win," regarding the rematch.

"We trained outdoors at Beacon because the show was originally scheduled for the Yankee Stadium," Grippo said, still intent on refighting the July 13 match, "and we continued in the open air after the bout was moved indoors. Melio would have been able to stand up better under the muggy air of the Garden."[17]

Grippo even paid a visit to Boxing Commissioner Havey Boyle and expressed many of the same thoughts and prejudices he wrote of in the *Sun-Telegraph*. His tiresome plea of an "even break" was repeated in the *Post-Gazette*. "We both think we won that fight [July 13], but Melio didn't get it. We think he's going to win next Monday, and we want an honest count. We don't want anything that isn't coming to us, but we want the rules observed and we are going to ask that the referee penalize Conn if he flicks with the open glove, as he did in New York."[18]

Jealous of the attention given to Conn prior to the first meeting, Grippo earnestly attempted to keep his fighter's name in the headlines during the days leading up to the ballyhooed match. Trying to replicate, and better, the publicized list of Billy's likes and dislikes that was released prior to the first fight, Grippo issued an extensive list of Bettina's favorite things.

Favorite ballplayer: Joe DiMaggio
Favorite team: New York Yankees
Favorite actor: George Raft
Favorite American: Fiorello La Guardia

On and on the list continued, through Melio's "favorite short story writer" (Francis Wallace) to "favorite orchestra" (Benny Goodman), "favorite radio star" (Kate Smith), and beyond; Grippo tried his best to cover all bases and interests—anything to keep his man's name on the people's lips.

Still, Johnny and Billy weren't concerned about media hype. They had the championship, and that's what really mattered. However, during a seemingly innocuous radio appearance, Bettina predicted on the air that he would knock out Conn when they met at Forbes Field. When the remark reached Billy's ears, his famous Irish temper flared.

"That wise guy said he'd knock me out," Conn said. "I never make predictions like that. I'll show him who he'll knock out—he won't win a single round. Every round I'll be in there fighting. I can take all he's got and plenty more."[19]

If anyone was more confident than Billy, it was Johnny. Visiting fight headquarters at the William Penn Hotel, Ray spoke to gathered reporters and expressed surprise that anyone could believe that his Junior would win by anything less than a knockout.

"Junior is punching harder than he ever did before, and there were four times in his first fight with Bettina when he had the guy badly hurt. When he gets him that way Monday night, he'll know what to do, because he isn't afraid of him any longer."[20]

Billy began training September 5 at White Mansions in Perrysville, but the Conn camp was quiet in comparison to the Grippo publicity machine. That's not to say the press didn't reach out to Billy. His rags-to-riches story seemed almost too much of a cliché to actually believe. New York writers in particular loved to pass on to their readers the story of Sweet William.

"Sure I was poor," Billy admitted to an interviewer. "Desperately poor. Not just a street kid. An alley kid. That's me. You ever see a rich kid fighting? I never did."[21]

The life of a champion, though, was quite different than that of an East Liberty street urchin.

"I have a radio and a swell shower in my room," Conn crowed. "I take four or five splashes a day. . . . I've sat there on an expensive chair looking at all my stuff thinking about what a sweet thing life really is. You don't think I'm going to let Melio Bettina take that away from me? I'll be thinking of that radio, my beautiful bed, the shower, the easy chair, and the rest of the furniture, all through the fight."

Furnishings and lovely household accoutrements weren't the only things Billy acquired with his newfound wealth. His wardrobe was second to none. In fact, he would be named the best-dressed man in sports for the year 1939. "I should have placed second," Jackie said upon learning of the award. "I wear all his clothes."[22]

Indeed, Jackie often helped himself to his brother's wardrobe, more often than not when Billy was traveling. On one occasion, Billy went to the county airport for an out-of-town venture only to learn that his flight had been canceled. He returned home and found Jackie about to embark on a nice evening on the town, decked out in a Chesterfield coat, cuff links, homburg . . . the works.

Billy took his brother by the arm and walked him to Maggie's bedroom, where she lay. "Maggie, I just wanted to show you how nice your son Jackie looks," Billy said. "Isn't he the dresser?"

He kissed his mother on the forehead and then took Jackie down to the cellar where he evaluated the ensemble piece by piece. "This is a beautiful one-hundred-and-seventy-five dollar coat," he said, helping Jackie take off the garment.

"Geez, that's a lovely ten-dollar shirt." And on Billy continued; the more layers that came off, though, the more nervous Jackie became.

"I was okay until I hit the silk underwear," Jackie later remembered. "Then bam! He let me have it with a right in the mush."[23]

The highlight of Billy's workout every day was the Conn–Conn sparring session. Cain and Abel had nothing on these boys. Pittsburgh writers had been privy to these familial fracases before; however, visiting scribes had never seen its like. Though Billy had three other sparring partners, nothing equaled the ferocity the siblings displayed when placed inside the ring together. "Both were hot-tempered Irishmen,"

Freddie Fierro explained, "who didn't know how to ease up and the riotous cat and dog battles they had in the gym made even the hard guys turn away. Nothing worried me more then when Billy and Jackie started to bang the hell out of each other. It wasn't sport or training, but plain murder."

Fierro beseeched Ray not to set the brothers on each other, but his pleas fell on deaf ears. Johnny's hands were tied because Jackie threatened to get another manager. It wasn't necessarily the prospect of Jackie finding someone else to represent him that bothered Johnny; in fact, Ray turned down an offer of $5,000 from a New York manager the week of the fight. No, Johnny was afraid another manager wouldn't look after Billy's little brother as conscientiously as he. So the frightful scenes were repeated over and over. Each day brought a new session, a renewal of a loving blood feud. Three days before the match, five hundred spectators gathered at White Mansions and watched as a frustrated Jackie continued to throw haymakers more than twenty seconds after the bell had rung. The timekeeper tried in vain to rein in Jackie's fury, repeatedly sounding the bell. The hostilities ceased only when Johnny jumped into the ring and intervened.

The next day, just forty-eight hours before he defended the long-sought title, Billy lay sleeping soundly in his grandiose new bed when Jackie came in and lifted the keys to Billy's new black Cadillac. With the Caddy stuffed full of friends, Jackie took his brother's new ride for a jaunt around town.

It wasn't until the next morning that Billy happened to look at the odometer. Immediately knowing who the culprit was that added mileage to his precious car, Conn let out a howl. He wanted Jackie's head, and there was no need for it to be attached to his torso.

He searched through their home, through the neighborhood, and looked in all of Jackie's haunts, but still Billy couldn't find a trace of his brother. He then let it be known that he was posting a $300 reward for information leading to the location of his delinquent brother. With cash as an incentive, an informant stepped forward in short time. Billy apprehended Jackie and led him into the family garage, closed the door behind them, and said, "Now you're going to get the beating of your life."

For the next quarter of an hour, the two Conn boys tore into each other with a little more exuberance than usual. Jackie, however, knew how it had to end, and decided to not put off the inevitable any longer.

He took one step back, held his chin out, and told Billy, "Okay, get it over with." With that, Billy uncorked a gorgeous right hand that sent Jackie off a wall into a crumpled heap on the grease-stained garage floor.

At that very moment, several cops busted into the garage with Uncle Mike and Johnny Ray in tow. Jacobs noticed the blood smeared about Billy's face and was stunned into silence, until he realized that the blood was actually Jackie's.

"You hurt, Billy?" he anxiously asked. "Are you hurt?

From the floor, Jackie piped in, "He's okay, but what about me?"

"You!" Johnny Ray shouted. "You!" and with that he reared back and delivered a swift kick to Jackie's ribs.

The weigh-in took place at noon in the Crystal Room of the William Penn Hotel. The room was filled with fight managers, radio broadcasters, photographers, and newsmen, a great many of them imported from New York. One figure was missing, however. The night prior, a friend from Maryland brought Billy and Johnny a seafood dinner from Baltimore. While Ray was stricken ill with ptomaine poisoning after sampling the fare from Charm City, Billy luckily escaped the same fate—he nearly ate from the same dish. With Ray unable to get out of bed for the weigh-in, Milt Jaffe stood in for him at the ceremony.

Dr. J. E. McClenahan conducted the examinations and declared Conn to be in perfect physical condition. Bettina, on the other hand, had a slight flutter in his heartbeat, an abnormality explained away by Melio's strenuous training regimen. Regardless of the slight irregularity in Bettina's heartbeat, Dr. McClenahan declared him fit enough to fight later that evening.

The acrimony between the fighters was obvious to all in the Crystal Room. Not a word had passed between the two since they met in July and the silence continued throughout the proceedings. While posing for photographs, neither man looked his counterpart in the eye. Bettina became particularly annoyed as the session continued. The challenger's grim mood and his animosity toward Conn were unmistakable. Billy was his usual good-natured self. He laughed and kidded with the boxing officials and spectators gathered for the ceremony. Conn's glance, however, changed drastically when focused on Bettina. His smile waned and all jocularity vanished. These fellas didn't like one another; that much was apparent.

Billy left the Crystal Room and retreated to a hotel room in the William Penn where he took a sound nap. Following his siesta, Conn visited Jaffe and then went to Johnny Ray's, who had recovered enough to be in the corner that night. From Ray's place, Billy went to Forbes Field, arriving at eight o'clock. His early arrival surprised those who saw him casually stroll onto the field and talk with a few friends. "I feel swell,"[24] he told them, before retreating under the stands to relax before his bout.

The streets of Oakland were often clogged when a major event was held at Forbes Field. The snarl of traffic was worse than normal the evening of the bout because a trailer became stuck on the streetcar tracks west of Craft Street. All motor traffic stopped for some while, and disgusted fans disembarked from trolley cars and grumbled all through their long walk to the park.

Though Jacobs was informed that fifty police officers would be enough for security, he nonetheless hired one hundred. Unlike so many previous big bouts in the city, there was no long jam at any of the gates. People actually got the seats assigned on their tickets. And thanks to the extra police on hand, there was no rush from the cheap seats to the more expensive variety. Uncle Mike certainly gave the city's promoters a lesson on how to operate like a pro, and the fighters themselves helped make the evening a near perfect night.

A full harvest moon shone down of Forbes Field, as Pittsburgh enjoyed a pleasant, warm late summer evening. It took a while, as it usually did when Billy slipped through the ropes, but once he got going, all the bitterness that had built up over the previous few weeks came pouring out in a parade of stiff right hands.

With the first two rounds even, Bettina took the next three. Some in Conn's camp laid the blame for Billy's slow start on a cold he had been fighting for the previous few days. The fighter himself offered no explanation or excuse. "It was a tougher fight than [the] first one," he said. "I just couldn't get started in the first six rounds. After the lucky seventh, began, however, I was back in form and never worried about the result. Bettina never hurt me with any of his punches, but he certainly did a lot of butting that had my nose bleeding so much."[25]

The alleged butting that Conn spoke of was the subject of a profane exchange between the boys during the third round. "He thought I had butted him and yelled about it," Bettina said later, cleaning up his language for public consumption. "And I told him I hadn't and not to try any butting on his own accord, or I would show him some real butting."[26]

Billy turned it on in the sixth and he set about trying to disprove his many critics who believed he couldn't dislodge one's hat. Through his long evolution into a champion, Conn rarely used his right hand. Against five former champs and two reigning titleholders, Billy never went to his right unless he was in dire trouble. In his rematch with Bettina, Billy used his right almost to the complete exclusion of his fabled left. "It was right, right, right, to the head, to the body, to the bell, once Billy warmed up after the fifth round," Regis Welsh reported.[27]

Midway through the fight, Billy had lost some steam, and as he reached his corner at the close of the tenth he was met by Johnny's stern voice. "Hey, you step on it again, do you hear?" Ray chastised Junior. "You'll blow this one."

"You're nuts," Billy shot back. "I'm licking the hell out of him."[28]

Try as he might, Billy couldn't take Melio down. Bettina, his legs weakened considerably, refused to wilt under the unyielding pounding. Having completely abandoned his skillful boxing techniques, Conn stood flat-footed in the center of the ring and delivered numerous rights to the challenger's jaw and midsection. The training with Jackie was paying off in spades. But like the younger Conn, Bettina continued to fight back. Though thoroughly beaten, Melio refused to give ground. With the tenacity and determination of a true champion, Bettina pulled out the thirteenth as the pace of the fight began to tell on both boxers.

The thirteenth was to be Melio's last hurrah. In the final two rounds, Billy battered Bettina from rope to rope, corner to corner. On several occasions it seemed to all that the challenger would find the canvas. But he took everything Billy had and kept his feet under him. At the start of the fifteenth, the two contestants met in the middle of the ring and touched gloves. "Nice fight, Billy," Bettina said. Conn nodded his appreciation.

"When the torturous hour of brawling had concluded, both fell into a loving embrace and began gabbing to one another, their first peaceful gesture in months. Conn had forgotten his enmity in the thrill of having retained his title. Bettina, then, for the first time, seemed to realize that the last hope of retaining his title had vanished."[29]

The revelers grew in number with each Conn victory. Being his first at home since becoming champion, this triumph was marked by an especially crowded dressing room. Friends, relatives, and newsmen (no longer just the Pittsburgh contingent following Billy) created a chaotic scene inside the victor's quarters. The room was crammed to capacity. In the crush, Billy was forced up against the wall, but his demeanor remained calm as he responded to reporters' questions.

Ever present, Harry Keck led things off, asking Billy why the drastic change in style. "I wanted to show some people who've been booing me that I can fight," Billy explained. "I didn't want to pedal around and box fancy and smell out the joint. I went in to punch and I left myself open for some pretty good return blows."[30]

Interestingly, on Billy's mind was not just retaining his title, but pleasing his fans *and* proving his detractors wrong. Quite an agenda and Conn successfully fulfilled his plans. "It was a good fight, wasn't it?" he said with a satisfied smile.

Fighting through the crowd, Westinghouse finally reached his son and offered his warm congratulations. This provided the shutterbugs with a great photo op. Then Johnny stepped in for some shots of him and Junior. They even got a few of Billy with his favorite Pirate, Jim Tobin, who stopped by with another Buc, Arky Vaughn, to offer their best wishes.

Billy slipped away from the crowded dressing room to pay his respects to his spirited foe. The two spoke quietly to one another, and then Billy turned to the few newsmen gathered in the loser's locker room. With an arm draped warmly around Melio's shoulders, Conn commended his opponent: "I've never been hit as hard and as often as I was out there tonight," he said.

The champion returned to his friends and family, leaving Bettina with his handlers. "He's tired," Jimmy Grippo said while sitting stretched out on a rubbing table. "He tired after the fifth round."

"He tired both times he fought Conn," Johnny Romano, Melio's trainer, interjected. "He can't beat him when he's tired." Both the trainer and the manager agreed that Bettina was in great condition before the fight, that he just couldn't withstand the rigors of a fifteen-round match against Conn. "That's right," Romano asserted. "In ten rounds, yes. But he can't go fifteen against a man with as much stamina and boxing skill as Conn."[31]

In the days leading up to the fight, Jacobs's publicists estimated that the fight would draw 30,000 and produce a $100,000 gate. Though the attractive card created much interest, the actual attendance fell far short of the much-hyped figures produced by Jacobs's men. Uncle

Mike ran a quality show, the likes of which Pittsburghers had never seen, but only 18,422 enjoyed the festivities. Some attributed the disappointing turnout to an out-of-towner running things; many would have rather seen the program put on by the popular Rooney-McGinley team. Again, the provincial thinking by Pittsburghers clouded their judgment as they missed a great undercard and highly entertaining championship bout.

"The point is not whether [Jacobs] should come back for another big promotion," Havey Boyle, an expert of the ins and outs of boxing, wrote. "The point is we should ask him back. His control over boxers is too tight, we think, on the contractual side, but the peculiar ramifications of boxing and its satellites probably call for special considerations. The chief consideration from the standpoint of the paying public is he puts on honest fights and puts them on in a class manner."[32]

Weary from an eight-week tour of "the sticks," which saw him put on shows in several cities, including Philadelphia and Detroit, Jacobs and his Cauliflower Caravan returned home to New York. Before departing, though, Uncle Mike indicated what he had in mind for the coming winter. "After I get home—and get a little sleep—I'm going to try to convince Jimmy Johnson that the best bet for him is to let [Bob] Pastor fight Conn. . . . He is the only heavyweight near Conn in weight."[33]

For Billy, before anything else, he wanted some rest. After the congratulations had faded and interviewers fell silent, he vacated Forbes Field and made the short drive up Fifth Avenue to his home. If escaping the ballyard for some peace and quiet was Conn's intent, he was rudely greeted when he stepped through the doorway. Westinghouse had set up a bar in the family basement and invited half the town over to celebrate, and celebrate they did—the Irish way. "I guess there were more fights than that part of Pittsburgh had seen since it was built," Billy said. "If Mike Jacobs could have moved the old man's bar to Forbes Field and let me and Melio have it out in the basement, what a fight show he would have put on!"[34]

Since there was little chance of Conn getting a good night's rest at home, after visiting with friends for a few hours, he retreated to Mercy Hospital where he was assured a therapeutic night's sleep. Early the next morning, the champion returned home where Maggie and the rest of the Conn brood waited with a hearty breakfast. The following days were filled with loafing about town before departing for

New York with Jackie and Johnny. The younger of the Conn brothers was slated to fight Mutt Wormer on the undercard of the October 2 Garcia–Apostoli match.

Following Jackie's fight (he lost on points), Billy went to Mike Jacobs's farm in Rumson, New Jersey, for a week's vacation away from boxing, New York, Pittsburgh, the works. His next fight was already set. Johnny and Jacobs certainly wasted no time agreeing that Billy's next title defense would be November 17 against Gustav "Gus" Lesnevich. Lesnevich was ringside along with his manager, Joe Vella, for the Bettina match. The very next day, the parties gathered and signed for the fight, which was to be held at Madison Square Garden.

In 1932, as a seventeen-year-old high school student, Gustav walked into the office of a Hackensack newspaper, found the sports editor, and asked, "Please get me a fight."[35] From begging for the opportunity to get into the ring, Lesnevich worked himself into a quality boxer, a rugged fighter no one liked to face. In the fall of 1939, Gus was ranked the New York state athletic commission's number-one contender. The National Boxing Association's title had remained unfilled since John Henry Lewis vacated it earlier in the year. For Conn to be recognized as the NBA's champion, he needed to defeat Lesnevich.

Lesnevich skipped the elimination tournament held the previous winter to name a successor to Lewis's vacant title. Instead, Gus traveled to Australia to work on his game. Down Under, the tough Russian lost to Ron Richards but defeated Ambrose Palmer, Alabama Kid, and Bob Olin, the latter a former Australian champion. He returned to the States in March and beat Larry Lane in April before catching the notice of the boxing press when he knocked out Joe Louis's stablemate, Dave Clark, in one round. That June 22 bout against Clark was the last time Gus had been in the ring.

Though neither Lesnevich nor Conn had yet thrown a single punch in anger or sport at one another, much of the commentary leading to the fight centered on Billy's farewell to the light-heavy division. With Jacobs's assertion that Pastor was lined up as Conn's next opponent, and little left to prove in his natural weight class, most assumed the change was a forgone conclusion (also implicit was a Conn victory over Lesnevich).

The light-heavyweight division had lost much of its luster in recent years. The class had fewer quality fighters than ever. Not so long before, the division bragged of great champions: Bob Fitzsimmons,

Georges Carpentier, Gene Tunney, and, of course, Harry Greb. And though the consensus was that Billy was a great and classy champion, who would be his foil? Without a worthy adversary, Conn's title lacked cachet. Money—the *real* money—was in the heavyweight division; there was no disputing that fact.

The potential of great riches and more fame was certainly a motivating factor for Billy to move up in weight class. Uncle Mike's impetus to see this happen was simple; it was the same incentive that always drove him: cash. Jacobs needed to find his heavyweight champion a formidable foe. In Billy he had the perfect foil for Louis. The million-dollar smile, the looks straight out of central casting—no doubt the public would buy into such a promotion. But Chester Smith wasn't going to line up to buy what Jacobs was hoping to sell, at least not yet. Such a move right now would be a reckless career move at this point for Billy.

"Conn, of course," Smith penned, "would do better to stay where he is, picking off a likely light-heavy here and there, and occasionally luring an overstuffed middleweight into the ring. Broadway Bill can't hit much harder than a Knox College halfback and, furthermore, it is a question whether he will ever be able to drape much more poundage on his angular frame. That means he will have to spend his time bouncing around twilight heavies, who come for a dime a bagful, and that any attempt to lift him into the upper crust will have to be on the same questionable platform that made a challenger out of that Galento man."[36]

All this nonsense could be placed at the feet of Jacobs, Smith believed. The relationship forged with Uncle Mike would no doubt be regretted. "Before he is through, I think he will be sorry for the day he became enmeshed in Mike Jacobs' spider web," Smith opined. "The fact is, if he allows Mr. Jacobs' trust to persuade him to bid the light heavyweight brigade a farewell and go gunning after Louis, he will have played his first wrong card—wrong that is, for Conn, but right up Mr. Jacobs' alley."[37]

Smith was dismissing Johnny Ray, and the influence he held over Billy, completely. In the days leading up to the November 17 match, Johnny and Jacobs found themselves at odds over Billy's prospects. The two had differing visions of their fighter's immediate future, with Jacobs eyeing a match against Louis the following summer, while Johnny wanted to take things slower and allow Billy to naturally fill out. He wanted to take time off after Lesnevich, go to California, and relax before entering the ring again.

All the prognostications, arguments, and opinions held no sway over Billy, even if it was him on whom all the conversation centered. His mind was firmly focused on Lesnevich—well, except for a brief respite from training. Without informing anyone, Billy left New York and flew home to Pittsburgh to be with Mary Louise. Johnny had given him the day off, but was clueless as to Billy's whereabouts until he received a phone call from his fighter. Conn's vanishing act reminded many of Tony Galento, who once disappeared for twenty-four hours prior to a bout with Lou Nova.

Lesnevich's manager, Dan Morgan, saw nothing humorous in Billy's antics. "Go out and bet that Conn will be back behind a soda fountain if he shows up to fight," Morgan said. "He's a good looking boy and should make a hit with any drug store's female trade. I'll tell you why Conn flew to Pittsburgh. He wanted to forget about Lesnevich, if only for twenty-four hours."

Gus chimed in as well. "Conn acts like Galento," he quipped, "but I don't think he can fight as well."

While Johnny wasn't enamored with Billy's vanishing act, publicly he stayed on message. "He'll beat Lesnevich, all right," he said. "Then we're going out to California and try to put a little weight on Billy."

Jackie was once again on the undercard. He was out to avenge the loss he suffered the previous month at the hands of the illustrious Maynard "Mutt" Wormer.

Wormer was, according to Billy, "a society bloke." The sardonic designation stemmed from Mutt's collegiate background, a rarity in the world of pugs. This much was for sure: Jackie had better cut this bookworm down to size, "otherwise," Billy said, "it'll be back to the steel mills for that young man on Monday. He will then be a retired prizefighter at the age of seventeen. Even if I put up with it, the old man wouldn't. It could cause trouble around our nice, new home. Just because we moved from Shakespeare to Fifth is no reason why we should have any society fella holding the duke over us."[38]

Though the press played up Billy's words as a humorous rant, there was conviction behind his statements. He wasn't in favor of Jackie entering the prize ring to begin with; once he had, there was no way Billy was going to stand by and let his younger brother embarrass the family name.

Jackie entered his four-round opener more than ten pounds under his normal weight of 163 and was noticeably lacking in strength during his brief rematch with Wormer. About two minutes into the opening round, Mutt connected with a solid left hook to the jaw that sent Jackie reeling backward into a neutral corner. He went down momentarily, rising quickly at the count of one. Sensing an opportunity for the kill, Mutt immediately moved in and assailed Jackie with a torrent of blows; once again, young Conn went down. This time he rose at two, but referee Johnny McAvoy had seen enough. The society bloke was declared the winner by technical knockout with just two seconds remaining in the first round.

Jackie managed a slight smile as he shook the victor's hand. He then left the ring and headed toward the dressing room, and that's when the sense of dread engulfed Jackie. On the other side of the door awaited Billy, who was relaxing and passing time until it was his turn to take to the ring. The tears were welling up before he opened the door, but the flow began freely once Jackie saw his brother. He collapsed across a rubbing table and began sobbing uncontrollably. A flicker of sympathy came over Billy; he went to his brother, rustled his sopping hair, and softly said, "Now listen Jackie, you're through, see? You're hanging up your gloves right this minute. I'm not going to have guys like that Mutt Wormer knocking you out. If anybody's going to lick you, I'll do it myself."

He wasn't through just yet. "I won't have total strangers coming along and punching the hell out of you. If anybody lifts a hand to you, I'll slap him silly. But that's only if it's out of the ring, because you're not getting in any more rings. I'm not going to have you disgracing me by getting yourself stiffened by some bum every time I'm waiting to do a little fighting myself. How does that look, huh? Don't you got any regard for my feelings?"

Billy then recounted for Jackie what *he* just went through, having to hear people talk about Jackie's defeat. "I'm sitting here in the dressing room a minute ago. The door's open. I'm wondering how I'm going to do with my guy. A couple of fellas come by, one says to the other, 'Who was that fat little punk who just got his lumps?'

'Why, that's Jackie Conn, Billy's brother.'

'Billy Conn's brother, huh? Geez, Billy Conn's anything like him, he must be a pip.'

"How do you think *I* felt?" Billy continued. "I ran out into the hall, but they'd gone. I'd popped 'em sure. They can't talk that way about you, or me either."

Jackie, his body now convulsing in sobs, realized what he'd done to the family name. "This is awful!" he cried. "That bum Wormer can't do this to me. He can't knock me out."

"He can't, huh?" Billy said with a chuckle. "Well, he just did. Now listen, get those duds off and get under that shower."

Jackie did as he was told. He stripped and headed to the shower. Everyone present thought the hysteria had passed when they heard a disturbance emanating from the shower room. The younger Conn had cracked. He was banging his head against the tile wall. When he was pulled from the shower, Jack was swinging wildly and kicking at anything within his reach. "I'm not through fighting!" he wailed. "I will come back! You can't make me quit, I tell you. I'll lick you someday if it's the last thing I ever do."

Standing back, watching the drama, Billy leaned over to Jack Miley of the *New York Post* and whispered, "That's what he thinks, but he's all washed up now. Maybe I shouldn't have let him try to be a fighter in the first place, but he talked me into it. But I'm not listening to him anymore. And if he argues with me, I'll throw him over my knee and fan his pants for him.

"Why kid ourselves? Jackie's just a baby, and this racket is too tough for babies. If Jackie keeps on the way he's going, he'll be punch drunk by the time he's eighteen. And then my ma will give *me* hell."

All through Billy's quiet discourse with Miley, Jackie's rant continued: *Nobody, not Billy, not Johnny Ray, would make him work in the mills!*

Taking in the frenzied incident was the boxing commission physician, William Walker. Walker approached Johnny and suggested that Jackie be admitted to the Polyclinic Hospital across Fiftieth Street for observation and a good night's rest. Ray agreed with the doctor's assessment and gingerly Johnny told Jackie their intentions. Surprisingly, given his state of mind, Jackie offered no objection. He slipped on his clothes, walked over to his brother, and shook his hand. "Goodbye Billy," Jackie said, still softly sobbing. "I hope you win."[39]

Another impressive contingent of Pittsburghers made the trip to New York. Greenfield Jimmy Smith, Milt Jaffe, Jack Zivic, and Billy Soose and his manager Paul Moss were all ringside. In the second row sat an empty chair, left vacant for Charley Wolk, a friend and adviser of Billy's who passed away shortly after the Bettina rematch. These Conn backers once again were frustrated by Billy's failure to actively join in the fight until it was several rounds old.

Were these slow starts intentional? Though he obviously risked falling too far behind to catch up, it was becoming more apparent that Billy was lying back deliberately as a means of sizing his opponent up and tiring him out. He blocked Lesnevich's rushes skillfully and bided his time until the fifth, when he turned on the offensive. It was an exemplary boxing exhibition put on by Conn. He whipped Gus thoroughly, beating him more decisively than he did Bettina in either of their matches. He intermittently switched from displaying his adroit boxing skill to slugging it out toe-to-toe, "Pier 8" style. The fine boxing exhibition surprised no one, but some observers were taken aback when Billy outslugged the hard-hitting Lesnevich.

In the thirteenth Conn exploded, which Regis Welsh captured in his fight report the next day. "His left became a punishing hook; his light, fencing right became a jolting smash to the jaw; his cool, cunning boxing with which he had bewildered Gus, was thrown to the winds as he buffeted Lesnevich into near senselessness under a terrific a two-fisted barrage as Billy had ever unloosed."[40]

Lesnevich was a battered man. A cavalcade of crashing lefts closed his left eye; dozens of blows to his rugged torso had exhausted his strength. As much of the crowd roared for the seemingly inevitable knockdown, Lesnevich weathered the storm of punches. He wobbled, buckled, and swayed, but the robust Jersey Russian remained upright. He stayed on his feet for the remainder of the bout, but there was no doubt in anyone's mind who had won. Columnists and fight reports were of one voice in describing Billy's performance: impressive. They were also unanimous in their opinion that Conn's obvious lack of a knockout punch was the lone element of his game that would keep him from contending in the heavyweight division.

At the close of the fight, Nat Fleisher presented Billy with his rightfully earned laurel, his championship belt: a solid-gold belt with a red, white, and blue sash. Conn graciously accepted the trophy from the editor of *Ring Magazine* with a beaming smile. In his dressing room, though, the grin dissipated when the champ offered a critical assessment of his performance.

"It was a stinkin' fight," Billy said. "I'm surprised the crowd liked it. I kept saying in my corner I couldn't get going. Why I oughta have nailed him in that eleventh. . . . He's a nice guy, though."[41]

Johnny wasn't as disparaging of Billy's perceived lackluster performance. It was Conn's weight, or lack thereof, that worried Ray. "I though he would weight more," he said, speaking of Billy's 171¼ pounds. "When he is in Pittsburgh he spends a lot of time in pool rooms and eats ice cream and drinks pop. But here in New York he goes to just about every movie in town and hits the hay at 9 o'clock. I guess he wasn't getting his side dishes."[42]

Billy slipped away from the Garden and went to his hotel for a few hours' sleep. The next morn, he arose early and caught a plane back home in time to catch the Pitt–Nebraska game at the stadium.

"Some call me 'Broadway Billy,'" Conn said to Regis Welsh on the flight home, "but you can tell them for me that any alley in East Liberty looks better than Broadway. I go to New York because it's the place to get the dough—but you notice how quickly I got away from it to get back home. I like New York for what it brings me, but I'll take Pittsburgh for what it has made me."[43]

Eight Toast of the Town

"The guy who licks Joe Louis is going to make a million bucks, and I'm the guy who's going to lick Joe Louis and become a boy millionaire."
—Billy Conn, February 1940

He was the toast of the town. Sure, some had come to believe his hat size had grown a bit, but Pittsburghers were proud to lay claim to the world's light-heavyweight champion. While others may have speculated among themselves about Billy's growing ego, in his own home Conn was confronted with such suspicion face to face.

Few days in the Conn household were staid, and their first Thanksgiving on Fifth Avenue proved no different. As Maggie prepared the family dinner, Westinghouse fell into a conversation with his oldest son. He believed Billy was forgetting where he came from. With a familiar air of confrontation, Westinghouse taunted his son. "You think you're a big shot now, huh," he said, accusingly. "You're not good enough to live at home, huh? Well, I'll tell you something. I think you're a bum. You're a bum and I'll prove it if you ain't too yellow."

No Conn ever turned his back to such a challenge, and the father and son marched out into the cold November air to settle their differences. A nearby vacant lot served as their proving ground, and each combatant removed his shirt in preparation for the fray. The Conn's neighbors, always on the watch for a good brawl, quickly gathered around the participants. The spectators who left their own holiday dinners were treated to a fine bout. The elder Conn held his own for a while, until Billy began landing some punishing blows to the old man's midsection. Just when it seemed as if Billy had gotten the best of his father, Frankie and Jackie came walking along on their way home for dinner. Sizing up the situation, Frankie jumped in on his father's side and the duo began pummeling Billy. Not one to stand idle in front of such a battle, Jackie joined in with Billy.

The brawling Conns fought unabated until a policeman was called to the scene by a neighbor, a neighbor surely eager to return to the Thanksgiving meal. With some effort, the cop separated the foursome and admonished the father.

"That don't look nice, a father fighting with his sons on Thanksgiving, now does it?"

Following a thoughtful pause, Westinghouse agreed. "No, I guess it don't at that."

With an arm wrapped around Frankie and the other slung over Billy's broad shoulders, Conn told his sons, "C'mon boys. Let's go home and eat that turkey."

The three began walking home with Jackie in tow several feet behind. After several steps, Bill Sr. abruptly whirled around. "Where do you think you're going?" he demanded of Jackie.

"Home to eat," Jackie said.

"Get outta here, you bum," Westinghouse said with a wave. "You was on the wrong side."

As Johnny had announced in the days leading up to the Lesnevich fight, he and Junior were returning to the West Coast. This time, though, the boys weren't going out to scavenge up a fight. No, work wasn't on the agenda for this trip. Hollywood was calling. The studios wanted to get a look at Conn, and Billy was anxious to see just how the movie business worked.

On November 28, 1939, Ray and Conn, accompanied by Milt Jaffe, boarded a train bound for California. "This time we're going in style," Billy said. "I got my baggage on early, and oh, boy, I got enough clothes to keep up with all those guys out there. And I brought along my golf clubs, too, because they tell me that's what they do when they go places where it is nice and warm all winter. . . . I don't know how long we will stay," Conn continued. "All depends upon what happens out there. If I make good in my screen test, then they will probably let me play Jim Corbett. I'd love to get the chance to do it. I'm not much of an actor—never did anything publicly in my life, except in the ring. But," Billy added with a gleam in his eye, "if they give me the chance I'll betcha I make a good Jim Corbett."

"We're going out to look at this proposition," Ray said. "If it is OK and Billy can fill the bill, it will be a swell thing have him do it. But, the reason I'm glad we are getting away to loaf awhile in the sun is that it might build him up into a real light heavyweight, or a heavyweight. There's a ton of money waiting for a fighter of Billy's style."[1]

Two days after departing Penn Station, the group reached Los Angeles. Upon arrival, Billy Marx greeted them. Playing the congenial host, Marx took the men to breakfast at Al Levy's and then on a tour of 20th Century Fox in the afternoon.

The *Los Angeles Times* noted Billy's presence in the city with an article extolling his exploits and detailed why the fighter was visiting. "Manager Ray has the bright idea if he can keep Conn away from Mike Jacobs's clutches for some kind of an extended period the boy will grow into a real heavyweight," Paul Lowry wrote.[2]

Billy didn't travel across the country just to fatten up. He was under consideration for the lead role in the upcoming film on "Gentleman Jim" Corbett, Lowry reported. Conn paid his visit to the movie studio and left with a less-than-flattering opinion of the business. "The guy playing the fighter in the fight picture was painted up as a mope," an incredulous Billy said. "A sissy! He has a part where the gal says, 'You've got give up fighting. Then I'll marry you.'

"Well this sissy, he yaps, 'Oh, I'm so happy, I could chin myself on a cloud.' He was a mope. A painted-up mope," Billy said, disgusted by the memory. Amazingly, the actor had the audacity to ask Conn for some fight tips, but Billy declined. "It would have been the joy of my life to put the gloves on with him, the mope. . . . I don't remember his name, the painted-up mope."[3] Billy was asked to test for a cowboy picture, but he declined. He wasn't no painted-up mope.

Hollywood wasn't a complete bust. Billy did get to meet teenage actress Bonita Granville, who starred in a number of Nancy Drew pictures. "Gee, she's pretty!" Conn also spent some time at Groucho Marx's ranch and appeared at a couple of fights. Billy was warmly greeted when introduced prior to the Georgie Hansford–Freddie Miller bout at Hollywood Legion Stadium. A few days later, the scene was repeated at the Olympic Auditorium before an Al Smith–Al Hagan match.

He didn't land the Corbett part. The weight he gained was negligible.

He certainly didn't need to travel across the continent to be introduced at run-of-the-mill boxing cards. But the trip wasn't a complete bust. Billy got a much-needed vacation . . . and there was Bonita Granville.

"A Bob Pastor–Billy Conn match is being smoked up back East," Bob Ray informed readers of the *Los Angeles Times.* "Probably for the powder puff title."[4] Ray wielded a sarcastic pen; unfortunately, he used the opinions of others to color his work since he had never seen Conn fight in person. To a man, boxing critics extolled Conn's many attributes. Billy's height and reach, which served him so well in the lesser weight classes, were not as big a feature among the heavyweights. His speed and adroit boxing ability, though, played even more of a role against the big guys. Still, the reputation of being a light puncher dogged Billy. Even with a string of impressive victories and a world championship title to call his own, Conn's critics continued to stay on point: He'll never make it against the heavies, not without a punch.

Billy wouldn't get the chance to take Bob Ray's facetious powder-puff belt, at least not yet. For reasons unexplained, Pastor wasn't next in line. Instead, Billy signed to fight a veteran heavyweight warhorse, Steve Dudas, in New York on January 10, 1940. The agreement was reached on December 17, and Conn began working out immediately in Pittsburgh. He enjoyed the holidays at home before leaving for New York and Pioneer Gym shortly after the new year. Upon arrival, however, Conn found out he was training for a different opponent. Due to a severe cold that Dudas was suffering from, Henry Cooper of Brooklyn was placed on the card in his stead.

In his three previous outings, Cooper had beaten Wild Bill Boyd and Buddy Knox and lost a ten-round decision to Gunnar Barland. The slow-moving Cooper was no match for Conn, though. Stepping out of character, Billy jumped to a quick start over his twenty-two-year-old opponent. He completely dominated the overmatched Cooper throughout the twelve-round bout.

"Billy Conn, the Pittsburgh phantom-weight, has started on the road he hopes will lead to the heavyweight title," the Associated Press reported. "But like the road to Tipperary, it's going to be a long and winding trail."[5]

Conn did as he wished against Cooper, and was handed a unanimous decision for his efforts. "For 12 rounds," penned Chet Smith in the *Pittsburgh Press,* "Billy slapped his clumsy, third-rate rival with everything but a copy of the rules."[6] The sparse crowd present in the Garden wanted more bang for the buck and let their displeasure show with a group raspberry. Unfulfilled though they were, the patrons' sentiment wasn't directed at Billy per se; he had put on a fine boxing exhibition, but the match was completely absent of blood, anyone's blood.

James Dawson smartly likened the bout to a race between a thoroughbred and a drag horse in his *New York Times* fight report. Despite Dawson's praise of Conn's performance, the reporter didn't believe Billy was ready for Joe Louis. "As a test to prove Conn's right to meet Louis, the fight was a complete flop," wrote Dawson. "It only served to prove what everybody already knew, to wit, that Billy is still the world's best light heavyweight, that he is a matchless boxer; that he can't punch hard enough to flatten a rugged heavyweight."[7]

Louis, Louis, Louis; that's all everyone could focus on. When would Conn be ready to face the imitable Brown Bomber, if ever? These questions overshadowed Billy's impressive exploits. With each succeeding fight, commentators noted Conn's fine boxing skill, but inevitably they mentioned that the light-heavy champ didn't have the punch to take down Louis. Certainly Johnny and Billy were partially responsible. Indeed, they had let it be known that the heavyweight championship was their ambition, but the growing infatuation of the boxing press with Louis–Conn was becoming a distraction. Perhaps the ruminations over Conn and Louis would cease if Jacobs could find a worthy heavyweight to challenge Joe. Instead, he was left with the likes of Two-Ton Tony Galento, which was a financial and artistic failure.

Conn was the best and only prospect on the horizon for the multitudes who wished to see Louis dethroned by a White challenger. The search for a "White hope" to save the heavyweight division had begun in the fall of 1935, almost two full years before Joe won the championship. The absurdity of such an undertaking was lost on most. Former champ Jack Dempsey even went so far as to propose a Great White Hope tournament. Nothing quite so organized was on the table at the dawn of 1940. All aspirations for the overthrow of Louis now were laid at the feet of Conn.

The Henry Cooper fight had failed to generate much interest among boxing fans. The match drew the smallest crowd yet for any of Conn's Garden appearances, with only 5,659 in attendance. The last-minute substitution of Cooper wasn't a factor, not considering that he had replaced Steve Dudas, whom no one would describe as a great-drawing card. Perhaps some of the blame for the paltry crowd could be attributed to the ever-present Louis question. Who wanted to see Conn fight run-of-the-mill heavies? Even the fans seemed to be looking ahead to Louis. The press just refused to let the subject rest. While in Pittsburgh to referee a Harry Bobo match at Islam Grotto, Jack Dempsey was quizzed about a possible Conn–Louis matchup. Though the great Manassa Mauler had only seen Billy at work once (against Lesnevich), he had an opinion on Conn's prospects.

"I do know that Conn's a swell kid and will go far in the boxing game," the former champ said, "but he's still a long way from a crack at Joe Louis."

In Detroit, Dempsey's great rival, Gene Tunney, was also asked about Conn. "Billy is a fine Irish kid, a colorful fighter and a credit to the game," Tunney offered. "I'd like to see him get up where he can make the money that a heavyweight contender can make. . . . But to me he seems a trifle short. Besides, he has small bones. And, worst of all, he is not a knockout puncher."[8]

Following his impressive defeat of Cooper, Billy remained in New York for an extra day. On the 11th, Conn was the guest of honor at the New York boxing writers' annual dinner. There he was awarded the Eddie Neil Award as the outstanding boxer of 1939. Part of the attraction members of the media had for Billy could be attributed to his extreme modesty outside the ring. In accepting the tribute, Conn remained true to his humble persona. "I could stand here a week and not thank the boxing writers enough," Billy told those in attendance. "I'll do all in my power to live up to this high honor."[9]

Who would be next? Lee Savold? Bob Pastor? Johnny Paychek? Paychek certainly wasn't shying away from any such proposition. In Orlando, the night after Billy took care of Cooper, Paychek knocked out Pietro Georgi in the fourth round. From his dressing room, the Chicago-born heavyweight let it be known that he was ready for the Pittsburgh pretty boy. "Bring on Billy Conn," he tersely told newsmen.[10]

Johnny Ray let it be known that Junior didn't care who would be his next opponent. "He'll fight anybody, that kid," he said. "I'm not the matchmaker, so I don't know who'll be next. Maybe we'll take on the winner of that Apostoli–Bettina business, but he [Conn] wants those heavyweights. They can't touch him."[11]

Ray wasn't a matchmaker, but he did have an enormous say in who his fighter was paired up against. For the moment, they were stepping away from the heavyweights. Uncle Mike wanted to extend his empire south. Since he had yet to put on a big card below the Mason-Dixon line, Jacobs saw Conn's rising popularity as a prime opportunity to finally do so. He had ruminated on such a possibility for some months, and the lackluster turnout for the Henry Cooper match confirmed the fact to him that he needed to take the show to new environs. On January 19, Jacobs announced that Conn would be defending his title against Gus Lesnevich in Miami's Orange Bowl the last week of February. The winner of that bout, Uncle Mike declared, would defend the light-heavyweight crown against the survivor of the February 2 Apostoli–Bettina fight.

Johnny left Pittsburgh on the 30th to set up camp in Miami, and Billy followed a couple of days later. Everything was in order as the night of the fight approached. In their Madison Square Garden match, Melio Bettina soundly thrashed Fred Apostoli, who failed to answer the bell for the start of the thirteenth. The former light-heavy champ patiently waited for the outcome of Mike Jacobs's Miami venture. Southern hospitality did wonders for Billy. Lounging in the sun gave the champ a nice tan, and Dixie delicacies helped him put on a few pounds. Ironically, Billy had finally gained weight—too much weight to reach the 175-pound limit. Following his February 25 workout, Conn tipped the scales at 179 pounds.

But something was amiss. In the preceding days, Billy wasn't sharp in his workouts. An infection of boils on Conn's right arm was bothering him to such an extent that Ray ceased workouts altogether for several days. The time off did nothing to help Conn's ailment, and reluctantly Johnny picked up a telephone and called Jacobs. "His arm is very sore and inflamed," Ray said. "I told Jacobs Billy couldn't get in good shape," Johnny later told reporters. "He said he didn't want any bad fights, that the best thing would be to call it off."[12]

Ray suggested that the fight be postponed a month, but Jacobs demurred; the peak tourist season would have passed by then. The fight was rescheduled for April 5, in Detroit. Jacobs was outwardly disappointed that his first southern venture failed to come to fruition. He had already laid out $10,000 in expenses, which of course was all lost. There had been $15,000 in advance sales, and Jacobs's Miami agents conservatively estimated a $50,000 gate.

"The most expensive set of pimples ever to grace an athlete in the cauliflower industry" was how Conn's malady was described in the *Washington Post.*[13] On the 28th, Billy had an abscessed gland under his right arm lanced at Mercy Hospital. He continued to make daily trips to the hospital to have the infection drained from his arm. Still the boils persisted. On Friday, March 22, Johnny had to once again inform Jacobs that Billy was unable to properly train for the upcoming match. Conn would not fight again until the boils were cured, "once and for all."

"He's just got a mess of boils in him that have got to come out," said Ray, who was confined to his home with the grippe. "Billy told me he felt pretty good Monday and Tuesday when he worked out in the Lyceum."

They crossed their fingers and hoped for the best, but Wednesday the boils reappeared in full bloom. The condition grew so bad that Billy could barely raise his arm twenty-four hours later, and, following visit to his physician, Ray and Conn decided to heed the doctor's advice and once again postpone the scheduled match.

"I though I could get that Lesnevich fight under my belt and then be ready to break right into the outdoor season with a heavyweight fight," Conn said. "I think I could have beaten Lesnevich easier than I did the first time. Then I planned on talking Mike Jacobs into letting me go with Bob Pastor in June. This would have been a good shot for me—because don't forget—I still have in mind that I might earn a chance to meet Louis before the summer is over.

"I figured this was to be the summer that I would prove I was ready to make my way among the big fellows. But I hate this business of being tabbed as sick, when there is nothing wrong with me—except that stuff that sunshine in Miami put into me is coming out the wrong way."[14]

The chairman of the Michigan State Boxing Commission, John J. Hettche, was cynical of Conn's illness and declared that Billy would not be permitted to fight anywhere else "until he defends his title here [against Lesnevich]."[15] He also ordered a doctor of his choosing to check up on Conn's condition every ten days and report back to him. All skepticism was erased after Hettche received his first update on Billy's health.

"The physician told me it will be at least two months before Conn will be able to begin training for his bout with Lesnevich and then it may take even a longer period for him to get into shape," the chairman said.[16]

Billy's ailment kept him from traveling with Johnny to New York for the March 29 Joe Louis massacre of Johnny Paychek at the Garden. As the weeks went by, however, the boils subsided and, following a ten-day vacation at Mike Jacobs's Rumson farm, Conn began training once again. The fight was rescheduled (once again) for June 5. Unbelievably, Hettche insisted that the bout be a twenty-round affair, though the contract called for fifteen. "I saw the last Conn–Lesnevich fight and it was very close," he said. "It was so close that, in my opinion, twenty rounds would have been required to prove anything."[17] Thankfully, Hettche didn't hang his hat on this ridiculous notion long. Common sense prevailed, and all parties agreed upon the originally scheduled fifteen rounds.

The Lesnevich camp was overflowing with confidence. No one was surer of impending victory than the Mad Russian himself. "I won't make the same mistake tomorrow night I did the last time," said Gus. "I've trained for endurance, and I expect to be just as strong at the finish as the start."

Of course, these comments were taken to Billy for a reaction. With a wry smile, Conn told reporters. "I'm going to carry the battle from the start and hope to win as quickly as possible," he said. "I certainly didn't come here to lose my title."[18]

Shortly after the weigh-in, Billy enjoyed his usual fight-day meal of an assortment of fruit. Anxious, and with nothing else to do in a strange city, Billy arrived at Olympia Stadium early. His deportment, as usual, was calm and relaxed but also extremely bored. He wandered the hall for a while before settling in down front, where he struck up a mostly one-sided conversation with workers who were busy preparing the ring. Yes sir, he told them, he was going to be careful. Not like most fighters. When he was through with the game, he was going to make sure he had enough cabbage to tide him over. The only vice he had, Billy admitted, was clothes. He liked to look good, and there was nothing wrong with that. Nope, when he retired, he was going to have enough money socked away so he never had to ask for a handout. He had taken out an annuity, Conn added, to make sure of his financial security.

The monologue was interrupted by Johnny, who had come looking for Junior. Ray examined the ring and exploded. The padding on the floor was excessive, Johnny said. It was designed to slow Conn down. Ray immediately threatened to pull Billy out of the building if something wasn't done. Local promoter Jack Nelson came running when he heard about the commotion. Nelson listened to Johnny's grievance and proceeded to inspect the ring, which he also found unsuitable. Instead of a "slow track," the canvas was left with a thin layer of padding, an alteration that met Ray's approval.

It wasn't Billy's best fight; still, he totally dominated the match from start to finish. There were slow spots during the bout, and during these lulls the sparse crowd present let their displeasure be known. Rhythmic hand-clapping, boos, and stamping feet were heard—the patrons telling each fighter to pick up the tempo. Billy didn't let the unhappy customers divert him from fighting his fight. The humidity in the arena was oppressive, and Conn was pacing himself throughout.

With the fight in hand at the start of the fifteenth, Billy suggested to Lesnevich that they slug it out for the final three minutes. The previous fourteen stanzas offered no great excitement, but Conn tried to make up for that deficit with a trainload of hooks and straight rights. One left to the jaw dropped Gus for no count. As he did in their first meeting, Lesnevich was game. Exhausted and thoroughly beaten, Gus continued to try to trade punches with Conn, but he was spent. The clang of the bell brought the evening to a close, and the two combatants fell into an embrace. Gus whispered into Billy's ear to ask whether he would fight him again. "Sure, Gus, but it won't be at 175 lbs," Conn replied. "I'm not going to kill myself to make weight again."[19]

Earlier in the day, at the weigh-in, Billy let it be known that this would be his swan song as a light-heavy. He reiterated this thought afterward. "I'm though with the light-heavyweight title," he told gathered newsmen. "I'm giving it back to the Indians. Lesnevich can have it if he wants it. It's worthless. The payoff tonight was the tip off."[20]

Billy was referring to the measly gate of $17,048, a far, far cry from the predicted $50,000. Several reasons were attributed to the poor turnout. First, and most obvious, was the two postponements. The interest in the fight had waned in the preceding weeks, and any excitement surrounding the bout had lost its edge. There were also the reports coming from Conn's camp (some emanating from Ray himself) that Billy wouldn't make weight, and thus would be forced to forfeit his title. Whatever the reason for the poor attendance, Billy didn't care.

"From now on I'm a full-fledged heavyweight, and I know I'll move better against the big, slow-moving fellows then against the guys I have to cut a leg off to fight. I'm a 180-pounder, and I'm growing everyday. In a year I'll be up around 190 or more, and that's plenty big enough to fight Joe Louis. There's nobody left for me to fight in the light-heavyweight class. If there was, I wouldn't have been fighting Lesnevich again tonight. At that, he's the best of the crop of contenders."[21]

As he was prone to do, Conn began asking reporters their opinion of the match.

"How was the fight? How did you like that last round?"

"How did you like that last round yourself?" Harry Keck replied.

"Gee," Billy said with a big grin. "I though it was swell. There sure was a lot of leather flying, wasn't there?"[22]

While Billy enjoyed the give-and-take with his friends in the press, Johnny was in a far corner of the dressing room conferring with Mike Jacobs.

"What do you want next?" the promoter asked. "Pastor? What do you want for it?"

Without missing a beat, Johnny replied. "Thirty-five percent. Billy's the card. We want the big end."

"All right," Jacobs agreed. "I'll see what I can do with Pastor. I'll let you know."

"Where are we going to fight?" Ray asked. "In Pittsburgh or New York?"

Always thinking about the bottom line, Jacobs countered. "Can we get a $16.50 top in Pittsburgh?"

Shaking his head, Johnny answered. "I don't think so. That's pretty steep. The fans aren't accustomed to paying such prices in Pittsburgh."

That settled things. "All right then. It'll have to be New York. I can get that kinda dough there," Jacobs said.[23]

Uncle Mike then walked to the middle of the room and addressed the press hovering around Billy. "Conn showed tonight that he has everything a great fighter needs," he declared. "Some people say he can't punch hard enough to mingle with heavyweights. Well, you saw what he did to Lesnevich—had him wobbly, down, out on his feet, cut and bleeding like no one else ever had him. And Bill showed the kind of fighting spirit I like, and the fans like. He is entitled to get something, and I'm going to try and get it for him."

Asked to be more specific, Jacobs complied. "I'm going to give Billy a chance to prove what I think he's worth. Pastor is the chance I had in mind. There are some things to be ironed out yet. But you are safe in saying it will be Pastor."[24]

So Pastor was next, but Billy had one thing left to do in Detroit. He left Olympia Stadium and retreated to his hotel and placed a call home to Maggie. He was fine, Billy informed his mother, and first thing in the morning he would be on an airplane back to Pittsburgh. Maggie was on his mind constantly. She had taken ill several months earlier, and now she was bedridden. Billy felt helpless. There was nothing he could do for Maggie except find the best doctors available to care for her, and round-the-clock nurses to tend to her needs. Yet still an immense feeling of helplessness overwhelmed Billy. The championship, the fancy clothes, the new cars—all of it he would toss aside in a moment to make Maggie well.

On July 18, the day after Henry Armstrong took Lew Jenkins out in six rounds, Billy and an increasingly growing number of companions set off for Grossinger Lake, in Ferndale, New York, some one hundred miles from Times Square. They needed two cars to carry the group. Johnny, Freddie Fierro, and Harry Mulford took one vehicle. In the other car, Billy rode with his sparring partners Joe Matisi, Willie Pavlovich, and Johnny Aicher. Modest though it was, Conn had himself an entourage.

The next afternoon, Billy began working out; six rounds with oversized gloves. Training was interrupted three days later when Conn made a previously planned trip to New York. From there, Billy caught a plane back home to Pittsburgh to be with Maggie before she underwent surgery. Unfortunately, the operation did nothing to relieve her suffering or heal her condition.

With his mind and heart still in Pittsburgh, Conn returned to Grossinger Lake on Wednesday the 24th and resumed preparations for Pastor in earnest. "This is a swell place, you know it's the first real training camp I've ever been in," Billy "wrote" in a guest column for the *Sun-Telegraph*. Actually, Conn dictated his thoughts to the camp's chief, Doc Morris, who hammered away at a typewriter recording every word.

"We have a lot of good clean fun here. My 'laugh department' is headed by Harry Mulford, who can eat four thick steaks in one sitting. . . .

"I have Jackie Heller, the tenor from Squirrel Hill, here with me. If there is anybody who can sing 'A Pretty Girl Is Like a Melody' any better than Jackie, I haven't heard him.

"Gabby Ryan was out making some motion pictures around camp. He bought himself a megaphone in a 5 and 10 cent store, turned the peak of his cap back and thought he was in Hollywood. . . . If this picture doesn't come out first rate, Gabby will swear that he's been double crossed.

"Jackie Lighting, who never rode a horse outside of a circus sideshow merry-go-around, is here with us. Jack's all right. He's shown me an easy way to make 10 bucks every day we've been here. Every time Milt Jaffe and Johnny Ray sit down and play pinochle we back Milt. . . . Johnny's been playing cards long enough, but he isn't happy unless he's tossing his dough away, and Jackie and I think we might as well get some of it as strangers.

"Maybe you heard me on that radio quiz program the other night. Well, I didn't win any championships in that league. They didn't ask me the questions I could answer, but I could lick anybody they had in the studio. But they didn't ask me to do that, either.

"So long, see you at the fight, and bring as many Pittsburghers as you can. We want to show Uncle Mike Jacobs he won't be wrong in putting on my fight with Joe Louis in Pittsburgh. I think I have a friend or two left there."[25]

Putting aside his journalistic responsibilities and instead fulfilling his duties as state athletic chairman, Havey Boyle met with Jacobs on August 7 to discuss the possibility of Pittsburgh hosting a Louis–Conn date in September. Though nothing would be definite until Billy defeated Pastor, Jacobs virtually assured Boyle that Pittsburgh would be allowed to host the championship match.

A rather unusual candidate for boxing promoter stepped forward to add his two cents concerning the potential bout. David Roberts, chief inspector of the State Inheritance Tax Department, proposed that the show be held at Pitt Stadium. The stadium, with its large seating capacity, was the perfect location for such a premier event. Roberts hoped to sell 100,000 tickets at $5 apiece, eliminating the high-priced ringside seats.

"I do not see why Pittsburgh cannot point out to the world the way these things should be done," Roberts explained. "The answer to put such gigantic proposition within the reach of all is capacity, and the Stadium easily could accommodate 100,000 persons on the field and in the stands."

With so many seats available within Pitt stadium, Roberts reasoned, the costs could be kept to a reasonable level. "At a $5 and tax top, with possibly some $10 ringside reservations, Pittsburgh would draw one of the largest crowds and one of the fattest gates in the history of boxing."[26]

For months the subject of Joe Louis and the heavyweight title had followed every move Billy made. Not that the connection bothered Conn, because if the champion's name was connected with his, then Billy was closing in on his dream. For the press, even for Johnny Ray, Pastor was practically an afterthought. The immense figure of the Brown Bomber loomed large, casting a mighty shadow over all things Billy Conn.

From Grossinger Lake, Johnny chatted up reporters. "Sure Louis is a great fighter," Ray admitted. "Sometimes I think that even Billy won't be as good as Joe when he had it. But everything's got to end. The greatest athletes in every sport fade eventually. Around Pittsburgh you'da had your head broke if you said—a long time ago—that some day Hans Wagner would be just another bum around shortstop. It's hard for the average fellow to realize that champions always collapse.

"You forget that Billy's still as fast as a middleweight. He can go around a heavyweight like a motorcycle through traffic."[27]

Louis did his part in fanning the publicity for a fight not yet scheduled. The champ visited both camps and quietly watched each man spar several rounds. As Pastor worked out in the Stillman's Gym ring in front of him, a reported sidled up to Louis and asked, "I see where Johnny Ray says you're about through, Joe."

The great champion let out a low chuckle, thought for a moment, and then answered. "Billy Conn's a champ, too, ain't he? Maybe he's all through, too, and nobody knows it."[28]

"I'll fight him," Louis added with a shrug of his shoulders, "'cause I could use the money. This has been my worst year since I started up. But Billy's too small for me. He's big enough for Pastor, all right, but for me. . . ."[29]

The good-natured (mostly) give-and-take vanished when Pastor's manager, James Joy Johnston, and Johnny Ray sparred with one another through the sports pages. If their entertaining war of words was a preview to the coming action at the Polo Grounds, the paying public was in for a volatile rumble on the evening of August 13.

With no prompting, Johnny offered his appraisal of Billy's next foe. "Pastor," Ray said to his friends in the press, "I went to see him fight in Buffalo not long ago [a ten-round victory over Charley Eagle], and if that's the kind of fighter he is, Billy might knock him out. And we don't knock people out. He looked slow and flabby to me, and even if he's only five pounds overweight, those five pounds will feel like 30 after 10 rounds."

Equally confident, and certain of an imminent victory, was Johnny's Junior. "Billy won't even look at moving pictures of him," Ray added. "All Billy says about him is, 'He's a college fellow ain't he? How can I lose to a college fellow?'"[30]

Neither Pastor's time spent at New York University nor his career on the school's football team unsettled Billy. However, Johnston was equally dismissive of Conn's ability and what he believed was Billy's inflated reputation in the fight game. "Conn's the most overrated fighter in the business," James Joy said. "He had so much trouble with Apostoli, Bettina, and Lesnevich that he had to fight each of them twice to convince the public that he could beat them. . . . This white hope bunk they're shooting about Conn is an old story to Pastor."[31]

Johnston had no doubt that his man could take Conn; that is, if everything was aboveboard. A quote attributed to a representative of the Twentieth Century Club infuriated Johnston, and the manager demanded that boxing officials conduct an investigation into the statement. Henry McLemore of United Press had reported a member of Mike Jacobs's organization as saying, "If the Conn–Pastor fight is close Conn is sure to get the decision. Conn is a flashy boxer and will catch the judge's eyes. Besides, who the hell wants to see Pastor fight Louis again?"

Understandably, Johnston was livid. He immediately asked the writers loafing about Stillman's to gather together. "That's pretty fine talk to be coming from an official of Mike Jacobs'," said Johnston. "But it doesn't surprise me a bit. I've known all along that Twentieth Century boys were out to give Pastor the works in this fight—if possible. I've tried before to get the commission to look into the situation. Now this statement is tossed right into the commissioner's teeth and they'll have to investigate."[32]

Johnston was convinced that the state boxing authorities had it in for him and his fighter. "Suppose you were a boxing commissioner and it was part of your responsibility to the state to check up on fighters in training?" he asked journalist Joe Williams. "Would it be more convenient for you to go to Ferndale or Stillman's?"

As expected, Johnston answered his own rhetorical question before Williams could open his mouth. The reason was simple, he said; they didn't care for the flamboyant manager. "They don't like me," Johnston said. "They don't like me because they know I don't respect them. I don't click my heels, bow from the hips and murmur, 'Good evening gentlemen' when I see them, which is no oftener than I can help, I assure you.

"But because of this, because I do not toady to their bloated sense of self-importance, they are conspiring against Pastor, who by an interesting coincidence, happens to be my fighter. . . . These men have conditioned themselves mentally in favor of Conn; there is a sinister significance in their trip to Ferndale and their utter indifference to our activities at Stillman's."[33]

That wasn't the end of Johnston's griping. He also took issue with the possibility that Arthur Donovan or Frankie Fullam might referee the match. These two, Johnston insisted, were, "too friendly with Conn."

"Well you saw that guy work in the Conn–Apostoli fight, didn't you?" Johnston asked, referring to Fullam. "You remember when Conn slipped on a wet patch in one of the corners and what Fullam did. . . . Fullam rushed over to him and tenderly picked him up. You'd have thought Conn was his little boy and had just been struck by a truck. There was concern on his face and for a moment I thought he was going to call for a nurse. . . . I'd just as soon have Conn's old man in there; he certainly can't be any more attached to him than Fullam is."[34]

Paranoid though he may have been, Johnston was doing his job in protecting his fighter (and, perhaps unwittingly, helping hype the fight). The first issue, concerning the possibility of prejudice on the part of Mike Jacobs's office, fell on deaf ears. Not that the public was naive; it was conceivable that Jacobs and his henchman wanted Billy to win—that prospect made good financial sense. After all, who *did* want to see Pastor and Louis for a third time? Probably no one outside of Johnston and Pastor's immediate family. No, Conn and Louis was where the money was and everyone understood that simple fact. To appease Johnston, and to quell any possible uncertainty, the referee for the fight would be someone other than Fullam or Donovan. To the satisfaction of all, Billy Cavanaugh was named to arbitrate the bout.

Unexpectedly, Billy broke camp at Grossinger Lake on August 9. "Why did you come to the city so early?" a reporter asked Ray.

"It was getting a little monotonous up there," Johnny explained. "We had been up there three weeks. . . . Junior had begun to get a little high strung, and I thought it better to take him away from the excitement of a high-pressure crowd of weekend visitors in the mountains."[35]

The fresh air was a nice deviation from Billy's normal routine, but he longed for the oppressive bouquet of Pioneer Gym. From the great outdoors, Conn returned to the familiar surroundings of Pioneer for the remaining days before the match at the Polo Grounds. With both fighters in the city, animosity between the rival camps reached a boil.

Ray showed no sign of letting up on his unflattering appraisal of Pastor's abilities. "Pastor is slow with his hands, awkward with his feet and, in short, moves around like a brewery horse."[36]

The lighthearted jab was met with a vicious air of sarcasm. "When Ray speaks of anything pertaining to a brewery, I must respect his opinion," James Joy Johnston said with a smirk. "While I am convinced he knows nothing about the prize ring, I must bow to him in his judgment of the swiggeries. His long association with them qualifies him as an authority."[37]

Johnston's invective filled the sports pages for weeks. The crookedness of the boxing commission, Ray's managerial incompetence, Conn's vastly overrated talent—any number of culprits could have been guilty of wanting to shove a cork in James Joy's mouth. When he finally did get his comeuppance, Johnston had his own distinct idea of where to point the finger of blame.

The day before the fight, Johnston stood outside the Brill Building in the midst of an animated conversation with Havey Boyle. The discussion was surely one-sided and undoubtedly centered on the universal inequity facing his fighter. In his right hand Johnston held an upturned black bowler hat. As Johnston was wildly gesticulating, a water-filled bag was dropped from Mike Jacobs's office, directly above. The anonymous prankster scored a direct hit into Johnston's hat. Angry that his diatribe was disrupted, a flustered Johnston put the water-filled hat on his steaming head. Furiously, he stormed into the building in search of the perpetrator. His chief suspect was Ray, but Johnston didn't dismiss the possibility that Conn was the culprit.

In his desperation for revenge, Johnston posted a reward for information leading to the offender's identity. Perhaps due to his own coarse behavior, Johnston insulted practically everyone associated with the match in the preceding weeks; no intelligence on the escapade was forthcoming.

When asked about the incident, with the innocence of an altar boy, Ray pleaded not guilty. Billy offered little in his own defense. Just a mischievous grin, followed by an ambiguous "I get blamed for everything."[38]

Fight day came and all the usual rituals were in place. The weigh-in was held; Billy, thanks to another boil and a row with dysentery the week before, came in at 175¾, down from the 185 he weighed at the beginning of training. Ray wasn't concerned about Billy's weight, or lack thereof. Regardless, "he'll punch Pastor full of holes," Johnny insisted.

Though he had been dismissive of Pastor's abilities for some time, Ray wanted to set the record straight. "No kidding," he said, "we're looking for a tough fight; one of the hardest Billy's had so far."

"Yeah," Billy agreed, "Pastor is a good fighter, and I'm not looking for a picnic. But I'm ready. I'll beat him no matter how good he is. I have to win this fight. It means everything to me. My whole future's wrapped up in it."[39]

Indeed, much was at stake for Billy, and though he had tenaciously prepared for Pastor, other thoughts filled his mind. Shortly after the weigh-in, Billy called Maggie, who was in St. Francis Hospital. He told his mother to listen to the radio broadcast of the night's fight. "Don't worry about me with that Pastor guy," he assured Maggie. "You just sit there and the news you will get will do you more good than all those doctors."[40]

And then the rains came.

The day began with the skies overcast and dark, but dry. For a brief while at midday the sun appeared, but within a couple of hours it had retreated behind foreboding clouds. Between two and four o'clock, the city of New York was blanketed with a summer rain. Shortly after four, Mike Jacobs announced the postponement of the fight; this conclusion was made even though the rain had stopped.

He held off his decision until he was assured that the rain would return later that evening and that the next day's weather forecast was no better. Original plans called for the fight to be held on the 14th in case of inclement weather, but now that option was out also. A one-week postponement was suggested, but both Ray and Johnston declined the suggestion. Each manager feared his man would lose the edge they had trained so diligently to attain. After some debate, all approved a September 5 rescheduled date. Jacobs's people didn't do their homework, however. One day later, the date was switched to the 6th of September to avoid a possible conflict with a benefit game between the Eastern College All-Star team and the NFL's New York Giants, which was scheduled for the 4th but had a rain date of the 5th.

Predictably, skeptics registered their belief that Jacobs had other motives for calling off the fight. "Some rain, no sale; result, no fight," John Kieran appraised.[41] These critics, Kieran included, claimed Uncle Mike postponed the show as much for the lagging box office as for the inclement weather. The cavernous Polo Grounds would have played host to tens of thousands of empty seats. Originally forecast as a $200,000 gate, at the time of Jacobs's announcement, only $12,000 in advance sales had been reached. Jacobs lost a good bit of money postponing the fight, but had the bout been put on with feeble sales he would have lost a great deal more, in addition to suffering a blow to his prestige. At the Garden, Uncle Mike would recoup his losses. "In three weeks," Jacobs promised, "this thing will draw $70,000 or $80,000 in the Garden."

To maintain peak interest in his product, Jacobs refused to dismiss the notion that the winner would face Joe Louis in the fall. But the East Coast was out, and that included Pittsburgh. Such a match would obviously be a premier event, which demanded a large outdoor stadium, and unpredictable weather that time of year kept the eastern seaboard off the negotiating table. If the proposed title fight came about in the fall of 1940, it would be held in Los Angeles.

In his Polo Grounds dressing room, Billy was disconsolate following Jacobs's decision. To Harry Keck, Conn rued his recent misfortune. "Did you ever hear of a guy having the luck I'm having?" he asked Keck. Though the newsman was well aware of Billy's bad run, Conn still recounted his dubious luck throughout the year. "First I get the boils and have to cancel the Lesnevich fight," Conn sighed. "Then I have to ask for a postponement of the same match in Detroit in March and then, when we fight in June, it doesn't draw.

"Then I get this match with Pastor and am a sure pop to fight Joe Louis next month if I win, and now this happens."

"Are you going home right away?" Keck asked.

"No, I'm going somewhere, but just where I don't know. Maybe out in the woods, or down to the shore, or maybe just drive around till I get over this. Breaks like these are enough to make a guy dive off the deep end."

Then, lost in his own thought, Billy slammed his right fist in the open palm of his left hand. "What a licking I'd have given that guy tonight. I was all set for him."[42]

Three weeks passed and, seemingly, so did the moment. All energy and excitement had been sapped from the fight. The run-up to the rescheduled date wasn't nearly as engaging or boisterous as the days leading up to the originally planned August 13 date. The entertaining give-and-take vanished from the sports pages. Billy returned home to be with Maggie for a week and when he resumed training, he was all business. The large throng of Pittsburghers who had made the trip on the 13th failed to return in September, leaving Conn with a hometown rooting section just a fraction of its usual size.

It seemed to all observers that Uncle Mike had a massive bust on his hands. On the evening in question, however, a surprisingly respectable crowd of 14,448 came to the Garden and enjoyed a vastly entertaining fight. Alternating between a stylistic demonstration of his adroit boxing skills and an atypical display of a relentlessly vicious body attack, Conn thoroughly took the fight to Pastor.

The fella who went twenty-one rounds over the course of two fights against Joe Louis before he was planted on his backside lasted but thirteen before he met the same fate at the hands of Billy Conn. Following another slow start, Billy aroused the crowd with a stunning offensive, an onslaught that left Pastor desperately looking for an escape hatch in the ring floor.

Seated in the second row ringside was a passive heavyweight champion. Surrounding Louis was a great number of animated Conn supporters who shouted their encouragement to Billy and offered their own analysis of the proceedings.

"Who says Billy can't hit?" shouted one man, who stood directly behind a seemingly bored Louis.

"The best left hand in the world!" another confirmed.

"Look at that speed."

Through it all—the great action in the ring, the enthusiastic commentary ringing in his ears—Ol' Joe sat, struggling to keep his eyes open. "He didn't pay the fight as much mind as he would a mess of pork chops, or a new pair of yaller shoes," Henry McLemore of the United Press noted.[43] If Joe was napping, he was missing a helluva show. Billy was determined to demonstrate to Bob Ryan what he could do with his powder-puff title, and proceeded to put on one of his finest punching exhibitions to date.

In his youthful exuberance, Conn delivered a couple of blows that landed below Pastor's belt. In fact, three times in the seventh round Billy threw punches that were on the wrong side of Pastor's highly worn trunks. Again in the eighth, Conn repeated the foul (twice) and referee Billy Cavanaugh took the round away from him and warned against further infractions. Throughout the next five rounds, Billy kept up his unforgiving attack. In the twelfth, with time ticking away in the round, Conn deposited Pastor on the canvas. Cavanaugh reached the count of nine when the bell rang, offering Pastor a brief reprieve. As Johnston helped his man to the corner, Cavanaugh walked to the judges and informed them that he was again taking the round from Billy for another low blow.

At the start of the thirteenth, Cavanaugh warned Conn to keep 'em up; Billy nodded, but his eyes were on his teetering opponent. This round, Pastor was going down to stay. They met at mid-ring, where Pastor offered no resistance as Billy threw three lefts to the jaw and two crushing rights to the body. Though visibly wilted, Pastor refused to go down. Another Conn hook, this one to the stomach, caused him to double over. A right uppercut followed and then a demoralizing left, which landed directly on the belt line.

"Pastor went down clutching at his groin," Regis Welsh wrote. "The blow was fair enough to all those ringside, but here a 'dead game' fellow's befuddled brain saw opportunity to grasp at the last chance to win, or at least, 'save his face' by going out claiming foul."[44]

Pastor rolled about the floor, hands between his legs, hoping to sway officials to penalize Conn. Cavanaugh disregarded the embarrassing demonstration and counted to ten in unison with the timekeeper. With just six seconds left in the thirteenth, Pastor was out, a limp pathetic figure lolling on the canvas.

In an attempt to quell anticipated controversy, Cavanaugh issued a statement to the press explaining his lack of intervention at the end of the fight. "The punch that ended the fight was not foul—but pretty close to it," read Cavanaugh's account. "Had Pastor been able to get up, I would have taken the round from Conn for low punching."

The referee's surprisingly ambivalent admission left many scratching their heads and opened the door for the Pastor camp to cry foul. "He has marks on his groin and is nauseated," Jimmy Johnston claimed.

"I don't know what kind of a rule that is—that a man can be knocked out by a foul blow."[45] He would go to the New York State Athletic Commission, Johnston vowed, "because the referee didn't throw Conn out after warning him."[46]

Though it took some time to drag his beaten self from the ring, Pastor gathered the strength to complain to the press. "I don't mind losing a fight, but I hate to lose it because of unfair blows," he grumbled.

Billy waved off all questions of fairness and criticism of his perceived dirty tactics. "A few of my punches might have been low," admitted Conn. "But Pastor just can't take it in the body."[47]

After meeting with the press, Billy veered from his normal routine of vacating his dressing room as quickly as possible. Instead of heading to his hotel room, Conn agreed to address the national audience tuned to the radio broadcast of the fight. Though Maggie had been advised by her doctors to not listen to the blow-by-blow descriptions of Billy's fights, she did join family and friends gathered in her living room to hear the ceremonies that followed the bout. In a moment, her Billy's voice filtered through the airwaves with a message especially for her. "I'd like to say hello to my mother and I hope she's feeling better."[48]

Before vacating New York City, Johnny huddled with Jacobs and discussed their favorite subject, Billy Conn; more specifically, young Conn's future. The men came to a mutual agreement that Billy wasn't ready for Louis. Another winter of seasoning and each was equally sure that Conn would be prepared for the challenge come spring. Next on Conn's plate was the well-traveled Buddy Knox. The match was to be a Rooney-McGinley production, September 30, at Forbes Field. The Knox fight was contingent on Buddy's winning his fight against Tommy Martin on the 14th.

From Joe Louis to Buddy Knox? What happened? Conn's detractors, many of whom emanated from the West Coast, wondered in print about these questions.

"Why, if he had graduated from 'slap artist' to a 'knockouter,' would Conn be rushed into a fight with Louis," Paul Zimmerman of the *Los Angeles Times* wrote. Sure, in eight months Louis would be older, there was no disputing that fact. But the real reason, Zimmerman surmised, was that Billy simply was frightened and "postponing his execution."[49]

Zimmerman certainly didn't know Conn, and it is unlikely that the West Coast sportswriter had even seen Billy fight. Had he been in Conn's presence, Zimmerman would have recognized Billy's dominant personality trait: confidence. Putting Louis off several months was not Conn's doing . . . he would take Joe on anytime, anyplace. Ray, however, recognized that there were still some things in Junior's technique that needed to be ironed out before he took on the champion. Uncle Mike also considered Billy's best interests. He wanted Conn to succeed. In the previous eighteen months, Jacobs had developed an enormous affection for the affable kid. Mike's Rumson estate had practically become a second home to Billy. With all that noted, there was also no doubting the fact that Jacobs thought in terms of dollar signs. Billy's success would also equal success for Jacobs, of course. Los Angeles was a viable venue, but Conn's name lacked panache on the left coast. To maximize the gate, Jacobs wanted Louis–Conn in New York or Pittsburgh.

Buddy Knox didn't hold up his end of the bargain, unfortunately. Tommy Martin upset the Dayton, Ohio, native when the duo squared off in Hollywood. The defeat eliminated Knox as an opponent for Conn, and the loss canceled the September 30 Forbes Field program. With just a little over two weeks to find a suitable opponent for Billy *and* promote the show, Art Rooney opted instead to just cancel the whole affair.

Billy Conn, the newest Celtic fistic star, and Boston were a natural fit. With the Knox match fallen by the wayside, Johnny went in search of a worthy opponent and a decent payday for his fighter. Boston promoter Rip Valenti had expressed an interest in Billy since Conn hit the big time. A swashbuckling Irishman couldn't miss in Boston. Following a brief round of negotiations, Ray signed for Billy to open the city's indoor boxing season at Boston Garden on October 18. His opponent, Al McCoy, was a twenty-six-year-old veteran with ten years' experience as a pro. On the surface, McCoy looked like a pushover for Conn, despite the fact that the Boston heavyweight had knocked out Nathan Mann and took a decision from Melio Bettina earlier in the year. Prognosticators hedged their bets, however. The bout was scheduled for just ten rounds. The perpetually slow-starting Conn could conceivably fall too far behind the aggressive McCoy to catch up.

Come fight day, Billy weighed in at a ridiculously low 172¾. This was a matter of growing concern for Johnny Ray. Try as he might to put some meat on Junior's bones and make him a bona fide heavyweight, Billy's frame refused to acquiesce. Officially, McCoy had a nine-pound advantage, though some expected that was with just one foot on the scale. Regardless of the weight differential, Conn had little trouble with the New England heavyweight champion. Only in the second and third rounds did Billy show any vulnerability to the portly McCoy's advances. The Bostonian missed his chance, though. After the first four rounds had been furiously contested, with each man giving as good as he got, Billy took over the fight in the fifth. He boxed brilliantly from long range using his most potent weapon, punishing left hooks to the body, to great effect. The attack slowed McCoy and left him resembling an animated heavy bag. All the fight had been sapped from the plump McCoy by the close of the round.

During the seventh, Billy slipped to one knee in the midst of a close exchange. As Conn attempted to rise, McCoy struck him. Accident or not, Billy refused to accept his opponent's gesture of apology. He angrily spat at McCoy; with a controlled fury, Conn moved in and retaliated for the perceived foul with a terrible vengeance.

Boston Garden was well packed with more than 15,500 in the hall, the finest crowd the city had seen in a number of years. Through the remaining rounds, Conn tried desperately to deposit McCoy on his behind in front of the large partisan crowd. His efforts were to no avail, however. Billy's failure to knock out his overstuffed opponent was the only disappointment of the evening. The referee and judges were unanimous in their opinion; Conn was undefeated in four bouts against the heavyweights.

On October 21, Conn signed for a November 29 fight against the rugged blond heavyweight, Lee Savold, in Madison Square Garden. Savold was a virtual unknown to all but hard-core fight fans. The former bartender had put together a nice eight-match winning streak, but the victories came against a group of tin cans. Just after the first of the year, the twenty-four-year-old Savold took just three rounds to take out big Jim Robinson. That performance catapulted him into a March 1 match against Bob Pastor. A victory in that bout would get Savold a shot at Louis, but he never got the opportunity. Instead, Savold suffered from a case of influenza that forced a cancellation of the bout. "Lethal Lee" returned to the ring before he had fully recovered from his illness. In St. Louis on March 28, Savold surprisingly lost a ten-round decision to Johnny Whiter. After that, he took a newspaper decision over Whiter and knocked out seven other nondescript opponents.

The smart dope said Conn would have an easy time with the heavyweight from the corn country of Des Moines, Iowa. If Billy fell to Savold, he would have no legitimate claim to a match with Louis. Conn himself wasn't concerned. He finished training two days before the fight, full of vim. "I feel so good that I wish I was fighting Louis instead of Savold," he told reporters.[50]

The fight did little to assuage critics who believed Billy wasn't ready to dethrone the heavyweight champ. Throughout the twelve-round match, Conn thoroughly outboxed his opponent, but once again media attention focused only on his failure to knock out his adversary. Billy couldn't even make the stouthearted Iowan take a step backward. The fight was dull and the crowd allowed its annoyance to be known. Boos and derisive calls for more action filled the hall numerous times throughout the evening.

Billy won ten of the twelve rounds, losing only the tenth and twelfth (the twelfth was taken from Conn by Arthur Donovan for a low blow). He blamed his poor showing on Savold's style. "If I hadn't forced the fight there wouldn't have been any," Conn said afterward. "That guy couldn't land a punch on me in a week if I merely wanted to out box him."[51]

Savold's ballyhooed right failed to make an appearance all evening. The only damage inflicted by the Iowan was a left hook in the eighth that opened a gash beneath Billy's right eye. Conn left the Garden with a slight blemish on his face from the blow, a still-undefeated record against heavyweights, and $9,000 richer.

Hollywood once again expressed interest in Billy. Though nothing had come from the screen test Conn had taken a year earlier, studio executives remained intrigued with the Pittsburgh Pretty Boy. On December 15, Ray met with motion picture magnates concerning a possible movie contract for Conn. The offer intrigued Johnny. Junior on the silver screen; wouldn't that be a hoot? Still, Ray spurned their $10,000 proffer. Six weeks of filming was too much time for Billy to take off at the moment. Plus, Ray was concerned that the bright lights of a movie set would harm his fighter's eyes.

Having put Hollywood on hold for the time being, Ray attended the Joe Louis–Al McCoy title match at Boston Garden on December 16. McCoy earned his shot at the heavyweight crown by losing to Buddy Knox, Gunnar Barland, and Conn in succession. The fight was viewed as little more than a paying sparring match for Louis. No one honestly believed McCoy was in the same class as Joe, and no one expected much more than a quick knockout of the challenger.

Surprisingly, McCoy put up a game, albeit brief, fight against the Brown Bomber. With a bobbing and weaving style, McCoy frustrated and befuddled Louis. The champion, however, was still too much for the Boston heavyweight. McCoy may have failed to answer the bell for the sixth round, but his style of fighting showed a weakness in Louis's game and raised the eyebrows of many in attendance.

"I know Billy would have become heavyweight champion if he had been in the ring with Louis in Boston," Ray noted. "He won't be an easy target to hit when he faces Joe and he'll land plenty of punches."[52]

Following more than a year of anticipation, the much speculated-upon pairing of Louis and Conn was made official on December 21. Coming to a satisfactory agreement proved difficult for Mike Jacobs and Johnny Ray, however. Though the men had enjoyed a mutually profitable relationship over the previous two years, their genial rapport went by the wayside over a forty-eight-hour period as they haggled back and forth before finally reaching an accord on conditions for the match. To the surprise of no one, Jacobs came out on top of nearly every disputed point. After all, Uncle Mike held all the cards. That's not to say little Johnny Ray didn't put forth a full-fledged effort in representing his fighter, though.

Earnings for the bout, which was slated to take place the following June, were to be 40 percent for the champion, 20 percent for the challenger. Should Conn pull off the upset, he was obligated to give Louis a rematch within ninety days. Despite Johnny's tenacious negotiating, the percentage each fighter would receive in such a return engagement was 30 percent apiece. Ray argued in vain for the customary 37½ percent usually given the champion. Billy was also compelled, should he wrestle the title from Louis, to defend the crown exclusively for Mike Jacobs and the Twentieth Century Club. This is where Ray won his only significant point. Johnny absolutely refused to relinquished control of Billy's exhibition matches to Jacobs as Mike requested. Agreeing to such a stipulation would have made Conn a virtual slave to Jacobs. Uncle Mike could still secure control of Billy's career, but for that to occur, Conn would have to have captured the heavyweight crown.

The Pittsburgh Chamber of Commerce immediately began a campaign to bring the fight to town. The president of the chamber, Frank Duggan, wrote a letter to Jacobs explaining that "there are about 2,100,000 persons in the metropolitan areas of the Pittsburgh district." People who were enjoying "prosperity unequaled in more than a decade. . . . In Pittsburgh," Duggan wrote, "the fight would be a big affair. While in New York it would be merely another in a series of assaults on the championship."[53]

The decision on the venue for the big event notwithstanding, the overdue agreement reached by Jacobs and Ray set off a firestorm, which played out over the ensuing weeks in sports pages across the nation. Several days after the pairing of Louis and Conn was made public, Joseph Triner, president of the National Boxing Association, wired Billy inquiring "whether you are ready to sign immediately in defense of your title or whether you have relinquished the same."[54]

Triner's telegram was not out of line. NBA rules deemed that a title-holder defend his championship a minimum of once every six months. Conn had not risked his title since meeting Gus Lesnevich the previous June 6, and now having signed to fight the heavyweight champion, Triner believed it a foregone conclusion that Billy was no longer interested in defending his light-heavy belt.

Initially, Johnny did little to dissuade this mode of thinking. "If there were any outstanding opponent, I'd be ready to put Billy in with him before we take on Louis," Ray said. "But I don't know of any good light heavyweights who would make it worthwhile."

Ray continued with his ambiguous statement. "So we very likely will give up the title but we haven't yet decided on the date the announcement will be made."[55]

Then, as if to further muddy the question, Jacobs announced that Jimmy Webb and Tommy Tucker would meet on February 28 and the winner would be recognized as the light-heavyweight champion. Clearly, though, Uncle Mike hadn't consulted with Ray on this matter.

Shortly after the dawn of 1941, two Cleveland promoters, Ben Goetz and Bob Brickman, were behind the first concerted effort to break Jacobs's monopolistic hold on the championship tier of the fight game. At the center of the controversy was Conn. Just a month earlier, the Cleveland businessmen tried to entice Ray with a $15,000 guarantee to bring Billy to their fair city. The offer was rejected, in part because Johnny and his fighter were more interested in chasing heavyweights than defending Conn's light-heavy title. The announcement made on

December 21 matching Billy against Joe Louis set off the "small-time" promoters.

"Conn," the Clevelanders argued, "having signed to meet Louis—whether by 'private' or 'public' agreement—abrogated his right to the 175 lb crown." Goetz and Brickman scheduled a match between Melio Bettina and Anton Christoforidis, which their publicity releases claimed was "for the world's light heavyweight championship."

Goetz and Brickman asked Ohio senator Harold H. Burton to introduce a congressional investigation of what they believed was "a monopoly on boxing held by Promoter Jacobs in violation of the Sherman Anti-trust Law."[56]

An outraged Johnny Ray addressed the controversy. "They've got no right to do that," he claimed. "We won that title in the ring and we're ready to defend it in the ring against a worthy opponent."

Johnny also added that he offered to defend the title against Tommy Tucker in Chicago, a fight that Triner refused to sanction, "and now," Ray said, "[Triner] wants to go ahead and take the title away from Conn. He can't do that."[57]

On January 5, Jacobs released a statement declaring that Conn would sue the Cleveland promoters if they continued to bill their upcoming fight as a "championship" bout. "The fact that Conn signed a private contract with me to challenge Joe Louis for the heavyweight title in June has no bearing now upon his light heavyweight championship in New York or any state. He's still champion and we defy anyone to advertise otherwise," Jacobs wrote, "to obtain money from the public under false pretenses. I'll back his suit to the limit."[58]

Jacobs continued, "For the protection of everyone connected with boxing, titles must be won and lost in the ring, and anyone who attempts to fool the public by advertising phony title matches from now on will run into plenty of trouble."[59]

Uncle Mike was forced to backpedal. In declaring the February 28 match between Tommy Tucker and Jimmy Webb to be a title match, a title still not vacated by Conn, Jacobs was guilty of the same "crime" as his Cleveland adversaries. Subsequent to an angry encounter with Johnny Ray, Jacobs amended the publicity release for the Tucker–Webb fight. The men, it was now announced, would fight for the right to face Billy Conn and a chance at the light-heavyweight title.

Jacobs's threat of a lawsuit (in Billy's name) did not intimidate Joseph Triner, who followed with an announcement of his own: the NBA no longer considered Billy Conn a champion. His reasons were neatly laid out.

1. Conn automatically relinquished his title when he signed to fight Joe Louis for the heavyweight championship in June.
2. Conn's manager, Johnny Ray, announced to the press that Conn had relinquished his title when he agreed to fight Louis.
3. Conn had not defended his title within the six months required by NBA rules against idle champions.

"The N.B.A. has served notice on Conn by two telegrams calling his attention to the fact that defense of his title was overdue," Triner said. "Neither Conn nor his manager has seen fit to accord the N.B.A. courtesy of a reply to the official inquiry."[60]

Noticeably silent through the entire controversy was the individual in the center of the tumult. Billy allowed Johnny to speak for him and permitted Jacobs to toss around threats of litigation in his name. He intrinsically trusted each man, and as of yet, neither had let him down. So, for the time being, Conn stayed on the sidelines and silently sat back as the debate ensued.

Keeping a low profile did little to prevent others from dragging Billy's name into print. After defeating Pat Comiskey on the 10th of January, Lou Nova asked Jacobs for a bout against Conn, the winner earning the right to fight Louis in the summer. Uncle Mike duly ignored this request. Instead, the promoter offered Nova a direct chance at Louis and his crown in late summer. Nova's manager, Ray Carlen, met this proposal with great skepticism.

"Gosh!" Carlen exclaimed, "That's a brand new one. Jacobs is using Louis, the world champion, as a policeman to protect his fair haired boy, Conn, from getting mussed up by Nova."[61]

The NBA failed to be intimidated by Jacobs's threatened lawsuit. Anton Christoforidis won a unanimous decision over Melio Bettina and was given the (forcibly) vacated light-heavyweight title. Conn still remained the acknowledged champion in the state of New York, however. The New York State Athletic Commission ignored the NBA-sanctioned title fight in Cleveland and refused to accept Christoforidis as the light-heavy champion.

"We will continue to recognize Conn in this state," commission chairman John J. Phelan said. "He has not relinquished the title and has expressed willingness to meet any challenger designated by the commission."[62]

At the same time the Conn–Louis summer match was announced to the public, Johnny Ray told reporters that Billy would remain idle until meeting the champion. Reporters present duly noted his statements, but few actually believed Johnny's words. The question wasn't necessarily if Conn would fight before summer arrived. Rather, the debate centered on the type of opponent Billy would face. Would he defend his light-heavy title? Certainly there was ample pressure to accept a challenge for his belt. Still, for the time being, Johnny refused to relent to any coercion. Junior was taking a vacation, getting away from the game for a month.

On February 12, the New York State Athletic Commission announced that Conn had agreed to abdicate his title "whenever asked." Simultaneously, the commission revealed the four top contenders for the soon-to-be-vacated crown, Tommy Tucker, Jimmy Webb, Gus Lesnevich, and Anton Christoforidis. These revelations were preceded by a meeting at Mike Jacobs's office one day earlier. There, in the Brill Building, Johnny Ray met with Uncle Mike and Philadelphia promoter Pat Moran, who also served as Danny Hassett's manager. Ray agreed to take his fighter to Washington's new ice palace, the $700,000 Uline Arena, on March 6. Billy's opponent, Hassett, mattered little. What did matter was Jacobs's ambition to see if big-time boxing would go over in the nation's capital.

Hassett had been curiously missing from the boxing scene since the previous July when he lost by a TKO at the hands of Bill Boyd at Washington's Griffith Stadium. Following his first training session for his fight with Conn, the Philadelphian reintroduced himself to the district's sporting press in case they failed to recognize him.

"I am Fighter Hassett," he declared with a stately air.

"I am Sleuth Hassett," he added. And then with flavored zeal, "I am the one who is going to beat Billy Conn when I get him in the ring Thursday night. . . . I don't see why there's so much concern over the fact that I am what they call an 'in and out' fighter. Honestly, I don't have to fight. I was doing pretty good as a refrigerator salesman around Philadelphia until a few months ago when I accepted a job as a private detective under Captain Jimmy Ryan. I'm still in the embryo stage as a detective, but I'm doing all right."[63]

In the days prior to the fight, the newly christened PI was blissfully at ease despite possessing a modest pedigree. Some attributed Hassett's relative comfort to his previous role as Conn's sparring partner a year earlier when Billy was preparing for Gus Lesnevich in Florida. Perhaps, they thought, Irish Danny was counting on his old boss taking it easy on a Fridgidaire huckster trying to make an honest buck.

When Billy arrived in Washington three days before the match, he was fresh off a victory over Ira Hughes in Clarksburg, West Virginia—the first match Ray lined up as they began their preparatory run toward the heavyweight crown. Hughes, also a native of Pittsburgh, offered little competition for Conn, as the two fought in front of an embarrassingly small crowd of 1,100. Billy won by technical knockout in the fourth round of a scheduled ten-round match, which was hastily put together by Ray to secure his fighter some work.

Two fights in six days, questionable scheduling for sure, but Conn wasn't looking back to Hughes or ahead to Hassett. On Billy's mind when he met with Washington sportswriters was a report out of New York that directly implied that Louis's managers were dictating Conn's opponents. This supposed "censoring" of Billy's foes was allegedly an effort to protect Conn before he faced the champion.

"Louis' managers don't have a thing to do with the selection of my opponents and never will," Billy said from his training headquarters at Catholic University. "In fact, I think I can qualify as Louis' advance man. Look what I did to Al McCoy and Gus Dorazio before he got around to them."

Still steaming from that perceived slight, Billy then faced a question from a local writer that further infuriated him. "And if you lose to Louis, Mr. Conn, will you go back into the light heavyweight division and try to reclaim your title?"

"What are you talking about?" Conn shouted at his naive inquisitor. The impudence of the question outraged the normally unflappable fighter. "Nobody can beat me—especially Louis. I'll drive him crazy with my left hand. Hell, they talk about my small size and say I can't punch. Maybe there are some who can out punch me, but they don't outthink me."

Eventually Billy's temper eased and his questioners wised up. Asked about Hassett, Conn replied very diplomatically. "He's a good tough boy and a dangerous puncher," he offered. "He's not what you call a good boxer, but I'm going to have to be careful to keep out of the way of those wild punches."[64]

Obviously—but left unsaid—Conn wasn't worried in the least by Irish Danny Hassett. The fight was simply a promotional tool for Jacobs to test the southern waters of the capital city.

On fight night, Uncle Mike couldn't have been more pleased. A record D.C. crowd came to Uline Arena; 8,000 patrons jammed the hall to the rafters and an additional 3,000 were turned away at the door. No question—Washington fight fans came out not for the aesthetic value of the fight, but rather for curiosity's sake . . . curious to see this Pittsburgh Adonis that they've read so much about.

"Didn't I tell ya," Johnny excitedly yelled to Jacobs as they watched fans fill the arena. "There's money in this town, Mike. Look at that crowd. They're turning 'em away in droves at the door. Look at this arena—perfect!"[65]

Unfortunately, the fight itself didn't live up to the anticipation and excitement that filled the hall. In the initial four rounds, Billy did little more than play with his former sparring partner. Then, in the fifth, the crowd shouted for Conn to end it and he acceded to their wish. Finally, Billy turned it on for the first time all night. At the start of that stanza, Conn planted a hard left in Hassett's bountiful belly. That was followed by a combination: a right above the heart and another left that landed directly on Irish Danny's chin.

Hassett fell to the canvas like a great oak under the hand of a mighty woodsman, where he smartly decided to stay. Thirty-five seconds into the fifth round, Detective Danny Hassett was counted out.

The match was little more than a paid sparring match for Conn, which brought to bear some questions. Where was the value in fighting stiffs like Hugheses and Hassetts? Wouldn't Billy have been better served squaring off against the Novas, Comiskeys, and Pastors? Certainly the purse from a fight with any of those men would have been substantially more than the fairly meager earnings gathered in Clarksburg and Washington, where, despite the record attendance, the gate was only $11,396.

Billy arrived in Chicago March 25. He was in town to fight Finnish heavyweight Gunnar Barland in an April 4 match at Chicago Stadium. Though not among the top contenders, Barland held the notable record of never losing a fight to a favorite. He was described by one news outlet as the "biggest and perhaps the most dangerous heavyweight" Conn had yet faced.[66] Regardless of the threat Barland may have posed, Billy's mind was focused on his June opponent rather than his next foe.

"I'm going to box him," Billy said of Louis. "I'll feint with my left, for every time I've seen Joe, a left feint makes him step back and blink his eyes before he can get set again. . . . If I can hit him I think I can knock him out. Anyway, he marks up easy. Didn't he get a bad eye from that Abe Simon? And the guys who hit him—Galento and Braddock—showed he knocks down pretty easy. Trouble is, most of the guys he's fought were scared stiff. They thought just because it was Louis who hit them, they had to go down. If that guy Simon could get to the thirteenth round, I'm a cinch."[67]

Despite giving sixteen and a half pounds, Conn easily handled the plodding Barland. If anything, Billy struggled to maintain interest in beating his clearly inferior opponent. Only in the third and seventh rounds did Conn open with an offensive that indicated a desire to take out the overmatched Finn. In the seventh, Billy threw a number of hooks and jabs, the effect of which left Barland's face a blood-caked mess. Following that round, the physician present examined Barland and declared the fighter fit enough to continue. Referee Barney Ross then spoke a few words with Barland, informing him that he would give Gunnar every opportunity to make a fight of things; otherwise, he would end the proceedings. Intently listening in was Barland's manager Paul Damaski. Like the ringside physician before him, Damaski had also examined his man and his diagnosis differed from the medical professional. Barland's manager informed Ross that the cut above Gunnar's left eye was too severe for the fighter to continue. Ross retreated from the Barland corner waving his arms and walked across the ring to raise the gloved fist of beaming Billy Conn.

The abrupt surrender shocked and angered the crowd. Though most in attendance recognized Conn's dominance over Barland, few present thought the beating harsh enough to throw in the towel. Making matters worse was the complete lack of fight put up by Barland, whose most effective offensive weapon all night was hugging and grabbing onto Conn for much of the evening, perhaps an ingenious effort to squeeze the zest and energy from Billy. One who questioned Damaski's decision was Sheldon Clark, chairman of the Illinois Athletic Commission. Clark issued an immediate directive to hold Barland's share of the purse pending an investigation.

Maybe he was looking past his Finnish opponent, but once again, Billy failed to impress many ringside reporters. H. C. Warren of the International News Service opined, "If Conn is the number one contender for Joe Louis' title, the Negro champion's crown is safe for a long time to come."

Warren's evaluation of Billy's performance continued, "Conn showed only a couple of flashes of anything that looked like championship fighting. If he is still serious about challenging Louis for the heavyweight title, he will need a lot of improvement to stand up long with the champion."[68]

Nationally, many boxing experts began to question Conn's legitimacy as the obvious choice to face Louis in the coming summer. Though Billy handled Gunnar Barland with relative ease, the victory wasn't enough to quell long-standing cynicism of his abilities. Lou Nova, some believed, was the rightful number-one contender for the heavyweight crown. Nova himself had just disposed of former champ Max Baer the same night Billy met Barland, again renewing the debate.

"We're not worried about Lou Nova," Johnny said after the Barland match. "Billy Conn will box Joe Louis in June and, after he beats him and becomes the heavyweight champion, Lou will get his chance, but he hasn't done anything so far to displace Billy as the natural opponent for this summer's big crack at Louis."

Ray was unusually verbose following the fight in Chicago. The criticism of his Junior was unfounded, he believed, and what's more, Nova hadn't done anything worthy of undue praise. "Barland quit to Billy and Baer quit to Nova, both in the eighth round," he explained. "That makes them even. But Billy made a game guy quit while Nova made a quitter quit. Baer has quit before and he plainly quit this time, unless what I hear about his fight is wrong."[69]

Ray then detailed Barland's reputation as a courageous fighter, having never been knocked out in his career. Conn's ruthless body attack wore the Finn fighter down, Johnny explained, and prevented Barland from answering the bell for the eighth round.

"I'll grant you it wasn't a spectacular fight, but that was because Billy hurt the Gunnar early and kept him hurt and Barland kept grabbing him at every opportunity. . . . If Barland hadn't quit in his corner after the seventh round, Billy would have knocked him out and everybody would have been happy."[70]

The Illinois state commission held up Barland's purse immediately following the fight. This act cast an undeserved light on Conn's performance and Barland's ethics, Johnny contended. "Holding up his money is preposterous, and unfair to both Billy and Barland," Ray said. "Anytime a fighter's purse is held up the first thing the fans think about is that there was something wrong with the fight. No fighter ever earned his money more honestly or harder than Barland in this fight. He went as long as he could. What do they want to see, a man killed in the ring?"[71]

On the 14th, the Illinois Athletic Commission suspended Damaski and Barland for one year and ordered Gunnar's share of the purse, $3,899.50, be returned to the state treasury.

Ray's explanation and the commission's suspension notwithstanding, Nova remained dismissive of Conn and stepped up his campaign following his defeat of Baer. "I've stopped both Baer and Pat Comiskey this winter," Nova told newsmen. "What has Conn been doing all this time? Oh, yes, he did manage to beat Gunnar Barland last night in Chicago, didn't he? That must be the same Barland I whipped here several years ago when I was learning the business."[72]

As could be expected, Nova's comments were carried to Johnny for a reaction. Ray listened impassively. "That is a decision for Mike Jacobs to make," he said. "He is the promoter. Our main job is to win the heavyweight championship and we are not going to surrender any of our hard earned rights. Sure, an elimination between Conn and Nova might mean a bigger gate against Louis in September, but we're not going to give any ground to Nova. When you get right down to it, who'd he ever lick? Galento murdered him and he was out a year, and since he has come back he has come back and beaten a green kid in Pat Comiskey and the champion quitter in Baer."[73]

However, there were other factors at play. Though Billy had indeed signed a contract to fight Joe Louis, Louis himself had not yet put his name to anything; therefore, the agreement was worthless. Joe's managers, Jack Blackburn and John Roxborough, feared that Louis, who had a low draft number, would be called into service at any time. Rightfully, Blackburn and Roxborough hoped to garner at least one more substantial purse for Joe before his number was selected. And, though some would question their judgment, they believed Nova offered a more lucrative payday for their fighter than Conn. The opinions of Louis and his men did hold some sway, but the final decision, of course, lay with Jacobs.

With pressure mounting in the press over Conn's perceived weak opponents, Jacobs hedged when answering inquiries and refused to confirm anything for the summer's season. "What's the rush?" he replied. "Let's wait and see how Louis makes out with Musto and Abe Simon. Maybe we won't have to worry about who fights him for that title. Anyhow, Nova doesn't need to worry. He'll get his chance."

His answer came equipped with a straight face, but not one of the scribes present believed a word that passed through Jacobs's lips. Uncle Mike was clearly disingenuous. No one expected Louis to have any problem with Simon or Musto. Those ingrained to be cynical about Jacobs only had their beliefs reinforced. Clearly, these critics believed, Conn was a favorite of Mike's and nothing was going to prevent Billy from having the first chance at the champion. A neutral party could evaluate the controversy and be sympathetic to Jacobs's point of view. Undoubtedly, Conn offered a bigger gate attraction than Nova. Should Billy upset Louis, there would be a rematch, another huge draw for Jacobs. If Billy lost to Louis as so many expected, then Nova would be in line for his long-sought-after opportunity. From Mike's point of view, it was just plain good business to go ahead with the originally planned Louis–Conn showdown in June.

Further complicating an already muddled picture was Louis's lackluster performance on the 8th against Tony Musto. On paper the fight looked like a continuation of the Bum of the Month Club. However, like Abe Simon before him, Musto forced Louis to expend more effort than anyone could have expected. Of course, in the end, Joe won and Musto suffered terrible cuts around his eyes, which bled profusely. Still, a weakness was displayed in the champion's game. Perhaps age was beginning to show or maybe Louis had simply grown indifferent to the endless parade of palookas lined up for him to dispatch. Whatever the cause, Joe certainly looked vulnerable to a worthy challenger, should one be found.

Ray and Jacobs had been butting heads through much of the year. Each man had Billy's best interest at heart, but Johnny's responsibilities to Junior went beyond dollars and cents. Money could not be made unless everything else was in line. The previous December, Ray indicated that Billy would remain idle until meeting Louis. Jacobs, who believed Conn's stock could only abate if he entered the ring against middling opponents, instituted that strategy. No, Mike was sure that public interest had reached its zenith, and all concerned parties needed to conspire and keep the curiosity at such a peak. Ira Hughes and pugs of his ilk were not the answer.

Regardless of Jacobs's wishes, Ray knew his fighter. Johnny knew Junior needed to stay active, needed more work against the heavies. And so Johnny bucked Jacobs. This gnawed at Uncle Mike, who more than anything liked control (well, perhaps he liked a buck more). Sure, Jacobs went along with the Hassett bout; even then Ray had to convince the promoter that there was a healthy dollar to be made down in Washington. But Barland, that's another story. Jacobs was not pleased when Ray accepted the offer to fight in Chicago. His reservations were realized when pundits and fans left the hall that night questioning Billy's worthiness as the number-one contender.

With great reluctance, Jacobs agreed to endorse one more Billy fight before the June 18 date tentatively set for Conn–Louis. One more fight allowed Conn the opportunity to regain some of the prestige he'd lost in the preceding months and hopefully once again stoke the paying public's enthusiasm.

A deal was made to bring Billy back home for the first time since he beat Melio Bettina in their rematch. Rooney and McGinley, working loosely with Jacobs, copromoted the May 27 card with Dapper Dan Charities. Though the local agents put together a fine undercard, for the main event, Conn's opponent was the decidedly unexciting Buddy Knox.

A native of Dayton, Ohio, Knox's recent history was suspect, to be kind. He began 1941 with a victory over Dan Merritt but followed that with consecutive losses to Tony Musto, Melio Bettina, and Jimmy Bivins. His last outing before meeting Conn was a draw against Buddy Walker.

"Billy and I could make a good living for years fighting bums," Johnny Ray said, in what could be viewed as a thinly veiled reference to Conn's recent, uninspired opponents. "But," he added, "we're giving up all that to fight Louis. Some guys say I'm crazy; that Louis will knock Billy out and make us start near the bottom again. Don't you think I've figured all that out? Don't you realize that Louis isn't much more than one-half the fighter he was a few years ago, and that both Billy and I are afraid that Buddy Baer will beat him before we can get a shot at him?"[74]

Amazingly, Ray's trepidation, mentioned in an offhand manner, came uncomfortably close to realization. Knowing his future was distinctly tied to the Louis–Baer match, Billy sat at home listening to the bout on the radio. "I heard the fight on the air and then went to bed and slept peacefully," Conn told Harry Keck. "If it took Louis that many punches to finish off Buddy, I know I have nothing to worry about. . . . I'll tell you, though, I was scared for awhile. That was when Buddy knocked Joe out of the ring in the first round. I thought, 'uh-oh there goes my title chance right out the window.'"[75]

Indeed, the deservedly unheralded Buddy Baer put the champion through the ropes with a terrific left hook. Baer also inflicted a cut on Joe's left eye, the first time in his career that the champ suffered such an injury. Still, despite being dazed momentarily, Louis regained his composure and took the fight to Baer. At the close of the sixth, Louis struck Baer after the bell had rung. According to the official timekeeper, the blow came three second after the round ended. In the chaos that followed Joe's inadvertent foul, Baer's manager, Aneil Hoffman, entered the ring. Hoffman protested loudly and bitterly to referee Arthur Donovan that his fighter should win by disqualification. Instead, Donovan awarded the fight to Louis due to Hoffman's presence in the ring. Though much comment and second-guessing ensued, Donovan dismissed such talk. He believed Baer wouldn't have survived the seventh round, he argued; Buddy was already a badly beaten fighter.

The events at Griffith Stadium added even more intrigue to the Conn–Louis soap opera. On the one hand, Baer's initial showing gave renewed hope for Billy's chances against Joe. If the slow-footed Baer could break through Louis's defenses, then the nimble legs of Conn could certainly trouble the champion.

Publicly, Jacobs continued to play coy and refused to commit to any particular matchup. In fact, following Baer's surprising showing in Washington, Uncle Mike hinted that Buddy might be given the opportunity to avenge the controversial ending at Griffith Stadium. And, Jacobs let it be known to all, if Conn failed to make a strong showing against Knox, then Baer it would be come June.

"I'll look good, all right," Billy said from Monk Ketchel's gym, where he was busy training for Knox. "And, how good did Louis look in that first round and when he got his eye cut later against Baer, and how good did Baer look when he got knocked out?"[76]

A beautiful spring day helped contribute to the record-breaking attendance. The largest fight crowd in the city's history turned out for Billy's homecoming—27,042 ticket buyers shattered the old record of 20,005, which was set in 1934 for the Teddy Yarosz–Vince Dundee middleweight title bout at Forbes Field.

Seemingly, any of the ill will that a portion of Pittsburgh felt toward their native son had either been forgiven or forgotten. Local adversaries like Yarosz and Zivic, who had drawn some parochial support away from Conn, were no longer in the same class as Billy. The East Liberty flash was now representing the town, the entire town, as he neared completion of his quest for the most revered sporting championship in the world.

The streets of Oakland were abuzz with anticipation and activity early in the day. Fans began milling outside Forbes Field as early as three o'clock waiting for the general admission gates to open at five. The typically congested roadways were overflowing with autos, streetcars, and buses, backing traffic up for miles around the city.

Though the streets around Oakland may have been hectic, order was kept inside the ballpark thanks to prodigious planning by Rooney and McGinley. Some fifty Duquesne Dukes football players served as ushers, rectifying an age-old problem at local matches of patrons not locating their proper seats. Approximately three hundred policeman and an additional fifty Allegheny County and Pittsburgh detectives were assigned to the event for security and traffic concerns. Yes sir, the Rooney-McGinley team went first class this time around. There was also the added incentive of an attractive undercard, which included Harry Bobo–Lee Savold and Pat Comiskey–James Johnson.

As the headliners entered the ring, jeers filled the air. The throng was vociferously objecting to the verdict awarding the previous match to Harry Bobo. The boos and catcalls overwhelmed Harry Krause's attempt to announce Conn and Knox.

Conn didn't disappoint the large gathering. He gave them a slow start, as they had come to expect, but when Billy finally turned it on, he assailed Knox with a murderous body attack. In the sixth, Knox went down on what was officially counted as a knockdown, but the fall could have been viewed as a slip. The following round, however, Buddy went down and there was no doubting the cause of his demise.

As he danced to the middle of the ring to start the seventh, Johnny shouted the admonition, "Not to get wild," which was duly ignored. With one of the most dynamic displays in his career, Conn landed a left hook to Knox's head. The blow sent the Ohioan reeling into the ropes. Billy quickly moved in on his staggered opponent and struck him with a solid right, which sent Knox to the canvas. At the count of eight, obviously stunned, Knox rose, only to be returned to the floor with a lethal right to the stomach.

With great grit, Buddy arose once again at the count of eight. Obviously dazed, Knox stood at mid-ring, bent at the waist, as the bell brought the round to a close. It took Buddy's handlers only a moment to realize their fighter had seen enough, and they wisely threw in the towel.

"A left hook to the temple was the blow which knocked me down the first time, and my mind went blank after that," Knox explained. "I don't remember being knocked down the other two times. . . . He doesn't have much of a right," he added, unprompted. "That left is a honey, though. I thought I would lick him when we first started out, but that blow just knocked everything out of me."[77]

"I needed the workout," Conn told the large contingent of Gotham scribes who traveled to Pittsburgh for the fight. "I'm ready for Louis now, and I'm going to give him the same kind of medicine."

A writer informed Conn that Joe had failed to turn out for the bout as had been anticipated. "Say," Billy quipped, offering a display of confidence that the newsmen would hear much of in the ensuing weeks, "he must have been afraid to show up."[78]

Nine That Conn Boy Talks Too Much

With a wink, Ray assured Chester Smith that he and Billy were running things, not Uncle Mike. In his *Press* column two years prior, Smith questioned the prudence of Ray tethering his fighter to Jacobs's authoritative jurisdiction. Johnny dismissed Smith's worries that he and Billy relinquished their independence to the New York promoter, "We're not going to be bossed, and you'll see what I mean," Johnny told Smith.[1]

Following the Barland fight, a match that Jacobs decidedly opposed, Ray looked up Smith when he returned to Pittsburgh. "See what I told you, we're doing as we please."[2] Stubbornly, Johnny again forsook Jacobs's wishes when he matched Billy against Buddy Knox. Ray's reasoning was sound. His fighter needed the work against heavyweights, a lucrative payday in front of the home crowd. . . . The downside was also present: a poor showing by Billy or, heaven forbid, a loss. These negative possibilities played no part in Ray's decision-making process, and the boastful manager crowed to Smith in the dressing room following Billy's victory. "Now you know who's running the show—it's Billy Conn and Johnny Ray and nobody else. We do what we please, and if they don't like it they know what they can do."[3]

Full of himself and his managerial dexterity, Ray arrived in New York prepared to dictate terms to Jacobs. Louis may have been the champion, but it was Billy the public was clamoring to see. Uncle Mike wasn't a naïf, however, and no one imposed his or her conditions on him.

The summit took place in Mike's office on May 28, and any notion Johnny had that he was directing the meeting was quickly dispelled.

Ray and Jacobs wrangled as they tried to arrive at terms—again. The initial agreement, reached the previous November, was breached when Billy fought Barland in Chicago. The disagreement between the two reached such a fevered pitch that Jacobs played his ace in the hole. Present at the conference was Lou Nova and his manager, Ray Carlen. At the height of his argument with Ray, Jacobs looked to Carlen and asked if he and his fighter would like to step in and face Louis on June 18. Carlen readily agreed.

Though he had a good hand to play himself, Ray was not willing to call Jacobs's bluff. Humbled and peeved at Jacobs's tactics, Johnny restrained his gaming instincts, which usually failed him, in any case. Sober and clear thinking, a gambling condition in which Ray never found himself, Johnny capitulated and gave in to Uncle Mike. He and Junior were too close to let this chance slip away in a fit.

Formalities were still to be met. Louis needed to place his signature on the contract also. That ceremony would also take place in Jacobs's office, more for the benefit of the press than anything else.

Since the Knox fight, Johnny was wearing out the rails between Pittsburgh and New York. Ray returned from his showdown with Jacobs, only to depart for Gotham once again two days later. Leaving Pittsburgh on the afternoon of the 1st were Ray and Conn's sparring partners, welterweights Johnny "Red" Cregan, Mike Lucas, and Steubenville's Jack Stauffer.

Just prior to Ray's exodus, Billy had his final workout before leaving for New York himself. He closed out his session at the Lyceum brimming with confidence. "I think I got a good chance to win—otherwise I wouldn't want to be in there," he said. "Louis is not the fighter he was a year ago, and as for his punching—well, he ain't going to hit me with those sucker punches."[4]

Later that evening, under a veil of great secrecy and with a private police escort, Billy quietly boarded the midnight train from Pittsburgh to New York. The covert maneuver was an effort to avoid a disruptive send-off party for the departing hero. Free from unnecessary hoopla, a relaxed Conn slept through much of the trip. Well rested when he arrived in the city, the first stop for Billy was Pioneer Gym and five rounds of limbering exercises in addition to several rounds of sparring with Cregan. The smaller Cregan wore headgear with a nose guard, which, according to one witness, made him resemble Boris Karloff. Billy pulled his punches on his stablemate lest he knock poor Red out for the duration of camp. He didn't, however, pull his punches when speaking of his opponent.

"I'm in shape now," Billy declared following the brief workout. "Louis has been in training for those bum-of-the-month guys since December. He must be getting stale."[5]

He could win. He would win. This he was sure of. Not because victory was preordained or anything like that, but because he had the smarts, the ability, and a plan. That's why he was going to beat the champion. There were some in the press who thought he had a shot also. That is, those writers cautioned, Billy had a chance as long as he didn't allow that Irish temper to get the best of him.

A match of such magnitude demanded more space; room for Billy's newfound entourage and the enlarging press corps who were entranced by Billy the Kid. Following his session at Pioneer, Billy, Johnny, and company left the city for Pompton Lakes, New Jersey, their home for the next two and a half weeks.

Pompton Lakes was selected as Conn's training site over Long Branch, New Jersey, on the advice of Billy's physician, who thought seaside air would not be beneficial to his preparation. The location had certainly proved advantageous for Louis, who used Pompton Lakes for each of his New York title defenses. For his date with Conn, Joe set up camp at Greenwood Lake, New York.

On June 3, the long-anticipated match was made a reality. Sitting at a desk in Jacobs's office, Conn and Joe Louis sat side by side as they signed their names to a binding agreement to meet June 18 at the Polo Grounds.

Reporters present were anxious to interpret Conn's body language when Billy met with Joe face to face. This would be the telltale sign. Was the kid intimidated by the champ? The fight could be over right here, some of them thought, if Conn exuded any anxiety and trepidation upon encountering Louis in the flesh. Anyone who *knew* Billy, however, understood that fear was not an emotion inherent in his makeup.

With an outstretched hand, a relaxed and genial Conn greeted Louis, "Hello, Joe, how are you?"

"Hello, Billy, how do you feel? You look like you're gaining weight."

"I am, Joe, weigh about 180. I saw your pictures the other day of the Baer fight."

The cordial but unsubstantial conversation continued.

"You did?" Louis asked, "You trainin' at Pompton?"

"Yes," Billy replied.

"You don't train much in the country, do you?"

"No, not very often, I always trained at Pioneer for my fights around New York."

"Pompton is okay. Everything is together."

"I hear you got quite a farm."

"Yes," Joe said, "nice place." Before he could elaborate on his newly purchased spread, the commission president, John J. Phelan, brought the meeting to order.

The contract specified that the champion would receive 40 percent of the gate, while the challenger was to get 20 percent. Ray also agreed that, should his fighter win, they would give Louis a rematch within sixty days. Both Louis and Conn posted a $5,000 forfeit with the New York Athletic Commission, which guaranteed their appearance for the match. Jacobs also posted $5,000 to ensure that he would put on the fight in accord with state commission requirements.

Together for seven years in a professional relationship, Johnny and Billy had always worked without a written contract. For the two, their word was their bond. For the New York State Commission, however, something on paper was needed to meet its standard. At the meeting in Jacobs's Twentieth Century office on Broadway, Ray and Conn met the state requirements by signing a one-year contract.

Johnny used the occasion to flex his muscles, and asked for something he knew was out of line, especially for a challenger. Due to Billy's proclivity for starting off his fights slowly, Ray made the appeal that his boxer be allowed to enter the ring "hot," rather than forcing him to sit through prefight festivities and introductions.

"Ridiculous," Phelan said of Ray's request. "Conn must come in as usual. If he wants to be hot, then his handlers had better bundle him up in plenty of clothes, towels and bathrobes."[6]

The following afternoon, sports sections across the country reported that a New York company came to Johnny with a solution: an electric blanket that could be plugged into an outlet in Conn's corner. The innovation was so unique and the idea so absurd that amused sportswriters had a field day with the proposal. One writer suggested Billy could "squat on his stool and be simmered or done medium rare," depending upon the setting Ray chose. And following introductions, Conn could be served to Louis "piping or just well done."[7] The "Kilowatt Kid" denied that he ordered electric booties to match the new blanket.

The notion of an electronic coverlet amused and inspired Havey Boyle.

> It might also be well for the Conn retinue to consider the virtues of the electric eye. This device, so popular in horse racing to determine the winner of a nose-and-nose race, might be installed so that as soon as Louis' gloves would get within a certain distance of Conn's façade an alarm would be sounded and Conn could take to a storm shelter.
>
> The storm shelter would be a simple thing to rig up under the ring. A series of trap doors in the ring floor could be cut and perhaps the spring would synchronize with the electric eye so that when Louis' glove would cross the controlling beam a trap door would fly open and Conn would be furnished complete coverage until the storm blew over.[8]

When the fun was over, it was a unanimous verdict among writers that the "electric blanket" debacle was a work of the imagination of Jack Miley, who had taken leave of his position at the *New York Post* to work as a publicity man for Jacobs. Once the hilarity passed, Jacobs stepped in and offered a solution that he hoped would placate Ray.

"I'm going to have both of them warm up in their dressing rooms and send them into the ring wrapped in blankets. Their weights will be announced and the fight will begin. Tape, bandages and gloves will be donned in the dressing room."[9]

Pompton Lakes was nestled in the quiet hills of Jersey, about an hour's drive from the city. Conn's headquarters, known as Dr. Bier's camp, was a spacious white frame house that sat among elms, maples, and poplars. In front of the home sat a picket fence that was at one time cream colored before the years faded and chipped away the once-fresh paint.

The rustic retreat, hired to offer Billy a respite from the city, instead became "about as exclusive as a four-alarm fire." The days had long passed since it was just Junior and Moonie; Apostoli had put an end to that. Sure, there were others around before they hit New York, like Johnny McGarvey and Milt Jaffe, but they had a vested interest in Billy. And Fierro joined the team in time to prepare for the Fightin' Bellhop. But other than family, Conn had no entourage to speak of—that is, until he arrived in New York and readied to prepare for Louis. Sportswriters from all corners of the country came to Pompton. So did friends of Billy's, "pals" that he couldn't recall ever meeting. Complete strangers also dropped in and found what looked to be "a combination convention, barbeque, and picnic."[10]

Excluding a handful of members of the fairer sex who stopped by to watch Billy's workouts, the camp was an all-male proposition. In the yard, two or three fellas could be spotted playing catch. On the porch, there was almost always a game of cards being played.

Inside the main house was organized chaos. One reporter described the atmosphere very simply: "The joint is jumpin'," he wrote. A constant rabble of conversation filled the halls as the hangers-on, newsmen, and luminaries who visited camp harangued to and fro. Down a tiny flight of stairs from the commotion sat the dining room. Hospitality was the order, and the chef cooked enough for all. A typical midday meal consisted of roast duck sandwiches, coffee, bread and butter, and Jell-O. Dinner was more taxing on the overworked chef. "I fed 43 yesterday," the hapless Willie Handeler commented, "but it looks like a new record today."

All the commotion didn't bother Billy one bit. In fact, he relished the attention and camaraderie. "Gosh, ain't it grand?" he gushed. "Don't let any of 'em leave. Why, I used to fight before crowds that were smaller than this."[11]

Curious onlookers peeked over the picket fence. They watched Johnny play pinochle under an elm, ruing his poor luck. On the back veranda, Billy lounged in an oversized chair, though a large hedge blocked the view from the road. Joe Becker, the Pittsburgh detective hired to watch over Billy, sat, as always, nearby.

"Johnny gives me the devil when I sit here in the sun without a shirt. Says it saps my strength," Conn joked, before becoming engrossed in conversation about the Pirates' fortunes. He was so preoccupied that he hadn't noticed that Johnny took leave of his card game. "Get outta that sun and put on that shirt," Ray commanded.

Looking over to his companion, Billy smiled as he pulled his shirt on over his head. "I catch more hell from him than I'll ever get from Louis."[12]

On the premises was an ancient edifice, the Colonial House, which was built during the days of the Revolutionary War. Billy prowled through the hallway of the old dwelling, peering into each room, oblivious to all history but the most recent. "Joe didn't leave any old left hooks around here, did he?"[13]

Johnny freed himself from his game of pinochle and went on a search for any available heavyweight in the city. "Conn has had almost enough experience against big fellows," Ray explained. "What he needs from now until we break camp the day before the fight is strong, tough fellows who can punch. Billy realized that Louis is going to hit him sometime, and there is no use in making it a surprise party. I'm going to get all the 200 pounders I can grab because Billy needs the kind of roughing up they will give him."[14]

He brought back with him from New York several fighters: Battling Monroe, a light-heavyweight who wore a "puzzled expression"; George Higgs, a Harlem heavyweight "long of leg and fast"; and the best of the trio, Teddy Wints, who possessed "strong legs" and whose frequent weaving and bobbing would prove mystifying to Conn. Another, Babe Ritchie, described as a "lumbering Californian," took a sound beating at the hands of Billy during their first session together.

Between the boxers brought along from Pittsburgh and those recruited from New York, Johnny was comfortable with the stable of fighters he had assembled for Billy's training. Ray then set out to implement a battle plan and exercises to prepare Conn for Louis. Among boxing experts, the overwhelming opinion was that if Billy had any chance in the ring against the champion, he would have to jab and move; to stand and exchange punches would be tantamount to committing suicide in the ring. Therefore, onlookers were both baffled and impressed as they watched Conn whale away at the midsection of his heavyweight sparring partners, using his bare strength to muscle his mate from rope to rope.

The plan, Ray told the inquisitive journalist following the workout, was to sharpen Billy's body attack. "He'll give Louis a terrible body beating—then knock him out," Johnny predicted. "We know Billy can outpoint Louis, but we want a Kayo. We want Conn to win the title impressively."

Reporters were perplexed by Ray's statement. Was this just a bluff? Surely Billy wasn't going to try to outpunch Louis. Credence could be found in this thought for Billy continued to work out with the faster welterweights in camp. Ray, however, called to mind history when emphasizing their strategy. "We all know about Louis," he said. "We know he is a total loss at infighting, although he might have looked good against certain stumble bums. Conn is one of the greatest infighters that ever lived. He punches twice as hard to the body as to the head."

Johnny called to mind recent Conn bouts against Pastor, Barland, and McCoy when Billy "went to work on the breadbaskets." Louis was, after all, twenty-seven years old, and an "old" twenty-seven at that. "He won't be able to take it downstairs for long."[15]

Ray's assessment had some validity; Louis had never faced a fighter of Billy's speed. But in his many prognoses, the manager overlooked the fact that Conn had not yet confronted a foe with the power of Joe Louis. Forgotten in Ray's frequently spouted appraisals were the opponents, Schmeling, John Henry Lewis, and Paulino Uzcudun, who were dispatched easily by the champion. More recently, Louis played around with second-rate "bums" such as Abe Simon, Buddy Baer, and Red Burmen. These lackluster performances were what Conn boosters were hanging their hopes on, and bolstered Ray's arguments.

Previously, in each weight class, Billy relied on his ability to avoid punishment, using his jab and hook as an effective counter. As a heavyweight, however, Conn seemed to forego the defensive and began to exchange punches with his heavier opponents. To do so against Louis would be pugilistic suicide; on this, all commentators agreed.

The odds were certainly against it all. Johnny in the corner, his fighter with a shot at the heavyweight title—it was a remarkable accomplishment for Ray, maneuvering his spindly fighter within one bout of the title, and with very little risk! When others questioned Billy's ability as he was coming up, if not his heart, Johnny always maintained complete faith in his boy. Likewise, many observers underrated Ray's capabilities in the corner. One thing not in question was the pair's loyalty to one another.

"If it were a two-bit piece Johnny needed, Billy was the happiest punk in the world if he had it in his pocket," Chester Smith wrote. "When Johnny turned up missing, as he did occasionally, Billy would lead the search. They were as loyal to each other as two men can be, and remember, that was before there was any indication that Conn was on the way to the top. Only Johnny Ray thought Billy would make a name for himself, and only Billy Conn swore he'd be true to no manager except Johnny."[16]

"It's a funny thing about boxing, you know it or you don't," a philosophical Ray told Havey Boyle. "Do you know I couldn't teach Billy anything now? I taught him all I knew early and all he did was improve on it. Now and then, if I see him drop into an old fault, I can remind him. But when you get a fighter like Billy, most of it's easy. It's him that does it and knows how. I never get over the thrill of seeing him when he's jabbing, hooking, dancing and blocking the way he does."[17]

Ray obviously relished his moment in the spotlight. The old lightweight spent years fighting for a pittance in virtual anonymity and he was not about to let the opportunity pass to bask in the attention being paid to him and Junior. For the big fight, Johnny forsook imbibing his beverage of choice. He may have been on the wagon and clear-headed, but Ray was no less a tangled bundle of nerves than he had been prior to earlier important fights. While Billy was enjoying the hype and excitement surrounding the buildup to the match, Ray was dying a thousand deaths. Conn did not fail to notice this juxtaposition of attitude and emotion.

"Look at him," Billy said while watching Johnny from across the veranda. "He'll be turning green almost any time now. He can't eat and he can't sleep. Well, that's what he's getting paid for. He's my vice-president in charge of worrying."[18]

He was nervous for sure, but Ray was also certain. Johnny was as convinced of Conn's imminent victory as Billy was himself. Much of the news emanating from Pompton Lakes consisted of Conn's supremely confident boasts of his impending triumph. Havey Boyle, concerned that Billy's remarks might stir unnecessary animosity in Louis, asked Ray if Billy should be a tad more modest in his prefight commentary.

"Do you think we should announce that Conn is an appeaser?" he sarcastically asked the *Post-Gazette* columnist. "Do you think he should go in saying, 'Hello, Mr. Louis' and 'I am all apologies for getting in the same ring with you?' Nuts. The world loves a fighter, a game, stand-up guy who's not afraid and besides, Conn hasn't been talking just to hear himself talk. He just feels he's going to be the champ. Me, I won't be surprised if he knocks Louis out."[19]

Rain kept the fighters indoors on Friday the thirteenth. Following his workout, Billy sat with the esteemed sportswriter Grantland Rice and introspectively analyzed the opportunity that awaited him. "Maybe it sounds crazy to you," he said, "but I'm a few days from the greatest dream I've ever known. I mean the chance to meet Joe Louis. I've been dreaming of this chance ever since I was a middleweight and whatever happens, I'm ready for it.

"I know it may sound cockeyed, but I've got the answer. In the first place I'm moving up and Louis is moving back. In the second place, I know I can out speed him and out box, I believe I can out think him. I know this too. I can take a harder punch than you fellows think I can take. And I can also punch harder. I may not knock Louis' brains out but when I tag him he'll know it."[20]

For months Conn had been verbalizing how he was going to defeat Louis. The words flowed freely and unabated, only increasing in detail and expansiveness following his arrival at Pompton. He may not have been reading the daily papers, but word of Billy's loquacious commentary reached Louis's ears nonetheless. Reporters were quick to convey Conn's pronouncements to the champion's camp at Greenwood Lake. Still, Louis was not one to easily ruffle. In response to Billy's incessant chatter, Joe austerely said, "That Conn boy talks too much." A simple, unadorned statement; nevertheless, Louis's words sent Billy into another verbal flurry.

"What does Joe want me to do, be a dummy?" he asked an amused press corps. "Doesn't he like the things I've been saying about him? What am I supposed to do, ask the great Joe Louis for permission to talk? My answer to Joe is 'Nuts.' Say, you don't suppose the Brown Bomber could be getting cold feet and start to crack up already, do you?"[21]

The *Pittsburgh Courier,* one of the leading race newspapers in the country, openly campaigned for the continuation of Louis's championship reign. Foregoing impartiality was a questionable decision on the part of the *Courier's* editors, but Louis was an icon to Black America. Conn was certainly not without his rooters. He had behind him the Irish contingent and trainloads of rooters from his hometown. However, there were also others in Billy's corner for more nefarious reasons. These backers simply wanted to see a White man defeat a Black man. For them, Conn was the Great White Hope.

Louis was not the century's first Black champion. Jack Johnson had come before him and, unlike Louis, was considered an "uppity" Black. Joe, on the other hand, had been schooled from the beginning not to repeat the seemingly offensive behavior of Johnson. The earlier champion flaunted his lifestyle, a lifestyle that included the taboo practice of dating White women, espousing unpopular opinions, and arrogantly wearing his wealth on his sleeve. Quite the opposite, for public dispersal, Louis was obsequious and reserved, keeping his comments short and to the point. Thoroughly tutored on behavior diplomacy, Joe remained staid and reserved throughout his career.

When Jack Blackburn met Joe, he offered the then-promising fighter some insight into the sport. "Let me tell you something right off," he said, "it's next to impossible for a Negro heavyweight to get anywhere. He's got to be very good outside the ring and very bad inside."

Louis heard Blackburn's words of warning. Outside the ropes, for public consumption at least, Joe was a model citizen. Inside, he was the consummate boxer, rarely placing the decision in the hands of the judges, where a Black man struggled to get a fair shake.

"Let your fists be your referee," Blackburn lectured Louis, and Joe heeded the sage advice.[22]

Perhaps because of Louis's mild manner, his intelligence was consistently under examination. The champ certainly wasn't Albert Schweitzer in boxing trunks, but neither were any of his contemporaries. When in search of great intellectual prowess, one doesn't usually seek such evidence inside a boxing ring.

Wittingly or not, Harry Keck, like many others in press row, downplayed Louis's cerebral abilities in the ring. He got by on natural instinct, was the accusation. "When he has to think or change his tactics under pressure he is lost," Keck wrote.

Billy, on the other hand, "goes about his work in a way that makes you sense instantly what he's doing," according to Keck. "You can see him think ahead in his every action."[23]

Keck's assessment of Louis's mental aptitude was curious in light of the champion's twenty-five consecutive victories, including eighteen straight successful title defenses. Curious, but not atypical. Reporters had long been guilty of peppering their prose with racially tinged commentary when assessing Louis. He was the "Dark Destroyer" and "Ol' Black Joe." The most oft-repeated stereotype was the allegation that Joe lacked smarts. Whether Billy bought into these readings, or if Jack Miley imposed his thoughts in print under the auspices of a Conn "interview," is unclear. Regardless, these beliefs were rampant. Louis was a respected champion and a "credit to his race."

The words were attributed to Conn, though most likely they were the creation of the fertile pen of Jack Miley. "Louis is just a big, slow thinking Negro," Billy supposedly said. "Nobody knows this better than Joe himself. He's a dangerous fighter because he can punch and because he's been taught well. But he's a mechanical fighter."

The quote continued, denigrating Louis's intellectual capabilities. "He can't think under pressure in the ring, and he knows it. He showed this every time he met a man who wasn't a rulebook fighter. Schmeling started hitting him with right hands in the second round of their first fight, and kept hitting him with those sucker punches until Louis was out. In 12 rounds Louis lacked the savvy to put his left hand up and block those punches."

Such supposition was not restricted to Keck, Miley, or Conn for that matter.

"Yeah," Johnny Ray said, "he waffled. Louis is as slow on his feet as he is in his brains. When he breaks out of his shuffle, he's gone. He gets all tangled up in his feet, like he did in the first Pastor fight. Billy'll move around him so fast, Louis won't be able to hit him with a shot gun. . . . Louis knows he's slippin' fast—that he ain't the fighter he used to be. Ain't got the old punch. Showed that in his last six fights. And he's stale from too much fightin' and trainin'. Can't get back the edge. He's worrying about these things. He's licked already."[24]

Years of tracking Billy's career, in and out of the ring, made a marked impression on Harry Keck. The *Sun-Telegraph*'s sports editor wasn't necessarily picking Conn to win, but he did know that the Pittsburgher exuded class.

"Class is what makes champions, and Billy has it. He is and acts like a big leaguer. He carries himself with the air of a man who is sure of himself and is not afraid to tell the world that he doesn't think there is a man in it who can beat him. . . . Class is something that is definable. It is the difference between greatness and mediocrity. It is what makes a thoroughbred in any line."[25]

Ten days in the wilderness and the country life began to wear on Conn. With playing catch banned by Johnny for fear of Billy jamming his thumb, shooting pool was the extent of extracurricular activity at camp. He had hoped to take one evening off to see the Pirates play the Dodgers at Ebbets Field. Billy's hero, Pittsburgh shortstop Arky Vaughn, stopped by camp on a Pirates day off, and Conn wished to repay the favor. Out of the question, Johnny said. "[He] said that if I did, I'd be out till 1 or 2 o'clock in the morning and it would interfere with my sleep. You'd think I was a kid. I've got more straw bosses around here than you can shake a stick at. They say, 'Willie don't do this,' or 'Willie don't do that.'

"They regulate my life from the time I get up in the morning until I go to bed at night. They do everything but fight Louis for me, but they tell me just how to do that whenever I stand still long enough to listen.

It is nice to know, though, that there are so many fellows around who know just what to do. Because if anything happens, I can just stick my head over the ring ropes and yell, 'Hey, boys, what do I do now?'"[26]

"I'm tired lookin' at nothin' but birds and rabbits. I'm going to town and stay at the Waldorf. I'll work Tuesday at the Pioneer Gym, so my Irish friends in New York can get a look at me."

Monday was a slow day for the newsmen covering Conn. Havey Boyle found material so sparse that he described Billy's attire for readers back home. Wearing a pair of slacks several inches too long, with the cuffs rolled up, and a "nightmare"[27] of a shirt, the tail of which hung casually outside his pants, Billy's last day at Pompton Lakes began with a trip to the local barber for a shave and a haircut. As he had been for the duration of his training period, Conn remained the most relaxed man at camp. His free and relaxed demeanor eased the tension for others, though Johnny continued to worry enough for everyone.

For his last workout before moving into the city, Billy donned a protective helmet and oversized sixteen-ounce gloves. He went two rounds each against three heavyweights, Battling Monroe, George Higgs, and Teddy Wints. Before sending out Monroe, Ray instructed him to go out there swinging and "don't stop." "I'll give ya a bonus if you keep punching."[28]

Most onlookers agreed that it was Conn's least impressive workout to date. Both Monroe and Higgs were able to land hooks to Billy's midsection, and easily found the range to connect jabs to Conn's head. Johnny diverted attention away from Billy's poor showing, and instead expounded on Louis's strange training tactics. Ray habitually grew more pessimistic as Billy's fights drew nearer. Something had taken hold of him, though, as his confidence continued to build as the witching hour drew nearer.

"Who ever heard of a defending champion working only four rounds two days before a fight?" Johnny asked, "That's what Louis did today. You know why—he's tired. Tired out!"

The prognosis was made with the lack of firsthand evidence, but Johnny continued unrepentant in his analysis. "Joe has been in the gym and in the ring for almost a year without a break. Very few fellows can do that—and be themselves. I am the first one in the world to admit that Louis was a great fighter, but I am almost convinced that he is not a great fighter anymore. And he realizes that his title is in danger because he will be facing the gamest, fastest challenger."[29]

A number of Billy's contemporaries had stopped and paid their respects in the days leading up to the fight. Jim Braddock came. So did Lou Nova and Fred Apostoli. No visitor captured Billy's interest, or startled Ray, more than Lew Jenkins. The lightweight champion had made himself at home at Pompton Lakes. He arrived at camp on his motorcycle and spent much of his stay riding recklessly about the countryside. Under different circumstances, Billy would have surely tried out Lew's ride; instead, Mother Hen Ray stood watch while Conn enviously watched Jenkins from a distance. Zipping along at forty miles an hour with no hands on the handlebars, Jenkins was obviously *not* accompanied by his manager.

Before leaving for New York, Billy spent his remaining hours at Pompton negotiating with Jenkins over a proposed swap of automobiles. "Whattya think of a guy like that?" Ray asked. "There's a half million dollar gate, and a championship waiting for him, and he wants to trade automobiles."

The fruitless bartering session marked the close of Billy's stay at Pompton. Later that afternoon, the team packed up and relocated to the Waldorf. Billy spent the evening with Jacobs.

On Tuesday the 17th, Johnny took his fighter to midtown Manhattan for one final workout at the Pioneer Gym. Ray walked away from the session feeling good. "You saw Billy today," he told the now-familiar faces of the press corps. "You saw him do things that no one else has ever done when fighting Louis. And he will do that to Joe, too. He is hard as a rock, game as a pebble and will be fast as lighting. And don't think that because he is fast, it will be all running."[30]

The story wasn't nearly as fresh at Greenwood Lake, a once-quiet retreat in Orange County, New York. Reporters watched, in rapt attention, for any chink in the champion's armor that they could ascertain. Onlookers agreed that Joe was showing Conn more respect than he had recent challengers. His workouts were aptly described as "serious" and "savage." Other than searching for a weakness in Louis's game, writers had little original to convey. They resorted to asking the Louis camp about Conn. Their editors had told them that the Pittsburgher was the story of the fight, and that was the lead to take.

Sitting with Harry Keck, Jack Blackburn expressed the desire to have had a chance at Billy. Blackburn harkened back to the days when he fought Al Grayber in Altoona and Harry Greb in Pittsburgh. He looked to his days in the ring and yearned to have the years back, if only for one more fight. "I wish I was younger and in there fighting Conn. I fought 'em all from Joe Gans on up to Sam Langford, and I liked to fight those boxers. Ah, Billy and I would have made a good fight."[31]

Keck asked Blackburn if all the talk coming from Pompton was annoying his fighter. "He knows most of it is ballyhoo, and anyway, he don't read the papers before a fight. They can say anything they want. It don't bother him none, like I said."

Louis confirmed Blackburn's utterance with a beautiful simplicity. "Well," he said, "the way I look at it—if Conn wants the title, it ought to be worth fighting for—and if he fights me, I'm liable to knock him out in a hurry; 'cause if he comes to me I can get a full shot at him—and if I get a full shot—well, he just ain't gonna be there long."[32]

"The Most Beautiful Girl in the World"

Exactly when their relationship became serious was difficult to pinpoint. Certainly, Billy's intentions were clear from the moment he met Miss Smith. She, on the other hand, barely gave him a second thought. It was only Billy's dogged persistence that won over her young heart.

Time passed following their first meeting in the summer of '39. The weeks ran into months, and Billy made no inroads in wooing Mary Louise, on whom he bestowed the nickname "Matt." He would send cards, letters, and flowers to her at school to no avail. Though flattered, she was hardly without other, equally determined male admirers. Her resolve broke a bit when, some months after meeting in Ocean City, when Mary was home from school, Billy asked if she would like to go to a fight. Mary Lou's answer was immediate and firm.

"No." She had no interest whatsoever in sports, especially boxing.

"Well," Conn said, not willing to give up so easily, "how about a movie?"

To this offer, Mary Louise reluctantly agreed, and to her surprise she found that she enjoyed the company of this young ruffian. He was vastly different from the more refined boys she was used to dating. He had an attractive edge to him, an irresistible sense of worldliness that the prep school boys sorely lacked. The two continued to date, and with each date, Mary Louise's infatuation with Billy deepened.

Though the romance was budding right under his nose, and despite his vigilance, Greenfield Jimmy was oblivious to the serious turn the relationship had taken. Smith and his wife Nora even accompanied the youngsters to the Pittsburgh premiere of *Gone with the Wind* at Warner Theater. At worst, Jimmy thought, it was a little harmless infatuation between the two. Smith was sure that Billy would lose interest in the much-too-young Mary, and she would come to realize that a prize-fighter offered her no real future. Surely, after a couple of dates, this flirtation would come to an innocent conclusion. One thing was for certain—Greenfield Jimmy was adamantly opposed to his daughter seeing anyone in the field of sports, and there was no athlete he was more determined to keep away from his girl than a prizefighter.

To Jimmy's consternation, however, Mary and Billy's feelings for one another only deepened. When he recognized this turn, Smith ordered Mary to stop seeing Conn. She loved her father. He was everything a father should be: providing, loving, ambitious, and, most of all, protective. There wasn't anyone in the world Mary Louise loved more than her daddy, but she couldn't abide by his wishes.

Upon Mary's graduation from Rosemont, the couple began to discuss marriage. Though no date was set, they both agreed that shortly after Billy's match with Louis would be ideal. They applied for a marriage license on May 28, which, when made public, made Daddy Smith fully aware of their true intentions. The hard part, harder than beating Joe Louis, was getting the approval of Greenfield Jimmy. In fact, Billy stood a better chance with the champ than he did wooing his prospective father-in-law to grant him permission to marry his daughter.

In his playing days, Smith earned the reputation of a fighter. In retirement, he steadfastly held to that standard, refusing to back down from anyone. He didn't care if Billy did knock out Louis and become the heavyweight champion of the world—Conn *still* couldn't take him.

Yes sir, Greenfield Jimmy would see hell freeze over before that pug married his little girl. "Win or lose, I know where those fellows end up," Smith said. "My daughter has just turned eighteen, and at her age I wouldn't want her to have anything to do with the greatest fellow in the world. . . . But they won't get married. I'll see to that. I'll beat the hell out of him, and he'd probably be the first one to say I could do it. I hope that fellow wins, but I want him to stay away from my family."[33]

The unfolding drama began playing itself out in newspapers around the country. The story was irresistible: the teenage beauty queen in love with the striking fighter, who was about to face his toughest opponent in the biggest match of his life. As if Billy didn't have enough to concern himself with, now Greenfield Jimmy was threatening his life and limbs. "Now I see I got to lick two guys," Billy said from Greenwood Lake, "Louis and Smitty. I know I can lick Louis, but that Smitty is pretty tough. I think I'll steer clear of him."[34]

Reporters, knowing a good story when they saw one, went to Westinghouse and asked his opinion of the unfolding love saga. They came from different worlds, Westinghouse and Greenfield Jimmy, and were as different as two men could be. Smith had an education and was erudite with his words. Conn was a workingman who spoke with the rough hue of the streets. A challenge to a Conn, any Conn, was an affront not to be ignored.

"He [Greenfield] might lick Billy," Conn said, "but I'll be damned if he can lick me. Who does this guy think he is? There is one thing for certain, he ain't ever punched a Conn. And it'll be a sorry day for him when he tries. . . . So he'll punch my boy Billy, will he. Listen, that guy never punched anybody without having a couple of guys hold the other fellow's arm. He was even a light hitter with a baseball bat."[35]

Mary Louise wasn't the only member of the Smith family who counted themselves as a Billy Conn fan. Her fourteen-year-old younger brother Jimmy III desperately wanted to make the trip to New York for the fight. Greenfield was adamant. "No, go upstairs where you belong."

Like his sister, though, Jimmy wasn't going to be deterred. With two and a half dollars in his pocket, Jimmy talked his pal Buzzy Kane into making a road trip to New York. The two boys hopped a streetcar in Wilkinsburg and rode it to the Pennsylvania Turnpike at Irwin. From there, Jimmy and Buzzy hitchhiked their way to Gotham. Two Irish immigrants, also on their way to the fight, picked up the adventurous boys. Along the way, the two Irishmen began venting their feelings about Greenfield Jimmy, not knowing that they had his namesake in the backseat.

"Who the hell does he think he is?" one said. "Why is he bothering Billy Conn?" These were but two of the printable diatribes the men spewed. In the backseat, Jimmy stewed, and only a constant salvo of elbows from his traveling companion kept his young Irish temper in check.

Maggie's condition had worsened while Billy was training for Louis. She had been diagnosed with terminal uterine cancer. Still she was able to offer her unique appraisal of the upcoming match. "I don't know much about boxing, but everybody's heard of Joe Louis," Maggie remarked. "He must be a great fighter and a fine man. I know he is much bigger than my Billy. But I'm not worried about that, Billy was always fighting with the boys of the neighborhood when he was six years old."[36]

Billy slipped away from Pompton to pay a visit to his mother. Nothing was ever too good for her, and now that he had a few bucks, Billy wanted her to enjoy some of the good life. He brought with him a beautiful diamond bracelet. Hell, it was probably worth more than the whole damn tenement on Shakespeare. When Billy gave it to her, though, Maggie softly refused.

"It's beautiful, but no, son, give it to Mary Louise." She then told him, that if indeed he loved Mary, then he was to marry her. Regardless of what Jimmy Smith said, follow your heart.

There was a plane to catch. Billy leaned over and kissed his beloved mother. "Maggie, I gotta go now, but the next time you see me, I'll be the heavyweight champion of the world."

Her doctor was amazed that Maggie was hanging on. She was living on sheer willpower now. But, she told her sister Rose, "I've got to live, I can't worry Billy."[37]

The war in Europe was half a world away; the reality of the escalating tragedy had not pierced the consciousness of most Americans. Following years of hard times, employment was on the rise. People were feeling optimistic about their prospects, and once again had discretionary income to spend. This new era of good feeling added greatly to the already-swelling coffers of Mike Jacobs. Herman Lewin, Jacobs's "chief box office man," set up a local ticket agency in Hotel William Penn. Tickets were also available at Owney McManus's restaurant and Goldstein's Restaurant on Fifth Avenue, and the restaurateur moved a lot of ducats for Uncle Mike. Owney alone accounted for more than $7,000 in ticket sales.

The streets of New York were flowing with revelers from the Smoky City. Over the previous two and a half years, Pittsburghers ventured to the city for Billy's fights at the Garden, but never before had this many fans made the journey. Up to 1,500 arrived in New York on one of three special trains, by automobile, or by airplane. The Shamrock Special carried 300, as did the Brown Bomber Special sponsored by Chester Washington of the Pittsburgh *Courier,* and McManus's Ham and Cabbage Special brought 400. They came to cheer for their hometown hero and they came to put their money where their hearts and sentimentality lay. With their "vulgar displays of bankrolls," these Pittsburghers put on the air of a Mellon or a Schwaub, and placed their wager on the Irish kid.

Though Jacobs had experienced the fanaticism of Pittsburgh enthusiasts with Billy's previous fights, he wasn't prepared for the deluge of requests he received. "I've got trouble enough of my own," he complained. "Them Pittsburgh people. They write in for seats, like that steel fellow today; he wants 50 seats and he wants them all in the first row or doesn't want them at all. Them Pittsburgh people, they think they got the championship already."[38]

Fight day, June 18. At noon, more than one hundred writers and nearly as many photographers gathered in the expansive New York Athletic Commission office for the official weighing-in ceremony. Dr. William H. Walker was present to conduct a physical examination of each fighter. After checking over Conn, the doctor offered an appraisal of Billy's health for the media. "Conn's pulse showed 64—and his blood pressure 128 over 70, proof that Billy is not much disturbed over what is going on or what may happen tonight. I would say that he is physically perfect—and so far as his reflexes show, he is not under any great mental strain—if any."[39]

Having already undergone his physical, Conn began spontaneously speaking into a portable microphone set up for radio broadcasters. He told his unseen audience that he was sure he'd be champion come midnight. "I'm in good shape. I think I got a good chance," he proclaimed. "I'll give him more fight than he ever got before—and I'll beat him."[40]

It was well past noon and still no sign of Louis. Peeved at what he perceived as a sign of disrespect, Conn demanded to weigh in, with or without Louis present. Billy's weight was a closely guarded secret. Reports out of Pompton Lakes claimed that Conn was hitting the scales at 180, though some speculated he was actually closer to the light-heavy weight of 175. Jacobs feared that the lesser weight would not be good for the box office. He had learned how to stretch the truth from his mentor, Tex Rickard, who implemented this practice when he promoted Jack Dempsey against Georges Carpentier, who, at 172 pounds, was knocked out in four rounds.

Either 180 or 170—it made little difference to Conn as he stepped on the scale. With a scrutinizing eye, the commissioner reported that

Billy weighed in at 174½, though that was a figment of Jacobs's fertile imagination; the challenger's actual weight was 169½.

Stepping off the scale, Billy looked around and didn't see Louis anywhere. "Where is that Louis?" Billy asked John Phelan. "I was told to be here at noon. I was here 15 minutes early. I'm not going to wait for him."[41]

With that, Conn dressed and, with Johnny in tow, headed toward the door. Phelan grabbed Ray by the elbow and asked that they wait a few more minutes; maybe Joe and his people were hung up in Manhattan traffic.

Johnny angrily pulled his arm from Phelan's pleading grasp and fairly spat at the commission chairman. "Louis ain't gonna make no chump out of us," he said. "We were here at 12 o'clock. We weighed—and we are leaving."[42]

Even the photographers present to document the moment asked Conn in vain to remain. They settled for several shots of Billy leaving the commission office. Just as Conn and his entourage reached the outer reaches of the office, the word passed that Louis had arrived. Surrounded by two policemen, his managers Julian Black and John Roxborough, and trainer Jack Blackburn, the champion entered the building. As they took their hurried leave, Ray and Conn practically brushed elbows with their opposing numbers. Not a word was spoken as the groups passed one another.

Now it was time for Louis to submit to the standard prefight medical ritual. Without a hint of emotion, Joe stepped on the scale. A deputy commissioner looked at the dial, adjusted it, and declared that the champion weighed in at 199½.

The quartet retreated to the Waldorf, where Billy was to rest until it was time to go to the Polo Grounds. When the Conn boys were involved, however, relaxation was a relative term.

In mid-afternoon, a restless Billy hollered to Fierro, who was in the next room of the suite reading the day's paper.

"Fat," he called, "come here a minute."

Fierro did as asked and set his paper down and went to Billy.

"Get a hold of Jackie and bring him up."

Reaching for the room phone, Fierro called down to Johnny Ray in the lobby. "Get Jackie and bring him upstairs, Billy wants him," Freddie instructed.

Ten minutes passed and in walked Jackie, decked out in a brazenly colored suit and with a cigar clamped in his mouth. With a flourish, Jackie announced as he entered the room: "My brother is going to be heavyweight champion tonight." Fierro had long ago grown accustomed to Jackie's bellicose ways, and he simply shook his head at the sight in front of him.

"Billy wants to see you in the bedroom," Fierro said.

Jackie didn't break stride as he continued on into the boudoir, closing the door behind him, leaving Fierro and Ray, who had also come to the room, behind. In a few moments, Johnny and Freddie heard a familiar tumult coming from the bedroom. The two exchanged knowing glances before jumping off the couch and charging into the chamber. There they found Jackie and the heavyweight challenger rolling about the floor in a mad flurry of arms and legs. With great effort, Ray and Fierro tore the two brawling brothers apart.

"What the hell are you doing, Billy, you're fighting for the biggest thing in the world tonight," Fierro chastised him. "It's the greatest night of our life and here you are taking a chance of getting your head busted open on a bed post or a cut eye or something else that will call the fight off."

Laughing, Billy shrugged off the censure. "Aw, Fats," he said, "we were only playing."

Ray and Fierro separated the two and escorted Billy into the living room, leaving Jackie alone in the bedroom. Conn took several phone calls and relaxed for the short while that he could sit still, listening to the radio and twiddling his thumbs. Finally, Billy couldn't stand the inactivity any longer. He went into the bedroom where Jackie lay asleep, his mouth agape, dead to the world and the imminent threat of his brother. Quietly, Billy left the bedroom, closed the door behind him, and phoned room service.

"Send me up a full seltzer bottle, right away."

Again, Ray and Fierro looked at each other. *This can't be good for Jackie, Billy, or our nerves,* they each silently thought.

Room service came and their apprehensions were realized. Billy took the bottle and slipped back into the bedroom, where he carefully straddled his brother's chest. Taking aim, Billy let fly the seltzer water into Jackie's open mouth. Startled and gagging, Jackie jumped to his feet and desperately tried to catch his breath.

A proud Billy doubled over in hysterics, enjoying his latest antic.

Recovered from the shock of near suffocation, Jackie found no humor in the incident and wanted blood, his brother's blood. He started chasing Billy about the room. Both Ray and Fierro made futile grabs at the boys before the brothers Conn took their act out of the living room and into the hallway. With great maturity, Billy turned to his pursuer, thumbed his nose, and stuck out his tongue. Cursing and shouting, a near-delirious Jackie crashed into a bellhop and his food cart. Au jus beef, peas, cherry Jell-O, applesauce—and Jackie—were scattered and sprawled. The pursuit was halted long enough for Ray to grab Billy and hustle him back into the hotel room, while Freddie took Jackie down into the lobby.

No day was complete without a Conn family scuffle, and this, the biggest day of Billy's professional life, was no different. *Now* he could relax until show time.

Ten Reckless Son of Erin

He reached the Polo Grounds two hours early. Without a hint of anxiety, Billy looked out the window of his elevated dressing room and looked down upon the growing crowd. For the moment, Conn's mind wasn't on Louis but rather how big the gate for the evening would be.

Well, Bill Joos told him, there are estimates that receipts could hit half a million.

"Gee," Billy said in amazement, "if there's that much dough in the house, I'll take you downtown when we get back and buy you a lot of new clothes and make a gentleman out of you."[1]

For the next two hours, Billy restlessly paced about the dressing room waiting for his moment. Eager, but certainly not nervous, in the minutes before entering the ring for the biggest fight of his career, Conn remained the essence of confidence. "I'm coming back the champion," Billy assured Johnny Ray and Joos.[2]

"From the Polo Grounds in New York City . . ."—the final preliminary had been fought, and for a moment, ring announcer Hank Balough took center stage—"the heavyweight championship of the world. Joe Louis, the champion, versus Billy Conn, the challenger. . . ." The massive crowd of nearly 55,000 drowned out any additional information Balough may have provided. On their feet they stood as one, shouting and whistling, filling the Polo Grounds with a spontaneous echo of clamor and exhilaration. Conn had made his entrance. With a smile sewn naturally on his face and his arms raised high above his head, which was covered with a white towel, Billy made his way down the aisle to the ring. Once there, he slipped through the ropes and began dancing about lightly in his corner.

From the opposite end of the park, the champion made his first appearance. With both hands hanging loosely at his side, Louis made his way slowly toward ringside to respectful applause. Once in the ring, Joe removed the towel that lay on his head and began shadowboxing in his corner.

Following the customary introduction of luminaries in the crowd, the timekeeper rang the bell three times, a signal for Balough to introduce the fighters. "The heavyweight champion, from Detroit, Michigan, weighing 199, wearing red trunks, Joe Louis."

Respectful applause welcoming the champion was soon drowned out by the roar that greeted Conn. "From Pittsburgh, Pennsylvania, weighing 174 and wearing purple trunks, the very capable challenger, Billy Conn." The crowd was still cheering Billy's name when both men met at center ring before referee Eddie Josephs. Louis listened, his head bowed, not realizing that Billy was staring directly at him, grinning broadly throughout the instructions.

"Let's have a good, clean fight, now touch gloves and come out fighting," Josephs told the fighters, who finally made eye contact for the first time, touched gloves, and retreated to their respective corners to wait for the bell.

In Pittsburgh, play between the Pirates and the Giants was halted and the lights at Forbes Field were lowered as the public address system delivered the fight via WCAE. Most ballplayers retreated to their clubhouses to listen, but several stayed behind and took the game in from the dugouts.

At 5435 Fifth Avenue, Maggie kept a vigil from her sickbed and sent word downstairs to her girls huddled around the radio to "keep praying." Up to seventeen family members or friends gathered and listened to one of three radios playing throughout the house.

The young Pittsburghers, Smith and Kane, successfully reached their destination. Once in New York, the duo's adventure took a downturn when Jimmy lost Buzzy somewhere on Broadway. Young Smith looked and looked, but in the hustle and bustle of the city streets, Kane was nowhere to be found. Jimmy abandoned the search and went to his uncle's hotel. Thomas Smith, in town for the fight, took his nephew in and plied him with a much-needed meal. More important, Thomas had an extra ticket to the fight.

On his own, Buzzy made his way to the Polo Grounds, where he proceeded to take a nap outside the ballpark. Luck was on Kane's side when five fellas from Greenfield were walking along and saw the youngster taking a nap.

"Hey, isn't that Buzzy Kane?" one of the men asked.

Indeed, it was Buzzy Kane, who encountered another stroke of luck when the boys from Greenfield told him they had an extra ticket.

Back in Pittsburgh, Mrs. Kane was fit to be tied, and she let Nora Smith know just how she felt. "I told my Buzzy not to loaf with your boy; he would get him in trouble."

At the Waldorf in Manhattan, Mary Lou anxiously sat waiting for word from the Polo Grounds with her Aunt Katherine, who was serving as Mary's chaperone.

Billy set the tone for the fight immediately. He stayed on his toes and danced, moving in, sliding out, this way and that. Conn's constant movement made him an evasive target for Louis, who stayed steady, patiently tracking his elusive prey. The second round was more of the same. Early in the stanza, Billy planted a hard left to Joe's head, which caused the champ to involuntarily blink. While the blow may have scored a point for Conn, it also served to wake up Louis, who then launched an attack to the head and body of Billy. Sensing an opportunity to close out the fight early, Joe tried to finish off Conn. With Billy pinned up against the ropes, Louis delivered a right to the midsection that doubled Conn, followed with another right to the jaw. Though clearly shaken, Billy was fighting back when the round came to a close.

When exactly did onlookers realize they were witnessing something special? Through the first two rounds, Conn's tactics surprised no one. His only chance to win was to avoid the knockout and outpoint the champion. In the first six minutes, though, Billy succeeded in evading a knockout only. (Though he did fall to the canvas in the first when pivoting himself to elude a Louis charge, Josephs waved it off as a slip.) Beginning in the third, Conn showed what an advantage his speed was, as he continually made Louis miss. Mixing great footwork with jabs and hooks, Billy won his first round of the evening. The next few rounds were split, and at the end of six, most scorecards had the fighters even at three rounds apiece.

"Billy," Regis Welsh wrote, "during the first six rounds made Joe look as though the champion were trying to wing a hummingbird on the fly with a baseball bat."[3]

Always a slow starter, Billy continued that trend with this, the biggest fight of his life. Still, despite spotting Louis the first two rounds and sporting a nasty cut above his right eye, Billy found that his and Johnny's plan of a "retreating attack" was proving effective. Conn continued to move backward and to Louis's left, a tactic that baffled Joe. By the seventh, Billy was finding his spots and scoring regularly with hooks and jabs. "Do as I tell you—move!"[4] Johnny shouted from the corner, and Conn dutifully heeded the advice.

The eighth began a stretch of five magnificent rounds for Conn. The retreating halted momentarily and Billy went on the attack. The action was intense and one-sided. Billy used everything in his arsenal: hooks, jabs, overhand rights—he was clearly inspired. Conn peppered Joe from the jaw to the belt. A right to the chin brought a collective gasp, and then a roar, from the crowd. The round closed when Billy knocked the champ back on his heels with a left hook to the chin.

The confidence was oozing from Conn. "I got him," he told his seconds as he approached the corner.

All those title defenses, all those bums; Louis had yet to run into anything like this. This kid was brash, *and* good. "You're in a fight tonight, Joe," Billy informed the champ as they met at mid-ring to begin the ninth.

Louis agreed with the assessment. "I know it," he replied.

Seemingly at will, Billy drilled a number of straight rights to Louis's chops. In rapid succession, Conn threw full-armed rights to Joe's midsection. A left jab brought blood from Louis's nose. By the close of the ninth, the champion seemed to be in a fog, his title in serious danger.

In the tenth, though, Louis demonstrated why he was a great champion and sportsman. His title on the brink moments before, Joe came out of his corner seemingly outraged that this young punk was making a chump out of him. For the first time in several rounds, Louis pressed his opponent. At one point, Conn slipped on the canvas and went down. For the better part of four years, Louis wore the heavyweight belt with class and had been nothing but a gentleman as champion.

As Billy rose from the canvas, Joe demonstrated why he was held in such high esteem. Rather than take advantage of Conn in his vulnerable state, Louis took a step back and allowed Billy to gain his composure before he once again pressed his attack. The combatants stood toe to toe furiously exchanging blows when the bell sounded the close to the stanza.

In the Conn home on Fifth Avenue, Aunt Annie McNeely fled from the radio at the opening bell. She was too anxious to listen. Conversely, Billy's sisters edged ever closer to the sounds of the broadcast. While the adults in the house cautiously tempered their enthusiasm, Peggy Ann and Mary Jane couldn't control their building excitement. "He's gonna do it! Billy's going to do it!"

At Forbes Field, the normally bright fluorescent lights were dimmed as the eerily quiet crowd sat forward on their seats intently listening to Don Dunphy detail the action from the Polo Grounds.

"Conn, a hard left to the champion's head. Louis winces but moves back in. Ten seconds to go in round ten, ten seconds. Conn a left hand to the jaw misses. Louis, a short left, Conn moves away from it. There's the bell for round ten."

Through the eleventh, Billy demonstrated his mastery of boxing. Louis appeared tired and confused; an easy target for the wily and willful Conn.

The remarkable contrast separating the fighters was evident to their respective corners between the eleventh and twelfth. Conn was an animated chatterbox throughout the rest period, telling Johnny and Bill Joos just how easy the whole thing was—Louis was a fixed mark for him. Ray, ever the cautious man, reminded Billy that he needed to keep on the move. There were still four rounds to go.

On the opposite side of the ring sat a dazed, seemingly drugged, Joe Louis. He appeared to be a beaten man. This feeling was not dispelled through the anxiety displayed by his cornermen. Roxborough and Blackburn furiously worked over their man, offering encouragement and instruction despite the dire circumstances.

Billy resumed his running dialogue with Joe during the twelfth. He backed up his words with a full-armed left that shook Louis back on his heels. Staggered, Joe fell forward into a clinch. Sensing Louis's vulnerability, Conn tried to put the champ down. With an array of blows,

Billy emerged from the clinch with his sights set on Joe's chin. These blows were not the variety Conn's critics had long ago dismissed as being "powder puff." Louis was obviously shaken, if not hurt. The fans, sensing an impending upset, were on their feet, the volume of their cheers rising with each Conn punch. Louis returned to his corner at the close of the round, still standing after enduring fifteen unyielding blows to his stomach and noggin.

Blackburn saw that Billy was too eager, too confident, and was occasionally missing with his left, which left him wide open. He told Joe just what he was seeing, and to watch for such an opening. Though dazed, Louis listened intently and nodded wearily in agreement.

Freddie Fierro met Billy at mid-ring and escorted him back to his corner.

"I'm going to knock that sonofabitch out." Ray and Fierro couldn't believe their ears. No, no, they pleaded. Coast in, stick and run. Keep movin'.

Billy's mind was already envisioning Louis lying beneath his feet. The crowd's roar was ringing in his ears, their anticipation, his visions of grandeur, Louis's desperation—all were intertwined as the timekeeper reached for his mark.

It immediately became apparent that Ray's counsel was not being implemented. With a broad grin creasing his face, Billy met Joe in the middle of the ring. The dancing had stopped; Conn was measuring Joe for the big blow. A minute into the round, Billy moved in with a terrific combination: a dozen or more punches furiously launched, most finding their mark. Still Joe remained standing and kept his right cocked, patiently waiting for the opening he knew would arrive.

Then it came. Billy hit Joe with a left to the body and one to the head, allowing Louis the chance he needed. A devastating right hand to the mush stunned Billy visibly. For the first time all evening, a look of bewilderment filled his once-assuming eyes. He had lost his ring sense, and Joe knew it. His knees buckled and Billy fell back into the ropes and Louis pursued.

It happened that quickly.

Meticulously, Louis proceeded to pummel Billy with a terrifying barrage, up to twenty blows. Billy tried to protect himself from the murderous onslaught, but to little effect. After nearly knocking Conn's head off his shoulders with a right, Louis went to work on the body. These punches sapped whatever life remained in Billy's legs. His body stood momentarily wavering with uncertainty when Joe delivered an overhand right to the jaw, shattering Billy's dream.

He's on his back.

An eerie calm enveloped the crowd. The sudden turn in the fight stunned onlookers. Eddie Josephs picked up the count from time-keeper George Bannon at four.

At seven, Conn willfully tried to reach his feet. On eight he was sitting up, staring bleary-eyed into Louis's corner; nine, he remained in that position . . . and with a wave of the hand, Josephs counted Billy out. Louis's eighteenth defense of his title, the sixteenth victory Joe had recorded by knockout. Still, Conn had done much to differentiate himself from all of Louis's other victims. No, Billy's name wouldn't be added to the Bum of the Month Club. His spirit, will, and Irish courage, if not his tactical sense, separated him from the long line of palookas that had become fodder in the Jacobs's gristmill.

Billy had just managed to reach his feet when Eddie Josephs completed his count. There were two seconds left in the thirteenth round.

Ray and Fierro were through the ropes and by Billy's side immediately. The two carefully ushered Conn to his corner before a mad rush of radio broadcasters, photographers, and police filled the ring.

Walking side by side with Johnny, Billy made the long, lonely journey to his dressing room. He walked up the flight of stairs, weak-kneed, supported by Moonie. Once there, Ray locked the door momentarily to allow Junior a moment alone. The tears had begun to softly flow before they approached the room. However, by the time Conn reached the shower, he was overwhelmed by his emotions. In the shower, with the hot water beating down upon him, Billy fell to his knees, convulsed in sobs.

Standing with his fighter under the steady stream of water, Johnny softly patted Billy on the back. "Go ahead," Ray soothingly said, "have a good one. Let it all come out."

Through the tears, Billy began spouting apologies to his manager and trainers. "I let you all down," he cried. "I let you all down." For a moment the room fell silent. Along with Johnny and Billy, Joos and Fierro stood. They had all come a long way to see such a great opportunity slip away. Finally, Johnny broke the sullen quiet that had enveloped the room. "That's all right now, Billy. Everything's all right."

Within a minute, Conn had regained control of his emotions and was ready to greet reporters with a smile. The first person through the door, however, wasn't a member of the fourth estate but rather Mike Jacobs. The normally staid Jacobs let his feelings show in a room quickly filling with reporters and Conn supporters. Uncle Mike reached a seated Billy, bent over, kissed him on both cheeks and, as a few tears trickled down his crotchety face, whispered into Conn's ear. The young fighter's face lit up. "Sure, Uncle Mike. I'll fight him again, but I'll beat him the next time."[5]

A look of warmth and affection filled Jacobs's face as he pulled away; he pinched both of Billy's cheeks and left the room.

Dozens of photographers took their stations while newsreel cameras set up their equipment. A long procession of friends came through and offered a hand and congratulations on a well-fought battle. He stood up through it all so well. "Thank you, I tried awfully hard," he quietly murmured.

"What happened Billy?" a reporter asked. "You had it in your pocket and all you had to do was hold him off for three more rounds."

"I'll bet it's the first time a fella ever lost a fight because he had too much guts," Conn answered through a weak attempt at a grin. "After the twelfth, I thought I had him and I simply couldn't do anything else but go out after him. Then it happened. . . . What's the sense in being Irish if you can't be dumb.[6]

"I have no alibis. He beat me. He's a great fighter."

What about Louis's punches? he was asked.

"All they say about his hitting is true," Billy answered. "His punches feel like a kick mule, and they really hurt when they land."[7]

"Wasn't he swell?" Johnny asked of the few newsmen still lingering in the dressing room, but he seemed lost in his own thoughts. "You bet he was—he was swell in defeat—but we'd rather have won."[8]

Across the sprawling ballyard, an unusually expansive champion held court.

"I figured it would end just as it did," Louis explained in his normally polite manner. "I felt sure that sooner or later he would be very wide with one of those lefts and that I would nail him with my right. That's just what happened."

"Billy Conn is a great fighter with a lot of heart," a gracious Louis said. "He was much faster than I was and I had a hard time catching him. . . . Anyone who says Conn can't hit hard enough to hurt you doesn't know what he's talking about."[9]

Do you think Conn stands a chance in a rematch, Joe?

"If he would fight the same fight I'd say he would have a good chance," said Louis. "I was behind, you know, going into the thirteenth."[10]

"For our money," William G. Nunn wrote in the *Pittsburgh Courier,* "Joe Louis is still the greatest champion ever to grace the ring. He proved tonight that he had it in him. With the chips all down . . . with the cards stacked against him . . . with 50,000 white folks pleading for Conn and 5,000 Negroes praying for Joe to win . . . the winner and still champion, Joe Louis. . . . Thank God!"[11]

"It was one of the most heartbreaking defeats any boxer ever suffered," Harry Keck wrote in a postmortem, "with the richest of ring titles at stake, and Billy beat himself, just as many predicted before the bout he would. They said he would lose his head and make the mistake of slugging it out with the champion and would be battered down."[12]

Too much courage. Too much Irish. In defeat, Billy enamored the public as few ever had in victory. They were charmed by his audacity. Certainly, the championship was his for the taking. Entering the thirteenth, all he needed to do was stay on his feet for three additional rounds. Foolish as it may have been, Billy wanted to earn the title by beating his opponent, not just "outboxing" him. Conn envisioned standing over the vanquished champion. He owed that much to Maggie. He wanted that much for Mary Louise.

Just two seconds more—if only he could have reached his feet before Josephs counted ten. Maybe he could have cleared his head between periods. Maybe then he would have listened to Moonie and kept moving the remaining two rounds, danced his way to the championship.

If only he had kept his head. *If only . . . if only.*

While Billy was in the shower, movie cameras were brought into the cramped room. "I fought a good man," he said, looking into the lens, "and he beat me. But if Uncle Mike will give me another chance, I think I can beat him. Yes, I'll knock him out."

Into a radio microphone, Billy sent a greeting to Maggie. "Hello, Mother. I hope you're all right. I'm okay."[13]

Maggie's sister Rose waited a few moments after the fight before carrying the bad news upstairs. Mrs. Conn showed little emotion. "That's all right Rose," she whispered. "I know. I'm very proud of Billy." Rose then conveyed Maggie's thoughts to Eddie Beachler of the *Press,* who was present to document the reaction to the fight at Fifth Avenue.

Twenty-year-old Mary Jane stifled a scream when she heard Don Dunphy describe Billy's fall to the canvas; she then broke down convulsing in sobs. Of all the family gathered in the house, none was more animated than Mary Jane. She gave a running discourse throughout the fight, yelling encouragement to Billy through the radio receiver and chastising unseen critics. "Yeah," she quipped after the tenth, "and the smart guys said he wouldn't even last that long."[14]

Through her tears, Peggy Ann told the room, "Aw, he'll get another fight and he'll beat that Joe Louis, I'll bet you."[15] The eleven-year-old redhead then went tearing out of the house and down the street. Knowing that little Rusty possessed the same scrappy traits as Westinghouse, Mary Jane called after her sister, "Don't you go fighting with anyone, no matter what they say."

For reporters, Conn had said all the right things. For the newsreels, he offered a bashful smile. For photographers, he flashed a dazzling grin. But beneath the façade, Billy was crestfallen.

The opportunity lost began to set in when Billy and Johnny vacated the Polo Grounds. Once outside the ballpark, they couldn't find a car to carry them to their hotel. The two began walking. They walked through the streets of Harlem, avenues filled with revelers celebrating the Brown Bomber's great victory. Then someone noticed the two and recognized Billy. Rather than jeer or belittle the challenger who had just fallen to Harlem's hero, a spontaneous celebration erupted when dozens of people made their way to Conn and congratulated him on his heroic effort.

Moonie and Junior continued their trek through Harlem and into Manhattan. Though each replayed the bout in his mind, little was said as they made their way. As Johnny chain-smoked, Billy walked with his head down, lost in thought. Nearing their destination, Conn and Ray parted as Johnny continued on to the Edison while Billy went to the Waldorf and Mary Lou. With a handshake and a hug, the two said goodnight; neither man dared speak of what could have been.

At the Waldorf, Mary Louise had been anxiously awaiting the phone call that Billy promised to make following the fight. He couldn't bring himself to do it, though. He didn't know what to say. The championship, all the trapping of glory that came with the crown, he wanted to share with Matt.

Finally there came a knock on the hotel room door. Mary Louise opened it to see Billy standing, tears streaming down his cheeks. "I tried my best," he said, and fell into her arms.

Eleven Where's Billy?

The next morning, Jacobs invited a number of writers to his office to listen to a recording of the Mutual Broadcasting Company's radio transmission of the bout. Ray was among those present. He sat on the windowsill of Mike's office, looking out on the bustling Manhattan street below with vacant eyes, oblivious to the blur of activity on the avenue. When the recording ended, Ray finally spoke up.

"Jeez," he cried, "what a chance my Junior missed. He had the champ going in the twelfth and the fight in the bag from the eighth round on. Then he winds up on the floor."

In an attempt to console the forlorn manager, one of the writers present said Billy had surprised them all. But the pugnacious Ray wasn't going to take any halfhearted empathy from some typewriting bloke. "Listen," Johnny said. "You guys were all wrong about that fight from the start. You guys had it doped all wrong. In the first place you said Conn would box; that he had to box to win. Well, we did just the opposite."

The newsmen agreed en masse, but all thought it was foolish to try to outslug Louis. "You don't know what you're talking about," Ray told them. "The only way to beat Joe Louis is to fight him every single minute. Louis will knock the hell out of all boxers you can find for him. You've got to find a guy who can take his punches and give them some of his own at the same time. My Billy almost did it last night. Billy fought Louis tooth and nail for twelve rounds. He moved all the time and kept punching. When he got in a corner he fought his way out, which is something no other fighter has had the nerve to do with the champion. Billy was great last night, but Louis was just a little greater when the chips were down.

"That Louis is a great sport, too," Johnny added. "That was one of the finest examples of sportsmen I've ever seen. Jeez, the guy was losing his crown and still gave my Billy a chance to get up and fight back. He had a perfect right to hit Billy then, but he wouldn't take advantage of him."

The reporters then began peppering Ray with questions they didn't have the opportunity to ask the evening before. Johnny's heart wasn't in the Q&A, though, and pulling information out of the little man proved a difficult task.

"How many rounds did Billy shadow box before he went into the ring?" Harry Keck asked.

"About two more than he usually does," Ray replied.

"There's an answer for you," a contemptuous Chicago writer snorted. "How the hell many rounds does he usually box in the dressing room?"

The previously verbose Ray had gone quiet. "I don't know," he said in a barely audible mumble, "I won't talk."

"When are you going back home?" Keck queried.

"As soon as I get word from Billy that it's safe for us in Pittsburgh," Johnny said. "I want him to make peace with Jimmy Smith first. Like Billy, I'm not too proud to fight, but I'm all tired out."

"Where's Billy?" another reporter asked. Indeed, that was the question on the minds of many. Placed side by side with the fight account in most of the country's newspapers was the story of Billy's "disappearance." The whereabouts of both Billy and Mary Louise was a mystery bandied about the front pages of dailies everywhere. Johnny, however, knew nothing more than he read in the New York tabloids.

"How should I know!" he sneered. "I'm only his manager. I don't know where he goes after a fight."

With that, the conference broke up, leaving only Ray, Jacobs, and Harry Keck. The three men sat mostly in silence, with the fight broadcast playing in the background. Keck interrupted the quiet when he broached the subject of the inevitable rematch, and what that show might draw.

"This fight means more to us than money," Johnny said. "We're not mercenary are we, Uncle Mike?" Not forgetting (or forgiving) the difficulty Ray gave him negotiating for the fight, Jacobs grumbled, "Not much, I guess you'll want a million dollars for the return fight."

"Go on and get mad," Johnny shouted. "Get mad. See if I care. I got the guy who packs 'em in. Four hundred and fifty one thousand dollars we drew. And all those guys saying Nova was the guy to fight Louis. . . . Listen, Uncle Mike. You're not taking all of the fifteen grand I owe you out of this fight. Only half of it, I'll owe you the other half so I'll have you on a string."[1]

The tension was broken when Jacobs's secretary, Rose Cohen, entered the room—there was a long-distance phone call for Mr. Ray, she said. Johnny took the receiver; Billy was on the other end of the line. The two spoke for a few moments when Keck spoke up, "Tell that guy I want to talk to him." Johnny had heard enough anyway. He threw up his hands in frustration and handed the phone to Keck.

"Where are you?" the reporter asked.

"Broadmoor, I think it is," Conn answered, though he was actually in Brockway, Pennsylvania.

"How about this marriage business, Billy? Come clean and we'll call off the hounds. Are you, or aren't you?"

Feigning ignorance, Billy asked, "Aren't I what?"

"Are you married or going to get married?"

Conn wasn't having any of that. Though he'd had a long, pleasant relationship with Keck, Billy wasn't giving Harry any scoops. Besides, Greenfield Jimmy could be listening in. You could never be too careful. "How did you like the fight?" Conn asked Keck.

"It was a great fight. You were wonderful," Harry said. "But what about this other business?"

"I can't talk."

"Who's with you?" Keck the investigative reporter queried.

"I can't say," an elusive Billy replied.

Remembering that Conn had his driver's license revoked in Pennsylvania, Keck asked, "Are you traveling by auto?"

"Yes."

"Do you want to make a statement?"

"Yes, just say I am not in a position to talk. I can't say anything."

The next few days were a blur, abuzz with activity and rumor. Where are they getting married? *Were* they married yet? Who was going to marry them? Was Greenfield Jimmy really going to "punch the hell out of" Billy?

A report came from Brockway that the couple was to be wed by Father Francis Schwindlein of Holy Cross Church. Indeed, Father Schwindlein had supposedly requested permission from the Pittsburgh diocese to perform the ceremony. This false story was born when Billy and Mary Louise drove to Brockway on the morning of the 19th. In Brockway, they were given their marriage license; from there, they called Greenfield Jimmy and asked for his blessing. Seemingly, Smith had softened his rigid stance and asked Mary to please come home. If she insisted on marrying this bum, could she at least have the ceremony at St. Philomena's? The couple, their hopes lifted, hopped in the backseat of their car and drove across state with Gabby Ryan at the wheel, arriving in Pittsburgh later that evening.

Before departing Brockway, Billy and Mary spoke with a newsman who asked the question that was on the minds of many. "All of our troubles have been settled and daddy has given his full consent and blessing," an ebullient Mary Louise gushed.

"And," Billy added, "tomorrow I'm going to marry the sweetest girl in the world."[2]

The news of the sudden change of events spread quicker than Billy's spanking Chevy could reach home. Early the following morning, hundreds of kids gathered outside St. Philomena's while several newsmen staked out Conn's Fifth Avenue home. At 5:00 A.M., Greenfield Jimmy was spotted briefly visiting the parish house at St. Philomena's. Was he there to arrange the wedding, or politicking to prevent one?

Shortly after 9:00 A.M., Billy emerged from his home, decked out in a checked coat over a sport shirt open at the collar and gray pants; hardly an outfit befitting a groom-to-be.

"Where are you going Billy?" someone shouted as Conn moved toward a waiting taxi.

"I'm just going to see a fellow," he hollered back, from across the street.

"Are you going to get married today?"

Billy paused for a moment before ducking into the car. "I don't know yet," he answered.

The ambivalent response kept alive the hope of a ceremony at St. Philomena's later that day. Into their cars the newsman leapt, hot on the heels of Conn's cab. The taxi drove for a couple of miles before pulling up to the home of Mary's grandmother on Greenfield Avenue, where Billy jumped from the car and went directly through the front door without fielding any questions.

Mary was present also, having spent the night at her paternal grandmother's. Speculation and conjecture grew as men of the cloth came and went from the residence throughout the morning. Surely something was happening in there. Perhaps they were negotiating a compromise on the reading of the banns. The banns of marriage required that approaching weddings be announced for three consecutive Sundays in one's parish, unless the bishop gave special permission. It became apparent, as a downcast Billy emerged from the home, that good news was not forthcoming.

"No wedding today," he glumly told those huddled along the sidewalk. "It may not be for sometime yet. . . . You can say that I'd love to be married today, but I can't."[3]

The press wanted specifics, though. What happened, Billy? Why no wedding today? Conn politely demurred, though. "Joe Louis caught me with my mouth open, so I'm keeping it still now."

He then subtly changed the subject. "Johnny Ray is bringing the cake tomorrow," Billy offered.

Wedding cake?

"Naw, I mean the dough, the money I got for fighting Louis. That's the only kind of cake I'm interested in cutting."[4]

Conn didn't give a reason for the cancellation, or postponement, or whatever it was that happened. He politely excused himself and slipped into a waiting car.

What happened? Had the Pittsburgh diocese not waived the customary reading of the banns? Perhaps. More likely, Jimmy Smith applied pressure to the local diocese. Jimmy insisted that the Church not marry his child, and with the influence Smith wielded, the Pittsburgh diocese didn't want to buck him, despite the public clamor for a marriage.

For the moment, Smith had won. Whether it was premeditated or not, Jimmy had misled his daughter into coming home when he spoke with her on the telephone. If the couple wanted to exchange vows, the ceremony wouldn't take place in the Smith's home parish of St. Philomena's.

With the wedding on indefinite hold, Billy went about his business. He and Johnny traveled to New York for a meeting with officials from Republic Studios. Conn was wanted for the lead role in the film version of Octavius Roy Cohen's magazine serial, "Kid Tinsel." Ray extended his managerial responsibilities beyond the fight game and into the world of film. Johnny publicly stated he wanted a hundred grand for Billy's first acting role, because "money doesn't mean anything to the people of Hollywood, and $100,000 is a cheap price for Billy as he stands today."[5] Though Ray couldn't get his price, he did negotiate a $25,000 fee for Conn—not bad pay for a novice.

The New York newsmen were interested in Conn's prospective film career, but they were even more curious about his forthcoming marriage. They peppered Billy with questions, most of which he answered solely with a smile.

"It will take me some time to soften up the old man," was all he offered his inquisitors.[6]

The visit to New York was shortened when Conn received an urgent call from home. Maggie had suffered a relapse, he was told. Billy was on the first flight to Pittsburgh.

There was little he could do for her now. She was slipping in and out of consciousness. It was only a matter of time; Billy sensed it and Maggie knew it. Though he wanted to stay by her side, Maggie insisted that Billy go ahead with plans he and Mary had made to visit Atlantic City. He balked at the suggestion. "No," Billy said. "I want to be here for you."

In a voice too weak to rise above a whisper, Maggie told her son, "Go Billy," she insisted. "Go be with Mary Louise."

Reluctantly, and with great hesitancy, Billy finally agreed to Maggie's wishes. "OK, mom, I'll go to the shore, but I'll see you in a few days when I get back."

"No, son," Maggie said, "the next time I see you will be in Paradise."

The next evening, Billy and Mary Louise were dining at the Marlborough Blenheim on the Atlantic City boardwalk when a newspaper reporter approached.

"Billy, you're wanted on the telephone," he said.

Conn went to the phone and listened quietly to the voice on the other end of the receiver. A moment later, Billy hung up the telephone and returned to Matt. He didn't need to say a thing; his face revealed more than a thousand words could ever hope to say.

"My mother died," Billy simply told Mary.[7] He knew the day was coming for some time. Only Maggie's steely determination kept her alive so long. Still, the news numbed Billy. As the tears streamed down his face, the only life he could feel was the comforting warmth of Mary Louise's arms.

Conn accompanied Mary to Ocean City where she remained while Billy went on to New York, where he flew home to lay Maggie to rest. He found a place for her in Calvary Cemetery, in the closest spot to Harry Greb's final resting place available.

Etiquette deemed that Mary and Billy wait an appropriate amount of time before marrying. Out of respect for Maggie, Conn believed, a proper period of mourning should be acknowledged first. Nonsense, Westinghouse told his son; Billy's brothers agreed with this. Before she passed, Maggie gave them her blessing and she wanted her Billy to wed Mary Louise. There was no need to wait. Furthermore, if Billy was waiting until Jimmy Smith gave his approval, well, then the wedding would never come to be. The Conn family was furious with Smith. This whole affair wasn't about Billy's chosen career path, they believed. Rather, Jimmy disapproved of his daughter's suitor because he came from "the wrong side of the tracks." Smith wasn't just judging Billy; he was judging the whole Conn clan—at least, that's how they saw things.

Billy took his family's counsel to heart. He left home and returned to the Jersey coast with Gabby Ryan. The two picked up Mary Louise and left the shore for Philadelphia. Before leaving Pittsburgh, Billy had made arrangements for him and Miss Smith to marry in the City of Brotherly Love. On July 1, the couple quietly slipped into St. Patrick's Church. Father Schwindlein received special dispensation to perform the modest ceremony, which took place at two o'clock. Standing as witnesses were Billy's best man, Gabby Ryan, and Mary Louise's maid of honor, Mary Byrne. In fact, Miss Byrne didn't even know who the couple was; she worked in the rectory of St. Patrick's.

The beautiful bride had a red rose in her hair, which matched her alligator slippers, and wore a white playsuit dotted with brown. They exchanged their vows, each promising to love and cherish the other. Through triumph and tragedy, until their dying breath, Billy and Mary Louise swore allegiance to one another. In front of God, their love was confirmed, and to symbolize this commitment, Billy slipped onto his bride's finger a simple band of gold, the same wedding ring his mother had worn.

The newlyweds retreated to Atlantic City for a few days. Amazingly, despite all the scrutiny in the preceding weeks, the wedding escaped the notice of the press. In fact, for three days the marriage remained a secret from all but those present, until the Conns met with the press at Mike Jacobs's farm in Rumson, New Jersey. Prior to speaking with the media, though, the news needed to be broken to Greenfield Jimmy, who was in Ocean City.

The first question was the obvious one: how did Mary Louise's father react when informed of the wedding?

"You wouldn't be able to print what he said," Billy said.[8]

Did they receive Smith's blessing?

"We got blessed all right," Conn answered ruefully. "But it wasn't the kind of blessing you could print. Mary's father was mighty sore. He had been trying to block the wedding, but we managed to sidestep his operatives. We had to work fast because her old man is tough and he's madder than hell."[9]

Mary stepped forward and softened the tone. "My father and mother both think we are a couple of kids, but this wasn't one of those spur of the moment things, and we're going to be happy, terribly happy, just as we are now."

"Mary's father just don't like me," Billy interjected. "I'm a fighter, that's why. Just because a fellow's a boxer, you shouldn't hold it against him. I think I'm a fine gentleman. Everybody in the world says I'm all right. My wife loves me because she believes I'm an all right guy, with no fancy airs like a lot of people might want me to have. Just a plain everyday guy with nothing phony about me.

"In the Catholic Church, when a priest marries you, you're married forever. It goes for keeps, and I'm mighty happy about it.

"Understand," Billy added, "I'm not running away from him. I'm not running from anybody. I want to meet him because I want him to be my friend. I never hurt anybody and I don't think this will hurt him or Mary Lou. But what can you do with a wild man."

What's next?

"I think we'll go see my friends Bob Taylor and Barbara Stanwyck and stay out there about a month." Conn was referring to their upcoming Hollywood excursion, set for the 15th. He wouldn't stay out west, Billy assured his questioners; boxing was still his game.

"I'm not a movie star," he said. "I'm a fighter. And if I ever get another shot at Louis, I'll be the heavyweight champion."[10]

Since releasing their first film in 1935, Republic Studios had specialized in B movies and serials such as *The Lone Ranger, Captain Marvel,* and *Zorro,* among others. *The Pittsburgh Kid,* as the film was now titled in the hopes of capitalizing on Billy's vastly increased national profile, fit Republic's formula perfectly. Good wholesome fun, with a little murder mystery tossed in. The script may have been lightweight, but it was a fine vehicle to showcase the handsome, gutsy kid from the Smoky City.

The shoot was scheduled for sixteen days; Billy's contract read that should filming run over, he would be paid $1,200 a day on top of his contracted fee of $25,000. And, as Conn told a Chicago reporter on the way to California, "That ain't hay, is it?"[11]

Accompanied by Johnny Ray and Milt Jaffe, the Conns arrived in Los Angeles on July 14, following a brief stay in the Windy City where they spent time on Charley Bidwell's yacht cruising Lake Michigan. Their first day in Hollywood was a whirlwind of activity as Mary and Billy were honored at a noon luncheon at the Biltmore. From there they were taken to Republic Studios on Radford Avenue, where a group of ingenues greeted Billy. Having seen photos of the couple, studio heads were taken with Mary's natural beauty and wanted to find a part for her in the picture. A screen test was set up for the new Mrs. Conn. While his bride was put before a camera, Billy was given makeup tests. After he was finished being painted up like a mope, Conn spoke with a *Los Angeles Times* reporter.

"I should have knocked Joe Louis' block off," he said.

Well, the writer asked, we know about your boxing abilities, but what about acting?

"No, I've never done any acting in my life. But what the heck. They say they are going to have a fellow there to show me how to box. That's all I need. If Max Baer can act, so can Billy Conn."

Standing nearby, fulfilling his mother-hen role, Johnny spoke up. The visit was all acting, he said, dispelling rumors that Conn would box while on the coast. "There won't be fighting while we are out here," Ray added. "We don't want to go near any gymnasium."[12]

Filming began the next day. Apparent immediately, Conn hadn't learned the art of diplomacy, which was an important facet in negotiating the fragile egos of movieland. Hollywood was a far cry from the streets of East Liberty where people cracked wise to one another and didn't sugarcoat opinions. From the start, Billy made producers nervous with his candor and humor. When Conn asked his makeup man if he was an out-of-work barber, the quip almost caused union difficulties.

Upon meeting his leading lady, Jean Parker, Billy mentioned that he had once seen her in Pittsburgh on a publicity tour for one of her early films.

Well, Miss Parker asked, what did you think of me?

"I didn't think you were much good," he told her.[13]

Always comfortable in his own skin, Billy was no different on the set; that is, until he was required to kiss his costar in one scene. Take after take, boxing's leading man looked as if he was kissing "a brick wall." Finally, director Jack Townley recognized the problem: Mary Louise had been on the set every day watching the filming. Townley realized that Conn was uncomfortable smooching another lady in front of his bride, and asked Mary to leave the set for the duration of the take. That did the trick. Billy was able to complete the scene, though the on-screen buss still lacked the passion portrayed in a Tyrone Power kiss.

While he couldn't be described as a temperamental actor, Billy did refuse to follow the script in one particular scene. The screenplay called for Conn to be knocked flat on the canvas. Too proud to lie down for anyone, even fictitiously, Billy adamantly refused to do as directed. The scene was altered so Conn would just have to go down to one knee following a solid punch to the jaw. Even that he couldn't do convincingly.

Between scenes, Townley asked Billy if he would mind doing a re-take.

"Sure, what will I do?" Conn asked.

"I'd like to get a shot of you flat on the canvas," the director asked.

"No sir," Billy said, shaking his head. "Only one man's spread me on the floor and even then I wasn't really flat. I don't need this job that bad."

His other "job" became a topic of conversation when Mike Jacobs came to Los Angeles, ostensibly to meet with Ray and Conn, but also to appear in *The Pittsburgh Kid.* A month had passed since the Louis fight and still Billy wasn't lined up to meet anybody; Jacobs wanted to strike while Billy was prominent in the public eye. "I have several fights in mind for Billy if they will listen," Jacobs explained. "I want to see what they think about Max Baer."[14]

Surely Jacobs wasn't serious. At that stage of his career, Baer was no longer a viable opponent. However, after Billy attended the Bob Pastor–Turkey Thompson match at Gilmore Field, L.A. writers began speculating that Pastor and Conn would meet again. Pastor, who had been denigrating Billy's performance at the Polo Grounds, seemed to be building interest in such a bout. His manager was also open to such prospects. "Sure," he said, "We'll fight that bum anytime, anywhere."

Ray told reporters that he was also open to the possibility—for the right price.

Filming wound to a close without the participation of Uncle Mike. Jacobs left for New York early due to a stomach disorder. Though Mike's screen debut would have to wait, there were several cameo appearances by members of the boxing fraternity. Freddie Steele was briefly on-screen, as was Henry Armstrong, who sparred with Conn in one scene. Ironically, Arthur Donovan was hired to play the referee in Billy's movie bouts.

How did Billy feel about such casting after he and Johnny had refused Donovan for the Louis fight? "Oh, that's OK," Billy laughed. "I've read the script. I already know who wins this time."[15]

Jacobs wasn't the only one not appearing in the film. Despite her great beauty, Mary Louise wouldn't be embarking on a career in the movies. Though her screen tests impressed producers, Billy refused the studio's offer to place her in the picture as a cigarette girl. "One actor in the family is good enough," he explained. "Besides, she's too pretty and talented and might want a picture career."[16]

Truth be told, neither Billy nor Mary Louise was cut out for the Hollywood life. "We were too young," she later said, "and we weren't sophisticated enough for Hollywood."[17]

Before the couple left for home, Jack Warner offered Billy another role. This time, he wouldn't be playing himself but rather the lead role in a film based on the life of Gentleman Jim Corbett. Despite the chance to pocket another $25,000, Billy turned it down. No thanks, he said, this life ain't for me.

The Conns returned home from their "working" honeymoon on August 3. The local media wanted to know what Billy thought of Hollywood.

"It's OK."

Not satisfied with Conn's unrevealing reply, he was pressed to be more expansive. "Well, Billy, what did you think of the whole Hollywood scene?" he was asked.

Conn wasn't playing along today, though. "It's just okay," is all he said. Some four decades later, Billy was a little more verbose in explaining his thoughts on movieland.

"That's the last place I'd be," he said. "I don't like actors and all those fake bastards."[18]

The finished product certainly wouldn't be mentioned in the same breath as the year's leading films, *Citizen Kane* or *How Green Is My Valley*. The picture opens with Billy, who did an admirable job of portraying himself, squared off in the ring. A moment later, the camera cuts to a blonde vixen sitting ringside, staring longingly at the action in front of her. She strikes a match to light her cigarette, but is so taken by the gorgeous creature before her she absentmindedly allows it to burn down to her fingers.

"Hot?" a man seated next to her asks.

"Plenty hot, and I don't mean the match," she replies wistfully. The shrew is Babs Ellison, daughter of a malevolent manager who wants to get Billy in his clutches. The snappy dialogue couldn't rescue the anemic plot. What began as a poorly acted film centered on a struggle for control over Billy's career took an abrupt turn into a poorly acted movie focused on a bum murder rap pinned on Conn. The vivacious Jean Parker played Patricia Mallory, daughter of Billy's beloved manager, Pops Mallory. As the picture progresses, Miss Mallory becomes a tepid love interest for Conn, but the two elicit no on-screen sparks.

The premier of *The Pittsburgh Kid* was held at Liberty Theater in East Liberty on September 24. Professional critics thumbed their noses at the effort, but they didn't speak for the great number of fans all across the country who enjoyed seeing the Celtic boxing god on the silver screen. Upon the release of *The Pittsburgh Kid,* the *New York Times* brutally appraised Conn's acting abilities. "Battling Billy shows the faults of most prominent boxers who are lured into thespian ventures: he misses all over the place," opined *Times* movie critic Bosley Crowther. "He does not know what to do with his hands. He is obviously no good in the clinches. And he throws such lines as 'Well this is a surprise,' or 'I'm in a jam,' like a fellow ordering a bromo-seltzer. As an actor, the Kid is a dud."[19]

One thing all critics agreed on, Billy acquitted himself well in the boxing scenes. "Conn makes a good showing in the ring, which is where his fans want him," ready the *Daily News* review. "When he dusts off the resin and puts away his gloves, he's not of the caliber to engender sleepless nights for Messrs Boyle, Cooper, and Gable."[20]

Though he had not produced a film classic, Conn had the last laugh. Before the film ended, celluloid Billy was the champ and he had the girl. He came home to Pittsburgh $25,000 richer, and in his later years, Conn had a potent weapon to use against guests who overstayed their welcome. For those visitors, Billy would break out a copy of *The Pittsburgh Kid,* which, according to his personal review, was "a real stinkaroo."

The day after Billy fell to Louis, a large portion of the boxing fraternity assumed there would be a rematch between the two. Most likely, the bout would take place in late September, before the weather turned harsh. However, such hopes were quickly dashed when Mike Jacobs revealed that the champion's next opponent would be Lou Nova rather than Conn. A displeased Johnny Ray met this news with skepticism. "I know how Mike operates," Ray said. "This announcement that he has Nova is to soften me up to make me rush in and sign for a Louis fight for Conn in September. He knows I was a good price. He can get Nova cheaper. So what? With Nova, who has a 'cosmic punch' and no color, he can draw peanuts. With Conn he's back in the million dollar class again."

Whatever Jacobs's game, Ray let it be known that he and Billy wouldn't be muscled by the promoter. "I've got offers from all over the country and even one outside the country, and if Uncle Mike wants to lose his real meal ticket all he has to do is to keep on kidding about his Nova match. Billy and I will go out and build up some other promotion."[21]

Johnny may have been ready to put it to Jacobs, but his Junior was preoccupied for the remainder of the summer. With Maggie's death, his marriage, and burgeoning film career, Billy gave little thought to stepping back into the ring. To Ray's great frustration, Conn did not help him try to drum up a public clamor for an immediate rematch with Louis. There was no doubt following their scintillating meeting at the Polo Grounds of what the public wanted to see. But Billy remained silent. He was content to relax with Matt and enjoy an extended honeymoon.

Indeed, very little was heard from Billy as summer turned to autumn. Though he continued to appear in public, Conn very rarely spoke for attribution. Not until visiting New York for the September 29 Louis–Nova fight did Billy demonstrate any desire to enter the ring again. News that Louis's induction into the army was imminent led Bill Considine of the *Washington Post* to ask Conn what he thought of the state of the heavyweight division without the champ.

"I can't say for sure," Billy responded, "but I have an idea they'll furlough Joe for one or two important fights. I certainly want to fight him again." Of course, Billy then swore that the next time would be different than the first. Yes, Conn said, he wouldn't make the same mistake twice. But there was someone he wanted to face even more than Louis.

"I'd like to get that Nova in the ring. I'll never forgive that guy for something he did the night I was fighting Louis."

Billy then recounted for Considine Nova's breach of propriety. "He went around the ring betting nickels . . . imagine that *nickels* . . . that I wouldn't come up for this or that round. I'd fight him winner take all. Or I'd bet you my end of the purse that he wouldn't hit me once in 15 rounds."[22]

To Conn's immense satisfaction, Nova was knocked out by Louis in the sixth round of their meeting. Even in the aftermath of his disgraceful performance, Nova continued to needle Billy through the press. Most definitely, he wanted to fight Louis again, Nova asserted, but "I'd like to fight Conn next. He's popping off pretty good. I'd like to hush him up. . . . I can't believe they'll put Max Baer in there against Conn. It's my spot."[23]

Yes, there was still talk of pitting Billy against Baer, but no one seemed interested in the matchup except Jacobs. In fact, after their little spat in the press, Conn seemed to lose interest in Nova also. Boxing remained far back in the recesses of Billy's mind. Instead, Conn spent the fall months traveling to various sporting events. In addition to the first game of the World Series at Yankee Stadium, Conn was spotted at several professional and collegiate football games. He also took in a few boxing matches as well as served as a guest referee at a couple of others. Billy was ubiquitous, seemingly everywhere in the sporting world. Everywhere, that is, but in the ring himself.

Not that there weren't any offers for Conn to mull over. West Coast promoter Tom Gallery wired Ray with a tender of a $15,000 guarantee to fight Ceferino Garcia at Gilmore Field in October. Though the money was tempting, Johnny turned down Gallery's proposal. His fighter had been on a honeymoon for three months and couldn't get into proper fighting condition in time.

Hollywood was also calling again. Douglas Churchill reported in the *New York Times* that Billy was to costar with John Wayne and Jerry Colonna in a Republic Studios production, *Down Mandalay Way*. The film was to tell the tale of a prizefighter who joined the U.S. Marines. Shooting was to begin in January if Billy's boxing schedule permitted.

The movies were good for a decent paycheck, but Johnny rightly believed that Billy's meal ticket was earned with the gloves on, and so Ray began trying to drum up business for his fighter without regard for the proposed filming timetable. In mid-November, Johnny promised a schedule of fights that failed to titillate the public interest. Billy would face three "not outstanding" opponents, by Ray's own measurement, which would serve as tune-ups for Conn in preparation of a June rematch with Louis. Tentatively, Billy would face Frankie Hammer in Toledo on January 12, Babe Ritchie a week later in Washington, and then J. D. Turner in Baltimore on January 26. As could be expected, this announcement was met with muted enthusiasm. Hammer, Ritchie, Turner—they were hardly three of the elite fighters in the heavyweight class. In addition, three fights in three weeks; cynics believed that Johnny was going to get his man in shape in the ring.

The day following Ray's statement, the Washington Boxing Commission let it be known that it would "look with disfavor" upon the proposed Conn–Ritchie fight. The district commission released a statement to the press declaring that Ritchie was not, at that time, a proper opponent for Conn; "therefore [the commission] feels that it should make its stand clear to both the press, public, and promoters that a permit for such a contest might not be granted."[24]

Scratch Ritchie and Washington. Ray's original plan was an obvious attempt to try to circumvent Mike Jacobs. In light of the criticism his tentative schedule produced, Johnny turned back to Uncle Mike for a more viable, publicly acceptable opponent for Billy. Jacobs's choice was peculiar. Tony Zale, the recently crowned middleweight champion, signed to fight Conn on November 29. The match was to take place February 13 at Madison Square Garden. A drastic step back in weight class for Billy, Zale still provided an interesting matchup for Conn.

Obviously, Billy was present for the contract ceremony in New York.

But, except when absolutely necessary, Conn continued to abstain from the business side of his affairs. The life of a newlywed agreed with Billy, and training, at least for the time being, held little appeal. He made no secret of his distaste for the Hollywood lifestyle, but if Johnny could work out a good deal, Billy would consider working with those bastards again. And Conn never questioned who Johnny placed him against in the ring. But now, for the time being, Billy was enjoying his idyllic married life. Conn had bought a beautiful English Tudor house in Squirrel Hill for him and Matt to raise a family in. And a new addition to that family would be arriving soon. As December dawned, Mary Louise was three months' pregnant with their first child. A lovely bride, a baby on the way, and a new home in which Billy would enjoy their warmth. He had the world by the tail. All that was missing was the heavyweight crown, but even that wasn't quite as important as it was months earlier.

Shortly after noon on December 7, Mary Louise sat on the steps in front of their home on Denniston Avenue. Billy was inside rushing about, as Gabby Ryan waited patiently for his boss in the street, by the automobile. Out the door Billy came, pausing only to kiss Mary good-bye. When Conn reached the car, an obviously agitated Ryan spoke briefly with him. Alarmed, Billy turned on his heels and ran back up the driveway to the house. "My God," he explained. "Matt, we've been attacked by the Japs."[25]

Like so many on that fateful day, the Conns couldn't fully digest the information or what it would mean to their lives.

Twelve I'm Afraid of No Man Living

lightly more than a year earlier, on October 17, 1940, Billy was among 16,000,000 American men who adhered to conscription registration and signed up for possible military training. In the angry wake of Pearl Harbor, however, thousands of young men weren't waiting for their draft number to be called, and instead directly volunteered to serve their country. One week before Christmas, Billy purchased $5,000 worth of defense bonds and declared his intention to report for physical examination. He expected to join the navy as a petty officer, Conn explained, and serve under Gene Tunney in the physical education program.

Still, the new year arrived and Billy remained a civilian. In fact, Johnny's plans to have Conn lace up the gloves in January had not been altered. What had changed, again, was Ray's chosen opponent for Billy. This time it was the Missouri Athletic Commission that declined to approve of James J. Johnson as Billy's adversary on January 21 in St. Louis. Sounding like a replay of the Washington Commission's objection to Conn's selected foe, the Missouri Commission chairman released a simple, straightforward statement: "Conn has to meet a better opponent," Arthur Heyne declared.[1]

J. D. Turner of Dallas, who was originally slated to face Billy in a canceled Baltimore show, replaced Johnson on the card. Before Turner, though, Conn traveled to northwest Ohio. In his first outing since June 18, 8,000 fans came to Toledo University Field House to watch Billy fight Henry Cooper.

In wartime, promoters of all sporting events needed to be respectful when plying their trade. In order to survive with their good reputations intact, promoters must not come off as profiteers while men were dying in service to their country. The proceeds of the January 12 card went to a police and fire fund, the first "charitable" bout that Billy would headline. As was expected, Conn defeated Cooper easily in a nondescript twelve-round decision using his left almost exclusively.

Next up, the 220-pound J. D. Turner. "We are fighting our way into condition," Johnny Ray said. "Turner promises to be just another workout for Billy and I hope he goes a few rounds because Conn needs the work."[2]

A pedestrian heavyweight with a middling record, Turner's pedigree offered little reason for the crowd to anticipate a classic match; thus, the crowd of 7,000 was a tribute to Billy's great drawing power. Those in attendance didn't come to see a "workout" session. No, they paid their hard-earned cash to witness Glamour Boy Billy knock out his much larger opponent. But Conn failed to fulfill their wish. The crowd's disappointment was vocalized with a spattering of jeers when Billy proved unable to satisfy their desire. Officially, Conn won four of the ten rounds, with the other six called even. Though the crowd was unhappy, Ray was pleased that Junior got a much-needed workout. The road back to Louis now made a strange detour through 165-pound Tony Zale.

Maybe his boxing skills weren't refined, but Conn's sense of style had never been better. He was hired to pen his thoughts on women's style for publication.

"The first time I got to know about women's clothes was when I married Mary Louise," Billy wrote. "I found out what they cost and I found out that you had to like them or else she'd buy some ones I might like better, but keep the others, which made it a double crash on the purse. But her clothes are pips."

Conn knew what he liked and he knew what he didn't like. "Some of women's clothes are really out of line, but those hats are the worst things. I wouldn't wear a boxing glove for a hat, but some girls do.

"I think most of their shoes are too high, and when shoes are too high, you know, with that heel about a foot high, the ankle looks too skinny. I don't like big round fat ankles, but I don't like 'em looking like matchsticks.

"Most women look swell in evening dress, just because of the lights and the fact that it's a party or a theater or something like that. It's the idea more than the dress, I believe, although that thought's liable to get me in a jam."[3]

Keeping Billy's mind on training and off women's fashions proved a difficult task for Ray. Around boxing circles, it was a well-known secret that Johnny couldn't get Billy in the gym for either Cooper or Turner. When Conn and Ray moved to New York's Pioneer Gym for the last days of training prior to meeting Zale, Billy had seemingly found the ardor obviously missing in recent months. Some attributed this renewal to the news that Conn, win or lose to Zale, was guaranteed to face Louis in June. In his first session at Pioneer, Billy impressed onlookers with three speedy rounds against Mickey McAvoy, three more with Harvey Massey, and two with Joe Brown. Against Massey and Brown, Conn displayed his undervalued power, repeatedly staggering the former and knocking down the latter.

"Billy will be ready for any style of battle Zale offers," Ray told the handful of curious newsmen on hand. "He's in grand shape right now and I hope he can hold his edge. Georgie Abrams floored Zale in the first round of their bout and maybe Billy will be able to repeat the trick and keep Zale down.

"At any rate, Billy will be out there trying for a knockout."[4]

Why Conn was fighting Zale at all was more apt a question than whether he would knock Tony out. Why would a man who came within a whisper of defeating the heavyweight champion risk his reputation against the middleweight champ?

"Maybe Conn took this bout for the money that is in it," John Kieran speculated in the *New York Times*. "Good exercise; easy money." A new car? Kieran wondered. Billy used to buy those, but surely he had enough vehicles by now. Maybe his wardrobe needed an updating.

"Possibly he is contemplating a trip to Miami and needs a line of light fabrics to wear while strolling along the line at Hialeah. He's a handsome gent, is Pittsburgh Billy, and he's cut quite a figure in his swanky suits."

More likely, thought Kieran, with March 15—tax day—approaching, Conn would be required to make at least a partial payment on his 1941 earnings. "If he's worried about that," the *Times* columnist mused, "he isn't the only citizen in the same fix."[5]

Regardless of Conn's and Ray's reasoning, fighting Tony Zale was a no-win proposition. If he knocked Zale out—well, that's to be expected. If Billy won a decision, critics would dwell on the fact that he should have knocked out Zale. And, heaven forbid, should Conn lose to his much-smaller opponent, then certainly any mystique and allure attached to Billy would have been dashed.

The biggest ovation of the night came when Private Joe Louis Barrow was introduced to the Valentine's Day Madison Square Garden crowd. Billy outweighed Zale by slightly more than eleven pounds (175¾–164½) and won a lopsided, if unmemorable, twelve-round decision. In both the ninth and eleventh rounds, Conn had Zale staggered, but his punch was lacking the necessary zip to put his smaller foe on the canvas. The victory was hollow for Conn. As Billy made his way from the ring, the once-adoring New York crowd booed and hooted their tarnished hero.

The raspberries baffled and hurt Billy's feelings. "If the customers only knew how earnest I am," a downtrodden Conn said from his dressing room. "I always try my best to give them a run for their money. Often I deliberately stick my chin out so that the customers will get a run for their money. . . . Zale wouldn't have hit me with a broom if I hadn't walked in at times just to make a fight of it. . . . Gosh, how I hate to get razzed."[6]

"I'll never fight a little guy again," Conn vowed. "Yes, I found out plenty in this fight about crowd psychology. I know now why everybody was for me in my fight with Joe Louis. They're always for the little guy, the underdog."[7]

"I've been dreaming about getting at Conn for two years now," a tanned Lou Nova declared. Nova was in Coral Gables where he was rehearsing for his stage debut in *Is Zat So*. With Conn's prestige taking a serious hit, Nova thought the time was ripe to pick a fight with his newspaper nemesis. "He's been ducking me for a long time, but he will have to meet me soon."[8]

Nova wouldn't get his wish; nor would Bob Pastor, who'd been recently moaning about getting another shot at Billy. Neither Conn nor Ray was going to be drawn into another sparring session with Nova in the press. There was talk of matching the two in late March or early April, but that's all it amounted to—talk. Billy had other, immediate priorities. He had delayed signing up for the service long enough. On March 7, Conn finally decided upon joining the army, but not before some politicking.

The competition between various branches of the service was fierce.

Each branch desperately sought to enlist high-profile recruits, for both cosmetic and practical reasons. The prestige of snaring a Ted Williams or Joe Louis was an obvious help in recruiting other young men. But there was also the role these prize recruits played in raising contributions for their given branch. And, in early 1942, there were few more desirable recruits than Billy Conn.

On March 5, Billy had paid a visit to the Naval Recruitment Office in New York. He emerged from the office declaring to reporters that he would be joining the navy "in a couple days." This pledge wasn't written in stone, however. Billy first wanted to see Gene Tunney, whose recruits had become known as "Tunneyfish"; there were a couple of details that needed to be covered before he finalized a decision.

Conn wasn't too keen on the trousers that navy men wore; the wide cuffs were too swishy, he believed. Would I have to wear those funny pants if I join? Billy inquired of Tunney. The ex–heavyweight champ didn't care for Conn and the feeling was mutual. The erudite Tunney saw himself as a cut above his pugilistic colleagues. The cultured Tunney was well versed in life's finer things; he even knew which fork to use at the dinner table. Yes sir, using his own personal method of judgment, Tunney was a better man than most and he made no secret about his discovery. And, in the case of Conn, Tunney not only looked down his nose at the younger boxer, but also resented the publicity Billy garnered.

This good-looking punk was getting all the headlines. Tunney's jealousy and pretentious ways wouldn't permit him to be diplomatic with Billy and Conn's unusual request. He would wear the regulation navy-issue pants, Tunney told Conn, and he would damn well like it. With his own distinct flavor, Billy responded, telling Tunney to "shove the Navy up his ass."

The navy's loss was the army's gain. Billy left Tunney and went to the Army Recruiting Office and, along with bodyguard/pal Joe Becker, was sworn into service by Colonel John F. Days. Billy emerged from the brief ceremony to the questions of the press, all of whom wanted to know why the change in plans.

"I just changed my mind, that's all," Conn shrugged, keeping from the public his private exchange with Tunney over naval attire. "I came in from Pittsburgh this morning, thought about joining the Army, and enlisted."[9] Billy was due to report for duty nine days after his March 7 enlistment. Following his basic training, Conn said he intended to study to become an officer. But, he added, "right now, I'm just plain-Buck Private Billy Conn."[10]

Early on April 12, Mary Louise went into labor. Later that same afternoon, she gave birth to a six-pound, four-and-a-half-ounce boy, who would be named David Phillip. Present to welcome their first grandchild into the world were Nora and Jimmy Smith. If nothing else, Greenfield was a stubborn man. Billy's courageous performance against Louis earned Jimmy's respect, but that didn't change anything. "Understand that doesn't alter the situation one bit," Smith clarified, in one of his only public comments following the wedding. "I'm more opposed to him now than ever. I'll never consent to their marriage." And true to his word, more than nine months had passed since Jimmy had last spoken with his son-in-law on the telephone (and on that memorable occasion, the nicest thing Smith said to Conn was "I'm going to pin your ears back"). When Mary came home from her honeymoon in Hollywood, she found herself back in the good graces of her family—but Billy remained on the outs. Indeed, Jimmy acted as if Conn didn't exist, and for his part, Billy avoided Greenfield at all costs.

Eluding Smith wasn't difficult for Conn. Though his home was just a short drive from the Smiths', he simply steered clear of any social function that Jimmy might attend. And while the situation proved straining on Mary, she did her best to keep the peace. When Billy was out of town, which was fairly often, then Mary visited with her family. Months passed before the possibility of an altercation arose, and that occasion came when Mary took ill.

Over the previous winter, Mary Lou had been admitted to Mercy Hospital with a severe throat infection. After visiting hours one evening, Billy stopped by to check on his girl. Tiptoeing into the darkened room, Conn saw a familiar broad-shouldered figure sitting by Mary's bedside with his back to the door. In an instant Billy recognized the silhouette, and slinked back out of the room, thus avoiding the first confrontation.

But the initial encounter between father-in-law Smith and son-in-law Conn would have to come eventually. Obstinate though he was, even Greenfield Jimmy couldn't shun his daughter's husband for perpetuity. The birth of David Phillip seemed to friends of the family like the opportune moment for amity between the two conflicting men. The possibility seemed unlikely to Billy, who held out little hope for reconciliation with Jimmy. With a furlough in hand to return home for his son's christening, Billy had one thing on his mind: Joe Louis. Before leaving Camp Wadsworth, Conn told a newsman that he would begin training for Louis immediately upon his return Monday. The reporter reminded Conn that with blackout restrictions and army regulations, the fight was far from a sure thing.

"We're going to fight on June 24," Conn assured him with a wink. "And I'll be ready."[11]

Sunday, May 10. A beautiful spring day, and Mother's Day at that; surely Jimmy would break down and come to St. Philomena's for the ceremony. But still Smith refused to recognize his daughter's marriage, or acknowledge Conn, even at the expense of missing the christening of his first grandchild.

Rather than attending the traditional gathering of family and friends that usually followed special occasions of this nature, Mary and Billy returned to their home after the ceremony. Art Rooney, who had developed a strong fondness for Billy over the previous few years, stood as the godfather to David Phillip. Upon leaving St. Philomena's, Rooney went to the Smith home. The soft-spoken, well-respected Rooney was hoping to talk some sense into his longtime pal, Greenfield Jimmy. Their friendship went back more than a dozen years, when Art played for Smith's sandlot baseball squad. If anyone could get through to Jimmy, surely Rooney could.

C'mon, Art persuaded with his gruff voice, isn't it time to bury the hatchet? This is the perfect occasion to mend fences and make your family whole. Why don't we all go over to Billy and Mary's and celebrate?

Smith listened silently until Rooney suggested they go *over there*. No, absolutely not. I am not going to his home.

Rooney the peacekeeper wasn't going to give up that easy. Well, then, what if they come over here?

Even an unreasonable man can see reason on occasion, and reluctantly, Jimmy agreed to Art's revised idea. With Smith's assent, Rooney picked up the telephone and called Billy.

"C'mon over," Art said into the receiver. Billy was skeptical—with good cause—and hedged for a moment. "It's all right," Rooney insisted. "Jimmy's ready to end the feud."

He had been waiting to hear those words for months. Though he had shrugged off Smith's intimidations and threats for the most part, the rift bothered Conn. If going over to Jimmy's house would put an end to all the nonsense, Billy was willing to go along.

An impromptu party was thrown together. There was a band, dancing, and enough food to feed all of Squirrel Hill. A who's who of Pittsburgh gathered on Beechwood Boulevard to celebrate David's baptism and nurture the fragile truce between Jimmy and Billy. In addition to Rooney, Milt Jaffe and Pittsburgh mayor David Lawrence, among others, were the celebrants, and all three were present in the Smith kitchen when the party began winding down several hours later.

The afternoon's good feeling began to give way after Jimmy, emboldened by a few drinks, started heckling Billy, who sat perched on the stove.

With an unmistakable edge to his voice, Jimmy asked, "Why don't you go to church?"

Billy was succinct with his answer. "I don't want to," he said.

"You have a son now, you've got to go to church," Smith insisted. Billy well knew where this was headed, and he desperately tried to defuse the rising tension.

"Hey, Jimmy, just leave me alone."

Smith wouldn't let up, though. "You're afraid of me, aren't you?" Greenfield asked. Whether Jimmy was making a statement or issuing a challenge was uncertain, but he was speaking to a Conn, and the blood of that clan naturally flowed hot.

Not pausing for a clarification of Smith's intentions, Billy replied in kind. "I'm afraid of no man living," he said as he leapt from his roost on the stovetop and threw a left, which skidded off the side of Jimmy's head. Jaffe and Rooney were at the ready. Both men were wary as the tone of Smith's rhetoric picked up an obvious edge. As soon as Billy delivered his blow, Milt had jumped in, trying to pull Conn off Jimmy. Then Rooney, a former boxer himself, grabbed hold of Billy, hoping to ensure peace. But Jaffe and Rooney's actions only made it easier for Smith to land a few punches himself and let out the anger and frustration that had been pent up for some time. From the living room came Nora and Mary; with their addition, the peacemakers finally outnumbered the combatants and sanity was restored.

The instigator, Greenfield Jimmy, emerged from the scrum unscathed, but there were several casualties. Jaffe had a swollen left hand and a twisted ankle. Also injured was Mary Louise, but the extent of her wounds was minimal bruises. Not so lucky was Billy. His face wore the marks of a man fresh from a scuffle, a few scratches under his left eye and a bruised nose, but these injuries were superficial. More important, with his initial clout, Conn had thrown away another chance at Joe Louis; again, his Irish temperament had gotten in the way of the heavyweight championship. With his roundhouse hook, in that moment of imprudence, Conn had fractured his left hand.

Earlier in the day, Billy placed an order with Tommy Silverblatt, the William Penn Hotel's florist. Conn asked Silverblatt if he would deliver an arrangement for his mother-in-law. Because of a backlog of orders, Silverblatt was just arriving at the Smith's home as the kitchen brawl concluded. As he drove up to the home, the florist saw Conn, stripped to the waist, and Mary Lou come out the front door. "Take me to the hospital, Tommy," Billy said. "I'm badly hurt."

The Conns hopped in the backseat and Silverblatt directed the car toward Mercy Hospital. The vehicle hurtled down the avenue, but not fast enough for Mary Lou. "Go faster Tommy! Go faster," she cried. "Billy is in awful shape."[12]

Shortly after six o'clock, Conn was admitted to the emergency room where Dr. Harold Keuhner examined the injured hand. X-rays confirmed what Billy already knew—a metacarpal fracture of Conn's left hand, which would require a cast for a minimum of six weeks. Keuhner also treated Billy for an abrasion on his right elbow and brush burns on his face.

Upon release from the hospital, Billy called his commanding officer at Camp Wadsworth. After explaining the day's fateful events, Conn requested a twenty-four-hour extension of his weekend pass, which was granted.

News traveled slowly. The morning papers, the *Sun-Telegraph* and *Post-Gazette,* carried no word of the Battle of the Pantry. But by mid-afternoon Monday, the story broke. With a banner headline that crowded out news of the war, the *Press* informed readers, "Billy Conn Breaks Hand in Brawl with Father-in-Law." The story was billed above news of a U.S. sub sinking three "Jap" ships and an account of a Winston Churchill speech in which the British prime minister issued a warning to Hitler that the use of poisonous gas in battle would not be tolerated. Indeed, in Pittsburgh, Billy's bad break overwhelmed the war, if just for a day or two.

Journalists about town tried desperately to learn the specifics of the kitchen fracas. Little information could be garnered from the principals present in the pantry. Jaffe was busy applying iodine to his battle scars, and Rooney was lamenting his failed attempt of bringing harmony to the Smith and Conn families. Neither man was quoted for attribution in the days immediately following the altercation.

A reporter tracked Mary Louise down at home hoping for an explanation but came away disappointed; she just wanted to be left alone. "Ever since Billy and I have been married our private life has been made public property," she said. "I don't want to be in the limelight. I have a young baby to raise and I want to be allowed to live like other people."[13]

Greenfield Jimmy gave newsmen no satisfaction either. Contacted at home and told of Mary Lou and Billy's condition, Smith was coy. "Is that so?" he grumbled into the line. "Maybe they were in an auto accident."[14]

Local reporters were stonewalled. No one in Pittsburgh would elucidate the events. Only Billy remained, and he was out of reach, on his way back to Camp Wadsworth in New York. Looking for some type of story line, Chet Smith tracked down a heartbroken Johnny Ray, who was drowning his misfortune in a downtown saloon. "It just goes to show you that you can't do anything about love," Ray mused, staring bleary-eyed at a half-empty glass. "My Billy and Mary Lou fell in love, and now we aren't going to fight Louis next month. I guess nobody just can't interfere with love."

There was no mistaking where Johnny believed the blame for the entire affair lie. "That's the second time Jimmy Smith knocked this kid out of the heavyweight championship of the world," Ray said, his voice rising in pitch and his face reddening as he continued. "You have no idea how his action before the fight last June upset Billy. He didn't sleep or eat for a couple of days before the fight and that kept his weight down. Now when it looked like a sure thing that Billy would win in the return bout, this had to happen." Ray may have been a bit presumptuous declaring an assumed victory over Louis, but one thing was certain, he and Billy had lost out on the biggest gate of their careers.

"I didn't even get a percentage from that Smith crap," Johnny muttered.[15]

"I guess the only place he wanted to bury the hatchet was in my skull," Billy explained to the horde of reporters that met him upon arrival in New York City. "Well, I went over, but instead of a love fest it turned out to be the same old thing. He [Smith] wanted to argue. We had some words in the kitchen and he said he had promised to give me a licking and he might as well do it then. . . . He swung a punch at me and we closed in. I broke my hand hitting him on top of the head and got all these scratches in the face from his nails. Before I could do much damage to him, friends and relations pulled me off."[16]

That was his story and he was sticking to it. Conn's version was significant for he had other worries beyond blowing the Louis match and a potential $125,000. As a private in the U.S. Army, it was possible that Conn would face a court-martial if it was judged he was not injured "in the line of duty." If charges were brought and Conn was found guilty, he would be stripped of his monthly pay of $21.

As could be expected, Billy endured an appreciable amount of grief from his comrades at Wadsworth.

"Next time you go home, better take a bodyguard."

"You'll be a big help when we meet the Japs. You can't even lick your father-in-law!"

Billy took the ribbing good-naturedly. He even managed a smile when the army medical board cleared him of any wrongdoing, having decided that Conn was injured in the line of duty since he was "attacked" while on furlough.

"That fight would have made a barrel of money for our soldiers," the philanthropic Mike Jacobs said. Billy had called Uncle Mike with the bad news the night of the incident. Obviously irritated at the loss of an enormous gate, like Ray, Jacobs pointed the finger of blame squarely at Greenfield Jimmy. "If Mr. Smith feels proud of what happened to a boy who is one of Uncle Sam's soldiers, then he must be the only one who is proud."[17]

It took a couple of days, and he needed a proxy to verbalize his feelings, but Jimmy eventually regretted the sour affair. "You can take my word for it, there's nobody sicker over what happened than Jimmy," Art Rooney, speaking for his friend, explained. "I don't think he'll talk about it, but I know how badly he feels. Despite what has occurred recently and in the past, Jimmy always has been rooting for Billy, and he still will be. You mark what I tell you, they'll be pals yet."[18]

Former heavyweight champion Jim Jeffries was asked what he thought of Conn's future in the ring. Would he be able to recover from the injury and return to proper fighting shape? Did he see Billy taking the crown from Louis? With a bemused smile on his face, Jeffries answered, "Marriage and boxing don't go together."[19]

A potpourri of sporting events served as entertainment for more than 12,000 people gathered at the Polo Grounds on June 14. The main event was a five-inning baseball game starring Bob Feller of the Newark Training Base against an army all-star squad. There was also a lacrosse game, some track and field events, and a solo boxing pantomime by Ray Bolger. While Bolger, Al Schacht, and Zero Mostel provided comic relief for the crowd, Tommy Dorsey and Fred Waring, along with their bands, provided the music.

Billy was also in attendance. And though he had had the cast removed from his left hand eleven days earlier, Conn was still not ready to be a participant in the afternoon's events. Four days before the one-year anniversary of Billy's fabled match with Louis in the same venue, he was introduced to the Polo Grounds crowd just before Joe boxed a four-round exhibition with George Nicholson. It was the first meeting between the two since Conn's showdown with Smith. "Hey Billy," Louis said upon seeing Conn. "Is your father-in-law still beating the shit out of you?"

Theirs had become a friendly rivalry. Whatever Louis thought of Conn prior to stepping into the ring on June 18, 1941, Joe emerged from that victory with great respect for the mouthy challenger. Billy recognized that Louis was a gentleman and great champion, perhaps the finest champion their sport had ever seen. Joe saw Conn as a worthy challenger and enticing foil. And each man understood that together they stood to make more dough than any other pairing in boxing.

"I won't fight nobody but Billy Conn," Corporal Louis said following his exhibition match. "No sense fighting anybody else. Fact is; I won't fight anybody else . . . if they let me fight. He's the only fella I can draw with."[20]

Hanging over Joe's head was a delinquent tax bill of $117,211.75. The tax burden didn't worry Louis, though. "That's all right," he told Bill Considine. "They're going to let it ride until after the war."[21]

After several weeks' recuperation, Billy received his release from Governor's Island. He went home for several days while on furlough, declared his hand healed, and said, "in six weeks I'll be ready to fight anybody, Joe Louis included."[22]

However, a fortnight later, Conn was singing a different tune. When asked if the rumors were true, whether he had been secretly boxing daily in preparation for a coming fight with Louis, he cackled, "Ha! That's a laugh. I don't have time. I haven't had a glove on or been anywhere near a ring for a year. And I won't get near one until I get permission."[23]

Mike Jacobs was hard at work trying to obtain the permission necessary for Billy and Joe to begin training. This wouldn't be a typical promotion for Jacobs. Putting together a show starring two servicemen meant the involvement of the War Department. Not having complete control over the enterprise was an unwelcome change of policy, but Jacobs had no choice. Patiently he waited for the call that would okay the bout. In the meantime, Mike put together some figures estimating what the show would make; seat pricing and the like. When his phone finally rang on September 8, Uncle Mike was ready.

Jacobs immediately left his office for a meeting with Colonel Walter Wells, Major General Alexander Surles, and John Kieran of the *New York Times*. Kieran was serving as the head of the sportswriters committee, which was put in place to oversee the event. Wells and Surles explained to the usually totalitarian Jacobs exactly how this particular boxing card would be promoted. He listened to their instructions politely before handing each of the men a copy of his numbers and telling them just how much money the show could raise for the Army Emergency Relief. "And if you think I'm wrong about the money, "Jacobs crowed, "I'll buy the bout from you right now for $750,000."

Immediately, Surles set the promoter straight. "It's not going to be handled that way," the general dourly told Jacobs. "A committee will run this and see that nobody gets a cent of profit out of it except Army Emergency Relief."

"That's OK with me," Mike replied, "but General, you gotta get those boys into training camp."

Surles was a step ahead of Jacobs. "We'll have them turned loose right away," he said. "Louis is at Fort Riley. It won't take him long to pack up."

Jacobs excitedly interrupted, "Not when you tell him what it's for. I know he wants to fight Conn again."

Surles continued his thought. "Bill Conn is at Fort Wadsworth, which is right handy and . . ." Again, Mike interjected. "No, he ain't at Fort Wadsworth, not right now. He's sitting in my office. I just left him. Whenever he gets a leave he shows up at my place. He's probably walking up and down now, waiting for me to get back and tell him what it's all about."

"I don't suppose he'll run off and hide when you break the news to him," Colonel Wells added with a chuckle.

Jacobs let out a hearty laugh. "Ha! This is what he's been waiting for."[24]

Ever the straight man, Surles wanted to make clear to Jacobs that this wasn't a typical Twentieth Century promotion. "This whole thing has got to be clean all the way," he emphasized. "The bout has to be clean as far as the Army is concerned. But the committee in charge must see to it that no person makes a cent of profit anywhere along the line. The whole thing—and nothing less—is for Army Emergency Relief."

Though he had been under the impression that he and Louis would both be compensated for the fight, Billy shrugged off the terms. "So," he said when informed by Jacobs that he wouldn't be paid for the fight, "I'll whip him for nothing then."[25]

On September 9, Billy and Joe received their orders. Both men were given a thirty-seven-day furlough to prepare for the October 12 date. Before heading to New York, Conn returned home for a brief visit. In Pittsburgh, his mended fist passed the first test: three speedy rounds with the heavy bag. Conn was pleased following the workout. "I can give it everything I've got and figure if it was ever going to bother me it would be then," he said. "But it didn't. It feels great."

His time in the service and the injury to his hand did nothing to quell Billy's confidence. "I think Joe's ready to be taken by the first good man who comes along. None of them, not even the best, goes on forever. In my book he's a dead pigeon."

Told by an onlooker that his foe had just been made a sergeant, Billy beamed, "Yeah, and wouldn't a lot of privates like to be in my shoes."[26]

Indeed, a few hours prior to his departure from Fort Riley, Louis had been informed that he had been promoted to sergeant. When Louis arrived at Grand Central Station three days after receiving his leave, he looked good, maybe a bit heavier than in his prime. "I'm around 220 lbs," Joe hedged, but he was only eating two meals a day, he insisted. Sergeant Louis was still wearing his corporal stripes. "I didn't have time to sew on the new ones," the champ shrugged.

His first stop in New York was the Brill Building, where Jacobs and Conn were waiting. They were soon off to the War Department's local

Office of Public Information, where Joe and Billy sat in on a meeting with Jacobs, army officials, and the sportswriter's committee, which was dubbed War Boxing, Inc. Following the conference, Louis and Conn sat together behind the army bench as the NFL's New York Giants played a contest against an aggregate of army all-stars at Yankee Stadium.

Officially, Conn and Louis signed for the match on September 22. Each man was dressed in uniform as they stood next to New York Boxing Commissioner John Phelan, Joe to his right, Billy to his left, while a gleeful Mike Jacobs hovered behind the trio. The papers were signed, but not without some degree of difficulty.

If Jacobs believed Johnny Ray would stop at nothing to get Billy back in the ring against Louis, he was mistaken. Mike's lawyer, Sol Strauss, placed five contracts in front of Ray, each relating to Conn's activities should he become champion and what part Twentieth Century promotion would play in Billy's pursuits.

After carefully reading through the contracts, Johnny refused to sign any of the documents. "I'm Billy's manager in civilian life and no one else has anything to say about handling him, except the army, now that he's a soldier." Finally Strauss took away four of the contracts, leaving only one that stipulated Conn couldn't fight any other boxer before giving Louis a rematch.

Still Ray would not relent. He wanted the contract devoid of legalese. Johnny wanted them rewritten in simple English. No lawyer was going to sneak something—anything—by him. Sitting nearby was John Kieran, who found the whole scene amusing. After all, Kieran reckoned, a return bout wouldn't take place until after the war; why make such a fuss about it now?

"I don't know [when the match will be]," Johnny said, "but I ain't taking any chances."

Well, Kieran asked, do you have any other objections to the terms? Yeah, Johnny said, "My objection is I can't understand them." Just then Johnny was pulled aside and each paragraph was explained to him in detail, stripped of all legal mumbo jumbo.

Finally Ray yielded. "Well, if that's what it means, it's all right and I'll sign," he said, "but they shoved it under my nose at the last minute and I couldn't make head or tail of it. I'll sign."

Another reporter standing nearby mumbled that most likely Ray's objections were unnecessary. Chances are that, because of the war,

Louis and Conn would never meet a third time. Or, more likely, Joe would defeat Billy, making Johnny's dispute moot. Though the comments weren't meant for his ears, Ray heard them and set the writer straight.

"Mister," Johnny snapped, "you're wrong on one count. Conn is going to win the title this time. About the rest, I wouldn't know. Billy's in the Army. So is Joe Louis. They'll be going places and taking orders from somebody else until the war is over. But I don't know when peace will come and I want to be prepared. They tell me that was the trouble with us; we weren't prepared for this war. I'm getting prepared for peace just in case."[27]

Initially, the fighter's preparation seemed typical of a title match. Billy began training on the 15th, when Johnny arrived in Rumson along with Conn's sparring partners. Makeshift training quarters were set up in a garage behind Jacobs's home. Louis selected the familiar Greenwood Lakes as his headquarters, though Joe lacked some of the accoutrements Billy took pleasure in at Uncle Mike's estate. While waiting for Ray to arrive, Conn enjoyed Mike's outdoor pool and wandered the manor studying Mike's beautiful flower gardens.

Then it all began to unravel.

Several days before the official contracts were signed, it was revealed that both participants would be allowed to repay debts owed Jacobs from the fight receipts. Since joining the army, Louis had defended his title on two occasions: January 1 against Buddy Baer and March 27 against Abe Simon. Though his crown was on the line, Joe didn't receive a penny for his efforts, as all revenue went directly to the navy and army relief funds. He was, however, charged for training expenses by Mike Jacobs, and his manager John Roxborough still expected his usual percentage of Joe's take.

Exactly who proposed an amendment to the original agreement was never revealed, though the most likely culprit was the man who stood to gain the most, Jacobs. Word of the alteration was leaked to the press that Louis would be able to repay the debts he incurred while training for Simon and Baer, and Conn would be allowed to do the same for money owed from the Zale training session. Joe's obligation amounted to $109,951.53, of which $59,805.50 would go to Twentieth Century and the remainder to Roxborough. Billy would "receive" $34,500, which would go directly to Jacobs's Twentieth Century organization.

The sportswriters committee overseeing the affair revised the articles of agreement to allow the stipulation, with the implicit permission of the War Department. In a released statement, the committee revealed its reasoning for altering the contracts.

"It is impossible to conduct the fight under the original plan suggested by the war department. . . . Upon investigation it was found there were commitments and obligations with regard to sums of money owed by the soldier contestants in this fight. In order that the fight may go forward, it is incumbent upon the committee to meet the sums of money owed by these soldiers to private interests."

The War Department issued its own announcement, explaining the about-face. In addition to raising a large amount of money for Army Emergency Relief, "it also falls in with the original intention of the war department that it would be proper reward for those soldiers to clear themselves of debts incurred by their previous boxing activities for similar charitable purposes."[28]

With the headlines swirling with these new revelations, Billy and Joe continued to prepare themselves for the fight. Private Jackie Conn received special leave that allowed him to help his brother train for the fight. At Jacobs's Rumson estate, everything appeared normal. The two brothers were happily tearing into each other in the ring, and Johnny was pleased with Junior's exceptional progress. Three weeks out, Ray believed Conn was ready to go. "Billy's sharp enough right now to step into the ring with Louis," he predicted.[29]

Perhaps he would have taken Joe this time. If it hadn't been for a bellicose congressman from New York, he just might have done it—but Billy wouldn't get the chance. Representative Donald O'Toole grabbed hold of the issue, which he described as "apparent favoritism" being shown members of the military. He took to the floor of Congress and made certain the revised fight contract wouldn't be swept under the rug.

"This is evidently the beginning of a new policy on the part of the war department," an incredulous O'Toole said from the House floor. "What a mockery we are making out of the army and of charity. The United States army is being used for the first time to guarantee obligations that are owed to a fight promoter. Why is it not possible for the man who has enlisted and whose wife must now work in order to keep herself and her family to have this leave?"

"Let us stop all of these theatrical performances, football games, pugilistic encounters and devote ourselves and our fighting men to the successful termination of the war."[30]

O'Toole's House speech was carried prominently in all major newspapers, and his proved to be the dominant voice calling for the cancellation of the bout. Pennsylvania Representative Elmer Holland of Pittsburgh did his best to protect his constituency while discrediting O'Toole. Holland conducted a background check on O'Toole and found that his colleague from New York was once a professional wrestler and, Holland pointed out, no one connected in any way with professional wrestling should be casting stones. Still, O'Toole's criticisms won out over Holland's efforts. Harold Stimson, the secretary of war, couldn't ignore the objection raised by O'Toole, certainly not after all the publicity the congressman had been given. Initially, Stimson professed ignorance of the entire situation when questioned about the controversy, but promised to conduct a full investigation "within 48 hours."

The secretary, who described learning of the particulars of the contract as "shocking," needed less than twenty-four hours to come to a decision. "I have determined that Sergeant Louis and Corporal Conn shall be returned at once to their military duties. The standards and interests of the Army do not permit the proposed contest to be carried out."

Stimson's statement continued, absolving the fighters of any wrongdoing. "There is no reflection upon the principals. Furthermore, the Army appreciates that Louis had heretofore generously contributed his efforts to both the Army and Navy without return."[31]

Representative O'Toole's grandstanding failed to acknowledge the great amount of money raised for the relief fund, which provided aid to maimed soldiers and to the widows and orphans of soldiers lost to battle. Though not stated, clearly the onus of blame belonged to Jacobs. Still, virtually no criticism of the promoter could be found, either by O'Toole, Stimson, or the many reporters who covered the swirling events. The only individual who stood to profit from the affair pleaded innocent to any misconduct. Jacobs was quick to point out that War Boxing, Inc., and the War Department asked him to promote the fight in order "to raise a large sum of money for the army relief fund" and that the controversial financial arrangements "were approved by the war department and War Boxing, Inc. . . . . If Mr. Stimson thinks an investigation is necessary, it's all right with me," Mike stated. "A representative of the war department saw Joe Louis at Ft. Riley before the fight was arranged. Louis told him that he had certain obligations, which he would like to have met—if he was going to fight. So far as I'm concerned, whatever money Joe owes me, he can owe me for as long as he wants."

Ever the promoter, Jacobs added, "I think all this publicity will add $200,000 to the gate. And that's good."[32] Mike then sent a telegram to Stimson, asking the secretary to please reconsider his decision: "I offer my services free in an advisory capacity to any official designated by you to stage a championship bout between Sergeant Joe Louis and Corporal Billy Conn."

Jacobs continued his plea, explaining that both fighters would fight for free, asking only that training expenses be covered. He also requested that a previous commitment to the Mutual Broadcasting System be honored. A week earlier, NBC won a blind bid for the radio rights at $71,200, while Mutual tendered the third highest bid at $55,000.

"I have orders, checks and cash amounting to more than $250,000 for advance sale of tickets for this bout," Jacobs explained. "I will begin to return to the purchasers immediately if your decision of Friday is irrevocable."[33]

Billy was at Jacobs's estate when word reached him that Stimson canceled the fight. He expressed "terrible disappointment" at the decision before saying, "There will be time enough afterward for boxing, but this is just my luck. I'm convinced that I could have beaten Joe." Told that Louis had said, "I'll fight for nothing if they let the fight go on," Billy nodded his head in agreement. "That's okay with me too," said Conn.[34]

Stimson was resolute. There would be no fight, and his order was final. Joe was to return to Kansas and Fort Riley, and Billy to Staten Island. That left Uncle Mike in New York wondering who would cover the expenses he already incurred, expenses he claimed had reached $15,000.

Thirteen Mickey Rooney's a Sissy

In late October, Billy was reassigned to the army's Pennsylvania center in New Cumberland, located two hundred miles east of Pittsburgh. Conn discovered there was a perk in being appointed to his new post. New Cumberland's close proximity to Pittsburgh allowed Gabby Ryan to come get Billy and bring him home on weekends. His assignment at New Cumberland was to coach the camp's boxing team and assist the athletic officer at the center. "I don't find teaching hard," Conn explained. "I just tell them what my manager, Johnny Ray, told me. He's a great teacher."

Fighting Louis again remained foremost in Billy's mind. And though he didn't want to appear insubordinate, Conn wondered why he and Joe were being singled out and prevented from meeting in the ring. "I read in the papers where some sailor, marine, soldier or Coast Guardsman is in a bout," said Conn. "I don't see why they won't let us fight, but I'm willing to wait until the war's over because we all know winning that fight is the most important."[1]

Stimson's September dictate did not deter amateur promoters from envisioning Louis–Conn II. Al Abrams of the *Pittsburgh Post-Gazette* made a pitch to General Surles that a fight between Billy and Joe could be held with war bonds being sold for admission. As expected, Surles rejected Abrams's proposal. The fight was not, Surles stated, "in the national interest for the War Department either to sponsor or authorize such a boxing engagement."[2] In April 1943, a month after Abrams's brainstorm, Senator W. Warren Barbour of New Jersey wrote to 675 sportswriters asking their thoughts on the desirability of a Conn–Louis match. Barbour had some experience in the ring himself. In 1910, the senator claimed the amateur heavyweight championship of North America, and he was also the timekeeper of the Jess Willard–Jack Dempsey title fight in Toledo.

"Frankly," wrote Barbour, "I would like to see Joe and Billy given an opportunity of engaging in such a bout, and I believe that millions of boxing fans throughout the country must feel the same way." Regardless of Senator Barbour's wishes or those of fight enthusiasts, Secretary Stimson was not going to redact his order. There was a war on, and the War Department was busily trying to mobilize for battle. Though professional sports continued to hobble along during the effort, Stimson could not justify allowing two high-profile servicemen to partake in such an event. At one of the secretary's weekly press conferences, the question was brought forward and met with a terse reply. "I think I can assure you that the War Department will not sponsor or approve a Louis–Conn fight this summer."[3]

So Barbour's idea died on the vine.

Meanwhile, Billy had been transferred from New Cumberland to Camp Lee, Virginia, in December and was once again on the move the following spring. On April 12, army officials released a statement announcing that Billy had joined the Twelfth Armored Division at Camp Campbell, Kentucky. Billy's duties would include coaching the division's boxing team. Once again, Conn took advantage of his camp's location, and on several occasions he and Mary Lou would rendezvous in nearby Cincinnati for a weekend at the Netherland Hotel. These "second honeymoons" were a much-appreciated distraction from the tedious life found in the military.

Promoters finally took Stimson at his word and talk of Louis–Conn II disappeared during the summer months. Cleveland fight promoter Bob Brickman checked his calendar, though, and in the early fall of '43 wired Stimson with an offer to "guarantee $50,000" to any war relief for permission from the War Department to stage a Louis–Conn match. Perhaps Brickman believed his modest guarantee would appeal to the secretary's sense of munificence. Compared to Mike Jacobs's garish prediction of a $1,000,000 gate, Brickman's guarantee seemed quaint. Unfortunately for the bold Clevelander, his proposal was met with silence.

On October 5, the principal characters coincidentally met up with one another at Jefferson Barracks in St. Louis. Louis and Conn were serving in a similar capacity: Joe was in St. Louis on his tour of boxing exhibitions, which were put on to entertain servicemen, while Billy was stopping briefly to instruct the Jefferson boxing team.

Undoubtedly, each man wanted to enter the ring once again opposite the other. However, with each meeting since their first encounter, their personal warmth toward one another grew and, with that, familiarity came. They heard the talk and they both read the papers, and any time reporters gained access, the question was inevitable—the rematch, the rematch. At least together they could joke. In St. Louis, Joe uttered a one-liner that Billy would laughingly rehash for decades to come. "All I want, Joe, is to have the title for six months," Conn said.

"Hell, Billy," a deadpan Louis replied, "you had it for twelve rounds and didn't know what to do with it."

Conn's chance to avenge his loss to Joe was on indefinite hold. A different, almost as intriguing opportunity briefly presented itself to Billy: Conn was to fight an exhibition with Lieutenant Mutt Wormer in Richmond. Unfortunately, the brass called off the match before Conn could avenge the family name. Apparently the higher-ups didn't want an enlisted man fighting an officer, thus saving Lieutenant Wormer.

In Pittsburgh, on Monday evening, May 17, while standing on a Fifth Avenue curb waiting for a streetcar, Johnny Ray suddenly lost consciousness and fell to the street. A nearby police officer came to Ray's assistance and took him to the emergency room at Mercy Hospital.

Upon admittance, Johnny disclosed to his doctor, G. C. Weil, that he had been drinking up to a pint of liquor a day for a numbers of weeks, but recently he'd stopped. This, Ray reasoned, was the reason he'd passed out on the street. It had happened before when he tried to kick the bottle without tapering off. All he'd had to drink in the last few days, Johnny told Dr. Weil, was a couple of beers. The forty-eight-year-old Ray had tried to live a cleaner lifestyle since his health scare five years prior. Johnny hadn't smoked a single cigarette since his lung operation. But quitting drink proved more difficult than tobacco for Ray. His latest attempt at temperance wouldn't last for long. Dr. Weil released Johnny from the hospital after two days, having diagnosed the episode as posttraumatic encephalopathy.

Shortly after D-Day, Billy received word that his unit was leaving for Europe. He phoned Mary Louise. "I've got bad news, Matt. I'm shipping out tomorrow."

If his news was inevitable, her reply was unexpected. "Well," she said, "I've got good and bad news; I'm pregnant."

Two weeks after the Allies established a beachhead in France, Billy was bound for England on a massive transport ship. More than two years had passed since Conn joined the service and, not surprisingly, he disliked the army thoroughly. Being told what to do did not sit well with him. Other than Maggie and Johnny Ray, few people ever got away with it in civilian life. "You have a million bosses in the Army," he complained more than once. "All these hillbillies telling you what to do."

One such "hillbilly" attempted to assert his authority on the trip to England. With dozens of enlisted men lined at attention before him, an officer new to Conn's platoon bellowed out a challenge typical to the service mentality.

"Anybody here thinks they can lick me, step out of line right now!" The entire platoon remained in formation, though nearly every eye found its way to Billy. The officer repeated the challenge. Again, the platoon remained in formation, but this time a number of heads turned in Billy's direction. With great reluctance, Conn took a step forward. Bearing down on the obstinate soldier, the colonel barked out, "So, do you think you can take me?"

In a respectful but forceful tone, the corporal replied, "Yes, sir."

"What's your name, corporal?"

"Billy Conn, sir."

The startled officer paused for a moment, then slapped an arm around Billy's broad shoulder. "That goes for everyone but you; let's go see the admiral."

Following eighteen days on the Atlantic, Conn arrived in England on June 29. Within a month, Billy had his first of several brushes with mortality. He also met up again with Joe Louis, who brought his traveling boxing show to Europe. According to *Stars and Stripes,* a hospitable air force colonel took Joe and Billy up in a bomber so they could get a visual appreciation of England's landscape from high above. The scenic tour went fine until the pilot began to descend and discovered his landing gear was stuck. For the next forty-five minutes while the pilot tried to fix the problem and avert disaster, Louis and Conn said prayers and wondered to one another "what Uncle Mike will say when he reads our obituaries."[4]

From England, Conn left with the special services tour for Paris. Billy's role in the unit was fairly simple. He would box a few rounds with a GI who had some experience in the ring. Ideally, Conn would put on a show for the grunts watching, dancing around, throwing a punch here and there, but nothing too serious. On a few instances, however, Billy was placed in the ring with a guy who wanted to make a name for himself as the fella who took out Billy Conn. On one such occasion, immediately after touching gloves, Conn's opponent threw a haymaker in an attempt to knock Billy off his feet. Conn was dazed by the blow but, worse for the soldier in the ring with him, Billy was angry. For the length of the three-round exhibition, Conn skillfully carved up the smart guy. The referee tried several times to stop the bout, but Billy assured him everything was all right.

Entertainment for the troops was not limited to boxing. Traveling with the special unit were golfers Horton Smith and Lloyd Mangum, who exhibited their sport with driving demonstrations. Several ranked tennis players also traveled with the party, including Charlie Hare and his wife Fudge Patty. One of the oddest members of the group was the author of a book on horseshoe throwing. He was brought along to Paris with the belief that the troops would enjoy an expert demonstration of show pitching. Unfortunately, the author knew the sport well but was no master himself. Luckily, on hand with the unit was a quick-thinking Lieutenant Harold L. Gefski, who found an expert who happened to be stationed nearby. Gefski brought the expert in to demonstrate horseshoe tossing while the author talked; riveting entertainment.

Lieutenant Gefski served on General Eisenhower's staff as a member of special services. Gefski's role was that of an advance man for the USO tour. He was usually one stop ahead of the troupe, traveling to the next camp to set up the show and secure lodgings for members of the unit. He also, on at least one occasion, served as a buffer between a hotheaded mess sergeant who gave a hard time to soldiers who came back for seconds. Apparently, one serving didn't satiate Billy's appetite. Like the officer on the transport ship, the mess sergeant didn't know to whom he was giving a hard time. Words were exchanged when Billy asked for another helping. Sitting nearby, Lieutenant Gefski stepped between the two men.

"I think we can arrange for you to box if you would like," Gefski told the sergeant.

"Fine, I'll kill him."

"I think you ought to meet him first. Sergeant, I'd like you to meet Billy Conn."

The cantankerous mess sergeant's face went ashen, and a look of awe replaced his tough-guy demeanor. An outstretched hand mended the brief quarrel, and the sergeant, in a moment of largesse, declared seconds for everyone.

The USO tour, which was originally scheduled for three weeks, stretched to ten and covered many camps before ending in Paris. Immediately, Conn was placed with another unit, this time an all-boxing tour, which began in the French capital and covered a number of camps on the Mediterranean front. Before leaving the City of Lights, Billy spoke with a reporter from the newspaper *Liberation*. Conn expressed the hope that he and Louis would meet in an exhibition, which would be put on in the Palais de Sport. "Louis is a great champion," Billy told the French reporter, "but I am sure that I will beat him when I meet him again for the title after the war."[5]

Before a packed house in the triple-decked Bari Opera House in Bari, Italy, Conn gave the Tommies and GIs an entertaining three-round exhibition.

"Billy's timing was a bit off, which is only natural," wrote a reporter in attendance. "Prof. Joe Louis who was here three weeks ago exhibited the same lack of tonal quality—but Conn still moves around like a guy with a double hot foot and still has a left-hand that can spear a piece of chicken meat at five paces."[6]

Conn's opponent in Bari was Johnny Ebarb of California, but more often than not, Billy's ring partner on the tour was Harold Raskin from Chicago. Corporal Raskin drew some notoriety in his role as Conn's chosen sparring mate, a position he gained when the troupe's pilot, Lieutenant Maury Schwartz, learned that Hal was a former amateur champion and Eighth Air Force heavyweight champ. His job became known as the toughest noncombat position in the army.

Occasionally during the tour, Raskin would face Conn six times a week. "Some guys think this traveling around is a racket," Raskin said. "Sure maybe we do escape some of the chicken, but you travel all day by truck, fighting almost every night and eating and sleeping where you can. And you don't get any Purple Hearts for these," he said, while pointing to his cauliflower ear and a freshly blackened eye.

"We want to put on as good a show as the Louis troupe did, and the G.I.'s don't care to see Conn be a fancy dan."[7]

Late in the tour, just a week before Christmas, Billy and a few members of his group were traveling along a lonely Italian road when an American fighter jet crash-landed in a nearby swamp. The plane burst into flames, leaving the unconscious pilot trapped inside. Conn and his companions rushed to the wreckage, fought through the blaze, and saved the unconscious pilot.

In a little more than a week, Conn went from aiding in the rescue of a comrade to nearly losing his own life. Two days after Christmas, Billy and his boxing mates were taking off from a French airfield in a C-41. Shortly after the plane was airborne, the pilot discovered his elevator controls were locked.

"We circled over the field and sweated for two hours," Billy recounted, "while a mechanic chopped his way through part of the plane in an attempt to unlock the controls. It was 'no soap' and it looked like we'd all get killed."

The pilot, Conn explained, came up with an unorthodox plan. "He had me and three others run up and down the plane so overweight would lower the tail, then the nose, so we could land. We hit the runway at 150 miles an hour, and made it okay, but it left me shaking for two days."

The boxing squad arrived in Paris perilously, but unharmed. Later that same night, the Germans bombed the city for the first time in four months. One Nazi bomb landed so close to Billy's hotel that a number of windows were shattered by the concussion.

In six months, Conn had traveled more than 50,000 miles. From England to France, Italy, Sicily, Corsica, and back to France, Billy boxed an average of four nights a week. He also made a point of visiting hospitals in every stop along the tour, cheering up wounded GIs with his biting sense of humor. On a number of occasions, Conn was offered a promotion. Each and every time he turned it down. He liked being one of the guys, and besides, he wasn't in the service for the long haul.

"Boxing's my game," he explained. "I'm a corporal and I'll never get any higher. They can make me a private any day—you have about 9,000,000 bosses but it doesn't make any difference."[8]

The boxing tour ended shortly after the new year when Billy was assigned once again to Horton Smith's USO group. Conn traveled throughout the continent with an eclectic group of sports entertainers, including his brother Jackie. Billy was very popular with the troops, very amiable, and spent much of his time keeping his younger brother out of trouble. Jackie had joined the USO group for the new tour, and, as the saying goes, you can take the kid out of Pittsburgh, but . . . well, suffice to say, Europe did nothing to change Jackie's demeanor. Like the streets of East Liberty, the military was home to a prevailing machismo attitude. Thankfully for Jackie, Billy was often nearby to keep the peace—that is, Billy was nearby until he was laid up with an attack of lumbago. Conn returned to England where he convalesced at Hertfordshire military hospital.

After his recovery, Billy returned to the USO troupe, which by then was winding down the tour. In a Nuremberg hotel, he met Bob Hope, who was also in the city with his own USO tour.

"I think this unit is just about through and I'd like to get on your show," Conn told the comedian. At the outbreak of war, Hope had tried to enlist, but at the age of thirty-seven, he was politely turned away with the suggestion that perhaps he could better serve his country by entertaining the troops rather than fighting alongside them. Hope took the idea to heart and had spent much of the war traveling around the globe with a constantly revolving revue. One constant, though, was Bob's "pop-eyed" sidekick, Jerry Colonna. Hope and Colonna worked well together and developed a number of routines to entertain servicemen. Sometimes Jerry would sit in the audience, unmistakable with his oversized mustache, in the uniform of whichever branch the tour was performing for.

"Say, private, you look familiar to me," Hope would call to Colonna. "What were you before you were in the Army?"

"Happy!" Colonna replied, to the great amusement of the crowd.

Hope listened to Conn and thought for a moment. "I've just thought of a routine I can do with you," he said. Hope had remembered an old joke about Al Capone and his Chicago outfit, but Bob figured he'd just substitute names. "I could ask you how hard Joe Louis hits, stuff like that," Hope elaborated.

Billy was all smiles. "If you could do that it would be wonderful."

Moments after leaving Conn, Hope ran into Major General Ben M. Sawbridge. "I'd like to thank your unit for coming over," the general said. "If I can do anything for you, just let me know."

"You're timing couldn't be better, General. Billy Conn is here. He's about through with Horton Smith's unit. If you'll let me have him I think I can use him in my show and do some good with him."

Sawbridge consulted with a nearby colonel and quickly gave Hope his answer. "Billy Conn is now with your unit."

The comedian went back to the lobby where Billy remained. "Pack, boy, you're with me."

Conn wasn't biting. He thought Hope was practicing a shtick. "Stop it," Billy said. "I don't feel like kidding about it."

"I've fixed it. You're speaking to a man who goes to the top. You're with me, pack."

Conn remained unconvinced until a colonel came by with his new orders. He then looked at Hope. "We'd better get out of here because when my brother finds out that I'm ditching him like this, he'll beat the hell out of both of us."

Another precarious flight awaited Billy on his first trip with the Hope tour. The plane hit some bad weather as they traveled through the Alps. Hope awoke from a nap and saw Billy lying on his back with a rosary in hand, quietly praying. Moving close, Hope said, "I hope you'll make it a package deal and include all of us."

"Don't worry," Conn said looking up. "I've included everyone, especially the pilot."[9]

Billy enjoyed his experience with the Hope tour a great deal. Along with Hope and Colonna, Bing Crosby, Fred Astaire, Jack Pepper, and June Bruner were also among the other entertainers aboard. Meeting celebrities usually didn't excite Billy too much, though Crosby was an exception. In fact, Conn was decidedly unimpressed with most of the mopes he came across with the troupe. Of all the so-called celebrities Conn came across, none left a more unfavorable impression than Judy Garland's partner on the silver screen—"Mickey Rooney's a sissy," Billy said in sizing up the young actor.

When Conn's stint with Hope was through, so was his stay on the continent. On September 12, at 1:50 A.M., Billy's flight from Paris landed at La Guardia Field. Sol Gold, a friend of Billy's from New York, a small party of newsmen, and, of course, Mike Jacobs were there to meet him as he disembarked from the plane. Uncle Mike gave a much-heavier Conn a bear hug for the cameras.

Billy had several days before he had to report to Camp Lee, and he wanted to use that time wisely. With little time to spare, Conn rushed home to see his family. He was met by his gorgeous young bride, a newly named four-year-old who looked familiar, and a curly-haired toddler.

Fourteen He Can Run . . .

Once he escaped Uncle Mike's gripping embrace, Conn was on an airplane heading home. He had a few free days before he was required to report to Fort Lee.

The house that sat quietly in front of him as he pulled up Denniston Avenue was noticeably different from what Billy remembered. With his son-in-law in Europe, Greenfield Jimmy took an interest in remodeling the English Tudor home and also helped Mary Lou decorate the interior. "Pap" was a constant presence in the house while Billy was away. If he wasn't laboring on household improvements, Jimmy was doting over his grandsons, whom he obviously adored.

Another change while Billy was away could also be directly credited to Smith. "David Phillip," Greenfield decided, wasn't a good enough name for his firstborn grandchild. "David Conn doesn't sound Irish enough," Jimmy told his daughter. "Tim Conn, that sounds right. Tim Conn it'll be."

Mary Lou had no special attachment to David Phillip, and she thought that Tim was, indeed, a good Irish name. So, Tim it would be.

As Billy walked through the front door and saw his young family for the first time in three years, things had certainly changed. The baby he left behind was now up and walking about and answered to a new name. His beautiful Matt—well, she hadn't changed. If anything, she was even more beautiful than when he left. At Mary Lou's side wobbled an adorable toddler sporting long blond curls.

"Who's that kid?" Billy asked.

"He's yours," Mary told him.

"Well, he needs a haircut." Changing David's name, that was all right. In fact, Billy kind of liked the name Tim. But those prissy curls had to go. Conn swept his namesake up in his arms and carried Billy Jr. out the door and down the street to Johnny Boyle's barbershop in East Liberty.

A couple of days in Pittsburgh and then Billy had to return to New Jersey to serve out his remaining days in the army. On September 25, Conn was formally discharged from the service. For the next several weeks, Conn relaxed at home and got reacquainted with his family.

At long last, peace had come to Europe and the Far East; even more improbably, a cessation of enmity had been informally declared between Greenfield Jimmy and Billy. That's not to say that Smith welcomed Conn home with open arms and a loving embrace, but Jimmy's anger had conspicuously subsided. Certainly Timmy and Billy Jr. played a part in loosening Pap's heartstrings and helped Jimmy come to terms with Mary Lou's choice for a husband.

Indeed, Billy returned from the war a lucky man: a darling family, a charming home, his health intact, and, as for his financial prospects, the sky was seemingly the limit. The Louis rematch would no longer be a game of speculation, but simply a matter of time before becoming a reality. Jacobs was already spouting off about a possible $3 million gate. Whatever it would be, Billy promised to make more from the bout than he could have ever imagined when working out in Johnny's old gym.

Physically, Billy was noticeably different than he was prior to entering the service. His handsome face was now fuller, more mature looking, and his frame had filled out considerably. The weight Conn had put on seemed to go to the right places. He finally looked like a heavyweight, and though he could stand to shed a few pounds from his midsection, it was the broad shoulders that Billy now sported that had changed most dramatically.

On October 17, Ray and Jacobs sat down in Mike's office and began to hash out the terms for the contract. The first hour of the discussion was productive and cordial, as Johnny found no problem with Jacobs's proposals. The talks quickly turned combative when the matter of "tune-up" bouts was introduced. Jacobs was steadfast; he didn't want Conn to risk a defeat before entering the ring with Louis. Too much was at stake. Johnny was equally adamant. Junior needed the work. He was out of shape and couldn't possibly beat Louis without significant action inside the ring.

He could sell the fight as things were, Jacobs insisted; there was no need for any warm-up matches. Johnny sneered at the suggestion, "Yeah," he said, "but that's not getting my fighter in shape. I'm going to see that Billy is ready to go when he gets in the ring with Joe."[1]

"You can't manage my fighter," Johnny barked at the promoter, who retorted. "Who's the boss here anyway? The champion or the challenger?" Jacobs was referring to the fact that Louis had already agreed to have no tune-up fights. But Johnny dismissed this argument with a wave of his hand.

"What do I care what Louis is doing?" he hollered. "I'm not managing Louis, I'm managing Billy. You want to manage both me and Billy, Mike. But I'm not gonna let you."

Besides, Ray added, "Louis can't fight a tune-up fight. He's the heavyweight champion and anytime he goes to the post his title is at stake."

The flaring tempers were getting to Billy, who excused himself from the room. "This is getting too hot for me," he said. A reporter followed Conn out into the hallway and asked Billy what he thought about the disagreements. "It makes no difference to me," he shrugged. "I'll fight next week or anytime. But what Johnny says goes. He's the boss."[2]

And Johnny said the talks had ended—for the day, anyway. Uncle Mike always had his representative, Sol Strauss, standing nearby to offer advice. And what was good for Jacobs was good for him, Johnny thought. Ray broke off negotiations until his lawyer (and brother), Dave Pitler, could arrive in the city from Pittsburgh. The next afternoon, Dave joined his older sibling at the Twentieth Century offices to resume talks anew. Johnny arrived with a cooler head, but was no less resolute. With his calm approach, Ray was able to steer Jacobs to his way of thinking—sort of.

A compromise was reached on the contentious issue. Billy would be allowed to partake in warm-up bouts, but they would be exhibitions. There would be no official fights for Conn until Billy met Louis in mid-June. The challenger was also allowed to accept refereeing jobs and to appear on the numerous radio shows requesting interviews since his army discharge.

The remainder of the contract was very similar to the agreement reached for the first fight. A "ninety-day" clause was inserted: should

Conn win, he would allow Louis a rematch within ninety days. One of the few variations this time around was the inclusion of a share of the television and radio rights for the fighters, of which Billy was to receive 20 percent. It was also agreed that Jacobs would sell the television rights separately rather than include them as a package with the radio and movie-house rights.

With the *i*'s dotted and the *t*'s finally crossed, Johnny announced a tentative schedule of exhibition bouts for Billy, which would begin in Kansas City in early November. "Billy will do light gym work for the next several months while he's going through with these exhibitions and then be ready for heavy stuff March 1."[3]

Uncle Mike was happy and Johnny was pleased, so Billy was in good spirits as he returned home later that same evening. Only a few days of relaxation remained for Conn before his workouts began at the Pittsburgh Lyceum. The long and arduous climb back began on October 26 with a ninety-minute workout at the Lyceum. Ray limited his fighter to jumping rope and working the light and heavy bags initially. In fact, Billy did not face a sparring partner before entering the ring for his first exhibition bout, held in Cleveland on the 29th.

The three-round match with Bearcat Jones was fought with oversized gloves. Though his weight was not announced, Conn was obviously not in shape. A slight roll of fat protruded neatly over his trunks. Despite carrying a few too many pounds, Billy looked fast against Jones. Still, it was palpable that he wasn't ready yet. In the second round, Conn threw an adventurous hook at Bearcat's head, missing the mark completely. The effort caused Billy to lose his balance and he tumbled to the floor, falling on his hands and knees. Blushing, Billy returned to his feet, but for the remainder of the exhibition, Conn was careful to pull his punches.

Eleven days later Billy again met Jones, this time in Kansas City. The result of this affair was the cancellation of any remaining exhibitions Ray had slated. Billy was too out of shape for these public displays, and both manager and fighter recognized that fact. For the ensuing weeks, Conn trained in seclusion for the match that was still more than seven months off.

After the holidays, the serious training regimen began. Billy needed to get in shape in order to get in shape, and to accomplish this, it was imperative that Conn not be distracted during the process. The home life was out. Mary Lou did not know how to cook for a fighter in training. Additionally, the temptation to become lax was too strong if Billy remained in Squirrel Hill while preparing for Louis. No, Johnny wanted to take his fighter away from any and all diversions.

Owney Madden called Ray and suggested that he bring Billy out to Hot Springs, Arkansas, to train. To Madden, Johnny was noncommittal. However, word reached Owney that Ray wanted nothing to do with Hot Springs. Being told no, even through an intermediary, was not something Madden found acceptable. "You tell that Jew he better do what I say!" he ordered. The message was relayed to Johnny, who understood completely. Hot Springs it would be.

In the mid-thirties, Madden relocated from New York to Arkansas. Actually, Owney went into "retirement" as ordered by Charles "Lucky" Luciano. Though in his line of work that directive usually meant a permanent disappearance, Madden was allowed to move his operations west. In Hot Springs, Madden became a beloved man about town. He joined the chamber of commerce, donated money to local churches, and funded the construction of swimming pools; his generosity knew no bounds. Indeed, by all appearances, Owney was a well-respected and munificent businessman. Unbeknownst to most, the origin of the money Madden so freely handed out came from the Hot Springs gambling clubs, which Owney fronted for the New York mob.

Hot Springs was a resort town with a bustling nightlife, and that nightlife filled the coffers of Madden and his friends in New York. Billy's presence in Hot Springs could well bring the cozy town a great number of curious visitors. Madden hoped these tourists would come to see Conn work out in one of his daily sessions and, later, spend their evenings in one of his gambling joints. These joints were also effective hideouts for mobsters on the lam. Both Al Capone and Lucky Luciano used the town on different occasions when the cops began turning up the heat, as did a number of lesser-known gangsters.

Accompanied by Freddie Fierro and Milt Jaffe, Billy reached Hot Springs on January 4. "I fully expect to win this fight with Louis," Conn said to newsmen documenting his arrival, but he didn't expand on his perfunctory answer.[4]

The initial four weeks consisted of light training. In the morning, Billy got in his roadwork on the track of Hot Springs High School. Following lunch, Conn rested for three hours before entering the gym and beginning another hour of drills, which included weight lifting and work on the punching bags. Following the afternoon session, Billy liked to slip into one of Hot Springs' famous hot baths. Occasionally, Conn would deviate from his regular routine and take a hearty hike through the hills of Arkansas. For the time being, Billy was staying out of the ring. The experience with Bearcat Jones convinced Fierro and Ray that their fighter was not prepared for "live" action.

Though Billy's stint in the army was filled with boxing exhibitions, he had abstained from any type of training schedule. The only work he got was the brief time he spent in the ring with far inferior opponents. "Those three years in the army didn't help my ring condition any," Conn explained. "I'm not in shape for serious work but I'm trying to get ready for it."

Besides, Billy added, "I couldn't do any serious training right now even if I'm ready. I don't have any sparring partners."[5]

On January 16, Jacobs revealed the location, date, and ticket prices for the fight. Conn and Louis were slated to meet at Yankee Stadium in the Bronx on June 19, five years and a day since their first match. Uncle Mike proudly predicted that this card would surely be the greatest draw in the history of the sport. To help make his forecast come to fruition, Jacobs set the price for ringside seats at $100, with the cost gradually decreasing for the remaining ducats to $50, $30, $20, and $10.

The initial reaction to Jacobs's intention to charge a hundred bucks was derision and scorn. Two weeks later, Mike recanted; $50 and $40 would be the top prices, he announced, but the majority of the tickets would be $5 general admission. This plan, too, was retracted. Waiting two additional months, Jacobs again changed his mind. The top tickets would, indeed, be $100. The pricing scale remained the same as the original announcement with the exception of the $6 general admission. The hundred-dollar price exceeded the previous high by forty dollars, which Tex Rickard charged for the Jack Dempsey–Jess Willard match in Toledo.

Though the criticism of the pricing scale continued, the $100 ducat became a status symbol for some. The elite crowd and wannabe big shots all clamored for the high-priced seats. Since Jacobs never announced exactly how many of these tickets would be issued, it was a well-founded guess that anyone who wanted to purchase one would be accommodated.

One particular New York columnist decried the exorbitantly priced seats. It was a ridiculous amount to charge, he declared, for a couple of has-beens. Hell, the fight wasn't worth even $10 ringside.

"What's eating that guy?" Billy wondered. "He's a fine guy to be saying they're charging too much for the fight. That stuff he peddles for two cents a copy, and that's the biggest over charge I know of."[6]

On April 2, Billy began his "sentence"—seventy-five days in the rustic surroundings of Greenwood Lake. This vacation retreat was to play host to Conn as he began his serious preparations for the fight. Billy's everyday routine involved sparring, rope skipping, calisthenics, and roadwork. In his first workout, Billy boxed two rounds with Pittsburgh lightweight Sam Schipani. He then followed that with a round on the heavy bag, then the light bag for two more, and finally finished the drill with a series of calisthenics. In addition to Schipani, a number of sparring partners were on-site for Billy, including the pudgy and pugnacious Jackie Conn, Frankie Poreda, Mickey Bellusceo, and Irish Jimmy Smith. Each man employed a different style of fighting to prime Conn for Louis.

The country life wasn't Billy's cup of tea. The only time he didn't mind the pastoral atmosphere was when he was working out. "What am I going to do about those crickets?" he moaned when asked his thoughts on the beautiful surroundings. "They kept me awake all last night with their noise. If that's what you call 'country,' you can have it. Why don't they let me train in the city, anyway?"[7]

Conn's fight headquarters were located in Ted Gleason's Brown's Hotel. Behind the hotel, on the lakeside, Gleason constructed an outdoor arena, built exclusively for Billy's training. For a $1 admission, up to 1,200 people could be accommodated in the bleachers to watch Conn work out on Sundays. Inside, there was a large hall on the lower floor, which was outfitted with a ring, punching bags, and all the accoutrements needed to prepare a fighter for his profession.

For privacy, Billy lived with his trainers and Joe Becker in a brand-new log cabin, which was located about a mile from the hotel. "[Conn] eats anything he cares for anytime," Harry Keck told his readers. "I had dinner with him a few nights ago, and we started off with soup and then went for a mess of the biggest and tastiest chunk of thick beef liver I've ever eaten. There were fried potatoes and a couple of other vegetables, plenty of bread, a pudding, and coffee or milk."[8]

The champ began his preparations in mid-February, spending two weeks in a Los Angeles gym before moving to French Lick, Indiana, on March 1. By the beginning of May, Louis was on familiar ground in Pompton Lakes.

On May 3, he and Billy appeared before the New York State Athletic Commission. Surrounded by a horde of reporters, cameramen, commissioners, policemen, and a handful of curious gate-crashers, Conn and Louis underwent a physical examination by Dr. William Walker. Both men were declared to be in good shape; however, Walker said each fighter was a little slower than when he examined them prior to their first bout. Louis weighed in at 224½; Conn tipped the scales at 195½. To conclude the brief ceremony, the representatives of each fighter signed formal contracts with the commission and procured a deposit of $5,000 as appearance forfeiture.

The fight was officially on now and already Johnny began taking a defensive position concerning any rematch following Billy's victory. "Mike wants a September show for the heavyweight championship regardless of the outcome," Ray told reporters, "but if Billy is the champion he won't fight in September. Not against Louis or anyone else."

The reason, Johnny explained, was simple economics. The government took too big a share out of any purses earned. "The federal taxes on our dough will cut us down to a fraction of the original sum and if we have another fight after this fight, it'll be worse."

Ray's obstinate stance—though possibly it was simply posturing—was surely directed to pique Jacobs's ire. The two men had a considerable row at Uncle Mike's office concerning complimentary tickets, which Ray wanted for some friends. Procuring tickets gratis from the promoter was always a chore, and this request was no different. But this time around, Johnny took umbrage at Mike's miserly ways. A shouting match ensued and ended only when Jacobs ordered Ray from the building and left instructions that he not be allowed to reenter in the future.

"If that's the way you want it, okay," Johnny shouted as he was removed from the office, "but when my Billy wins the heavyweight championship you'll have to come to my office in Pittsburgh to see me. And when you do, I'll have two doormen on the door with orders to keep you out."

Ray's theatrics had drawn a nice little crowd of onlookers, which only fed his frenzy. "You're Louis' manager and protector," Johnny added, "and when he wants something you see that he gets it. He's got a lot going for him, and we don't have anything going for us. Well, we'll take care of that June 19."[9]

Billy's distress with living in the country only intensified as the fight drew nearer. "Everything you need for training you've got to drag out from the city anyway," he said. "First you bring out the ring, then the sparring partners, and your handlers, and your cook. The country doesn't have anything to offer except all those trees and lakes, and who wants them?"

Conn's antinature diatribe continued, "Monday I laid off and was in New York. Was up at Yankee Stadium and saw the Yankees bang the Browns around. That was all right—had a little bet on them. Then I had dinner in a good spot and lobbed around the hotel. Ain't that a lot better than waiting for your arteries to harden in the country?"

His contempt for the rural life knew no bounds. "Every time you want to see a movie, you got to drive for miles. I know so many towns around here, I could run a hack stand."[10]

Though Billy would gladly pack up and leave at a moment's notice, reporters covering both fighters found Greenwood Lake to be a wonderfully informal camp, especially when compared to Louis's "all-business approach" at Pompton Lakes. The main house at Brown's Hotel was always jumping. Two bars were set up to supply guests with their cocktail of choice, an always-popular perk for sportswriters. The house was overflowing with reporters, Billy's sparring partners, countless friends from Pittsburgh, and the curious who made the trip from the city. Whereas Louis had a strict rule of no autographs until he was finished with his workout, Conn was a delight to all his visitors. He spoke with everyone and signed anything put in front of him, even while wearing his gloves.

To inspire Billy, a photograph of Gene Tunney was hung in a prominent spot. The shot held a special place in Conn's heart; it depicted Tunney lying flat on his back in the famous "long count" fight against Jack Dempsey. Tunney had been talking to the press, and talking a lot, about how Billy wouldn't last two rounds against Louis.

"There's the guy who's taking cracks at me," Conn said. "Ain't he a great one? He's losing the title the first time he defends it if he don't get that long count. He ought to mind his stocks and bonds. . . . I wish I was going in there with Tunney. He's got nerve poppin' off the way he's doing. Who did he ever lick that was in shape?"[11]

Unlike Junior, Ray enjoyed the ambiance of Greenwood Lake. "We've got the same air the millionaires get over at Tuvedo," Johnny crowed. Ray didn't spend much time outside, though. Often he could be found inside the house where there was a running game of gin rummy, which Johnny seemingly always had a stake in. His luck since the start of camp had been poor, but that was certainly nothing new to Ray. Nor had Johnny's accounting habits changed any since the days long before, when he himself would slip through the ropes to earn a buck. He hadn't saved a dime of the money he had earned while managing Billy. This worried Ray not a bit. "Uncle Mike will bring me some more money," he shrugged. If not for Milt Jaffe, Johnny would have fallen on hard times during the four years Conn was out of action. Jaffe was there, however, to stake Ray enough to get by.

Unfortunately, Johnny's trouble holding onto a dollar wasn't the only weakness he failed to control. Since his stay at Mercy Hospital more than three years prior, Johnny's struggle with the bottle only intensified. In times of high stress, Ray depended on his addiction even more. Five years had been an unendurable wait for the rematch he wanted so badly, and now, with the fight just a handful of days away, Johnny increasingly turned to drink to help him cope with the building tension. Unlike previous training sessions, though, Johnny's dependency was now affecting his ability to conduct his job properly. Conn often said that Ray knew more about boxing drunk than anyone else did sober. But this time around it was different. Billy had never seen Moonie like this. Ray's dereliction was obvious to all who visited Conn's camp. However, thanks to newsmen who looked the other way, Johnny's condition remained unreported. Harry Keck, however, hinted that Ray was in a weakened condition. "Johnny is a very tired man," he wrote. "He has had little sleep during the past week. He'll need a long one when the fight is out of the way. Hardly a minute passes that some newspapermen or other friend is not tugging at his sleeve and asking him questions. He's all worn out and should be given a sedative and put to bed for a good sleep right now."[12]

On June 4, following a two-day rest, Billy put on one of his best workouts since training began. In front of 500 spectators, Conn danced around Teddy Gleason's makeshift ring, looking sure-footed and fast. The eight rounds he sparred brought the total to 217 boxed during his preparations. Immediately following his lengthy drill, Conn stepped onto a scale; the needle stopped at 182.

That same day, Jackie was sent on a mission to scout Louis at his camp. Joe, Jackie told reporters before leaving, "looked awfully easy to hit and Billy will punch him silly."[13] Not having access to the next day's papers just yet, following his workout, Billy inquired about his brother's trip to Pompton Lakes.

"You might just as well have had a blind man watching," he said with a laugh. Then Conn expressed his satisfaction with his own workout. "I feel great right now, near the peak. I'll be all right when I sharpen up just a bit more on the boxing. We'll box everyday the rest of this week."[14]

For reasons not made public, Conn fired his younger brother as sparring partner, but Billy kept him around camp to serve in the role as a "bouncer" and for the laughs Jackie always provided. Along with Steve Belloise, a middleweight who was being groomed for a match with Rocky Graziano, Jackie kept visitors on edge with his pranks. One evening, Belloise and Jackie removed the hubcaps from the automobiles parked in the lot at Brown's Hotel. They loaded the hubcaps with gravel and then replaced them. The jokesters then sat back and laughed as unknowing drivers headed out, stopped, lifted their hoods, and then headed for a service station to learn the cause of the strange noise emanating from their vehicles. They even got Johnny Ray, who borrowed a car to run an errand. "That was the best laugh of all," Jackie said. "He wouldn't know whether there was an engine in the car or not."[15]

The first sparring mate hired for Conn was Mickey McAvoy. Though McAvoy hadn't amassed much of a record in the ring, he had built a substantial résumé as a sparring partner to the previous six heavyweight champions: Jack Sharkey, Max Schmeling, Primo Carnera, Jimmy Braddock, Max Baer, and Joe Louis.

McAvoy had worked with Conn when Billy first entered the heavyweight ranks in 1940, and the two struck up a good working relationship. During the war, the Irishman from Brooklyn hung up his gloves and took up honest work driving a brewery truck in New York. After much enticement, Johnny Ray was able to persuade McAvoy to take a leave of absence and join the Conn team at Greenwood Lake.

"If Mickey never even boxed with Billy he'd been worth every cent we're paying him," Freddie Fierro said. "Did you ever stop to think that a sparring partner is a constant companion to the man he trains with? It's just as important for Conn to like the men personally, as it is for Billy to be pleased with their boxing."

McAvoy's value to the Conn camp went well beyond his role as sparring partner to Billy. His love of storytelling relieved many a tedious day. Mickey reveled in sharing tales from his days as a bodyguard in Hollywood, and often had the camp in stitches with his humorous tales.

Another hired gun at Greenwood Lake was Marty Clark, who was awarded the Purple Heart while fighting in Italy. Clark's specialty was his ability to pack a wallop with either hand. "We expect to use a total of fifteen sparring partners before we break camp," said Tony Tomacci, a newcomer to the Conn team. "Most of them, if we can obtain the type we want, will be good punchers. We'll have a middleweight or two for speed, but there's one thing you can be sure of—no matter whom we hire for Conn, when they step into that ring at Greenwood Lake, both he and Billy will be leveling. Conn will box an unprecedented number of rounds, traveling ten to twelve heats per day, with perhaps one day off from boxing every two weeks."[16]

Not everyone was awed by Conn's practice mates. Doc Kearns, onetime manager of Jack Dempsey, came away from Greenwood Lake unimpressed. "Conn has a bunch of nondescript sparring partners so you can't tell too much about Billy except that he's in shape. Louis, on the other hand, is training with a bunch of fighters any of whom might give Conn trouble."

As expected, especially with an unprecedented number of reporters covering the buildup, Billy was repeatedly asked about the first match. He answered the queries politely and with candor. "I should have gone down from the left hook," he said, referring to the thirteenth. "Going down for nine is no worse than going down for one. I should'a gone down and then got up, and Louis would never have found me for the rest of the night.

"It seemed like a fast count to me, but I'm not alibiing. I guess I was a sucker, at that hook, I got mad and punched back like a fool, I guess. I was wide open when he uppercut me, and I don't blame him."

Conn wanted to make one thing clear—all the talk was just show. He liked Louis. "Joe's a nice guy. I ain't mad at him. I just want that title of his; that's all. He's had it a long time, now, and I'd like to have it. . . . I'm 28, but look at Joe. He's an old man. He's 32. They tell me he isn't moving so good. I'm glad to hear that, because if he doesn't keep moving, I'm gonna have that title. If it goes the limit, I ought to be the new champion."[17]

More than 700 press credentials were issued for journalists arriving from every corner of the country and beyond. Interest in the fight reached far beyond American borders as reporters from Australia, Sweden, Mexico, South Africa, South America, England, France, Belgium, Bermuda, Italy, Hawaii, Russia, and Switzerland converged on New York. Shortly before noon each day, the newsmen would gather at the Twentieth Century offices. They would then all jump into a long procession of autos for the thirty-five-mile trip to Pompton Lakes or the fifty-mile hike to Greenwood Lake. No accredited writer captured the subject with quite the verve as comedienne Gracie Allen.

"I went to Mr. Conn's camp at Greenwood Lake to see how he looked," Ms. Allen, wife of comedian George Burns, wrote for the North American Newspaper Alliance. "I wore a blue and yellow checked dressmaker suit with a Navy skirt and my little blue hat. He looked for about ten minutes.

"Mr. Conn is terribly handsome, and, of course, has a simply gorgeous physique. I was puzzled at first by some odd bumps on his arms that I had never seen on George's, but I soon learned what they were. They're called muscles."[18]

In her next column, Ms. Allen attempted to handicap the fight. Condition of the principals, she was told, was an important component when picking a winner. "Well," Allen wrote, "both Joe and Billy are wearing white satin robes with green trim, so there's no choice there."

Next was speed, and there, Allen decided, Louis had the edge because "he noticed my new hat right away, while Billy took quite a few seconds.

"As to their respective ages, I asked my sister Bessie and she says there's no difference between a man 28, and a man 32, especially if they both have money."

With so many factors to weigh, Allen came to a succinct conclusion. "If Louis doesn't knock Conn out, Conn will get the decision, unless, of course, he knocks Joe out, which can't possibly happen if Louis outpoints him, and he may."[19]

Mary Louise changed her plans and decided against coming to New York. Rather, she would stay home with her boys and listen to the fight on the radio. "I'm not particularly worked up about the fight," she told a reporter. "I have my two youngsters to take care of, you know. They keep me pretty busy."

When asked if she believed Billy would win, Mary Lou didn't hesitate. "Certainly," she confidently replied.[20] An Associated Press poll found that a large majority of fight experts disagreed with Mrs. Conn. Fifty-seven of seventy-four writers questioned selected the champ to retain his title. Ironically, despite Louis being the heavy favorite, reports from Pompton Lakes were mixed at best. Jack Dempsey paid a visit to the Louis camp and declared himself undecided.

"But you picked Joe to win in four or five rounds," a writer quizzically asked.

"I didn't do that," Dempsey said. "The ghost writer did."[21]

George Jaffe and Johnny's brother Dave replaced Jackie as Billy's spies. They, too, reported back that the champ was vulnerable. Like Dempsey, they found Louis to be slow and lacking fire. "I've beaten a lot of champions, but this is the only one that counts," Billy said. "All I know is that I'm going to win. A knockout? Maybe. But put this down in your little book—I'm taking over for Joe Louis. He's been a great champion, but his days are done. I'm going to be the new champion. There's no question about that."[22]

Conn's predictions lacked the brazenness of five years prior. He mouthed the words, but his heart didn't seem to be into the statements. Surely he felt he had a chance to win. And certainly, Louis's days were numbered. Billy knew he had a puncher's chance, but he also knew that, even at his best, he wasn't known as a puncher. Whereas five years earlier Billy mapped out how he would win the fight in great detail, in 1946 Conn simply laid his fate on Louis's age. But he, too, had grown older. The war and the time away from the ring had done neither man any favor.

Louis always exuded confidence in his modest way, but Joe was rarely specific concerning upcoming bouts. This time was different. "I should knock Billy out sometime in the eighth round," Louis told writers as he broke camp. "I want to win this one bad; I'm going to get Conn as fast as I can."[23]

What about Billy's speed? Joe had trouble with Conn's quickness the first time around; why shouldn't fight fans expect more of the same this time? Louis had a concise answer to this query. "He can run, but he can't hide," Joe said simply.[24]

Louis's corner would be absent several men who helped forge the Brown Bomber into a champion. Jack Blackburn, Joe's friend and trainer, passed away on April 24, 1942, of pneumonia. Chappie's death came shortly after Louis's second fight with Buddy Baer. Joe's former manager, John Roxborough, was doing time in upstate Michigan on a gambling conspiracy rap. And Julian Black was shown the door by the champ when his contract with Louis expired in January of '45.

Johnny did a bit of psychoanalyzing for the papers. "I think Joe is a little bitter about the way things have turned out for him," Ray said. "Here he is at the end of his career with little to show for his nine years as champion. For the last four years he has not been able to fight and make any money. He has thrown away four of the best years of his fistic life."

The war robbed countless men the occasion to fulfill their earning potential, and certainly a professional athlete's window of opportunity was more finite than the average Joe, but Johnny's statement could also apply to his fighter. Louis did have good reason to be resentful, though. Despite donating his time and the purses of the prewar Simon and Baer fights to government charities, Joe's tax bill was astronomical. "He owes Uncle Mike and the government a lot of money," Johnny said. "and it may be that what he gets out of this one, with the additional taxes, will leave him as flat as he is today."

There was also the fact that Joe's longtime benefactors, Blackburn, Black, and Roxborough, were gone. "He's surrounded by strangers," Ray pointed out. "I feel sorry for him. The average man who works for a weekly paycheck and is able to live within his means is better off than Joe with all his obligations."

Regardless, Ray thought highly of Billy's adversary. "Louis is a fine fellow, a great fighter and a gentleman. My guy is different. He'd cut your throat to win. He has the instinct that goes with the fight game. I hope he doesn't become a gentleman until after we make some money. Being a gentleman softens you up in this business."[25]

The unprecedented hype was reaching its apex as both fighters closed their camps. On the afternoon of the 17th, Billy strayed from his schedule as he finished his work at Greenwood Lake. He sparred three rounds with Sammy Schipani, a Pittsburgh lightweight who was chosen for his speed and Conn's superstition that Sammy was a good luck charm because he had been the first to spar with Billy when camp opened on April 2. Later that evening, Conn slipped into the city behind a police motorcade. He couldn't vacate the rustic retreat fast enough and plant his feet on the soothing pavement and bustling streets of Gotham, arriving early enough to venture to the theater with Joe Becker and take in the show *Billion Dollar Baby*.

Unlike Billy, Joe stuck to the script for his final workout at Pompton

Lakes. Louis boxed four rounds, including his usual warm-up, and concluded the session with some work on the heavy bag.

A hotel room within the borough of Manhattan was next to impossible to find. Hotel officials placed cots in ballrooms, banquet rooms, and in any nook allowed by law.

For the first time since the start of the war, Owney McManus chartered the Ham and Cabbage Special, though not nearly as many fans took this mode of transportation. "The train won't have the entertainment and free beer of pre-war times," McManus said. "You can't get that 'bevo' to sell, much less give it away. Oh, well, we'll make our own entertainment coming back in honor of the new heavyweight champ. I tell you Billy is a cinch to win."[26] Though only seventy Pittsburghers took advantage of the McManus train, more than five thousand Smoky City fans ventured to New York for the fight, many more flying than ever before. The Edison Hotel served as the headquarters for Pittsburgh enthusiasts.

Jake Mintz was among the many Pittsburghers who had ventured east. But ol' Jake was not on vacation. No, this was a working trip for Mintz. The assiduous promoter was seen tacking a placard up in Times Square pushing his upcoming July 1 match between Ezzard Charles and Jimmy Bivins.

Greenfield Jimmy was among the Conn backers. Indeed, Smith had quietly become one of Billy's biggest supporters and had spent a number of days at Greenwood Lake. He expected his son-in-law to win. Jimmy said, "I won't settle for less, although I know Billy has his work cut out for him. But Billy will do it—I'm not worried about that."[27] Not everyone in the Conn family had faith in their prizefighter. Pap asked Timmy whom he thought would win, and without so much as a pause he replied, "Joe Louis."

Mike Jacobs was a whirlwind in the last couple of days before the fight. He divided his time between his headquarters at Madison Square Garden and at Yankee Stadium, overseeing every detail of the production. At the venue, Mike supervised a veritable army of 200 workers who spent the day before the fight arranging the stands. In addition to the normal flat sections of seats, an additional 15,000 elevated seats were put in place.

The Twentieth Century offices were swamped with last-minute requests, but the demand was largely for the lower-priced seats. Other customers were angered by Jacobs's "no-refund" policy. It seemed a number of people purchased more tickets than were needed. Uncle Mike, though, would not relent. He instituted the plan to thwart counterfeiting.

Jacobs also busied himself seeing to the last-minute needs of NBC. The television network had five cameras ready to go on-air an hour and a half before the main bout. The broadcast would only be seen in Washington, D.C., Philadelphia, Schenectady, and New York City. An estimated 1,000,000 fans were expected to view the fight in restaurants and bars, and it was carried by more than 1,200 Muzak outlets in greater New York.

Jacobs garnered $100,000 for the radio rights from the American Broadcasting Company. The State Department would also broadcast the fight via a relay to France and Latin America. Between television and radio, Louis–Conn II was going to be the most elaborate and extensive transmission of a sporting event ever.

To maintain a semblance of order and to accommodate the enormous media demand, the weigh-in was scheduled for Madison Square Garden rather than the typical gathering at the office of the athletic commission. Admission was by ticket only, and an estimated 400 cameramen, "movie men," and sportswriters assembled in the Garden's arena for the ceremony. Having just arrived in the city at 12:15, Louis was the first to climb into the ring. Wearing a white bathrobe and purple trunks, Joe stepped on the scale weighing 207 pounds.

While Dr. Clilan Powell examined Louis, Billy stood ringside, intently watching the activities. When Powell asked Joe to run in place, Conn looked over to Johnny, who was standing nearby, and winked. Ray was vainly trying to keep an eye on the examination also, but the numerous photographers crowding the ring hoping to capture the ideal shot of the champion were hounding him.

"They are chasing me like a thief," Ray exclaimed.[28]

Billy was up next. Rather than a boxing robe, Conn sported over his shoulders a gray coat, which matched the suit he wore into the arena. Discarding his pants, Billy too wore purple trunks and stepped on the scale. At 182, Conn, like Louis, was at the heaviest weight of his career. As the number was announced to the gathered throng, Joe leaned over to Billy, "You're big enough for a heavyweight now, you're growing."

"Yeah, Joe," Conn said with a smile, "I'm getting bigger."[29]

To some in attendance, Billy's normal confidence was absent at the weigh-in. Harry Keck later described Conn's disposition as "tight as a drum."[30] Earlier, in the dressing room of the Garden, Billy asked for a stick of gum and then was observed chewing with nothing in his mouth. As Conn stepped off the scale, shutterbugs yelled to him, asking Billy to turn this way or that, each photographer vying for the best possible shot. The whole scene seemed to perturb Conn, who turned away from the throng with a strong hint of irritation. Ray and Fierro quickly jumped in for their man and told the cameramen to "lay off." Billy needed a chance to contemplate the task awaiting him. Harry Keck had been to many of Conn's fights, and knew the fighter as well as anyone outside his immediately circle of friends. There was nothing scientific to the reporter's estimation that Billy was tight, but his opinion was based on great familiarity with the subject.

Following the examination, chairman commissioner Eddie Eagan conferred with Ray and Conn before speaking with Louis and his manager, Marshall Miles. Though both factions had previously expressed the desire to keep their fighter under the stands until the ceremonial introductions had concluded, neither group brought the matter up at the Garden. Eagan assured both sides that, though they would enter the ring immediately following the final preliminary bout, the announcements would be made as quickly as possible. At the close of the weigh-in, Eagan confirmed the cornermen for each side. The champion's seconds were Miles, trainer Mannie Seamon, assistant trainer George Nicholson, and Larry Amadee. In Billy's corner were the usual faces of Ray, Fierro, and Billy Joos. Joining the old team was trainer Tony Tomacci, who united with Conn's merry band at Greenwood Lake.

The evening before the bout, Art Rooney was speaking with Shirley Povich of the *Washington Post.* In his heart, Rooney was pulling for Billy to come through; still, the Pittsburgh sportsman couldn't envision a Conn victory. "I've still got a little bundle riding on him," Rooney admitted, "but it's sentimental. Billy can't win. He knows he's over-matched and he doesn't have much enthusiasm for this one. You could see it in all his training."

Rooney wasn't the only visitor to Greenwood Lake to come away with this belief. Though most reports from the Conn camp were glowing, those in the know questioned if Billy was prepared, mentally or physically, for Joe Louis. "He's like every guy who's been knocked out by Joe Louis," Rooney explained. "Sure, Billy was great the first time he fought Louis. He'd never been tagged by Joe before and he never knew how hard Joe could hit. He knows now, and it's not good. No guy going in there against Louis a second time has the same confidence. I don't like Billy's chances."[31]

Billy arrived at the Stadium at 7:30, his car following a police motorcycle escort. Pulling up to the gate, Conn was met by attendants determined not to allow entry. Someone in the Conn party decided that they should try the office door for the Yankees. After much discussion and persuasion, the guard on duty there decided to permit Billy into the park. "After all," he surmised, "the guy is fighting here tonight and he has to get in somehow even if it isn't supposed to be through this door." Twenty minutes later, Louis experienced a virtual replay of Billy's attempt to enter the stadium.

In his later years, Billy was always affable. Running into an old fan on the street, he was always available for a word or willing to rehash an old memory from his days in the ring. But whenever the second Louis fight was brought up, Billy shut down. That was one memory he'd rather not conjure.

To his dying day, Harry Keck carried with him the belief that something untoward happened to Billy in the hours leading up to the fight. The day following the bout, Keck reported Conn's strange behavior at the weigh-in; however, at the time, he attributed Billy's actions to nervous jitters. Two years later, though, Keck was a little more to the point. "You never saw a better conditioned or more confident challenger in camp than Billy or a more unimpressive looking heavyweight champion than Louis."

Then came the day of the fight, Keck wrote, and "Billy suddenly went limp. He doesn't remember going to the weigh-in, has only a vague recollection of the fight. He was walking like a man in a dream. There have been many rumors that he was drugged by persons interested in the betting angle."[32]

Prior to the fight, Conn seemed to be in a complete daze, barely recognizing the faces of people he'd known for years. Just before entering the ring, Billy turned to Greenfield Jimmy and said, "This will be the worst fight ever."

The next morning's paper carried Gracie Allen's coverage of the fight, which concluded with an apt summary. "Billy was the first in the ring," Ms. Allen wrote. "He came in at 10:08 and that was where he made his first mistake of the evening. He should have gone home at 10:06."[33]

The fight began inauspiciously. For three rounds Billy circled, circled, and circled some more. Occasionally the challenger threw a jab. Or a hook. But these halfhearted punches appeared to be a formality, an effort not intent on bringing harm or instilling fear in his opponent. These initial stanzas were as perplexing as they were numbingly dull. What was Conn's plan? His defense in the initial bout was a strategic fighting retreat. This time, Billy completely left out the fighting part of the plan and simply retreated. He stayed on the balls of his feet, bouncing and dancing, fleeing at the hint of a Louis feint, never mounting an attack of his own except one solid right in the second. But Billy didn't follow this jolt with anything but more dancing. During the first minutes of the bout, Conn began talking to Joe. The banter lacked the buoyancy Billy delivered five years earlier. His statements obviously belied Conn's state of mind.

"Hey Joe," he groused, "take it easy. We got fifteen rounds to go."

Louis, though, had no intention of taking the fight to the limit.

Little changed in the fourth except that Joe began to read the pattern of Billy's strange choreography. Finally Joe landed a few telling blows; Billy reciprocated with several of his own. Though they lacked the steam to hurt Louis, the punches did serve notice that Conn remembered the objective of his profession. Still the tedious dance continued. On occasion, Joe found the range and scraped his glove across Conn's nose, but those in the hundred-dollar seats surely began to wonder if they'd been better served to invest in fine theater tickets instead.

It took until the sixth, but for a brief moment a flash of fire showed in Billy's eyes. A combination was delivered with the full intention of bringing the champ down. Then, as quickly as it came, the flame was extinguished. Through seven rounds, the only good thing that could be said was that Billy had escaped any serious punishment. The same must be said though, that Conn had failed to inflict any himself. Those who had seen him at Greenwood Lake thought they were witnessing another fighter. The Conn who stood against Louis in front of them looked old, slow, unmotivated, perplexed. He wasn't the brash exuberant challenger of twenty-three that so many had etched in their minds. Certainly age had wearied his legs a bit. Perhaps the clarity of family had sapped some of Billy's impetus. Others held out hope that Billy had something up his sleeve. Maybe Conn was luring Joe into a trap of some sort. One look into his corner, however, and all such optimism vanished.

There, outside the ring, Ray paced to and fro, anxiously rubbing his hands. There was no sign of confidence or hope in Billy's corner.

Between the seventh and eighth, Joe sat passively in his corner as Mannie Seamon talked to him, giving a running dialogue of instruction and encouragement. Louis silenced his trainer with a brief statement of purpose. "I'm gonna go out and fight now and see how he can take it."[34] Strangely, as the two fighters came out at the sound of the bell, they touched gloves, a custom usually followed at the beginning of the final round.

Billy ran and ran, but within the strict confines of the roped canvas he could not hide from the menacing and lethal fists of Louis. A minute into the eighth, Louis threw a telling hook that caught Billy under the left eye, opening a nasty cut that immediately sent a flow of blood down Conn's cheek. With the blow, and Billy's humbled reaction to it, Louis knew the fight was his. Sixty seconds passed before Joe followed with a right to Billy's side, which obviously hurt Conn, sending him into a stagger and bringing a telling sneer to his face. Then came a short right uppercut landing square on the jaw. That blow appeared to be enough to bring Billy down, but Louis was brooking no chance. A left flush to Conn's jaw sent Sweet William tumbling to the canvas.

There he lay, flat on his back, his left gloved hand raised slightly as if to shield his eyes from the blinding lights overhead. Picking up the count from the timekeeper at three, Eddie Josephs continued, 4, 5, 6 . . . Conn continued to lay prone beneath the referee. Josephs persisted to ten and with a wave of his arms, mercifully stopped the fight.

Before the count reached ten, Johnny had already thrown in the towel and slipped through the ropes to retrieve Junior. Dazed, Billy rose to his feet and, with the support of Moonie, gingerly found his way to the refuge of his corner.

As the battered Conn stepped down from the ring, a supportive member of press row called out to the fighter, "Nice going, Billy."

A bemused smile formed on Conn's face. "Nice going, my ass."

A police escort cleared a path to the dressing room for Conn. Soon he would be surrounded by reporters, but for a moment, Billy was alone in the room with his entourage and one member of the press, Harry Keck. Weary, Conn sat down for a few moments with his head in his hands. The moment of solitary reflection was broken by the arrival of a flock of newsmen.

"This was the kid's last fight, I'm putting the cue stick back on the rack," Billy said, struggling to smile as he said the painful words. "I can't fight anymore. I just haven't got it, and there's no sense continuing and getting killed."

Before the reporters could begin to ask their questions, Conn supplied the answers. "I know it was a stinking fight, but I had a definite plan. I kept backing away, trying to tire him out. He hit me a good shot and that was all. He's still a great fighter. Me, I'll never fight again. I should reenlist in the Army, I was so lousy tonight."[35]

A few steps away, Johnny Ray stood watching Junior speak to the press. With tears streaming down his cheeks, Ray agreed with Conn's acknowledgment. "Billy hasn't got it. He's finished."[36]

"Will it stick?" Harry Keck asked. "Are you sure he won't change his mind after the disappointment wears off?"

"No," Ray answered. "I told him. And you know it's final."[37]

Ray admitted that he realized something was amiss early in the match. "Before the fight started," Johnny said. "I never thought there was a chance that Billy would lose, but after the first round, I knew it was all over. Billy just didn't have it. We have no excuses, no alibis, nothing. He's all washed up as a fighter. But he was a great one when he had it."[38]

Greenfield Jimmy waded through the press surrounding Billy and reached out for his son-in-law's hand. "The hell with it," Jimmy said. "Just as long as you didn't get hurt."[39]

Billy took Smith's hand in his. "Timmy was right," he told Smith.

Across the way, the champion was surrounded by a horde of inquisitive reporters. Holding a water bottle with one hand and eating an orange with the other, Joe deadpanned, "The toughest fight I've had tonight was getting into this dressing room."

"What did you think of Billy?" Louis was asked.

"Well, I'll say this. Billy wasn't the fighter he was the last time. He was much slower and didn't bother me at all. I was taking it easy until the eighth round." A reporter then told Louis that Conn had announced his retirement; what do you think of that, Joe?

Over the course of the previous five years Louis had grown close to Conn. The two would never be the best of friends, but they certainly liked each other and enjoyed one another's company. For five years, their names were constantly linked in the conjecture of a possible rematch. History would indelibly bind their names thanks to that unforgettable night in June of '41, before the war reached American shores. Defeating Billy was not an enjoyable task, but his competitive drive and devotion to his sport demanded nothing less than full effort. Indeed, Joe wanted to beat his rival as quickly and decisively as possible, but he hated bringing about the obvious verity that Billy Conn was no longer the brash gunslinger of old. Hearing the news that Billy was hanging up his gloves saddened Joe, but he didn't offer any comment. No, the great champion silently looked off, lost in thought, and softly shook his head.

The big celebration party for Billy that was planned at Toots Shor's place was canceled, as were a number of other gatherings and the hope of painting the town green. A great exodus from the city began shortly after Josephs counted Conn out. A number of Pittsburghers who'd planned on remaining in the city in the afterglow of a victory by their native son opted instead to drive home that very night. Others sought space on trains or airlines. A somber cloud enveloped Billy's many supporters as their much-anticipated night of revelry was dashed.

The reviews, as could be expected, were scathing.

Dan Parker wrote for the INS perhaps the most vicious indictment that could be laid upon Conn—that he was afraid. "Billy Conn was scared out of his wits when he entered the ring and acted during most of the fight as if his wits had actually deserted him," Parker opined. "Conn backed up far enough to be in the suburbs of Pittsburgh if he had traveled in a straight line."[40]

"He [Conn] won the Arthur Murray cup," Joe Williams quipped, "and very likely a job on the maestro's staff where his genius will be appreciated. But he lost the boxing contest." It seems as if Williams was miffed that so much of the commentary afterward was centered on, and critical of, the boxing exhibition rather than the impressive dance contest he had just witnessed.

Williams continued, "I believe any right thinker and decent sportsman will argue that Conn proved to be the most gifted dancer since the Castles, though perhaps lacking comparable stamina, especially that of the glass-fragile Irene."[41]

With best vantage point in the house, Eddie Josephs was ruthless in his evaluation of the fight. "That was not only the worst title fight I ever refereed, but it was the worst stinkaroo I ever saw," said Josephs. "And I sure feel sorry for the fellows who laid out a hundred bucks a copy."[42]

The star-studded crowd that filed out of Yankee Stadium was disappointed that the fight didn't come close to living up to the great buildup. The much-ballyhooed hundred-dollar seats were nearly sold out, but the less-expensive seats were nowhere near filled to capacity. To some commentators, this rated the production as a bust. Jacobs pledged on several occasions in the days leading up to the show that more than $2 million in tickets had already been sold, and he fully expected the final tally to approach $3 million. The official gate was $1,925,564; 45,266 came through the turnstiles in a ballpark that could accommodate 80,000. Were it not for the hype, the numbers would have seemed more impressive. But hype there was, and plenty of it. That fact, taken in hand with the disappointing show inside the ring, resulted in many who viewed the affair as a failure.

Television played a role in the low turnout. Like other prefight predictions, the viewing audience much lower than anticipated. An estimated 100,000 people saw the fight in the limited area where it was available over the airwaves. TV was a novelty and the picture transmitted by NBC lacked crystal clarity; still, large groups gathered in bars and homes to view the championship match. Certainly a portion of the television audience would have ventured to New York had the fight not been available for free over the airwaves. Sitting in Washington, D.C., was one person who had intended on witnessing the bout in person if only Uncle Mike had provided the complimentary tickets requested; a familiar voice from past Louis–Conn affairs. Though the fight was brought alive only through blurry images on his black-and-white console television, New York Congressman Donald O'Toole believed he could see that something crooked was taking place in Yankee Stadium.

At Eddie Josephs's count of ten, O'Toole was off his chair, busily dialing the number of every reporter in his book. The congressman announced his intention of going to the New York Boxing Commission and asking that the purses for Louis and Conn be held. He also issued a demand that Jacobs be prevented from using the mail system because "he has been defrauding the public." O'Toole's charges went beyond the poor show put on by the principals inside the ring and covered Jacobs's near monopoly of the sport. In a telegram to the state boxing commissioner Edward Eagan, O'Toole wrote,

> In justice to those who were swindled at last night's Conn–Louis fight the State Boxing Commission should hold up the purses of

both fighters pending investigation. This investigation should cover the preparations made for the fight, the agreements made between Jacobs, the fighters and others, the actual splitting of the purses and the existence of any debts on the part of the fighters to Jacobs.

The investigation should further cover the amount of control that Jacobs has not only over Conn and Louis but also over the entire boxing industry in the United States. One more fraud such as last night's and boxing will be ruined in the United States for many years to come. It is the duty of the commission to protect the public and this can only be achieved by an investigation such as I suggest.[43]

O'Toole hoped to address the issue from the House floor but was refused recognition during a busy House session. The grandstanding Brooklyn Democrat declared his intention of demanding that Jacobs be barred from using the mail system because "he had been defrauding the public."

Uncle Mike deftly responded to O'Toole's strongly worded charges. The congressman was only angry, Jacobs claimed, because he had been denied the free tickets his office requested. This reply only furthered O'Toole's crusade, which now alleged that Jacobs was "accusing me of extortion" and promised a civil lawsuit against the promoter. The squabble was already more entertaining than the passive punchless fest put on by Billy and Joe.

"Yes sir," Jacobs told reporters, "I'll welcome the suit. But I don't believe he'll dare to go through with it. He's just trying to get his name in the paper at my expense because he's coming up for election soon. He wants to dish it out, but he can't take it."[44]

Though Edward Eagan had not yet received O'Toole's telegram, he had read about it in the newspaper and found the politician's complaints curious. "I see no reason why any congressman would make inquiries about the fight if he had not the sporting instinct to come and see it in the first place," Eagan said.[45]

The give-and-take continued. "I saw the whole fight by television right here in Washington," O'Toole said. "What Eagan means is that I didn't have the sucker instinct."

Perhaps, the congressman continued, the commissioner should "turn in his papers" if he couldn't live up to his responsibility of protecting the public from such exhibitions.

For forty-eight hours, O'Toole's allegations filled headlines and nearly overshadowed the fight itself. The congressman refused to let the matter drop; he spoke briefly on the affair to the House the day after first being denied the opportunity, and he also granted an extensive interview to the *Washington Post*.

"The whole fight set-up in New York is as false as Jacobs' store teeth," O'Toole told Bus Ham of the *Post*. He had been to both camps prior to the fight and watched each man work out. "Louis had good men to toughen him. Conn had nobody that a girl couldn't have hit. Louis and Conn should never have been permitted to enter the same ring together."

"A fight such as the Louis–Conn affair becomes a national scandal when the mails are used to send out tickets, accept checks and ballyhoo the bout into the picture. . . . When such things go over the State lines, as they did for the Louis–Conn fraud, the Federal Government should look into it."[46]

Following O'Toole's speech to the House, the Justice Department issued a statement declaring "there is no reason for an investigation."[47] No investigation of the fight was forthcoming, but Representative O'Toole did raise several salient points, not the least of which was the questioning of Jacobs's monopoly of the game and the criminal element invested in the outcome of boxing matches. His hope of exposing the underbelly of professional boxing may have been curtailed, but O'Toole did follow through on his threat to sue Jacobs.

On June 28, the congressman filed a $200,000 libel and slander suit against Uncle Mike ($100,000 for slander and $100,000 for libel). The charges stemmed from Jacobs's allegation that O'Toole merely criticized the fight because he was denied free tickets. "The defamatory words uttered by the defendant and thereafter published were and are wholly false," the complaint read. "The said articles which appeared in numerous newspapers throughout the United States were calculated to and did hold the plaintiff up to public hatred, infamy and disgrace." (On January 31, 1949, the suit between O'Toole and Jacobs was settled for a "nominal sum.")

In the shadow of the fight, O'Toole was very public in expressing his misgivings. Others had their suspicions, though these doubts amounted to nothing more than a whispering campaign. Things weren't quite right in the days immediately leading up to the match, about that there was little dispute. Conn's decision to leave his hotel room and instead spend the night before the fight at Toots Shor's apartment raised a few eyebrows when the move became known. This switch was made without the knowledge of Johnny or Greenfield Jimmy, who were both frantically searching for Billy. Indeed, more than a few present in Conn's dressing room speculated that something was slipped into his food or drink the evening prior to the fight, and Billy's dazed and disheveled appearance only added credence to such conjecture. A Senate investigative committee, the Kefauver Committee, was formed in 1950 in order to gain knowledge of organized crime. This highly publicized commission began looking into the unsubstantiated allegations associated with the Louis–Conn bout, but nothing was formally brought before the committee. And Billy—he would never speak of the matter.

The reporting from Pittsburgh writers lacked the biting humor that was found in the coverage throughout the rest of the country. While frank in its appraisal of Billy's performance, the tone found in Pittsburgh's dailies was somber. Something special had passed. The exciting, effervescent young man who had entertained them for years was nowhere to be seen in Yankee Stadium on June 19. Of Conn's admirers on press row, few thought more highly of him than Havey Boyle. The *Post-Gazette* sports editor had followed Billy's career from its inception, and detailing Conn's porous performance proved difficult.

"Billy Conn not only lost to Joe Louis, but he lost ingloriously, he lost without furnishing a single palliative for the bitter dregs of the knockout."

If only Billy had put up a fight, Boyle lamented. "There was a hardly a saving thing about his ill-starred adventure with a great champion. Had Conn stood on the bridge as he did during his first sinking five years ago and gone with flags still flying, defeat would have been secondary as it must always be, in the display of great spirit."[48]

Boyle had touched on the aspect of Conn's defeat that most frustrated fans: Billy didn't put up a fight. The lack of "fight" led some to report that Conn was "afraid" and that he was "timid" in the ring with Louis. Billy himself was forthright when evaluating his performance. "Was I terrible? I stunk the joint out."

Conn walked out of Yankee Stadium and left his boxing career behind; symbolically, by leaving his equipment bag at the park, and mentally—mentally, Billy was through with the game before he got on his feet, if not before. What he needed when he left the stadium was his family. Thankfully, Mary Louise altered her plans once again and arrived in

New York several hours before the fight, but true to her word, Mrs. Conn neither attended the fight nor listened to it on the radio. With Timmy and Billy Jr. in tow, win or lose, Mary was waiting for Billy in the Waldorf Astoria.

Indeed, the sting of defeat wasn't as biting when surrounded by family. Conn arose early the morning after the fight and spent a long while playing with his sons. Try as he might, though, Conn couldn't wash his mind of the previous evening's events. He hadn't bothered to shave, his right eye was discolored, and he had a cut on his nose and a scar across the bridge of his nose; Billy looked liked the defeated man he was. Wearing the same gray suit that he wore the day before to the weigh-in, Conn emerged from the Astoria late in the morning and took a stroll through Manhattan to Uncle Mike's office. There a group of reporters gathered to kibitz and shake their head in wonder—what had happened to Conn? Five years earlier, many of the same writers had met in the same office; then they marveled at young Billy's Irish courage. Now, though some didn't verbalize it, Conn's bravery was brought into doubt. A few went so far as to say Billy was "timid" in the ring and "afraid" of Louis.

In Jacobs's office, Conn perused a few papers and read some of these critical reviews. The loss was painful beyond description. Billy had fallen before, but never had he been embarrassed. He prided himself on his fighting spirit, and last night, on center stage, he appeared listless and lacking in will. He lost and he lost big. But quit? Never. Afraid? Ridiculous. Some of the things being written disturbed Conn to no end.

"Imagine," he roared. "Those bums calling *me* timid!"[49] All of this—the questions, the way he was *looked* at, the loss—was weighing heavy enough on Conn; he didn't need people feeling sorry for him or, worse, doubting his toughness. He stayed with Mike and the reporters for a brief time. Conn's mind was elsewhere, preoccupied with faraway thoughts. He even left without inquiring about his share of the gate. Billy just wanted to leave New York and boxing, at least for a few days. Returning to the Waldorf Astoria, Conn, along with Mary Lou and their boys, lit out for Ocean City in a borrowed car. A couple of days of reflection and relaxation would do wonders for Billy's psyche. Or so he hoped.

"I'd rather have had Joe murder me out there than what happened," Billy moaned upon returning home. Yes, there was to be another round of queries when he arrived in Pittsburgh. Not facing the local press would bring about more criticism, that of a sore loser. So one more time, Conn sucked up his damaged pride and left himself open to interrogation about a very sensitive subject.

"I never quit to anybody in my life; never was afraid of any man living and my record will prove it. It makes me sick to read or hear that I was licked before I got into the ring with Louis."[50]

"I was just following orders, a planned strategy which everyone thought would wear out Louis, but it didn't work. I'm not blaming anyone. Johnny Ray and my handlers agreed that this was the best way to fight Joe, and I tried to follow instructions to the letter. If for one minute I thought it would turn out the way it did, I never would have fought this way. I would have gone right out in the first round and slugged it out with him. That business of me being through as early as the second round is all bunk. There was nothing wrong with my physical condition, either. I was in good shape and so was Louis. It was just a case of strategy backfiring."

Billy admitted wagering $7,000 on himself to win, but losing the bet didn't bother him as much as letting down all his friends who had backed him with their own dough. "I'm sorry I let everybody down, but don't let anyone tell you that I quit."

Hindsight is usually reserved for losers, and had Billy a chance to do it all over again, well—"It's no use crying over it now. I realize that in the two fights I went from one extreme to the other. That's what made it look so bad. I should have gone out there and thrown a hundred punches at the start, but that's a good second guess now. A couple of times I thought, here's the spot to open up, but remembered my instructions, and didn't.

"Right now, I'm definitely through with the ring. I should quit after that one. I don't know whether I'll change my mind about returning, but I'm not all washed up as a fighter. I can lick a lot of those guys around today."

What's next? He was asked. To this, Billy hedged. Maybe he would open a saloon or a restaurant. He admitted that he knew nothing about the business, but it sounded like a good idea. One thing he was certain of, Conn admitted. "All I want to do is to forget that fight."[51]

Fifteen Old Scores to Settle

For six months Billy didn't leave his house.

He was disgusted with himself, embarrassed. He struggled to come to terms with a whole range of emotions. For five years Conn had looked forward to an opportunity to redeem the mistake he made at the Polo Grounds. He was given the chance and he blew it. The humiliation of the defeat, of how he lost, ate at Billy. He'd let down friends, family, and the countless supporters who'd wished him well through the years. The paying customer, hell, some of them shelled out a hundred bucks to see that shit.

At first glance, Conn's cut of the gate was impressive, $312,950. That figure was deceptive, however. A number of obligations needed to be met before Billy could begin counting his dough. Ray and Jaffe, of course, received their one-third share. Then there was the old debt of $100,000 still owed to Mike Jacobs. On top of these commitments, Billy was still in arrears for his 1941 taxes to the tune of $26,478. When all bills were paid, Conn walked away with $81,885, but that was before his 1946 taxes were met.

Billy stayed beneath the radar until mid-January, and then it was only to pay a visit to Mike Jacobs at St. Charles Hospital. Several weeks earlier, Jacobs had collapsed and suffered a cerebral hemorrhage. The promoter was critically ill for the better part of a month before rallying. On January 15, just a couple of days before Conn called on Uncle Mike, the NBA removed Billy from its list of heavyweight contenders. And then, once again, Conn dropped off the sporting map.

Several more months passed without a word from or about Billy. In early March, Shirley Povich reported in his *Washington Post* column that Conn was coming out of retirement, but there was no immediate follow-up. In late May, the issue once again entered the sports pages when Sol Strauss traveled to Pittsburgh with the hope of enticing Billy back into the ring. Representing his client Mike Jacobs and the Twentieth Century Sporting Club, Strauss presented Milt Jaffe and Billy an opportunity to come back whenever the fighter was ready.

"He offered me anybody I want, anytime I want, anyplace I want," Billy explained, though he was quick to add that "anyone" did not include Joe Louis. That stipulation was okay with Conn. "I want a couple of tune-ups before I ever think of another title fight. . . . I'll try to get in shape. I'll see how it goes and if I find I still have it, I'll start fighting again. I'll need about two months to see if I can get into satisfactory shape."[1]

Strauss wanted Billy to make his return in New York, against, perhaps, Ezzard Charles, but both Conn and Jaffe disagreed. They weren't against fighting Charles, who was managed by Jake Mintz, but Conn needed to take things slow. "If I find that I'm in good shape, and I believe I will be, I will take a couple of tune-up bouts in smaller towns before coming to New York. I don't want to go to Madison Square Garden if I'm not ready."[2]

Louis defeated Jersey Joe Walcott on June 26 in a lackluster fight. Following the match, Joe announced his retirement, though he said he would tour the country in a series of exhibition bouts that would keep him active as well provide a steady income to help with his continuing tax woes. Billy read the reports of the Louis–Walcott fight. Joe was obviously slipping and still he defeated Walcott. Looking over the remaining contenders, Conn saw possibilities.

Quietly, Billy entered the gym. Conn had been working out at the Lyceum, but the sessions were nothing serious, he explained, just an effort to keep himself in shape. Billy's next public appearance was the Dapper Dan awards in early July. Billy's presence surprised a number of attendees, most of whom hadn't seen him since the previous summer at Yankee Stadium. A little more than a year had passed since Conn was one-half of the biggest boxing match ever seen, yet Billy sat far from the dais, toward the back of the hall. Still, other than the novelty of seeing Conn out in public, little fuss was paid Billy. Bill Considine of the *Washington Post* took note of the apathetic greeting the crowd gave their old hero and was intrigued by the paradox. "Conn today," he wrote, "is a prime example of America's appalling indifference to a runner-up, especially one who put up a bad performance." The Billy

Conn present that evening was a strikingly different person than the "fresh, grinning, cocky Dead End kid" Considine remembered from years before. "He now is shy, diffident and given to uneasy and embarrassed chuckles."

Remembering the report from a few weeks earlier, Considine approached Conn and asked if he was still training for a comeback. "I'm not that crazy," Billy laughed. "I'm just resting, and I think that's all I'm ever going to do. I'm okay in the dough department. Don't listen to anybody who tells you I'm going to fight again. I'm too old . . . and tired."[3]

Too old. Billy was still a few months shy of his thirtieth birthday—certainly not an ideal age for a boxer, but also not yet over the hill. Was the fire gone? He certainly didn't think so while preparing at Greenwood Lake. But how could he reconcile what happened at Yankee Stadium? He was older, heavier, and slower, all these things were true, but everyone thought he looked great in training. He was leaving something out of his explanation: Conn had lost his motivation. Beginning in 1940, Joe Louis and the heavyweight title was Billy's goal. He had his stab at it and missed, and for the moment, Conn wasn't fooling himself. He could come back and beat the also-rans of the heavyweight division, but Louis was another story. A few days in the gym and he understood that he couldn't take Joe, and that's all that mattered to him. He didn't need the money, and he certainly didn't miss the glory. The only thing he wanted from boxing was the heavyweight title, and that, realistically, was beyond Billy's grasp.

On November 3, without prompting, Billy again reiterated that he was done with the ring. "I'm definitely through," Conn announced in a press release. "I'll never fight in competition again. I'm getting too old, and it's too tough a game. . . . I still think I could lick most of the guys aiming for a shot at Joe today. But that training grind is too tough for a fellow my age. I'm a father with three great kids and for their sake I can't afford to risk getting permanently hurt. Too many fellows stay in there catching punches too long."[4]

Nearly a year went by. Nothing much had changed except that Billy had grown a year older. His reasons for remaining out of the ring apparently receded from Conn's consciousness, because his competitive desires began to again swell. Billy believed that he was a "young" thirty-one. After all, taking into consideration his time spent in the service and two years of retirement, Conn reasoned that he had the legs of a twenty-five-year-old.

Word began filtering out that Billy was working out daily in contemplation of a return to the ring. Conn even made his first public appearance in months when he came out to Forbes Field for the August 31 Pirates game against the Giants looking "trim and strong."

One look around at the heavyweight division and Billy was convinced that he could take any of the top contenders. He knew most of them well already: Lesnevich, Bettina, Savold, and Zale. The best of the group, however, was Ezzard Charles of Cincinnati. Nonetheless, Conn wasn't concerned about Charles either. "Let me get four or five good bouts under my belt and I'll knock Ezzard in Jake Mintz' lap."[5]

Was the public interested in a Billy Conn comeback? It was a fair question. The debacle at Yankee Stadium had not been forgotten, and what was foremost in the mind of most was Conn's lack of fight that night. Why should they expect anything different now? On September 23, Conn was in Jersey City for the Zale–Cerdan bout. Prior to the match, Billy was introduced to spectators along with other fistic notables. Conn bounded into the ring and stood before a fight crowd for the first time in more than two years. A brief moment of silence greeted Billy before a polite smattering of applause came from a mostly apathetic crowd.

If his appearance was meant to stir up interest and intrigue, then Conn's visit to Jersey was a bust. He did, however, offer a flash of his old cockiness when a writer yelled from ringside asking if Billy expected to fight again.

"Why not?" Conn replied from the ring apron. "I can lick a lot of bums like this guy."[6] And with that boast, Billy gave a nudge to Lee Savold standing next to him.

Jaffe was still in the picture as a representative of Conn's, but Johnny Ray most certainly was not. Ray continued to work with fighters. His favorite of the moment was Billy Neumont of East Liberty, whose fighting style recalled another young Billy from East Liberty. One Pittsburgh writer quipped that the only Billy on Johnny's mind now was Neumont, which was the first public acknowledgement of a riff between Conn and Ray. There was also Regis Agitole (who changed his name to O'Toole because Pittsburgh liked Irishmen), Ray Connelly, and a handful of other pugs, but none of them amounted to much in the ring.

Though Billy and Johnny maintained their friendship, professionally they were through. When asked, Conn offered little more than, "Johnny will be taken care of."[7] Whatever their differences, neither Billy nor

Johnny spoke one negative word about the other for attribution. Their fallout remained a private affair, and the local newspapers offered no speculation on the source of the estrangement. Undoubtedly, though, Ray's performance, or lack thereof, during the run-up to the second Louis fight played a part in the split. Certainly, Billy harbored some resentment about Johnny's debilitating condition at Greenwood Lake. Yeah, the bottle always had a hold on Moonie, but Johnny had never let it affect the job at hand before. But for forty days leading up to the fight, Ray was practically incapacitated. The annulment wasn't a one-way affair, however. Following Conn's final fight, Johnny had no qualms saying that he thought Billy was through. His Junior had had it and Ray wasn't going to endorse Billy entering the ring again.

The new guiding force in Conn's life, at least on a professional basis, was an oilman from Oklahoma City. Bob Jordan was introduced to Conn several months after the second Louis fight. Jordan quickly ingratiated himself to Billy and before long had talked Conn into speculating in several oil wells. It would be a solid investment for retirement, Jordan assured Billy. And the first returns proved Jordan correct. Though reports of Conn joining the "millionaires" club were a bit exaggerated, the dividends earned from the wells were sufficient enough that Billy never had to concern himself with fighting again.

Still, Conn planned on lacing the gloves up once again. Returning wasn't about money, anyway. It was about erasing the bad taste he left the game with.

Jordan put out the word that Billy was interested in entering the ring again. This news intrigued Chicago promoter Frank Harmon. Harmon had already approached Louis and asked the champ whom he would like to fight, to which Joe replied, "anybody."

"Well, what about Conn?" the promoter asked.

"We drew a lot of money in two fights," Louis reasoned. "I don't think Billy would be interested, but he'll be all right if you can get him."

Harmon wasted no time in picking up a telephone and contacting Bob Jordan, who passed the Chicagoan's offer along to Billy. Though Harmon's proposal was for an exhibition match, Conn did not hesitate. "I'd swim two rivers to get the chance at Louis again," Billy said.[8]

At the time, Joe was enjoying his "retirement" by touring the country with a series of exhibition matches. Louis's handlers readily agreed to Harmon's proposal also. On November 3, Billy appeared in Chicago and, seated between promoter Harmon and Louis's representative,

Harry Mendel, Conn signed to fight the champion in a six-round exhibition in the Windy City. "I am down to 190 lbs and hope to be in good shape before meeting Joe again. You can be sure of one thing; I'll make an effort to prove that I still rate as the number one heavyweight contender," Conn offered.[9]

"I'm coming back to boxing to redeem my bad showing against Louis," Billy explained. "I don't want to be remembered as a palooka because of the way I looked that night. I think I can lick most of the big fellows around today, and that goes for Louis, too. I never thought I'd get the chance to box him again, and I'm jumping at it."[10]

He had a plan, Billy explained. Following the December 10 exhibition at Chicago's International Amphitheatre, he would begin an earnest campaign to meet one of the leading contenders to the heavyweight crown. "I know I can whip any of those bums around today."[11] Scheduled the same night as the Louis–Conn reunion was an Ezzard Charles–Joe Baksi fight at Madison Square Garden, purportedly for the right to meet the champion. But if he was serious about making a run at the title, Conn could not enter the ring in Chicago cold. He needed some live action. Perhaps the biggest mistake made in 1946 was when Ray (begrudgingly) agreed to no warm-up bouts prior to the big match. Before meeting Louis in December, Billy knew he had to have at least two preparation bouts.

Down South, Bill Aiken and Saul Weingeroff desperately wanted Conn to begin his comeback in their hometown of Macon. They had recently put on a show headlining Fritzie Zivic and Eddie Steele. The success of that bout set the promoters to dreaming. Their ambition was to make Macon the fight capital of the South. A successful program with Conn at the top of the bill would bring them that much closer to their goal. Yankee Stadium and Madison Square Garden were a distant memory. The comeback trail would take him far away from the bright lights of New York. Billy's travels would take him off the beaten path to Macon, Savannah, and Dallas. Conn agreed to meet Mike O'Dowd on November 15 at the Macon City Auditorium.

Once word was out that Billy agreed to fight in Macon, Jordan was flooded with offers. Supposedly, the novice fight manager had booked eighteen fights for Conn, but Billy assured reporters that was quite an exaggeration. The Macon fight "and the one in Dallas on November 25 are the only two definitely scheduled," he said. "There may be one more, but that one is still tentative."[12] The unconfirmed fight was to be in Savannah, just three days after the Macon bout, against Whitey Bellier of New Orleans. But first came the test against New York's Mike O'Dowd, though how demanding the examination was a fair question to be asked. O'Dowd's résumé was suspect, to be kind. He hadn't fought since July 7, 1946, when he defeated Pete March. That ancient victory had been preceded by five consecutive losses. Still, Conn had to start somewhere.

Billy flew into Atlanta on the 14th and was met at the airport by Aiken and Weingeroff, who then escorted Conn to Macon. Though Billy's comeback barely caused a ripple of interest around the country, the quiet Georgia town heralded the upcoming fight as if a championship was on the line. Rival sports editors, Sam Glassman of the *Macon Telegraph* and Hank Drane of the *Macon News* were each granted interviews with Conn, the first given by Billy since his ignominious performance in June of '46. Drane reached Billy in his suite at Hotel Dempsey, while Glassman talked with Conn in the hotel's coffee shop as the fighter finished a shrimp cocktail. The questions each man asked varied little, as did Billy's replies.

Why hadn't he come back earlier?

"Just lazy, I guess."[13]

Well, then, why now?

"I got tired of sitting around doing nothing for two years," Conn explained. "And I never got over that second beating Louis gave me, see. I'd like to clear the stink of that fight. I was lousy that night." Billy continued, "I don't really need the money. 'Course it takes a lot to keep a fighter going. But I have some real estate property in Pittsburgh and my manager Bob Jordan has invested some of my dough in oil wells. When these oil wells pop I'll be in the clover."

The motivating factor wasn't money so much as getting another crack at Louis, Conn added. "I figure I have a chance to win the championship. You know why? There's only one good prospect in the bunch (of heavyweight contenders). Ezzard Charles." He then explained his plan of fighting a few matches stateside before possibly heading to England and fighting English champion Freddie Mills and Bruce Woodcock.

Well, Billy, what did the missus think of his comeback? "She doesn't care," Conn insisted. "She knows how much I've hated myself since that second fight. And she knows I'm tired of sitting around doing nothing."[14]

"I'm still as fast as I ever was, but you know fighting in a gymnasium and before a crowd is a different story . . . This fight means more to me than anyone will ever know. It means that I will either keep going up the ladder, or just forget the whole thing."[15]

"Comeback?" Joe Parham asked in the *Macon News,* "The Wild Irishman was so far superior to any other pugilistic talent seen in this precinct for a decade that it made a citizen wonder what manner of man beat him."

Billy entered the ring to a great roar of applause from the sold-out crowd of 3,200. They came out to see a great performance by the former champion, and they weren't disappointed. Throughout the fight, Billy completely dominated his overmatched opponent. From the opening bell, Conn was relentless, throwing his renowned left and moving well on his feet. O'Dowd went down in the eighth for three counts of eight, and once for eight in the ninth before referee Jackie Crawford stopped the proceedings. At the close of the fight, O'Dowd's nose shone a bright swollen red and his face resembled raw hamburger. What the decisive victory meant to Billy's comeback, though, was ambiguous. O'Dowd was little more than a run-of-the-mill fighter. However, Conn's performance, coming after more than two years off, was refreshing.

Billy emerged from the fight in fine condition with the exception of a swollen right hand, caused by inflicting too many blows on O'Dowd. The bruised hand forced Conn to cancel his next date against Whitey Bellier, which was scheduled just three days later in Savannah. Promoter Dick Leonard of that Georgia town threatened to ask the NBA to suspend Billy due to the short notice given. There was nothing to substantiate Leonard's complaint, according to Saul Weingeroff.

"There was nothing in writing that Conn would appear in Savannah," Weingeroff told the *Macon Telegraph.* Billy had given the Macon promoters permission to book several fights for him while he was in Dixie. "I had talked to Leonard about the fight, and we tentatively agreed on terms and the date. But the final contract was to have been signed Monday night after the fight provided Conn was not hurt. . . . There was nothing definite set. And when Leonard failed to show up in Macon with the contract and post the guarantee for Conn as agreed, then Billy decided to return to his home in Pittsburgh."[16]

Leonard's threat was groundless and died on the vine. Billy spent several days at home before flying to Texas. Instead of Bellier in Savannah, Conn would next fight Jackie Lyons in Dallas on November 25. Former heavyweight champ James Braddock had seen Lyons box in person and believed the Oklahoman would be a worthy opponent for Billy. "He's fast and he knows the score," Braddock said of Lyons. "He also packs enough punch to sting anybody. He can hurt Conn if tags him. I think [Billy] will have a real contest on his hands."[17] Braddock may have been overly generous when evaluating Lyons's capabilities. The record showed a string of wins for Lyons, but the victories came over a batch of second- and third-string heavyweights at a time when the division had few quality fighters in its ranks.

Billy arrived in Dallas several days early and looked good sparring with a variety of opponents at Compton Citadel. Local writers were impressed with Conn's condition and came away from the workouts believing that the Chicago exhibition could offer some fireworks. For his part, Billy expected nothing less. "As far as I'm concerned," he told George White of the *Dallas Morning News,* "a champion is just as much in jeopardy in a 6-round exhibition as he is in a 15-round title fight. If I can knock him out I'm going to do it. After all, I have a couple of old scores to settle with Joe.

"I don't claim that I'm a better fighter now at 31 than I was when I met Joe in 1941 or when I fought him last June [*sic*]. But he didn't have a whole lot on me then and I know positively that he has slipped more than I have since those bouts. I agree it doesn't look so good for the crop of heavyweights when the old men in the game, including myself, are the only worthy challengers, but this is true nonetheless. There isn't a good young heavyweight in the country. The fellows who have been around the top for a long time will have to furnish the competition for the champion.

"I'm on comeback and I'm not asking for any set-ups. The promoters have the right to sign any opponents they can get for me. I know I can't get back in top tune for a championship shot without having some competition. If I didn't believe I could whip Louis I wouldn't have any business with these other boys."[18]

In front of 2,500 at Dallas's Sportatorium, Conn continued his successful "comeback" tour. The degree of success, however, could be debated. As with O'Dowd, Conn dominated the less-talented Lyons. Evaluating Billy's skills in a one-sided fight was a difficult task. A writer reporting for the International News Service believed Conn would make a good showing against Louis in Chicago, which, in turn, would get

Billy another shot at Joe's crown. "Conn looked beautiful and displayed neat fighting tactics. His footwork was masterful and he displayed a left jab that carried plenty of dynamite."[19]

At the start of the ninth, Lyons's left eye was shut tight from Conn's repeated jabs. This injury provided an inviting target for Billy, who focused on Lyons's eye and body before a right uppercut to the jaw sent him to the canvas at 1:25 of the round. Whether Lyons was simply overmatched, or if Conn was sharp, was difficult to ascertain. If nothing else, Billy got a workout, but whether he could be considered a legitimate contender was impossible to tell against second-rate competition.

Though the affair in Chicago was only an exhibition, Louis was earnest in his preparation. For nine consecutive days, Joe pounded the roads and sparred as if his title was on the line. Most boxing exhibitions were purely for show; an entertaining dance in which the adversaries implicitly agreed not to inflict harm upon one another. Louis was fully aware, however, that Billy had much riding on their meeting. "I'm going to have my guard up every round," Joe said.[20] To Conn's cocky request that they forego the contract and use smaller gloves, Louis was welcoming. "Billy says he wants lighter gloves. He had two chances with six ounce gloves, so if he wants 'em lighter than 14 it's okay with me."[21] The provisions for the exhibition provided for no referee, fourteen-ounce gloves, and no judge's decision. The only verdict would be an unofficial newspaper ballot. The price for entry was well below Mike Jacobs's money-grabbing $100 ducats. Harmon set ticket prices at a more manageable $6 and $2.

In stark contrast to their meeting at Yankee Stadium, Billy came out in the first round as the aggressor. A parade of left jabs and hooks seemingly had Louis puzzled, unsure of what tactic to employ, bobbing or retreating. Soon, however, Joe realized Billy's blows lacked steam. His philosophy for the remainder of the show was to allow Conn to do most of the work. On a couple of occasions, most noticeably the third, Louis pressed Billy. To all in attendance, the champ obviously eased his attack when Conn was distressed. In the third, Joe's attack had Billy staggering. Had regulation gloves been in use, Conn surely would have fallen under the volley of Louis's blows.

Only 6,517 appeared at the International Amphitheatre. They left convinced that Louis remained Conn's master. Even more, many believed Joe took it easy on his pal to make Billy look good.

"No," Louis said to such a question afterward. "I was trying all the way."[22]

Any illusion that Billy rightfully belonged in the same ring with Joe had been erased by the end of the exhibition match. Indeed, any fantasy Conn might have entertained that the championship was within his grasp was stifled. The spring was gone from his legs and his punches were void of danger. While Billy treated the match as his chance to step back into the big time, Louis performed in the ring as if he were sparring in training camp. Still, Joe proved his dominance over Conn.

Louis received a 6-2 newspaper decision. Only one of the ballots cast by the writers "judging" the contest went for Conn, while another called the fight a draw.

What now? Ezzard Charles won in New York over Baski, and Louis acknowledged that the Cincinnatian should be considered the top contender. In the dressing room of the International Amphitheatre, though, Joe said he thought Conn should face Charles. From across the room, Billy heard Louis's suggestion and didn't shy away from the possibility. "I hope to fight him," Conn said. "I know I can beat all the heavyweights around. They're all a bunch of bums but Louis. He is great."[23]

Such postfight talk of taking on Charles, or anybody else for that matter, was just empty banter and Billy knew it. Since June 19, 1941, Conn had futilely been chasing glory that had long since escaped his grasp. He had his chance and the cocksure kid let immortality slip away.

No, Billy was through with the fight game, and the fight game was through with him.

Sixteen "You Only Get One Chance"

"**M**oney is made for one thing," Billy said at the height of his career. "Spending."[1]

Wealth was never Conn's sole motivation. He liked the things money could bring, certainly, but he never went chasing after the stuff. "I started with nothing, and I'll wind up with nothing. Nothing from nothing leaves nothing. I've had a lot of fun but I'll never have a quarter. The fellows I've met and the times I've had, I wouldn't take nothing for it."[2]

For the better part of the next decade, Conn was aimless. His investment in Bob Jordan's oil wells was modestly paying off. Though one report credited the value of Billy's speculation to be in the range of a $1,000,000, that number was a bit of a stretch, though it was reported that Conn had turned down $100,000 for his holdings. He had also invested in a twelve-unit apartment building in East Liberty. In the mid-fifties, Billy lent his name to an auto dealer on Baum Boulevard in East Liberty. His role was simple—show up at the dealership so people could come and meet their hero and occasionally make an appearance at a party. "Billy Conn's Big Three Motors" specialized in Nash Ramblers and could boast Jackie Conn as one of their salesmen. Glad-handing for a few bucks was easy enough, but it was too much like a job, and to Billy, work was one four-letter word he'd rather not utter, let alone do. "Who wanted to work? The only things that work are horses and mules and they turn their ass to it," he explained. "All you get from work is tired."

His aversion to physical labor was a subject Conn had given some philosophical thought. "You can't make money from working," Billy offered. "It's just like taking a racehorse and hitching his ass to a garbage wagon. You'll break his heart. He's going to pull that garbage wagon after he was a racehorse? He can't do it."[3]

Conn turned to the institution that he knew best, boxing. Initially he tried to get into the promotions racket, but receiving his license proved to be too much of a hassle so Billy let that idea fall by the wayside. He then moved on to the business of managing fighters. With a modest stable of two boxers, Waymon Dawson of Youngstown and Henry Hickman of Pittsburgh, Billy had under his tutelage two run-of-the-mill pugs. However, like many great athletes, Conn lacked the patience to teach less capable fighters and this endeavor, too, was quickly set aside.

"Who wanted to work?" indeed. But Billy needed to do something.

More than any other sport, professional boxing has held an intoxicating allure. Championship fights have always attracted a wide array of devotees and hangers-on. During his climb to fistic stardom, Billy encountered a great number of Hollywood stars, elected officials, and more than a few individuals who made their way unencumbered by restrictions of the law. Idols of the silver screen didn't impress Conn too much; his opinion of these fancy Dans was well documented. Politicians; now they were the real criminals. What's that old saying? You know they're lying when their lips are moving. Wiseguys and fellas of their ilk . . . funny thing was, you could almost always take them at their word.

Milt Jaffe had crossed paths with this element years before, prior to becoming a partner with Johnny Ray as Conn's manager. But after entering the world of professional boxing, Jaffe began meeting some of the more influential gangsters in the land. Milt nurtured relationships with a number of these fellas even after Billy left the ring. This networking served Milt well, and eventually landed him a position he would retain for a quarter of a century.

Moe Dalitz had made his name in Cleveland as the head of the Mayfield Road Gang, whose interests were varied—bootlegging, prostitution, gambling. Dalitz moved his operation to Las Vegas in the late 1940s when he took over the construction of the Desert Inn. He became one of the city's major players as the fifties wore on. There were other casinos for Moe; the Desert Showboat Motel and, later, the Stardust. He opened the Stardust in '58 with the help of Jimmy Hoffa and millions in Teamster "loans." To help him run his new hotel and casino, Dalitz turned to an old acquaintance with a relatively clean record,

Milt Jaffe. Jaffe readily accepted the offer and entered into business with some of the most notorious criminal minds in the country. In addition to Dalitz, Morris Kleinman and Longy Zwillman also held an interest in the Stardust. For years, he and Art Rooney ventured into this world, but these guys were in the big leagues, whereas Milt and Art were small time. Still, Milt felt at home with this crowd.

Jaffe had been in Vegas for nearly two years before he came to Billy with a proposition. He was aware that Conn had spent much of the fifties drifting about, aimlessly searching for some type of occupation that could hold his interest.

How would you like to come out to the desert and be a host at the Stardust? Milt asked Billy. The idea came to Jaffe when he learned that Joe Louis was holding a similar position at Caesar's Palace. Conn had no idea what a "host" did, but after Milt explained the undemanding duties, Billy promised to give the offer some thought. After all, how hard could it be; shake a few hands, reminisce a little? The income would certainly be nice, and he thought he could handle the workload, but Billy told Milt that he wouldn't think about coming out without Mary Lou and the kids.

"No problem," Jaffe said, "talk it over with Mary and get back to me." But, he added, you make sure to tell her that Vegas is a great place to raise a family.

Vegas was the mob's town then. The Chicago Outfit had an interest in a few different hotels, as did the New York families and the West Coast gangs. They all lived harmoniously; there was money enough for all in the desert.

The Desert Inn catered to the high rollers, while the Stardust was geared toward the blue-collar gambler. These Dalitz-controlled joints, in addition to the Riviera, were the three major hotel-casinos in the city when Billy arrived. This Las Vegas, the Vegas of the late fifties, was an adult playland where people went to indulge themselves. Food, drink, flesh, song and dance—the hospitable folks of Vegas were there to satisfy any appetite one might bring to the desert. But there was one craving more than all others that tourists came to quench: they came to try their luck against the one-armed bandits and at the green felt tables that littered the floor of the Stardust and all the town's casinos.[4]

It was a long way from home, both physically and spiritually. To Billy, Vegas was "Devil's Island." Everybody worked all night and slept all day. Every night was Saturday night. That kinda of lifestyle could wear you out, and quick.

Mary Lou found much to like in Vegas. Nevada's weather certainly had it all over Pittsburgh's, and needless to say, the nightlife on the Strip had it all over Squirrel Hill's sedate evenings. On more than one occasion, Billy would call their suite late at night from the lounge. "Matt, what are you doing?"

"I'm getting ready for bed," Mary replied.

"Well, there are some big players here, come down and help me." The effervescent Mary Louise found the fast pace to her liking; the Conn children, however, decidedly didn't like their new habitat. Suzanne was on the receiving end of typical adolescent teasing. Having worn penny loafers to school one day, she came home in tears. "They said I'm wearing my old man's shoes," she cried. Though her footwear wasn't the deciding factor, Suzanne hated Nevada so much that she moved back east to live with her Aunt Nora. Billy Jr., already resentful because he was relocated prior to his senior year in high school, also moved back to Pittsburgh. The move was also a cultural shock for Michael, but the youngest of the brood was only in grade school and had no option but to remain with his parents in the neon city.

Despite the agreeable climate and steady income, a few years in the desert proved to be enough for Billy. He heeded the prudent advice of Bob Hope, who recommended Conn take his family back east. You stay out there too long, Hope said, and you start to go a little goofy. He also reminded Billy that his partner in the movies, Bing Crosby, tried to raise a family out there and it didn't work out so well for his kids. After a few years in Nevada, Billy didn't need much prodding to return to his hometown. The house on Denniston Avenue, which Billy and Matt had been renting out while living in Vegas, was awaiting them upon their arrival.

In early 1961, the news had reached Billy in Vegas that Johnny was very ill. He had been in Veterans Hospital for some time, but word was that time was running short for Moonie. Most of the writers who covered Billy and Johnny's rise from the alleys of East Liberty to New York's Broadway were now gone, but Regis Welsh remained at the *Press*. The old reporter phoned Conn and asked for any thoughts Billy might have about his mentor. "John was the best," Billy wistfully recalled. "The best teacher and the best matchmaker. He taught me defense. He took me to the gymnasium every day like going to college." Then, as if transported back to Johnny's ratty old gym, a teary-eyed Billy continued. "He'd say, 'Keep your hands up; punch straight; don't get hit, Willie.' He said he'd make a fighter out of me and I believed him. He was the best."[5]

Life had continued much the same for Johnny. He and Billy may have parted ways but Ray continued with what he knew best. He had a retinue of fighters, though none exceptionally talented. He had a new wife, Jamie, and a son, Robert, born in 1949. But holding onto a dollar remained a difficult proposition for Ray. After the second Louis bout, Johnny never again had a significant payday.

Many years had gone by since they traveled the countryside together, Junior and Moonie. But the passage of time couldn't erase what they meant to one another. Billy flew east to be with Moonie as Johnny's days grew shorter. On a few occasions, he brought his boys with him to pay their respects. What they saw was a shrunken, frail man whose skin had taken on a yellowish tinge. Ray appeared aged well beyond his earthly years, and he and Billy both knew the end was near. One day, Johnny asked Junior to sneak him out of the hospital for a drink. Never known for his tact, Billy was bluntly honest with his friend. "Moonie, the only way you're leaving this place is with a tag on your big toe," he said.

A couple of days later, Billy again stopped by Veterans Hospital. He knew Moonie's time was short, and with a heavy heart, Billy took his friend's hand. "John, old pal, I won't see you anymore."

Johnny, too, knew this was good-bye. With mist-filled eyes, Ray patted Junior's hand. They'd known each other for the better part of three decades. Thirty years had passed and they'd never been maudlin—why start now? A moment's lingering glance articulated their affection more than awkward words ever could. With a voice wracked from years of abuse and significantly weakened by his illness, Moonie murmured good-bye to his Junior.

Less than an hour later, on July 16, 1961, Johnny Ray passed.

An associate of Conn's said of Billy several years earlier: "He's the only man I've ever known who has to scratch for an answer if you greet him with a hello."[6] And so it was with great irony that Conn was hired, along with Archie Moore, to serve as a color commentator for the March 30, 1965, light-heavy championship between Jose Torres and Willie Pastrone. The Madison Square Garden crowd of more than

18,000 was thrilled and roared with excitement as Torres won a ninth-round TKO. In his limited role, however, Billy failed to communicate to his audience the scene in front of him.

Apparently broadcasting was out, but Conn hadn't yet exhausted all employment opportunities in the fight game.[7] He had refereed before, usually exhibition matches; Billy was offered the chance to officiate on an international stage. Though Billy wasn't inclined to travel abroad, sometimes you have to get out of the house. With great reluctance, Conn agreed to journey to Mexico City where he would referee the October 21, 1966, world lightweight championship between Carlos Ortiz of New York and Sugar Ramos, a Cuban who lived in Mexico City. The aftermath of the match evoked echoes of Billy's early tussles with Teddy Yarosz, with Conn squarely in the middle of a controversial conclusion. Comparably, the disorder following Billy's epic battles with Yarosz resembled grade school miscreants acting up. Pittsburgh fight fans often demonstrated their zeal for the fight game, sometimes a little too boisterously. They, however, had nothing on latter-day Mexican fistic buffs. These fellas *really* knew how to vent their sporting frustration with style and clarity.

Following a second-round knockdown, Ortiz recovered and came back strong. In the fourth, he had Ramos in so much trouble that Conn wanted to stop the bout. "Where's the doctor?" Billy shouted from the ring, "Where's the doctor?" The ringside doctor was nowhere to be found, however, and Conn allowed the fight to continue.

The lopsided nature of the bout continued into the next round as Ortiz opened a terrible gash above Ramos's left eye. "If Ramos goes a couple of more rounds, he's taking a chance of losing his eye," Billy later said. Blood was pouring from the wound. "It was like a bullfight," Conn added. He then stopped the fight and sent Ramos to the corner and called the doctor into the ring. Billy informed the physician that he intended to end the match. "He was terrified," Conn said of the doctor. "He said I was doing the right thing—and then he lit outta that ring like a greased banana."[8]

At 1:45 of the fifth, Billy awarded the fight to Ortiz by technical knockout. To be kind, the crowd in El Toreo Arena did not greet the decision with enthusiasm. The ring doctor, however, decided to make an appearance, proclaimed that Ramos was able to continue, and ordered that the fight be resumed, but Ortiz refused.

Bottles, coins, and rocks began raining down on Ortiz as he tried to exit the ring, opening cuts on the fighter's head and face. Ortiz's manager, Bill Daley, tried desperately to help Carlos to the dressing room, but he was hit in the head with a bottle and knocked to the floor. While on the floor, Daley was kicked repeatedly and suffered two broken ribs. Through the chaos, Daley kept his composure. He rose from the ground and placed a bucket over Carlos's head and hustled his fighter to the dressing room behind a wedge of policemen.

Word reached Daley and Ortiz that they were expected to return to the ring and continue the match. Fat chance, Daley proclaimed. "We aren't going back in that ring if we got 18 machine guns behind us," he said.[9]

Ramon Valazquez, the secretary of the World Boxing Association, interpreted Daley's refusal to bring his fighter back as a forfeiture. He awarded the match to Ramos and added that, according to the laws of Mexico, the purses of both Ortiz and Conn were being withheld.

Like Daley and Ortiz, Billy had trouble vacating the ring. "I felt like the lone covered wagon," he said. "It was the loneliest feeling in the world. It looked like a bunch of Indians circling up. I thought I was a goner. It looked like the end of the line at age 49 for me. Cops came in but they were too scared to do anything."[10]

"That was the most exciting 15-round 'Hey Rube' I ever was in. When they busted my back open, and when I see all those people hollering at me, I say to myself—how am I going to get out of this jackpot? It did not look like it was going to be educational."[11] Conn walked amid a gauntlet of frenzied fans who threw punches, kicked, spit, and cursed their intended target, the culprit of their displeasure, the referee who halted the action before them. Though rightfully alarmed—his situation was perilous, to be sure—Billy refused to act frightened as he ventured through the angry mob. Conn furnished a compelling reason for maintaining his composure as he made his way to his dressing room. "If I had run and gone down, I would have had my brains knocked out," he explained. "If I had tried to fight back, I would have got lynched. I was thinking I might get one of those shivs in my belly."[12] It was only after some Mexican soldiers came that Conn escaped, albeit with some bruises and scrapes, but with his life intact.

In the ensuing days, Billy's gutsy decision was widely heralded throughout the boxing world. He was also vindicated by the fact that Ramos needed twenty-eight stitches to close the cut in question and would not be able to fight until April. Vindication was nice, but setting

foot on American soil was all Conn wanted. "That was the last time I
see old Mexico. . . . I was the happiest guy in the world when I crossed
over the border."

Sure, the governing body relented and Billy received his pay, but
think of what could have happened. He could have lost an eye or
maybe had his skull fractured by a heaved bottle. Or, "worst of all,"
Conn mused, "if I got killed I might have gotten myself buried in Mexico.
Imagine that. That would have been the worst of all."[13]

Like everything else Conn tried his hand at since hanging up the
gloves, refereeing wasn't going to become a full-time occupation. Two
decades into retirement, Billy still couldn't find a purpose. A few local businessmen, guys like Jack Cargo, a longtime fan, wanted to get
their hero in on the ground floor of something big. Cargo, who owned
a local candy company in Pittsburgh, tried often to get Conn involved
in some project or another. A regular man about town, Cargo was the
opposite of Billy in many ways, a big gambler and fun-loving guy. These
attributes made Cargo an enjoyable companion, and after some time
he was finally able to wear Billy down.

With some reluctance, Conn agreed to become a "partner" of Cargo
and Jimmy Fallon. Their venture: a nightclub named Jimmy and Jack's
New Arena located downtown on Grant Street. In a town not known for
nightclubs, the joint was a hit. The McGuire Sisters, Bobby Darin, and
Andy Williams were just a few of the popular acts that performed at the
New Arena. Billy's risk in the scheme was minimal, for, as always, he
put up no money. Officially, Cargo and Fallon were the owners. Conn's
role in the operation was familiar ground for him. He did what he did
best: nursed a drink, smoked a bit, and hung around. Billy was there
for a word or to rehash a memory if any patron would like.

Much as he didn't care for the practice, Billy also got on the banquet
circuit and began to make a variety of appearances. Such engagements
were always for money, though. He would show up for an event, but
he wanted to be paid. These things were a chore, not something to be
enjoyed. The Kennedys once called and asked if Conn would appear
at one of their charity events. Mary Lou was all for it. "C'mon, Billy,
it'll be a chance to meet *the Kennedys.*" But Billy wasn't interested. He
didn't give a damn who he was going to meet; if he was going to leave
the comfort of his home, Conn wanted a buck for his troubles.

Even vice president Hubert Humphrey tried to enlist Billy's services.
Humphrey phoned Billy and asked the champ if he would like to come

to D.C. and work with underprivileged kids. Working with kids was all right, but Billy wanted nothing to do with living in Washington. With diplomacy and tact, Conn told the vice president that his plate was full at the moment and politely ended the conversation. Standing nearby, listening to the conversation, was Timmy, amazed that his father could turn down the vice president of the United States.

"Remember, Tim," Billy told his son. "You're an asshole. I'm an asshole. We're all assholes."

The 1960s was a turbulent decade. Lines were drawn, sides were chosen, and no issue divided the country more than the Vietnam War. The concern entered the sports world when the famous boxer, possibly the most famous athlete in the world, Muhammad Ali refused induction into the armed services as a conscientious objector. He was, Ali asserted, a minister in the Nation of Islam serving the Honorable Elijah Muhammad. Famously, Ali told reporters that "I ain't got no quarrel with them Vietcong," and his voice of discontent struck a chord with the antiwar crowd. Others, though, thought Ali was a shirker. Conn was a member of this crowd. Billy didn't philosophize over politics, though his beliefs leaned to the right.

"I'll never go to another of his fights," Billy said. "And I think any American who pays to see him fight after what he has said recently should be ashamed. They should stay away from those closed circuit television shows in droves."

Conn was certain that others in the boxing community agreed with him. "He is a disgrace to the boxing profession," Billy asserted. "Other fighters and ex-fighters feel exactly the same way I do and it is about time that somebody spoke out."[14]

Without argument, Ali's circumstances were special, but Billy didn't limit himself to criticizing the exiled champion. He had little good to say about any current fighters, but that didn't stop reporters from asking Billy's opinion.

Q: What do you think of fighters today?
A: They can't fight at all.
Q: How would you rate a heavyweight like Gerry Cooney?
A: Terrible fighter. I saw him fight and I couldn't believe how bad he was.
Q: When you talk heavyweights, who do you consider the good ones?

A: Joe Louis was the very best and Rocky Marciano was very good, too.

Q: You didn't mention Muhammad Ali. What do you think of him?

A: He's a nice guy but he was a better actor than a fighter. I could've beaten him but because of our styles it would've been a dull fight.

This exchange was fairly typical. Louis, Marciano, Armstrong, Sugar Ray Robinson, the fellas from his era, were the best he'd ever seen, Conn would say, but the guys nowadays, they couldn't fight worth a damn. These often-repeated refrains would irk his son. Billy Jr. would tell him, "Dad, you're making yourself sound foolish, these guys look up to you," but these admonishments were met with a dismissive wave of the hand.

Conn continued to offer his candid opinions, and often appeared at championship bouts as a guest of honor. Billy used one such occasion to visit his ancestral homeland for the first time. On July 19, 1972, Conn traveled to Dublin for the Muhammad Ali–Al Lewis match, ignoring his personal boycott of Ali fights. Surprisingly, it was the first visit to Ireland for the onetime Celtic God of the ring. Despite Mary Lou's pleas to travel more and to visit the great European cities, Billy preferred to stay close to home. He had seen enough of Europe during the war, and had no desire to return. The opportunity to visit the Emerald Isle, and a chance to make a buck, presented itself when Conn was asked by the Irish government to appear in Dublin to help promote the fight.

As expected, Ali retained his championship and Billy enjoyed his stay in his ancestral homeland. He met Ulick O'Connor and amused the noted author with his pointed honesty and sense of humor. Others, however, weren't captivated by Conn's disarming tact. While loafing at the bar in the Gresham Hotel, Billy fell into conversation with a couple members of the IRA, who were neither charmed nor amused by Conn's pointed remarks concerning their political beliefs. Suffice to say, this tête-à-tête ended abruptly. Billy, with his urban sensibilities, wasn't overly impressed with the pastoral landscape. A reporter asked Conn how he felt about being in the land of his forebears for the first time. The idyllic setting had little impact on Billy. "All I can say about it is; I'm glad my mother didn't miss the boat."[15]

On those occasions when Conn appeared at championship bouts as a guest of honor, he was just another in a retinue of past boxing greats feted. He rarely allowed himself to be the center of attention.

Billy didn't care to bask in his past fame or hear others extol his greatness. The few times he allowed a testimonial in his honor, Billy usually brought Timmy or Mary Louise along to do his talking for him. Once, following a lengthy and praise-filled introduction, Conn stepped up to the podium, simply mumbled, "Thank you, I didn't know I had so many friends," and returned to his seat. Everyone in the hall looked to Mary Lou. She knew the people had come for more than a grateful grunt, and saved the evening when she went to the microphone and delivered an impromptu speech.

As Billy got older, he didn't warm up to people as easy as he did in his younger days. Sadly, even with his own boys, Billy was reticent. He was largely a disinterested father. "Sit down, shut up" was a mantra often heard by the Conn boys. Like most boys, Billy's sons all had dreams of athletic greatness. Realistic or not, such imaginings are a rite of passage. Still, Billy didn't want his kids wasting their time on such endeavors. "All athletes are bums," Conn would tell them, and discourage all his son's athletic pursuits. Billy didn't shy away from the fact that he made his way through boxing. But have his boys enter the ring? No way. "Sure, it was good to me [boxing]," Billy admitted. "I was a young kid when I started and didn't know anything else. I was fortunate that I made money out of boxing and acquired some real friends. But it's too tough a business. I don't want my boys mixed up in it."

These dictates hindered Billy Jr. more than his brothers. Easily the most athletic of the boys, Billy Jr. was also the most academically challenged of the Conn siblings. Billy encouraged his son to forego football and instead become a "lawyer" or "doctor," and the young man lost all interest in scholastic achievement. That was Billy's idea of "accomplishment"—doctors, writers, lawyers. He saw no future in the sporting world, and also didn't allow irony to hinder his beliefs. Where he failed, Billy aspired that his children succeed. Leaving school at such an early age was a lifelong regret of Conn's, and he impressed upon them the importance of an education. To Billy's great satisfaction, three of his kids went on to earn their college degrees.

Where Billy's parental skills were lacking, his younger brother stepped in and performed as a wonderful father figure to the Conn children, who loved their uncle and his mischievous ways. Of all his siblings, Billy remained the closest to Jackie. Following Maggie's death in 1941, he had lost some connect with his family. Westinghouse remarried the year after his wife's passing to Henrietta Wilshire and started a second family, which distanced Billy from his younger sisters, who remained with their father. He still loved them, he loved them all, Frank, Jackie, Rusty, Mary Jane, but nothing was the same; it couldn't be the same without Maggie. Through the years, however, the two old sparring partners sustained their sometimes boisterous relationship.

They were as different as night and day. Billy was an introvert who preferred to melt into the scenery, out of notice from all. Jackie, with a large stogie clenched between his lips and a loud sport coat worn loosely over his shoulders, was a garrulous soul who loved to stand out in any crowd of people. Jackie would sometimes play chauffeur when visiting notables came to Pittsburgh and drive them anywhere in town they wanted. Billy, however, remained at home in Squirrel Hill and let them come to him.

Jackie's adolescent jealousy of his older brother never faded. Jackie longed to be Billy, to have the looks, the talent, and the fame. One could conclude that Jackie would have better traded in on celebrity than did his brother. With his flamboyant personality and gregarious appetite for life's finer things, Jackie could win over even the stodgiest curmudgeon. In his back pocket, Jackie always carried with him a moneymaking scheme of one sort or another, but none of his grandiose ideas ever came to fruition.

Though he loved his brother dearly, Billy would sometimes tire of Jackie's yarns. Once the younger Conn was regaling an attentive audience about his time spent as a paratrooper during the war. This tale, like most coming from Jackie, was pure fabrication and Billy wasn't going to let it pass without interruption. "Hell, Jackie," chimed Billy, "you never even jumped off a front porch."

Little details, like the truth, never slowed Jackie, nor would he allow it to alter a good story. Since his forced retirement from the ring, he had bounced from job to job. Like his brother, Jackie struggled to discover work that proved to be a good fit for him. For a time, Conn was a security guard at the Meadowlands in Washington County. Jackie did similar work for Milt Jaffe in Vegas, but he spoiled that opportunity. Returning home, Conn tried his hand as an investigator for attorney Tom Livingston, but like all other pursuits, Jackie tired of this employment. What he did find suitable to his personality, though, was the role of bon vivant, which Jackie pursued despite being hampered by lengthy bouts of unemployment. Fittingly, Conn shopped for his wardrobe at LaMonts, "a rich man's taste, for a poor man's pocket book." He traveled often and widely. From Vegas to New York, wherever Jackie went, he was sure to be found in the midst of a group of celebrities.

Whenever Conn strolled into a room, the other occupants all took notice. "Here comes Jackie Conn!" would ring out. Regardless of who was in attendance, Conn took control of the room and became the center of attention. Sinatra, Crosby, Gleason—they all enjoyed Jackie's company and the tall tales that accompanied him.

One particular evening at Toots Shor's, a fair gathering of film, Broadway, and sport stars were breaking up following a raucous evening. At the close of the night, the check came and much fuss was raised over who would have the honor of covering the bill. Finally, over the din, Jackie Gleason demanded of Shor that he be permitted the privilege. Toots, not caring who paid for the evening, began to hand the bill over to the robust comedian when the grandiloquent younger Conn stepped up and took the check out of Shor's hand.

"The evening's on me, boys," Jackie declared with a sweeping panache. Though without employment of any note, Conn signed for the bill, which amounted to well over a thousand dollars.

Shor was very fond of Jackie and was tolerant of his unrestrained generosity; still, Toots was incredulous at Conn's unrepentant gall. "Jackie, it's bad enough you signed for a bill you can't cover, but you didn't have to leave a fifty dollar tip."

Even during his brief boxing career, Jackie struggled to keep his weight in check. Since the Mutt Wormer affair at Madison Square Garden, Jackie had continued to neglect his health, and as the years wore on, he became exceedingly overweight. Eventually, his bachelor lifestyle caught up with Conn. In 1972, Jackie suffered a cerebral hemorrhage and had a massive stroke. After just a week's hospitalization, Jackie Conn, who brought a smile to many, breathed his last.

The death of his younger brother forced Billy to take stock in his life and face his own mortality. Life with Mary Lou couldn't be better and the kids were all doing well. Still, he looked around and saw so many of the faces from the past disappearing. Uncle Mike had been gone for two decades, having died an embittered man, resentful of his successors in the promotion game and critical of the boxers who came in the wake of Louis.[16] Jimmy Greenfield passed away on New Year's Day, 1973, and Westinghouse died just a few years later.

Joe Louis was still around, though. He and Billy had remained close through the years. While Billy was working at the Stardust, Joe held a similar position at Caesars Palace. Their paths crossed often in Vegas, and Billy came away with many stories of Louis's largesse. Conn often recalled the night Louis won $10,000 while playing keno. After Marva, Joe's wife, left the champ alone for ninety minutes, all the winnings had been given away.

On another occasion, Billy and Joe were sitting together in a Vegas casino when a fella came by begging for chips. Louis had two stacks of chips, black $100s and green $50s. Joe handed the moocher a handful of the black. Taken aback, Billy yelped, "Hey, you could have given him the green ones."

"What's the difference?" Louis replied with a shrug of his shoulders. "I'll lose them all anyway."

Though in the ring he had won the admiration of millions, after hanging up his gloves for good in 1951, Joe found life to be a struggle outside the arena. Increasing pressure from the government, which offered Louis no reprieve from his ever-compounding tax burden, forced the great champion to enter the ring as a professional wrestler to earn a few bucks. And, as if his tax troubles weren't enough, Joe also developed a drug dependency. Through it all, though, Billy stood by his friend.

They often appeared together at various functions. Frequently, they would show a film of their classic 1941 fight. Usually, when the screening began, Joe would exit the room and head to the bar. Every so often, Louis would pop his head in and ask, "Hey Billy, are we to the 13th round yet?" to which Billy would laugh and turn his head back to the fight. When that fateful round did arrive, as it always did, Joe would pop back into the room and say, "Goodbye, Billy."[17]

After one such appearance at the William Penn Hotel, Billy walked through the lobby carrying the film in a Giant Eagle shopping bag. "Imagine this, I fought 11 champions 21 times and I end up carrying a shopping bag. They kiss your ass to get the film, and then when they're done they throw it at ya." At about this time Billy came upon Louis. "Joe," he said, "you should have knocked me out. You should have just killed me."

Conn was present at Caesars Palace on November 9, 1978, when Frank Sinatra threw a $500-a-plate dinner in honor of Joe. The evening was both a tribute and a benefit for the ailing ex-champ, who had been confined to a wheelchair since a heart ailment befell him a year earlier, which was followed by a stroke. The day before the dinner, Conn paid a visit to the champ at his home. Though Joe recognized Billy, he was unable to speak to his old friend. "He recognized me, that's all," Conn sadly explained.

That evening at Caesars Palace was the last time Billy and Joe saw one another. Louis's health continued to deteriorate until he passed away on April 12, 1981. President Ronald Reagan waived the eligibility requirements for burial at Arlington, and ten days after his death, Joe was laid to rest in the National Cemetery with Billy present at the graveside ceremony.

Louis's passing shook Billy. Certainly, he had seen it coming—Joe had been ill for some time—but so much of Conn's professional life could be measured by his relationship with the Brown Bomber. "Joe was such a big piece of my past," Conn said, shortly after Joe's death. "Joe put me in the big leagues. He put me in long pants.

"He's the only guy I know who never rapped anyone, never said a bad word about anyone."[18]

Many times Jake LaMotta told Billy to come to New York; that's where the action could be found, there was something going on in the Big Apple every night. But Conn always shook his head. "No, Jake," he'd say, "there's no place like Pittsburgh." Billy liked the slow pace of his hometown, and besides, Pittsburghers were his people. He was a humble man who didn't understand the meaning of the word "celebrity." The attention didn't feed his ego; it was an intrusion. When a crowd gathered around him, Billy would turn to Mary Louise. "Why do these people want to talk to me?" he asked. "Don't they have something better to do?" The fact that he was seen as something special, that to so many Pittsburghers he was a hero, was lost on Billy. He was one of them, a man who represented the city well.

In his later years, Conn loafed at Connelly's tavern nearly every day where he would nurse a few drinks. The inside of the saloon was lit solely by the orange neon glow emanating from a sign that told one he was in Connelly's. Cheap beer on draft and a room full of unsolicited opinions kept patrons company at Connelly's. The Lawrenceville tavern was owned by one of Johnny Ray's former boxers, Ray Connelly, who opened the joint in 1957. It was Billy's kind of place, a place where people would leave him be if that's what he wanted; like any respectable Pittsburgh bar, it held a portrait of Harry Greb in a prominent position. Occasionally his solitude would be disturbed and a barfly would approach, one who, emboldened by a drink or three, thought he could take the great Billy Conn. "You're not so big, Billy," they would say. "You don't look so tough." A younger Conn may have taken the bait and set the loudmouth straight. But a more wise and mature Billy played the scene diplomatically. "Let me buy you a drink and I'll put it in the record books that you knocked me out."

Frank Deford, a lyrical freelance writer, came to Squirrel Hill in the spring of 1985 in search of a story. Deford spent many hours with Billy and Mary Lou in the cellar of their Tudor home. The writer was completely taken by the couple. He became entranced by their love and the captivating story they had to tell. Deford's resulting piece, "The Boxer and the Blonde," was published in *Sports Illustrated* to great interest and acclaim. The summer of '41, the romance, the tragedy, and the brief kiss with greatness were captured beautifully by Deford.

A striking photograph accompanied the piece. Taken on the sands of Ocean City, Billy and Mary Lou are caught in midstride, holding hands, with radiant smiles spread across their effervescent faces, racing the tide to the shore. It was an irresistible tale and, thanks to "The Boxer and the Blonde," there was renewed interest in Billy's career. Talk of a movie based on Conn's life ensued, as did countless print interviews. Several months later, shortly after his sixty-eighth birthday, Billy sat down with a writer from *Pittsburgh Magazine*. "When you're a young guy and you see a guy who's fifty years old, you say, 'Look at that old bastard, he's fifty years old.' I'm sixty-eight. Jeez, I never thought I'd live this long."[19]

His Celtic Adonis looks had matured with the passing years. The dark and curly hair was now thinning and tinged with gray. Nowadays, lines creased his once-unblemished face. Indeed, time was beginning to show its effects on Billy. The journalist asked the obvious question: would Conn like to be young again? No, Billy answered. "You play your cards right, once is enough. You only pass through here one time. If you play your cards right, once is enough."[20]

He made the news again a couple of years later. This time, old memories weren't being rehashed; rather, it was Billy's determined use of his patented left that once again made headlines.

Following mass on a chilly January morn in 1990, Billy and Mary Louise stopped by a Uni-Mart convenience store for a cup of coffee. While Mary Lou went to the back of the store where the coffee machine was located, Billy stayed up front near the door. Suddenly, another customer approached the counter and told the clerk that he had a gun and demanded the contents of the register. Not one to fall for the old "finger-in-the-sweatshirt" routine, the cashier asked to see the weapon. Without brandishing a gun, the thief grabbed the cash from the register and began pummeling the clerk.

In the midst of the commotion, Mary Louise sped out the door and asked a school crossing guard to call for help. Billy stayed behind. "My instinct was to get help," Mary Lou remembered. "Billy's instinct was to fight."

Billy pulled the burglar off the cashier and with a hook that still possessed some zing, knocked the robber through a cookie display. The two rolled around the convenience store floor before the bandit escaped out the door with eighty dollars in cash. He may have gotten away, but the thief took a couple of shots from an old pro before escaping. "I interrupted him," Billy explained in his humble manner. "He won't be robbing stores for a few days, I think. I hit him with a left. You've got to go with your favorite punch."[21]

For the participant, between the ropes lay hope, a promise of redemption, and the fulfillment of starry dreams. To most, such imaginings were a futile mirage. Still, the temptation to take a chance outweighed the possibility of failure, or worse. The ring was a sanctuary and also, as Billy once described, "the loneliest place in the world." It could be an exhilarating exhibition. The poetry of a well-thrown jab, the beauty of the dance—in its finest form, boxing offered a thrilling display. But at its core, the sport was brutality unleashed, a performance that sated the spectator's darkest desires and quenched their bloodthirst. The residue of the profession left many of the combatants suffering a slow and debilitating erosion of their mental facilities, the effects of which began to be revealed incrementally as the fighter crept toward old age. This illness, known as chronic traumatic brain injury, occurs in roughly 20 percent of professional boxers. The plight struck a number of Billy's contemporaries, including his pal and onetime adversary Fritzie Zivic, who passed away in 1984.

In 1988, just prior to his seventy-first birthday, Billy started to show signs of memory loss. The onslaught of the illness came slowly; little things began to show. One day, Billy went to see a movie only to return home and not remember what film he'd seen. A little while later, the family was sitting together enjoying a drink before dinner. Billy began to get antsy; he looked to Billy Jr., glanced at Mary Louise, and then back to his son.

"Is that your girlfriend?" he asked.

"No," Billy Jr. answered.

"Is that my girlfriend?"

"No."

"Who the hell is she?"

Billy then looked at his wife: "It's nice to have a drink with you, but you better leave before Mary Louise gets home."

"Dad, that is Mary Louise, that is mom," Tim said. Still, Billy was unconvinced of the identity of the pretty woman in his midst. Mary Lou put her hand on Billy's arm. "Did you ever see *The Pittsburgh Kid*?" she asked. Billy shook his head. Tim went upstairs and found a videotape of the classic. While viewing the movie, Billy snapped out of his confusion.

Conn also began to panic whenever Mary Louise would leave the house. He would phone Tim in an agitated state. "You mother's gone, she's been gone for days," Billy told his son. "We've got to get the FBI in on this."

Knowing there was no reason for alarm, Tim always tried to ease his father's anxiety. "Dad, she just went to the Giant Eagle, she'll be home in a few minutes." Still, on many occasions, his son's reassurance did nothing to soothe Billy. Wanting action to be taken, Conn would call 911 in search of his wife. The local police, though, were accustomed to Billy's frantic calls. They would stop by the Conn home, have a cup of coffee, look at Billy's scrapbooks, and admire the large collection of photographs lining the walls. Conn could be placated only so long, however.

"What about Mary Louise?" he would ask.

"We're on it, Billy," the Squirrel Hill officers would assure him.

There were other signs that something was wrong with Billy. He stopped reading, even though he had long loved to sit down with a good western. He also, to a great extent, stopped eating and sleeping. Conn was constantly on the move, finding it difficult to sit still. At home, he would pace the floor as much as eight hours a day, often at night. The family's growing concern finally led them to seek a professional opinion on Billy's worsening state.

The name for Conn's condition was "pugilistic dementia." Dr. Paula Trzepacz, assistant professor of psychiatry at Pitt, explained. "Both frontal lobes and the right parietal lobes have defects in the blood flow," the doctor said. "That's a lot of regions. Almost all of them."[22]

"In all our testing, he doesn't show the Alzheimer's pattern. The symptoms are agitation, disorientation, and memory problems. He's confused about where he is. He's focused inappropriately."[23]

Caring for Billy became a terrible chore for the family, Mary Louise most of all. Though her boys helped her, the bulk of the caregiving was Mary's responsibility. With Billy sleeping little, someone was needed to stay awake to keep an eye on him. Different medications were prescribed to help Conn sleep through the night; more for the relief of Mary than anything else. Suzanne knew that for her mother's own sanity, Mary Louise needed to get away for a while. It took much convincing, but Suzanne was able to finally talk Mary Louise into traveling to Paris. The day after Mary left, Billy inquired into his wife's whereabouts.

"She's in Paris," Billy Jr. answered.

"You SOB!" Conn roared at his son. "If she's in Paris, you get the hell out of this house!"

True to his word, Billy tossed his namesake out in the street, but by the next day he had forgotten everything: "Where's your mother?"

Living at home became increasingly dangerous for Billy. One afternoon he jumped in the car and took off down the boulevard. She had put off this day as long as she could, but Mary Lou knew that Billy needed to be placed in the hospital. The inevitable came in the summer of 1992, when Billy was admitted to Western Psychiatric Institute. Sadly, Billy came to the hospital believing he was just paying a visit and was confused and alarmed when Mary Lou and Tim left him behind. Billy's stay at Western Psych was brief; soon he was relocated to the VA on Highland Drive. He had grown very thin, his walk had slowed to a crawl, and when he talked, which was rare, Conn would refer to people no one else knew.

Once in the VA, Billy took an immediate turn for the worse. His memory continued to deteriorate and Conn's physical capacity diminished drastically. Still, Billy continued to recognize everyone who came to see him. There were regular visitors, of course, his children and Mary Louise, but also Rusty, Mary Jane, and Frank came often to see their brother. Only Billy's immediate family was at the hospital more often than Ray Connelly, who made it a point to stop by nearly every day to see his old pal.

Several months into his stay at the VA, Conn's mental state had become so porous that the family didn't even inform him that his beloved Suzanne suffered a recurrence of the breast cancer she had been bravely battling for thirteen years. Billy could sometime be distant with his boys; however, he was unabashedly affectionate with his Suzanne. With her brown hair and big beautiful eyes, she was a classic Irish colleen. Though she had relocated to Lake Forest in suburban Chicago after graduating from Marymount College and had started her own family there, the distance didn't hamper the relationship between Suzanne and her parents. Billy had often taken the train to Lake Forest to visit his little girl. Like clockwork, though, as soon as he set his bags down, Billy would ask Suzanne, "What time does the train leave?"

"Daddy, you just got here," she would always say.

"This place is so boring, there's no place to hang out." The nightlife in Lake Forest was, indeed, lacking.

Billy's traveling days were over, and unfortunately, in her worsening condition, Suzanne was unable to come to Pittsburgh. Still, her illness was kept from Billy. On February 12, 1993, just three months before her forty-sixth birthday, Suzanne passed away.

Billy's condition continued to rapidly decline. One afternoon in mid-May, Tim stopped on his way to the hospital and bought his dad a milkshake. After one drink, it was obvious something was seriously wrong. Billy spit up the small portion he attempted to sip. He had lost his ability to swallow. To combat the latest setback, doctors inserted a feeding tube into Conn. Within a day, however, Billy was trying to pull the tube out. Frustrated and thrashing about, Conn refused the admonitions of doctors and nurses. Until they spoke with Mary Louise, there was no choice but to tie Billy's hands down. When she arrived at the VA with Tim, Mary Lou was pulled aside. "You'll have to make a decision," the doctor told Mrs. Conn.

If the feeding tube was left in, Billy could continue living for some time. Without the artificial assistance, however, he would only last another week, maybe ten days. As heartbreaking as the decision was, Mary Louise and her sons were in complete harmony. "He would hate us if we left him in this condition," they agreed. Billy never feared death. Paradise was awaiting when he was through here, of this he was always sure. The choice was agonizing, but Mary Louise was sure she and her boys were doing what was right by Billy. The feeding tube was removed, leaving the family to wait for life's only certainty.

Ten days later, Mary Lou was preparing herself to visit her husband when the phone rang. On the other end of the receiver was the chaplain at the VA. The news, however expected, weakened Matt's knees nonetheless. Billy's years of suffering were finally eased at 10:20 A.M., on Saturday, May 29, 1993. The end came quietly; death found Billy in his sleep.

Officially, his death was attributed to complications of pneumonia, though surely the end was hastened by the consequences of his chosen profession.

"The champ is gone," his adoring widow informed the local media.[24]

The line of mourners in front of John A. Freyvogel's Funeral Home stretched far down Centre Avenue. They patiently stood, waiting to say good-bye to Billy, not far from the beautiful home he bought Maggie on Fifth Avenue and a short distance from the site where their old tenement on Shakespeare Avenue once sat. The funeral mass was held on a beautiful morning on the first day of June. The sun shone through brightly as friends and family, all with a story to tell, congregated outside St. Philomena's. Following Mass, the funeral procession made the slow trek from Squirrel Hill to Calvary Cemetery. Mary Louise and her boys devotedly stood by as a brief graveside ceremony took place before Billy was laid to rest; forever close to Harry Greb, eternally near Maggie.

In late 1953, Hollywood had called Billy again. He was in the midst of doing a whole lot of nothing, so maybe Conn would consider the offer. This time he was wanted for a part in *On the Waterfront*. It took less than a moment for Billy to turn down the offer. Once a painted-up mope, but never again.

Some eighteen years later, in March of 1971, Billy sat down for an entertaining and illuminating interview with author Peter Heller. Much of Conn's career was rehashed during the course of their conversation and Heller captured a candid and honest Billy. "You only get one chance," Conn admitted, speaking of the first Louis fight. "Of all the times to be a wise guy. Serves me right. He should have killed me. What a bastard I was."[25]

The fight that took place on that wondrous night at the Polo Grounds brought Billy sports immortality. That immortality, though, came with the baggage of being on the losing end of an epic battle. After June 18,

1941, hardly a day passed for the remainder of his life that someone didn't bring up the subject of the bout to Conn.

He would be approached on the street: "What happened Billy? What happened in the thirteenth?"

"You saw what happened," a weary Conn would reply. "I got knocked on my ass."

The memory etched in the public's mind, though, wasn't the portrait of Billy, felled by Louis's lethal blows, prone, on the canvas. No, the enduring image for those present and those who learned of the night's events secondhand was that of Sweet William dancing confidently on that balmy June night, capturing the imagination of countless fans. Indeed, Billy Conn's name has lived on thanks to his courageous, albeit eventually obstinate, stand against Joe Louis.

Conn's refusal to sign with those Hollywood phonies did not prevent *On the Waterfront*'s screenwriter from invoking Billy's name in the movie's dialogue. The imagery conjured endless possibilities, imaginings stoked by only the starriest dreamers. In the picture, Charley Malloy, played by Rod Steiger, mournfully reminisced to his brother, Terry, portrayed by Marlon Brando: "When you weighed one hundred and sixty-eight pounds you were beautiful. You could have been another Billy Conn. . . ."

Sweet William's epoch, delightful and radiant, embodied the passion and bliss of aplomb and youth. Lived, of course, with a wink and a smile. Always a smile.

"This is easy, Moonie."

Notes

Chapter One: This Is Easy

1. *New York Daily Mirror,* June 19, 1941.
2. *Pittsburgh Press,* June 19, 1941.
3. *Pittsburgh Sun-Telegraph,* June 19, 1941.
4. *Pittsburgh Press,* June 17, 1941.

Chapter Two: A Kiss from Heaven

1. *Collier's,* May 24, 1941.
2. *Pittsburgh Sun,* January 29, 1924.
3. International News Service, February 11, 1939.
4. *Colliers,* May 24, 1941.
5. *Colliers,* June 3, 1939.
6. *Saturday Evening Post.*
7. *Pittsburgh Post-Gazette,* February 22, 1988.
8. *Colliers,* May 24, 1941.

Chapter Three: I Can Lick Anyone Johnny Ray Tells Me I Can Lick

1. *Pittsburgh Post-Gazette,* November 20, 1935.
2. *Pittsburgh Post-Gazette,* June 10, 1957.
3. *Pittsburgh Sun-Telegraph,* August 10, 1936.
4. Ibid.
5. Ibid.
6. *Pittsburgh Sun-Telegraph,* June 4, 1936.
7. *Pittsburgh Sun-Telegraph,* September 8, 1936.
8. *Pittsburgh Post-Gazette,* December 18, 1936.
9. *Pittsburgh Press,* December 3, 1936.

10. *Pittsburgh Post-Gazette,* December 19, 1936.

11. Ibid.

12. *Pittsburgh Post-Gazette,* December 23, 1936.

13. Ibid.

14. Peter Heller, *In This Corner . . . ! Forty-Two World Champions Tell Their Stories* (DaCapo Press, 1994).

15. *Pittsburgh Post-Gazette,* December 29, 1936.

16. *Pittsburgh Press,* December 29, 1936.

17. Ibid.

18. Heller, *In This Corner . . . !*

19. *Pittsburgh Post-Gazette,* December 29, 1936.

20. *Pittsburgh Post-Gazette,* December 30, 1936.

21. *Pittsburgh Press,* December 29, 1936.

Chapter Four: Like a Thief He Kept Running

1. *San Francisco Examiner,* November 9, 1937.

2. As reprinted in the *Pittsburgh Sun-Telegraph,* March 11, 1937.

3. Ibid.

4. *Pittsburgh Sun-Telegraph,* March 12, 1937.

5. *Pittsburgh Post-Gazette,* May 3, 1937.

6. *Pittsburgh Post-Gazette,* May 4, 1937.

7. Ibid.

8. *Pittsburgh Sun-Telegraph,* May 4, 1937.

9. *Pittsburgh Press,* May 28, 1937.

10. *Pittsburgh Sun-Telegraph,* May 28, 1937.

11. *Pittsburgh Press,* June 29, 1937.

12. Ibid.

13. *Pittsburgh Press,* July 1, 1937.

14. *Pittsburgh Sun-Telegraph,* August 1, 1937.

15. *Pittsburgh Press,* June 30, 1937.

16. *Pittsburgh Press,* July 1, 1937.

17. *Pittsburgh Post-Gazette,* July 1, 1937.

18. *Pittsburgh Sun-Telegraph,* July 1, 1937.

19. *Pittsburgh Press,* July 1, 1937.

20. *Pittsburgh Sun-Telegraph,* July 1, 1937.

21. Ibid.

22. *Pittsburgh Post-Gazette,* July 1, 1937.

23. *Pittsburgh Sun-Telegraph,* July 1, 1937.

24. *Pittsburgh Post-Gazette,* August 2, 1937.

25. Ibid.

26. *San Francisco Examiner,* August 11, 1937.

27. *San Francisco Examiner,* August 12, 1937.

28. *San Francisco News,* August 14, 1937.

29. "Corbett Butts His Way to Win over Conn," *San Francisco Chronicle*, August 14, 1937.

30. *Pittsburgh Post-Gazette*, September 30, 1937.

31. Ibid.

32. *Pittsburgh Press*, September 27, 1937.

33. *Pittsburgh Press*, October 1, 1937.

34. Ibid.

35. *Pittsburgh Sun-Telegraph*, October 1, 1937.

36. *Pittsburgh Post-Gazette*, October 1, 1937.

37. *Pittsburgh Post-Gazette*, October 2, 1937.

38. *Pittsburgh Press*, October 1, 1937.

39. *Pittsburgh Post-Gazette*, October 2, 1937.

40. *Pittsburgh Post-Gazette*, October 9, 1937.

41. *Pittsburgh Press*, November 9, 1937.

42. *Pittsburgh Post-Gazette*, November 9, 1937.

43. *Pittsburgh Post-Gazette*, October 2, 1937.

44. *Pittsburgh Sun-Telegraph*, October 1, 1937.

45. *Pittsburgh Sun-Telegraph*, December 16, 1937.

46. *Pittsburgh Sun-Telegraph*, December 17, 1937.

47. *Washington Post*, December 24, 1937.

48. Ibid.

49. *Washington Post*, January 14, 1938.

50. *Pittsburgh Press*, December 17, 1937.

51. *Pittsburgh Press*, January 24, 1938.

52. *Pittsburgh Post-Gazette*, January 25, 1938.

53. Billy Conn interview with J. Knox McConnell (late 1980s).

54. *Pittsburgh Sun-Telegraph*, June 12, 1937.

55. *Pittsburgh Press*, July 26, 1938.

56. Ibid.

57. *Pittsburgh Sun-Telegraph*, July 26, 1938.

58. *Pittsburgh Sun-Telegraph*, September 24, 1939.

59. *Pittsburgh Sun-Telegraph*, August 22, 1938.

60. Billy Conn interview with J. Knox McConnell (late 1980s).

61. *San Francisco Examiner*, October 15, 1938.

62. *Pittsburgh Press*, October 22, 1938.

63. *Pittsburgh Post-Gazette*, November 24, 1938.

64. *Pittsburgh Sun-Telegraph*, November 29, 1938.

65. Ibid.

66. Ibid.

Chapter Five: A Fistic Star Is Born

1. *Pittsburgh Press*, January 5, 1939.

2. *Pittsburgh Press*, December 20, 1938.

3. *Pittsburgh Press,* January 6, 1939.

4. *Pittsburgh Sun-Telegraph,* January 6, 1939.

5. *Pittsburgh Press,* December 18, 1938.

6. "The Champion Who Was Born for Laughs," *Boxing and Wrestling Magazine* [n.d.].

7. *Los Angeles Herald and Express,* December 19, 1960.

8. That same year, Rooney brought Carnera to the North Side for an exhibition at the Arena.

9. *New York Times,* January 7, 1939.

10. Bug Baer's International News Service, January 9, 1939.

11. *New York Journal American,* January 9, 1939.

12. *Pittsburgh Press,* January 8, 1939.

13. *Pittsburgh Post-Gazette,* January 8, 1939.

14. Ibid.

15. Daniel M. Daniel, *The Mike Jacobs Story* (Ring Book Shop, 1949–50).

16. Ibid.

17. Ibid.

18. *Ring Magazine,* May 1953.

19. *Pittsburgh Press,* February 9, 1939.

20. *Pittsburgh Press,* February 10, 1939.

21. *Pittsburgh Post-Gazette,* February 11, 1939.

22. Heller, *In This Corner . . . !*

23. *New York Post,* February 11, 1939.

24. *New York Journal American,* February 11, 1939.

25. *Pittsburgh Sun-Telegraph,* February 11, 1939.

26. Ibid.

27. *New York Journal American,* February 11, 1939.

28. *Pittsburgh Sun-Telegraph,* February 11, 1939.

29. *New York Post,* February 10, 1939.

30. *New York Post,* February 12, 1939.

31. *New York Times,* February 11, 1939.

32. *Pittsburgh Press,* February 12, 1939.

33. *New York Post,* February 11, 1939.

34. Ibid.

35. *Pittsburgh Sun-Telegraph,* February 11, 1939.

36. *Pittsburgh Press,* February 12, 1939.

37. Ibid.

38. Ibid.

Chapter Six: Gone to the Fight

1. *Pittsburgh Press,* May 11, 1939.

2. *Pittsburgh Post-Gazette,* May 12, 1939.

3. *New York Post,* May 12, 1939.

4. Ibid.
5. *New York Times,* May 13, 1939.
6. *Pittsburgh Sun-Telegraph,* May 14, 1939.
7. *Pittsburgh Post-Gazette,* July 13, 1939.
8. *New York Post,* July 10, 1939.
9. *Pittsburgh Sun-Telegraph,* July 14, 1939.
10. *New York Times,* July 13, 1939.
11. Ibid.
12. *Pittsburgh Sun-Telegraph,* July 13, 1939.
13. *New York Daily Mirror,* July 14, 1939.
14. *Pittsburgh Sun-Telegraph,* July 13, 1939.
15. *Pittsburgh Sun-Telegraph,* July 15, 1939.
16. *New York Journal American,* July 14, 1939.
17. *Pittsburgh Sun-Telegraph,* July 15, 1939.
18. *Pittsburgh Sun-Telegraph,* July 15, 1939.
19. *New York Daily Mirror,* July 14, 1939.
20. *Pittsburgh Sun-Telegraph,* July 14, 1939.
21. *New York Journal American,* July 14, 1939.

Chapter Seven: Fighting Is My Business

1. *Pittsburgh Press,* April 27, 1941.
2. Billy Conn interview with J. Knox McConnell (late 1980s).
3. *New York Journal American,* September 22, 1939.
4. *Pittsburgh Sun-Telegraph,* July 15, 1939.
5. *Philadelphia Evening Public Ledger,* August 10, 1939.
6. Ibid.
7. Ibid.
8. Ibid.
9. *Pittsburgh Sun-Telegraph,* August 15, 1939.
10. *Denver Post,* August 15, 1939.
11. *Pittsburgh Post-Gazette,* August 15, 1939.
12. *New York Journal American,* August 15, 1939.
13. *New York Mirror,* August 15, 1939.
14. *New York Times,* August 18, 1939.
15. *Pittsburgh Sun-Telegraph,* September 5, 1939.
16. Ibid.
17. *Pittsburgh Sun-Telegraph,* September 10, 1939.
18. *Pittsburgh Post-Gazette,* September 19, 1939.
19. *Washington Post,* September 23, 1939.
20. *Pittsburgh Press,* September 24, 1939.
21. *Philadelphia Evening Ledger,* August 10, 1939.
22. *New York Post,* September 10, 1939.
23. Ibid.

24. *Pittsburgh Post-Gazette,* September 16, 1939.
25. *Pittsburgh Post-Gazette,* September 26, 1939.
26. *Pittsburgh Sun-Telegraph,* September 26, 1939.
27. *Pittsburgh Press,* September 25, 1939.
28. *Pittsburgh Post-Gazette,* September 27, 1939.
29. *Pittsburgh Press,* September 25, 1939.
30. *Pittsburgh Sun-Telegraph,* September 26, 1939.
31. *Pittsburgh Press,* September 25, 1939.
32. *Pittsburgh Post-Gazette,* September 27, 1939.
33. *Pittsburgh Press,* September 27, 1939.
34. *New York Journal American,* November 16, 1939.
35. *Pittsburgh Post-Gazette,* November 17, 1939.
36. *Pittsburgh Press,* November 16, 1939.
37. Ibid.
38. *New York Post,* November 16, 1939.
39. *New York Post,* November 17, 1939.
40. *Pittsburgh Press,* November 18, 1939.
41. *Pittsburgh Post-Gazette,* November 18, 1939.
42. Ibid.
43. *Pittsburgh Press,* November 18, 1939.

Chapter Eight: Toast of the Town

1. *Pittsburgh Sun-Telegraph,* November 29, 1939.
2. *Los Angeles Times,* December 1, 1939.
3. *Pittsburgh Post-Gazette,* December 10, 1939.
4. *Los Angeles Times,* December 10, 1939.
5. *Pittsburgh Post-Gazette,* January 12, 1940.
6. *Pittsburgh Press,* January 12, 1940.
7. *New York Times,* January 11, 1940.
8. *Pittsburgh Post-Gazette,* January 13, 1940.
9. *Pittsburgh Sun-Telegraph,* January 12, 1940.
10. *Pittsburgh Post-Gazette,* January 12, 1940.
11. *Pittsburgh Sun-Telegraph,* January 11, 1940.
12. *Pittsburgh Press,* February 25, 1940.
13. *Washington Post,* February 26, 1940.
14. *Pittsburgh Press,* March 22, 1940.
15. *Los Angeles Times,* March 24, 1940.
16. *Los Angeles Times,* March 25, 1940.
17. *New York Times,* May 16, 1940.
18. *Detroit Press,* June 5, 1940.
19. *Pittsburgh Sun-Telegraph,* June 6, 1940.
20. Ibid.
21. Ibid.

22. Ibid.

23. Ibid.

24. *Pittsburgh Press,* June 6, 1940.

25. *Pittsburgh Sun-Telegraph,* August 6, 1940.

26. Ibid.

27. *Washington Post,* August 1, 1940.

28. *Washington Post,* August 3, 1940.

29. *Pittsburgh Press,* August 11, 1940.

30. *Washington Post,* August 1, 1940.

31. *Washington Post,* August 6, 1940.

32. *Washington Post,* August 12, 1940.

33. *Pittsburgh Press,* August 10, 1940.

34. Ibid.

35. *Pittsburgh Press,* August 11, 1940.

36. *Pittsburgh Press,* August 9, 1940.

37. *Pittsburgh Press,* August 10, 1940.

38. *Pittsburgh Sun-Telegraph,* August 14, 1940.

39. *Pittsburgh Sun-Telegraph,* August 12, 1940.

40. *Pittsburgh Press,* August 13, 1940.

41. *New York Times,* September 6, 1940.

42. *Pittsburgh Sun-Telegraph,* August 14, 1940.

43. *Pittsburgh Press,* September 7, 1940.

44. Ibid.

45. *Los Angeles Times,* September 7, 1940.

46. *Pittsburgh Press,* September 7, 1940.

47. Ibid.

48. *Pittsburgh Post-Gazette,* September 7, 1940.

49. *Los Angeles Times,* September 9, 1940.

50. *Washington Post,* November 28, 1940.

51. *Pittsburgh Sun-Telegraph,* November 30, 1940.

52. *New York Times,* December 17, 1940.

53. *New York Times,* December 18, 1940.

54. *Los Angeles Times,* December 24, 1940.

55. Ibid.

56. *Washington Post,* January 7, 1941.

57. *New York Times,* January 6, 1941.

58. *Los Angeles Times,* January 6, 1941.

59. *Washington Post,* January 6, 1941.

60. *New York Times,* January 6, 1941.

61. *Los Angeles Times,* January 13, 1941.

62. *Washington Post,* January 15, 1941.

63. *Washington Post,* March 3, 1941.

64. *Washington Post,* March 5, 1941.

65. *Washington Post,* March 7, 1941.

66. *Washington Post,* April 4, 1941.

67. *Washington Post,* March 26, 1941.

68. *Pittsburgh Sun-Telegraph,* April 5, 1941.

69. *Pittsburgh Sun-Telegraph,* April 7, 1941.

70. Ibid.

71. Ibid.

72. *Pittsburgh Sun-Telegraph,* April 5, 1941.

73. *Pittsburgh Sun-Telegraph,* April 9, 1941.

74. *Washington Post,* May 17, 1941.

75. *Pittsburgh Sun-Telegraph,* March 25, 1941.

76. *Pittsburgh Sun-Telegraph,* May 26, 1941.

77. *Pittsburgh Post-Gazette,* May 27, 1941.

78. Ibid.

Chapter Nine: That Conn Boy Talks Too Much

1. *Pittsburgh Press,* June 4, 1941.

2. Ibid.

3. Ibid.

4. *Pittsburgh Press,* June 2, 1941.

5. *Pittsburgh Press,* June 5, 1941.

6. *Pittsburgh Press,* June 3, 1941.

7. *Pittsburgh Press,* June 7, 1941.

8. *Pittsburgh Post-Gazette,* June 10, 1941.

9. *Pittsburgh Press,* June 5, 1941.

10. *Pittsburgh Press,* June 16, 1941.

11. Ibid.

12. *Pittsburgh Sun-Telegraph,* June 16, 1941.

13. *Pittsburgh Press,* June 5, 1941.

14. *Pittsburgh Press,* June 6, 1941.

15. *Pittsburgh Press,* June 12, 1941.

16. *Pittsburgh Press,* June 4, 1941.

17. *Pittsburgh Post-Gazette,* June 17, 1941.

18. *Pittsburgh Sun-Telegraph,* June 17, 1941.

19. *Pittsburgh Post-Gazette,* June 16, 1941.

20. *Pittsburgh Post-Gazette,* June 13, 1941.

21. *Pittsburgh Post-Gazette,* June 10, 1941.

22. Richard Bak, *Joe Louis: The Great Black Hope* (Taylor Publishing, 1995).

23. *Pittsburgh Sun-Telegraph,* June 15, 1941.

24. *Pittsburgh Press,* June 10, 1941.

25. *Pittsburgh Sun-Telegraph,* June 15, 1941.

26. *Pittsburgh Post-Gazette,* June 12, 1941.

27. *Pittsburgh Post-Gazette,* June 17, 1941.

28. *Pittsburgh Press,* June 16, 1941.
29. *Pittsburgh Post-Gazette,* June 17, 1941.
30. *Pittsburgh Press,* June 17, 1941.
31. *Pittsburgh Sun-Telegraph,* June 17, 1941.
32. *Pittsburgh Press,* June 16, 1941.
33. *Los Angeles Times,* June 18, 1941.
34. *New York Daily Mirror,* June 19, 1941.
35. Ibid.
36. International News Service, June 18, 1941.
37. Associated Press, June 28, 1941.
38. *Pittsburgh Press,* June 17, 1941.
39. *Pittsburgh Press,* June 18, 1941.
40. Ibid.
41. Ibid.
42. Ibid.

Chapter Ten: Reckless Son of Erin

1. *Pittsburgh Sun-Telegraph,* June 21, 1941.
2. *Pittsburgh Sun-Telegraph,* June 18, 1941.
3. *Pittsburgh Press,* June 19, 1941.
4. *Pittsburgh Sun-Telegraph,* June 19, 1941.
5. *Pittsburgh Post-Gazette,* June 19, 1941.
6. *New York Herald Tribune,* June 19, 1941.
7. *Pittsburgh Post-Gazette,* June 19, 1941.
8. *Pittsburgh Press,* June 19, 1941.
9. Ibid.
10. *Pittsburgh Courier,* June 21, 1941.
11. Ibid.
12. *Pittsburgh Sun-Telegraph,* June 19, 1941.
13. *Pittsburgh Press,* June 19, 1941.
14. Ibid.
15. *Pittsburgh Sun-Telegraph,* June 19, 1941.

Chapter Eleven: Where's Billy?

1. *Pittsburgh Sun-Telegraph,* June 20, 1941.
2. Associated Press, June 20, 1941.
3. *Pittsburgh Press,* June 20, 1941.
4. Ibid.
5. *Pittsburgh Sun-Telegraph,* June 24, 1941.
6. International New Service, June 26, 1941.
7. Interview with Mary Louise Conn, April 26, 2004.
8. *New York Daily News,* July 6, 1941.

9. *Washington Post,* July 6, 1941.

10. Ibid.

11. *Washington Post,* July 12, 1941.

12. *Los Angeles Times,* July 15, 1941.

13. *New York Times,* July 27, 1941.

14. *Los Angeles Times,* July 20, 1941.

15. *Los Angeles Times,* August 5, 1941.

16. International News Service, July 25, 1941.

17. Interview with Mary Louise Conn, April 8, 2003.

18. *Pittsburgh Magazine,* December 1985.

19. *New York Times,* September 23, 1941.

20. *New York Daily News,* September 22, 1941.

21. *Pittsburgh Sun-Telegraph,* June 22, 1941.

22. *Washington Post,* September 30, 1941.

23. *Washington Post,* October 11, 1941.

24. *Washington Post,* November 13, 1941.

25. Interview with Mary Louise Conn, April 26, 2004.

Chapter Twelve: I'm Afraid of No Man Living

1. Associated Press, January 6, 1942.

2. Associated Press, January 27, 1942.

3. *Washington Post,* December 20, 1941.

4. *New York Times,* February 12, 1942.

5. *New York Times,* February 13, 1942.

6. International News Service, February 14, 1942.

7. *Pittsburgh Sun-Telegraph,* February 15, 1942.

8. *Los Angeles Times,* February 17, 1942.

9. *New York Times,* March 8, 1942.

10. Ibid.

11. *Pittsburgh Press,* May 12, 1942.

12. *Pittsburgh Press,* May 11, 1942.

13. *Chicago Daily Tribune,* May 12, 1942.

14. *Los Angeles Times,* May 12, 1942.

15. *Pittsburgh Press,* May 12, 1942.

16. *Washington Post,* May 12, 1942.

17. *Los Angeles Times,* May 15, 1942.

18. *Los Angeles Times,* May 13, 1942.

19. *Chicago Daily Tribune,* May 22, 1942.

20. *Washington Post,* June 24, 1942.

21. Ibid.

22. *New York Times,* June 21, 1942.

23. *Washington Post,* July 4, 1942.

24. *New York Times,* September 9, 1942.

25. Ibid.

26. *New York Times,* September 11, 1942.

27. *New York Times,* September 23, 1942.

28. *Chicago Daily Tribune,* September 19, 1942.

29. *Washington Post,* September 22, 1942.

30. *Chicago Daily Tribune,* September 24, 1942.

31. *New York Times,* September 26, 1942.qa

32. *Pittsburgh Post-Gazette,* September 25, 1942.

33. *New York Times,* September 27, 1942.

34. *Pittsburgh Sun-Telegraph,* September 26, 1942.

Chapter Thirteen: Mickey Rooney's a Sissy

1. *Los Angeles Times,* November 20, 1942.

2. *Washington Post,* March 15, 1943.

3. *New York Times,* April 30, 1943.

4. *Stars and Stripes,* July 17, 1944.

5. *New York Times,* October 20, 1944.

6. *Washington Post,* October 25, 1944.

7. *Yank Magazine,* December 1944.

8. *New York Times,* December 29, 1944.

9. Bob Hope and Pete Martin, *Have Tux, Will Travel: Bob Hope's Own Story* (Simon & Schuster, 2003).

Chapter Fourteen: He Can Run . . .

1. *Pittsburgh Post-Gazette,* October 18, 1945.

2. *New York Times,* October 18, 1945.

3. *Pittsburgh Post-Gazette,* October 19, 1945.

4. *New York Times,* January 5, 1946.

5. *Washington Post,* February 3, 1946.

6. *Washington Post,* June 14, 1946.

7. *New York Times,* April 3, 1946.

8. *Pittsburgh Sun-Telegraph,* June 12, 1946.

9. *Washington Post,* May 29, 1946.

10. *Washington Post,* June 6, 1946.

11. *Washington Post,* June 14, 1946.

12. *Pittsburgh Sun-Telegraph,* June 18, 1946.

13. *New York Times,* June 5, 1946.

14. Ibid.

15. *Pittsburgh Sun-Telegraph,* June 13, 1946.

16. "The Shock Absorbers," *Ring Magazine,* June 1946.

17. *Washington Post,* June 10, 1946.

18. *Pittsburgh Press,* June 17, 1946.

19. *Pittsburgh Press,* June 18, 1946.

20. *New York Times,* June 19, 1946.

21. *Pittsburgh Sun-Telegraph,* June 14, 1946.

22. *Pittsburgh Press,* June 18, 1946.

23. *Pittsburgh Sun-Telegraph,* June 12, 1946.

24. Ibid.

25. *Pittsburgh Sun-Telegraph,* June 13, 1946.

26. *Pittsburgh Post-Gazette,* June 19, 1946.

27. *Pittsburgh Post-Gazette,* June 18, 1946.

28. *Pittsburgh Post-Gazette,* June 19, 1946.

29. Ibid.

30. *Pittsburgh Sun-Telegraph,* June 20, 1946.

31. *Washington Post,* May 30, 1947.

32. *Pittsburgh Sun-Telegraph,* November 7, 1948.

33. *Pittsburgh Press,* June 20, 1946.

34. Ibid.

35. *New York Times,* June 20, 1946.

36. Ibid.

37. *Pittsburgh Sun-Telegraph,* June 20, 1946.

38. *Pittsburgh Press,* June 20, 1946.

39. Ibid.

40. *Pittsburgh Sun-Telegraph,* June 20, 1946.

41. *Pittsburgh Press,* June 20, 1946.

42. *Pittsburgh Sun-Telegraph,* June 20, 1946.

43. *Pittsburgh Press,* June 20, 1946.

44. *Pittsburgh Press,* June 21, 1946.

45. Ibid.

46. *Washington Post,* June 22, 1946.

47. *New York Times,* June 22, 1946.

48. *Pittsburgh Post-Gazette,* June 21, 1946.

49. Ibid.

50. *Pittsburgh Post-Gazette,* June 23, 1946.

51. Ibid.

Chapter Fifteen: Old Scores to Settle

1. *Washington Post,* May 29, 1947.

2. *Pittsburgh Post-Gazette,* May 29, 1947.

3. *Washington Post,* July 6, 1947.

4. *Pittsburgh Post-Gazette,* November 4, 1947.

5. *Pittsburgh Post-Gazette,* September 24, 1948.

6. Ibid.

7. *Pittsburgh Sun-Telegraph,* November 4, 1948.

8. Ibid.

9. *New York Times*, November 4, 1948.

10. *Pittsburgh Sun-Telegraph*, November 4, 1948.

11. *New York Times*, November 4, 1948.

12. *Macon Telegraph*, November 15, 1948.

13. Ibid.

14. *Macon News*, November 15, 1948.

15. *Macon Telegraph*, November 15, 1948.

16. *Macon Telegraph*, November 18, 1948.

17. *Dallas Morning News*, November 25, 1948.

18. *Dallas Morning News*, November 23, 1948.

19. *Pittsburgh Sun-Telegraph*, November 26, 1948.

20. *Pittsburgh Post-Gazette*, December 10, 1948.

21. *Chicago Sun-Times*, December 9, 1948.

22. *Chicago Sun-Times*, December 11, 1948.

23. Ibid.

Chapter Sixteen: "You Only Get One Chance"

1. "Battling Billy Conn," *Sport Magazine*, 1964.

2. Ibid.

3. Heller, *In This Corner . . . !*

4. Celebrities were common fare in the Stardust; Hollywood stars and starlets were spotted nearly every night in the lounge or on the casino floor. They came and went so often that practically none made an impression on Billy. He did, though, long remember his encounter with presidential hopeful John Kennedy in the winter of 1960. Kennedy was in Las Vegas with his brother Robert on February 7, a one-day stop before a week of campaigning in the Pacific Northwest for the Democratic nomination. The junior senator from Massachusetts had long admired Conn, and the two cordially talked for a while. During the course of their conversation, Kennedy mentioned that he hoped to take in the spectacular French production, Lido de Paris, but had been unable to secure tickets. Billy said he'd take care of that problem, and reached for a phone to call Jaffe.

"The next president of the United States is here and wants to see the Lido show," Conn told Milt.

"You're crazy," was the only response Jaffe could muster.

"Well," Billy said, "Come down here and see for yourself."

As Jaffe made his way from his office to the hotel lounge, the candidate brought up the subject of politics to the apolitical Conn. "The governor of Pennsylvania isn't for me," Kennedy said, speaking of David Lawrence. "He's for Stevenson.

"I'll fix that," Billy assured the youthful senator. "Lawrence is a good friend of my son's godfather. I'll take care of it." Before Kennedy could ask just how Conn would take care of it, Jaffe arrived. Following brief introductions, Milt hustled the senator away; there was just enough time to get to the ballroom before the curtain went up.

After the show, an inquisitive Kennedy looked Billy up. "What you told me before the show, can you really do that?"

"Listen," Billy simply stated, "if I tell you that a chicken can pull a train, don't ask how, just hitch his ass up."

Laughing uproariously, Kennedy said, "I've never heard that one before." The presidential hopeful also didn't realize that Billy knew of what he spoke. A phone call to Rooney, who had known Lawrence since they both played sandlot baseball as children, would do the trick.

How could an old pug and the owner of a professional football team help persuade the governor of one of the Union's largest states to back their guy? Lawrence had long been one of Adlai Stevenson's biggest supporters, and backed the Illinois governor as the Democratic nominee in '52 and '56. His loyalty to Stevenson was strong, but Lawrence tipped his hand in early May, two months before the party's convention.

While not implicitly endorsing Kennedy, the governor did the next best thing and admitted that, as a Roman Catholic, he would like to see the senator receive the party nomination "to get rid of the old idea" that a Catholic wasn't suitable to run for the highest office in the land. Though splitting hairs, Lawrence emphasized that he was "remaining neutral."

By the time the Democrats gathered in Los Angeles to select their nominee, Lawrence had dropped all guise of whom he would support. He threw his considerable political weight behind Kennedy and delivered sixty-four of his state's eighty-one delegates to the Massachusetts senator, which, it so happened, put Kennedy over the necessary 761 needed to secure the nomination.

5. *Pittsburgh Press,* July 17, 1961.

6. *Washington Post,* July 9, 1959.

7. Billy was elected to the Boxing Hall of Fame on January 5, 1966, along with a class that included his old nemesis Young Corbett, among others.

8. *Los Angeles Times,* October 24, 1966.

9. Ibid.

10. *Washington Post,* October 30, 1966.

11. Ibid.

12. Ibid.

13. Ibid.

14. *New York Times,* May 27, 1966.

15. Interview with Tim Conn, March 21, 2001.

16. Jacobs had fought off death since suffering a stroke in late 1946. The end finally came January 23, 1953, at Hialeah racetrack in Miami Beach, when Uncle Mike was felled by a heart attack. Two months earlier, Jacobs gave his last interview. At seventy-two, it was a tired and bitter old man who sat down with Milton Richman of the United Press. "There ain't one good fighter around today, not one. They're a bunch of chorus boys. . . . And these promoters? What do these guys

know about promoting a fight? They ought to be promoting beauty contests instead of fights."

Richmond reminded Mike that he still had a lot of friends in boxing, to which Jacobs grunted, "Friends? I didn't have any in boxing. It was strictly business with me." *Washington Post,* January 25, 1953.

17. Frank Deford, "The Boxer and the Blonde," *Sports Illustrated,* June 17, 1985.

18. *Los Angeles Times,* November 12, 1978.

19. *Pittsburgh Magazine,* December 1985.

20. Ibid.

21. WTAE-TV, Pittsburgh; broadcast interview replayed May 29, 1993.

22. *Pittsburgh Post-Gazette,* November 4, 1992.

23. Ibid.

24. *Pittsburgh Post-Gazette,* May 30, 1993.

25. Heller, *In This Corner . . . !*

Bibliography

Books

Albert, Marv, with Maury Allen. *Voices of Sport*. Grosset and Dunlap, 1971.
Bak, Richard. *Joe Louis: The Great Black Hope*. Taylor Publishing, 1995.
Daniel, Daniel M. *The Mike Jacobs Story*. The Ring Book Shop. 1949 and 1950.
Heller, Peter. *In This Corner. . . ! Forty-Two World Champions Tell Their Stories*. Da-Capo Press, 1994.
Hope, Bob, and Pete Martin. *Have Tux, Will Travel: Bob Hope's Own Story*. Simon & Schuster, 2003.

Audio and Video

McConnell, J. Knox. Audio interview with Billy Conn. Late 1980s.
Video of Joe Louis–Billy Conn fight, June 18, 1941.
Video of Joe Louis–Billy Conn fight, June 19, 1946.
Video of *The Way It Was*, Curt Gowdy with Billy Conn and Joe Louis looking back on June 18, 1941.
Video of ESPN *Classic Game of the Week*, Louis–Conn.
Video of Billy Conn's funeral, June 1, 1993, KDKA-TV and WTAE-TV (unedited).

Magazine Articles

Albertani, Francis. "Mike Jacobs, Successor to Tex Rickard." *Ring Magazine* (July 1936).
Andre, Sam. "Billy Conn: Boy Millionaire." *Sport Magazine* (March, 1963).
"Billy Conn, Boy Millionaire." *Ring Magazine* (March 1963).
Campbell, Glenn. "Billy Conn Is 60!" *Pittsburgh Magazine* (October 1977).
Conn, Billy. "Unforgettable Joe Louis." *Reader's Digest* (July 1983).
Daniel, Daniel M. "Daniel Gives Conn a Chance." *Ring Magazine* (July 1941).

———. "The First Louis-Conn Fight Reconstructed." *Ring Magazine* (June 1946).

Dawson, James P. "Dawson Doubts Billy's Punch." *Ring Magazine* (July 1941).

Deford, Frank. "The Boxer and the Blonde." *Sports Illustrated* (June 17, 1985).

Fierro, Freddie. "The Champion Who Was Born for Laughs." *Boxing and Wrestling Magazine* (n.d.).

Fleischer, Nat. "Billy Conn Talks." *Ring Magazine* (July 1942).

———. "Cockiness Costly." *Ring Magazine* (August 1941).

———. "The Jacobs I Knew." *Ring Magazine* (May 1953).

"Interview with Billy Conn." *Pittsburgh Magazine* (December 1985).

McNamee, Laurence Francis. "In Memory of My Hero, Billy Conn." *Boxing Illustrated* (October, 1993).

Merrill, Eddie. "The Shock Absorbers." *Ring Magazine* (June 1946).

Miley, Jack. "In Conn's Corner, Mike Jacobs." *Saturday Evening Post* (June 7, 1941).

———. "Irish Eyes Are Smiling." *Collier's* (June 3, 1939).

Morey, Charles. "Battling Billy Conn." *Sport Magazine* (n.d.).

Pardy, George T. "Pittsburgh, the Home of Famous Fighters." *Ring Magazine* (May 1939).

Ray, Johnny. "My Boy Billy." *Collier's* (May 24, 1941).

Wood, Wilbur. "Teddy Yarosz, Uncrowned Champion." *Ring Magazine* (January 1934).

Zinberg, Cpl. Len. "Billy and the Kid in Italy." *Yank Magazine* (December 1944).

Newspapers

Atlanta Constitution

Chicago Daily Tribune

Chicago Sun-Times

Dallas Morning News

Denver Post

Detroit Press

Los Angeles Herald and Express

Los Angeles Times

Macon News

Macon Telegraph

New York Daily Mirror

New Daily News

New York Herald Tribune

New York Journal American

New York Post

New York Times

Philadelphia Evening Public Ledger

Pittsburgh Courier

Pittsburgh Post-Gazette

Pittsburgh Press
Pittsburgh Sun
Pittsburgh Sun-Telegraph
San Francisco Chronicle
San Francisco Examiner
San Francisco Press
Washington Post

Interviews

Billy Conn Jr.
Frank Conn
Mary Louise Conn
Tim Conn
Ray Connelly
Mary Jane Cunningham
Harold F. Gefki
Bob Jacobs
Al Lamphram
Jack McGinley
Roy McHugh
William Nunn
Robert Pitler
Allen Rothstein
Jimmy Smith

Index

ANDREW O'TOOLE is author of several books on sports and Pittsburgh, including *Baseball's Best Kept Secret: Al Oliver and His Time in Baseball; Branch Rickey in Pittsburgh; The Best Man Plays: Major League Baseball and the Black Athlete, 1901–2002;* and *Smiling Irish Eyes: Art Rooney and the Pittsburgh Steelers.*

Sport and Society

Touching Base: Professional Baseball and American Culture in the Progressive
  Era (rev. ed.)   *Steven A. Riess*
Red Grange and the Rise of Modern Football   *John M. Carroll*
Golf and the American Country Club   *Richard J. Moss*
Extra Innings: Writing on Baseball   *Richard Peterson*
Global Games   *Maarten Van Bottenburg*
The Sporting World of the Modern South   *Edited by Patrick B. Miller*
The End of Baseball As We Knew It: The Players Union, 1960–81   *Charles P. Korr*
Rocky Marciano: The Rock of His Times   *Russell Sullivan*
Saying It's So: A Cultural History of the Black Sox Scandal   *Daniel A. Nathan*
The Nazi Olympics: Sport, Politics, and Appeasement in the 1930s   *Edited by
  Arnd Krüger and William Murray*
The Unlevel Playing Field: A Documentary History of the African American
  Experience in Sport   *David K. Wiggins and Patrick B. Miller*
Sports in Zion: Mormon Recreation, 1890–1940   *Richard Ian Kimball*
Sweet William: The Life of Billy Conn   *Andrew O'Toole*

Reprint Editions

The Nazi Olympics   *Richard D. Mandell*
Sports in the Western World (2d ed.)   *William J. Baker*
Jesse Owens: An American Life   *William J. Baker*

The University of Illinois Press
is a founding member of the
Association of American University Presses.

———————————————————————

University of Illinois Press
1325 South Oak Street
Champaign, IL 61820-6903
www.press.uillinois.edu